AMERICA'S
TEST KITCHEN

ALSO BY AMERICA'S TEST KITCHEN

Desserts Illustrated

The Savory Baker

Fresh Pasta at Home

The Complete Modern Pantry

Vegan Cooking for Two

The Complete Small Plates Cookbook

Modern Bistro

Boards

More Mediterranean

The Complete Guide to Healthy Drinks

The Everyday Athlete Cookbook

The New Cooking School Cookbook:
Advanced Fundamentals

The New Cooking School Cookbook:
Fundamentals

Cooking with Plant-Based Meat

The Complete Autumn and Winter
Cookbook

Five-Ingredient Dinners

One-Hour Comfort

The Complete Plant-Based Cookbook

Cook for Your Gut Health

Foolproof Fish

The Complete Salad Cookbook

Meat Illustrated

Vegetables Illustrated

Bowls

The Ultimate Meal-Prep Cookbook

The Chicken Bible

The Side Dish Bible

The Complete One Pot

Cooking for One

How Can It Be Gluten-Free Cookbook
Collection

The Complete Summer Cookbook

100 Techniques

Easy Everyday Keto

Everything Chocolate

The Perfect Pie

The Perfect Cake

The Perfect Cookie

How to Cocktail

Spiced

The Ultimate Burger

The New Essentials Cookbook

Dinner Illustrated

America's Test Kitchen Menu Cookbook

Cook's Illustrated Revolutionary Recipes

Tasting Italy: A Culinary Journey

Cooking at Home with Bridget
and Julia

The Complete Mediterranean Cookbook

The Complete Vegetarian Cookbook

The Complete Cooking for Two
Cookbook

The Complete Diabetes Cookbook

The Complete Slow Cooker

The Complete Make-Ahead Cookbook

Just Add Sauce

How to Braise Everything

How to Roast Everything

Nutritious Delicious

What Good Cooks Know

Cook's Science

The Science of Good Cooking

Bread Illustrated

Master of the Grill

Kitchen Smarts

Kitchen Hacks

100 Recipes: The Absolute Best Ways to
Make the True Essentials

The New Family Cookbook

The Cook's Illustrated Baking Book

The Cook's Illustrated Cookbook

The America's Test Kitchen Family Baking
Book

The Best of America's Test Kitchen
(2007–2023 Editions)

America's Test Kitchen Twentieth
Anniversary TV Show Cookbook

The Complete America's Test Kitchen TV
Show Cookbook 2001–2023

Healthy Air Fryer

Healthy and Delicious Instant Pot

Mediterranean Instant Pot

Cook It in Your Dutch Oven

Vegan for Everybody

Sous Vide for Everybody

Toaster Oven Perfection

Air Fryer Perfection

Multicooker Perfection

Food Processor Perfection

Pressure Cooker Perfection

Instant Pot Ace Blender Cookbook

Naturally Sweet

Foolproof Preserving

Paleo Perfected

The Best Mexican Recipes

Slow Cooker Revolution Volume 2:
The Easy-Prep Edition

Slow Cooker Revolution

The America's Test Kitchen
D.I.Y. Cookbook

COOK'S COUNTRY TITLES:

Big Flavors from Italian America

One-Pan Wonders

Cook It in Cast Iron

Cook's Country Eats Local

The Complete Cook's Country
TV Show Cookbook

FOR A FULL LISTING OF
ALL OUR BOOKS:

CooksIllustrated.com

AmericasTestKitchen.com

PRAISE FOR AMERICA'S TEST KITCHEN

"A mood board for one's food board is served up in this excellent guide . . . This has instant classic written all over it."

Publishers Weekly (starred review) on *Boards: Stylish Spreads for Casual Gatherings*

"In this latest offering from the fertile minds at America's Test Kitchen the recipes focus on savory baked goods. Pizzas, flatbreads, crackers, and stuffed breads all shine here . . . Introductory essays for each recipe give background information and tips for making things come out perfectly."

Booklist (starred review) on *The Savory Baker*

"Reassuringly hefty and comprehensive, *The Complete Autumn and Winter Cookbook* by America's Test Kitchen has you covered with a seemingly endless array of seasonal fare . . . This overstuffed compendium is guaranteed to warm you from the inside out."

NPR on *The Complete Autumn and Winter Cookbook*

Selected as the Cookbook Award Winner of 2021 in the General Cookbook Category

International Association of Culinary Professionals (IACP) on *Meat Illustrated*

Selected as the Cookbook Award Winner of 2021 in the Health and Nutrition Category

International Association of Culinary Professionals (IACP) on *the Complete plant-based cookbook*

"The book's depth, breadth, and practicality make it a must-have for seafood lovers."

Publishers Weekly (starred review) on *Foolproof Fish*

"Another flawless entry in the America's Test Kitchen canon, *Bowls* guides readers of all culinary skill levels in composing one-bowl meals from a variety of cuisines."

BuzzFeed Books on *Bowls*

"Diabetics and all health-conscious home cooks will find great information on almost every page."

Booklist (starred review) on *The Complete Diabetes Cookbook*

"*The Perfect Cookie* . . . is, in a word, perfect. This is an important and substantial cookbook . . . If you love cookies, but have been a tad shy to bake on your own, all your fears will be dissipated. This is one book you can use for years with magnificently happy results."

The Huffington Post on *the Perfect cookie*

"True to its name, this smart and endlessly enlightening cookbook is about as definitive as it's possible to get in the modern vegetarian realm."

Men's Journal on *The Complete Vegetarian Cookbook*

"Filled with complete meals you can cook in your Instant Pot. Next time you're thinking of turning to takeout or convenience foods, prepare one of these one-pot meals instead."

NBC News on *Mediterranean Instant Pot*

"If you're a home cook who loves long introductions that tell you why a dish works followed by lots of step-by-step hand holding, then you'll love *Vegetables Illustrated*."

The Wall Street Journal on *Vegetables Illustrated*

"Here are the words just about any vegan would be happy to read: 'Why This Recipe Works.' Fans of America's Test Kitchen are used to seeing the phrase, and now it applies to the growing collection of plant-based creations in *Vegan for Everybody*."

The Washington Post on *Vegan for Everybody*

"A one-volume kitchen seminar, addressing in one smart chapter after another the sometimes surprising whys behind a cook's best practices . . . You get the myth, the theory, the science, and the proof, all rigorously interrogated as only America's Test Kitchen can do."

NPR on *The Science of Good Cooking*

"The 21st-century *Fannie Farmer Cookbook* or *The Joy of Cooking*. If you had to have one cookbook and that's all you could have, this one would do it."

CBS San Francisco on *The New Family Cookbook*

"The go-to gift book for newlyweds, small families, or empty nesters."

Orlando Sentinel on *The Complete Cooking for Two Cookbook*

"The America's Test Kitchen team elevates the humble side dish to center stage in this excellent collection of 1,001 recipes . . . Benefiting from the clarity that comes from experience and experiments, ATK shows off its many sides in this comprehensive volume."

Publishers Weekly on *The Side Dish Bible*

EVERYDAY
BREAD

100 Recipes for Baking Bread on Your Schedule

AMERICA'S TEST KITCHEN

Library of Congress Cataloging-in-Publication Data has been applied for.

ISBN 978-1-954210-39-4

America's Test Kitchen
21 Drydock Avenue, Boston, MA 02210

Printed in Canada

10 9 8 7 6 5 4 3 2 1

Distributed by Penguin Random House Publisher Services

Tel: 800.733.3000

Pictured on Front Cover Garlic-Herb Butter Rolls (page 123)

Pictured on Back Cover Whole-Wheat Rustic Loaf (page 196), Brioche Cinnamon Buns (page 196), Cast Iron Orange-Herb Biscuits (page 50), Rye Bread (page 214), Pita Bread (page 278), Chive Spiral Rolls (page 108), Zhoug Swirl Bread (page 172), Thin-Crust Whole-Wheat Pizza with Garlic Oil, Three Cheeses, and Basil (page 244).

Featured Photography by Daniel J. van Ackere

Editorial Director, Books Adam Kowit

Executive Food Editor Dan Zuccarello

Deputy Food Editor Stephanie Pixley

Executive Managing Editor Debra Hudak

Project Editor Sacha Madadian

Senior Editors Camila Chaparro and Sara Mayer

Test Cooks Olivia Counter, Hannah Fenton, Hisham Hassan, José Maldonado, and Patricia Suarez

Kitchen Intern Olivia Goldstein

Design Director Lindsey Timko Chandler

Deputy Art Director Katie Barranger

Associate Art Director Molly Gillespie

Photography Director Julie Bozzo Cote

Senior Photography Producer Meredith Mulcahy

Senior Staff Photographers Steve Klise and Daniel J. van Ackere

Staff Photographer Kevin White

Additional Photography Joseph Keller and Carl Tremblay

Food Styling Joy Howard, Sheila Jarnes, Catrine Kelty, Chantal Lambeth, Gina McCreadie, Kendra McKnight, Ashley Moore, Christie Morrison, Marie Piraino, Elle Simone Scott, Kendra Smith, and Sally Staub

Executive Producer, TV and Video Simon Savelyev

Managing Producer, Video Lee Jasmin

Social Media Manager Norma Tentori

Project Manager, Publishing Operations Katie Kimmerer

Senior Print Production Specialist Lauren Robbins

Production and Imaging Coordinator Amanda Yong

Production and Imaging Specialists Tricia Neumyer and Dennis Noble

Copy Editor Cheryl Redmond

Proofreader Ann-Marie Imbornoni

Indexer Elizabeth Parson

Chief Creative Officer Jack Bishop

Executive Editorial Directors Julia Collin Davison and Bridget Lancaster

CONTENTS

WELCOME TO AMERICA'S TEST KITCHEN

This book has been tested, written, and edited by the folks at America's Test Kitchen, where curious cooks become confident cooks. Located in Boston's Seaport District in the historic Innovation and Design Building, it features 15,000 square feet of kitchen space including multiple photography and video studios. It is the home of *Cook's Illustrated* magazine and *Cook's Country* magazine and is the workday destination for more than 60 test cooks, editors, and cookware specialists. Our mission is to empower and inspire confidence, community, and creativity in the kitchen.

We start the process of testing a recipe with a complete lack of preconceptions, which means that we accept no claim, no technique, and no recipe at face value. We simply assemble as many variations as possible, test a half-dozen of the most promising, and taste the results blind. We then construct our own recipe and continue to test it, varying ingredients, techniques, and cooking times until we reach a consensus. As we like to say in the test kitchen, "We make the mistakes so you don't have to." The result, we hope, is the best version of a particular recipe, but we realize that only you can be the final judge of our success (or failure). We use the same rigorous approach when we test equipment and taste ingredients.

All of this would not be possible without a belief that good cooking, much like good music, is based on a foundation of objective technique. Some people like spicy foods and others don't, but there is a right way to sauté, there is a best way to cook a pot roast, and there are measurable scientific principles involved in producing perfectly beaten, stable egg whites. Our ultimate goal is to investigate the fundamental principles of cooking to give you the techniques, tools, and ingredients you need to become a better cook. It is as simple as that.

To see what goes on behind the scenes at America's Test Kitchen, check out our social media channels for kitchen snapshots, exclusive content, video tips, and much more. You can watch us work (in our actual test kitchen) by tuning in to *America's Test Kitchen* or *Cook's Country* on public television or on our websites. Listen to *Proof*, *Mystery Recipe*, and *The Walk-In* (AmericasTestKitchen.com/podcasts), to hear engaging, complex stories about people and food. Want to hone your cooking skills or finally learn how to bake—with an America's Test Kitchen test cook? Enroll in one of our online cooking classes. And you can engage the next generation of home cooks with kid-tested recipes from America's Test Kitchen Kids.

Join Our Community of Recipe Testers

 Our recipe testers provide valuable feedback on recipes under development by ensuring that they are foolproof in home kitchens. Help the America's Test Kitchen book team investigate the how and why behind successful recipes from your home kitchen.

facebook.com/AmericasTestKitchen
instagram.com/TestKitchen
youtube.com/AmericasTestKitchen
tiktok.com/@TestKitchen
twitter.com/TestKitchen
pinterest.com/TestKitchen

AmericasTestKitchen.com
CooksIllustrated.com
CooksCountry.com
OnlineCookingSchool.com
AmericasTestKitchen.com/kids

getting bread on your table

In kitchens the world over, you're likely to find some kind of bread—from a basic flatbread that comes together from flour, water, salt, and leavener, to an intricate loaf with rich fillings. Bread's the first item to disappear from store shelves ahead of a storm. It's a go-to for breakfast, lunch, dinner, or a snack. It's built into a number of dishes, including bread salads like fattoush, soups like acquacotta, and breaded favorites like schnitzel. We'll likely never stop turning to bread in some form every day, and because modern life demands those days be more and more busy, the supermarket or, if you're lucky, a local bakery, may be your common source. But there are few things better than the aroma, texture, and flavor of freshly baked bread. Making bread at home is a chance to pause, to use our hands, and to better appreciate this foundational part of our diet.

In *Bread Illustrated*, our award-winning first book on the subject, we covered the principles of baking a wide breadth of breads. We're publishing this follow-up to further spread the joy of bread baking by giving you more—more recipes and more intriguing flavors, yes, but also more incentives to make the process routine. In this book, we tackle one of the most challenging aspects of bread baking for even advanced bakers: time. Maybe you love to make bread and you don't get to do it that often, not because it's difficult for you to pre-pare, but because it's difficult to work into your schedule.

The simplest way we lower the bar to baking bread on a regular basis is to give you options to make it fast. A large chapter of quick breads opens the possibilities of the category wide. These recipes aren't just cake; you'll find you can build a sandwich on supersavory breads that need just a few ingredients, some turns of a whisk, and minimal time, like savory Three-Ingredient Bread (beer gives the bread yeasty flavor) or Feta-Dill Zucchini Bread (not your garden average). You'll make biscuits and muffins (Miso-Scallion Biscuits or Manchego and Chorizo Muffins, anyone?) to accompany breakfast, a warm bowl of soup, or a dinner party roast in far less time than you'd expect for bread so satisfying.

Our yeasted breads offer a different approach that's not all about speed. We suspect spreading steps over a few days might be better for your schedule, so the breads in this book are engineered to be flexible. Many let you push the pause button—typically by refrigerating bread for an extended first or second rise—to stretch out the baking process. This allows you to enjoy bread at its very best without stress. Serve Cast Iron Garlic-Herb Butter Rolls perfectly shiny and warm for a holiday; instead of worrying about kneading and shaping them while preparing other dishes, you can take preshaped rolls from the fridge and bake them before dinner. Similarly, you can have sweet Sticky Buns ready for brunch without waking up at the crack of dawn. Bake beautiful Coques with Spinach, Raisins, and Pine Nuts for a weekday dinner by making them up to the assembly stage over the weekend. To help you visualize and plan your bread—and see where you can step away and do something else (including go to sleep)—every recipe comes with a timeline breaking down the stages.

You're likely to pick up dough more regularly if every step feels like muscle memory. For each category of bread, we devote a special feature to the friendliest—and most versatile—doughs you'll ever make, like white dinner rolls that shape like a dream and brioche with all the butter and none of the grease or sticking. But their value doesn't stop there: We give instruction on flavoring or molding these core doughs in a variety of ways for a catalog of breads that grows exponentially. The white dinner roll dough can turn into precious Crescent Rolls or aromatic Chive Spiral Rolls. Brioche becomes a statuesque Pumpkin Spice Brioche à Tête or an interactive Garlic-Thyme Pull-Apart Brioche.

The rest of the recipes in the book include special tips and tricks for making them extra workable: Use the tangzhong method from Asian baking to incorporate extra moisture (and therefore fluffiness) to doughs in a way that doesn't make them sticky. Coat sandwich loaves with fun toppings like quinoa, bagel seasoning, or furikake without disturbing their delicate structure. Learn these techniques through lots of instruction, step-by-step photos, and even scannable how-to videos.

Chief among our techniques: We're proud to present our new-and-improved No-Knead Rustic Loaf with the most airy, open, sink-your-teeth-in-it, crisp-crusted loaves you can make at home—of course, with no kneading. We use the recipe as the foundation for a whole chapter of no-knead breads that sound like they come from an artisan bakery. Adapt the recipe to use a range of nutty whole-grain flours (you just need to increase the water in the dough) for Sprouted Wheat Berry Bread or Cocoa Cherry Rye Bread. Fold piquant ingredients into Spicy Olive Spelt Bread or Cranberry Walnut Bread. Impress with golden-crumbed Sesame Durum Bread or cornmeal-coated Anadama Bread.

What you won't find in this book: an arsenal of bread-specific equipment. Instead, a common Dutch oven mimics the dramatic results of a steam-injected bakery oven. Similarly, you'll achieve extra-tall biscuits, rolls, and braided loaves with beautifully burnished exteriors with your trusty cast-iron skillet. While a pizza peel or baking steel or stone is helpful for charred flatbreads, you can get away with a set of overturned baking sheets, and we've eliminated specialty items like lames, bannetons, or couches.

Relaxing the bread baking equation adds up to bread when and how you want it, as often as every day. Let America's Test Kitchen make bread baking a source of immeasurable joy.

KEY BREAD BAKING STEPS

The breads in this book run the gamut from two-step quick breads to scoop-and-drop dinner rolls to Dutch oven–baked rustic loaves for a collection full of variety. But no matter the type of bread, there are steps that are common to all of them—you won't go through all seven for a simple quick bread, but you'll still make stops along the way. Here's everything you need to know to make bread, spelled out at a glance.

BREAD LINGO TO KNOW

Batter is a pourable or spreadable mix of dry and wet ingredients that turns into muffins, cornbreads, and loaf-pan quick breads. The well-hydrated mixture ensures an element of fluffiness in the product. Batters come together with simple stirring.

Dough is a malleable amalgamation of, at its most basic, flour, water, salt, and yeast. You knead (or fold) dough: This gives it structure to rise and hold air.

Gluten comes into greater play once kneading begins, but it announces its presence in mixing. Gluten is a protein in wheat flour that develops to give bread chew. When gluten proteins come in contact with liquid during mixing, they unwind so they can link up with each other to create chains.

Autolyse is a baking pause, short or long, that is sometimes incorporated right after mixing and before kneading. During this rest, natural enzymes help cut the gluten coils into smaller segments that are easier to align during kneading and so cut kneading time. (This is for breads where you want big chew.)

#1 MIXING

WHAT IS IT?

Gather your ingredients and go: Any bread recipe requires combining wet and dry ingredients, either to make a batter or to distribute the ingredients before working them further through kneading or folding (see page 9) to make a dough.

For a quick batter-based bread, mixing usually looks like whisking together dry ingredients, combining wet ingredients, and folding or stirring the wet into the dry until any dry pockets are moistened—you want a cohesive batter but you don't want to overmix it or the bread will be tough.

For a bread dough, mixing often happens in the stand mixer. You carefully add the wet ingredients to the dry on low speed and mix until they're combined. This usually means making just a shaggy dough, not something smooth and ready to form. It should take about 2 minutes. Alternatively, some recipes that don't require a stand mixer call for mixing the ingredients in a bowl with a rubber spatula. And for pizza doughs, which don't need a huge amount of structure, we use a food processor; a more conventional stand-mixer method might take 15 to 20 minutes to produce a shiny, elastic dough, but the food processor takes less than 2 minutes. (Though for many bread recipes, we would caution against the rough treatment of a food processor, which can tear apart the strands of gluten.)

WHAT'S HAPPENING?

The dry ingredients hydrate, which starts chemical reactions—between baking powder and/or baking soda and liquids or between sugar and yeast—that will initiate rise in your bread.

Hydrating the flour also unravels coiled gluten proteins within it that eventually cross-link and develop to give your dough structure.

HELPFUL TIPS

• **mind your weights and measures**
The most important part of mixing might not be combining ingredients but prepping them: Weighing ingredients, while associated with professional baking, really should be a home baker's skill—baking is a science so using ingredients in the proper proportion is the easiest step toward good results.

• **take the temperature**
Ingredient lists often call for bringing items to a certain phase—softened or melted butter, room-temperature eggs, warm milk. There's always a reason. Sometimes it's for easy, seamless mixing, sometimes it's to activate yeast and jump-start processes with heat.

• **add wet to dry**
Gradually and carefully adding wet ingredients to dry ingredients in mixing prevents pockets of flour from forming.

• **mix on low**
A gentle approach ensures that ingredients are properly combined and therefore fully hydrated.

• **take it easy**
Doughs shouldn't be completely smooth—just cohesive enough to allow gluten proteins to unfurl and start coming together.

• **hold the salt**
Salt strengthens gluten structure but don't add it until after your dough has been mixed, if you will be giving it a prework rest (autolyse). Salt slows the alteration of proteins that you want to happen during this period.

#2 WORKING

WHAT IS IT?

Now that your mound of dough is poised to strengthen and grow, you need to manipulate it to facilitate those processes. Tender quick breads don't require this step, but it's one of the most critical for yeasted doughs.

Kneading dough in a stand mixer is a common route. The mixed dough gets worked around the bowl with the machine's dough hook until it's smooth and just sticks to the bottom of the bowl.

Another satisfying route builds as much or even more strength than kneading does by combining sets of intentional folds of the dough over itself with resting periods. This is useful for well-hydrated rustic doughs, which may be too wet to engage with the mixer, and for silky enriched doughs.

WHAT'S HAPPENING?

Working the dough incorporates air, distributes ingredients further, and, most important, develops gluten to give bread chew. The mechanical action of kneading aligns unfurled gluten strands into a strong gluten network. How do you know when you've kneaded adequately? It's important because underkneaded dough will lack structure and overkneaded dough . . . will also lack structure. Check out the stages of dough kneading on page 9.

But when it comes to folding, how does such a seemingly gentle technique work to do this so well? The process brings wayward strands of gluten in these initially amorphous masses of dough into alignment. In addition, folding dough distributes gas bubbles evenly (that means nicely distributed holes within the matrix of a chewy crumb) and refreshes the yeast to give these bubbles flight. For more information, see page 9.

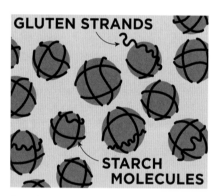

Protein strands glutenin and gliadin are wrapped around starch granules in flour.

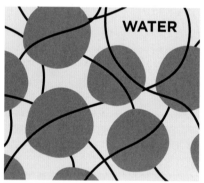

In the presence of water, the strands unwind and link to form a network of gluten.

BREAD LINGO TO KNOW

Hydration describes how wet a dough is (that is, how high the ratio of liquid to flour is). The more water in a dough, the stronger and more extensible the gluten strands, so they can best support the gas bubbles that grow within the dough. This results in an airier bread with good chew. Extra water also creates a looser dough, which allows steam to expand more easily. In brief, more water means a more open crumb, less water means a more closed crumb.

Rustic breads are the class of breads you find at an artisan bakery. Rustic doughs contain little or no fat and lots of water, and they develop a lot of gluten to support large air pockets. A good rustic loaf has a deeply browned, thick but crisp outer crust that breaks to a chewy, flavorful crumb.

HELPFUL TIPS

• medium-low is the way to go
The best machinery isn't infallible, and aggressive mixing can burn out the motor on your stand mixer or lead to overmixing dough.

• take help from a tool
A bowl scraper is probably one of our favorite extras for dough. You don't need one—you can use a spatula for folding—but the inexpensive hand spatula is ideal for folding dough or for transferring kneaded dough from a stand mixer to a bowl without ripping. Our favorite is the **Fox Run Silicone Dough/Bowl Scraper.**

how-to
PROPER KNEADING

how-to
FOLDING RUSTIC DOUGH

#3 FIRST RISE

WHAT IS IT?

Rising is what physically happens to dough when it undergoes a process called fermentation. When you set the dough to rest after kneading or folding it, you let it sit for a period during which it lightens and rises thanks to the yeast.

WHAT'S HAPPENING?

Mixing and kneading initiate fermentation by distributing the yeast throughout the dough and hydrating it so it can activate; that is, begin eating sugars in the flour and in turn releasing carbon dioxide and alcohol. The expanding carbon dioxide bubbles blow up the dough like a balloon. You're looking for the dough to about double in size. That's when most of the available sugar has been consumed.

Rising seems like magic, but it doesn't occur unconditionally just because a dough calls for yeast. Fermentation is also dependent on the gluten developed when you worked the dough. This gluten structure allows the yeasted dough to expand in a controlled manner, evenly and without bursting at faulty spots along the mass.

You'll notice that in our recipes, we often give the option for the first rise to occur in the refrigerator. This slows the process down, but slow and steady can win you a delicious loaf, as a refrigerator rise gives the dough more time to develop complex flavor. Steadiness allows for the most even rising as well.

how-to
RISING DURING BULK FERMENTATION

HELPFUL TIPS

- **lay to rest**
You can let dough rise in a glass bowl or in a transparent container. The bowl is easier to maneuver; the container lets you see very clearly how high the rise is.

- **prep properly**
Make sure to grease the vessel your dough rises in so it doesn't stick—any ripping of the dough disrupts the gluten network.

- **keep cover**
Cover the vessel the dough rises in with plastic wrap to prevent the outer dough from drying out and forming a skin. A waste-free alternative: an elasticized shower cap.

- **keep cool (enough)**
For room temperature–risen doughs, use room-temperature ingredients and keep the dough at around 70 degrees. Higher temperatures can break down gluten, forcing the yeast to work harder and faster to make the dough rise. That means the sugar-hungry yeast will take up 100 percent of the available sugar, which will result in bread with a boozy flavor and a pale crust.

- **take it fast or slow**
You'll learn more about scheduling your dough making on page 28, but this first rise is often a great place to build in a greater pause if you need it to tend to other responsibilities.

✳ **BREAD LINGO TO KNOW**

Yeast is a unicellular organism found in the environment (such as on plants) that initiates fermentation in bread doughs as well as in beverages like beer.

Bulk Rise (or Fermentation) also describes the first rise for dough. Most yeasted bread doughs rise twice; the first rise is the bulk rise because it happens when the dough isn't yet divided or shaped.

Fermentation is the chemical process that occurs when yeast consumes the available sugars and produces and emits alcohol and carbon dioxide. It can happen during both rises but some call the first rise "fermentation."

#4 SHAPING

HELPFUL TIPS

• **make clean cuts**

Often, dough needs to be divided (for smaller loaves or rolls and buns) before shaping. Every cut in the dough creates weak points in the gluten network, so slice cleanly. You can use a bench scraper or a sharp knife.

• **divide and conquer**

Make sure to cut even pieces of dough so they rise and bake evenly. You can use a scale to weigh them, if desired.

• **move decisively**

You want to shape dough with a gentle but decisive hand to avoid working out too much air while creating surface tension on the dough to develop a gluten sheath.

• **take a rest**

Dough that's hard to manipulate may need a little bit of time for the gluten network to relax.

• **cover up**

Make sure to cover pieces of dough you're not working with so they don't form a skin.

WHAT IS IT?

Your lump of dough might look close to round if it rose in a bowl, but if you try to bake that, you'll get a loose, low blob of a bread. Shaping does what it says—molds the dough into a shape—but it also determines the success of the loaf's trajectory in the oven. If you shape the loaf properly, you'll strengthen the loaf's structure a final time.

WHAT'S HAPPENING?

Much more occurs during shaping than you'd expect. First, you'll usually deflate the dough. When you do this, the gluten relaxes for better workability, the temperature of the dough equalizes throughout and, most important, the yeast is redistributed so new food sources become available for it to consume and give the dough more lift.

When you stretch, pull, or roll the dough into a shape, you'll be instructed to make tight, taut seals. This secures the outer gluten sheath so that the dough rises properly a second time and comes from the oven looking shapely.

 BREAD LINGO TO KNOW

Gluten Sheath is the outer network of gluten that forms around the interior gluten matrix. The sturdy sheath will get inflated during the bread's second rise (proofing) and serve as a barrier to keep the gases within. This ensures that the dough rises up and not out and holds onto carbon dioxide for an airy crumb.

Taut is a word you might know but not in the context of baking bread. We use the word to describe what the dough should feel like when it's properly shaped. The tension created on the surface of the dough when you shape it creates a strong gluten sheath. When a loaf, for example, doesn't have a taut surface, it can rise unevenly and bake into an unattractive shape from carbon dioxide escaping the bread at random points.

#5 SECOND RISE

WHAT IS IT?

This second rise of the dough after shaping it expands the dough to the appropriate size before baking. Another term for this post-shaping rise is proofing.

WHAT'S HAPPENING?

During this second rise, the dough relaxes, some more gas bubbles form to make up for those squashed during shaping, and a little more flavor develops through additional fermentation, as shaping unlocks additional sugars for the yeast to consume.

> **BREAD LINGO TO KNOW**
>
> *Proof* refers to the second rise for bread dough.

HELPFUL TIPS

• do not disturb

There might be a temptation to touch or move bread during its second rise. After shaping, transfer dough to the baking vessel (or to parchment that can be moved to that vessel) and then leave it to proof, so you don't deflate the dough before it hits the oven.

• it's all in the finger

To know the dough is done proofing, test it by gently pressing it with your finger. If the depression fills right in, the dough isn't ready. If it slowly fills in, you're good to bake. If it doesn't fill in, you've likely overproofed the dough.

how-to
RISING DURING PROOFING

how-to
TESTING PROOFING

#6 BAKING

WHAT IS IT?

Once your bread is properly proofed, you'll want to get it into the oven so it doesn't overproof. You might just give it a finishing touch like a brush of egg wash or a slash first. There's a variety of vessels your bread might be baked in but generally rustic loaves are baked at high temperatures and enriched and sandwich breads at more moderate temperatures.

WHAT'S HAPPENING?

When bread is in the oven, the chemical processes continue: Starches in flour gelatinize to form the bread's crumb. Further, enzymes convert starch to sugars to flavor bread and caramelize its crust. And the bread gets bigger still, despite its two rises. Water in the dough vaporizes when the loaf hits the hot oven, opening up the crumb, and causing the loaf to expand.

HELPFUL TIPS

• test internal temperature

Using a thermometer helps you know when to pull your bread: Properly baked lean breads should register between 205 and 210 degrees; enriched breads should register between 190 and 195 degrees. But internal temperature alone isn't sufficient: Your loaf won't overbake if you leave it in longer to get a browned crust.

• preheat your oven—and your pot

A blast of heat from your loaf's vessel can really help your bread finish with an airier crumb and fire-roasted crust—just be careful when handling hot equipment.

> **BREAD LINGO TO KNOW**
>
> *Gelatinization* is the process of starches absorbing water, swelling, and bursting. When bread reaches its doneness temperature, it is gelatinized and forms a solid mass that is its crumb.
>
> *Oven Spring* is the rise dough experiences when it hits a hot oven. The more spring, the taller and airier the loaf.

#7 COOLING AND STORING

HELPFUL TIPS

• resist the urge
Let most breads cool for a full 3 hours before slicing so they reach their full flavor and texture potential.

• elevate your bread
Cool loaves on a wire rack so air can circulate below and around them to prevent them from softening from trapped moisture.

• de-pan the pain
Yeasted pan breads trap steam in the loaf pan and are not fully set when they're done baking. Let the loaf cool in the pan for 15 minutes to set so it retains the proper shape, and then remove and transfer to a wire rack to let the crumb solidify.

• deep cuts
The tool you use to slice your cooled loaf is important. A chef's knife could squash your bread's crumb when you press down on it. A serrated knife is dragged across a bread's surface as it moves through so it preserves the crust and interior crumb.

• temperate climate
Keep bread you're storing out of the refrigerator; cold temperatures speed retrogradation.

WHAT IS IT?

Unfortunately, you can't eat most breads when they come out of the oven, no matter how glorious they smell (you can eat some quick breads like biscuits warm, and flatbreads are ideal fresh from the oven). You need to transfer loaves to a wire rack to cool, usually for about 3 hours, before slicing. And while it's called fresh bread for a reason, you can store bread at room temperature for a couple days (you'll find that sweetened and enriched breads last longer).

WHAT'S HAPPENING?

During cooling, starches continue to gelatinize, excess moisture evaporates, and the true flavor of the loaf comes to the fore. To preserve that, proper storage is necessary. Once exposed to air, bread starch undergoes retrogradation. When the bread bakes, the starch molecules absorb water and lose their structure, giving fresh bread its moist chew. But as the bread cools and sits, the starch molecules in the bread recrystallize, turning the bread hard and crumbly—what we think of as stale.

TO KNEAD OR NOT TO KNEAD

When we talk about physically manipulating yeasted bread dough to develop gluten, we call the process "working" (see page 3). That's because we know that kneading, the most common way to work dough, isn't the only way. Folding dough is a technique we use almost as often to stitch together a loaf. How do you know when to do what?

KNEAD

Kneading is for your average dough, one that's not superwet and that bakes up with a tender chew and a closed crumb. Breads that call for kneading include White Sandwich Bread (page 158), plush dinner rolls like Cast Iron Garlic-Herb Butter Rolls (page 123), simple flatbreads like Pita Bread (page 278), and enriched classics like Challah (page 308).

A goal of kneading is to develop plenty of gluten so a loaf can contain the carbon dioxide given off by yeast and rise tall and proud. To make sure that happens, it's important to know when you've kneaded enough. Dough that is adequately kneaded will clear the sides of the bowl (while likely still sticking to the bottom). It will be elastic, pulling like a rubber band without snapping and springing back into place. Dough that lacks the proper elasticity will break when pulled, signaling that the gluten network is compromised. Overkneaded dough becomes warm and can darken and dull slightly in color. See below.

FOLD

We use folding instead of kneading for well-hydrated rustic doughs (those that are too wet to engage with the mixer) that develop a chewy open crumb. Gently turning the dough over itself at regular intervals, usually after an extended first rise, accomplishes three things: It brings the wheat proteins into closer proximity with one another, keeping the process of gluten development going at a maximum clip; it aerates the dough, replenishing the oxygen that the yeast consumed during fermentation; and it elongates and redistributes the air bubbles that turn into chewy open pockets once the dough is baked. The result is well-risen bread with a moist crumb.

Our No-Knead Rustic Loaf (page 186) is the poster child for this method. Like with kneading, the dough evolves quite a bit just through this folding process, turning from a lumpy mass to cohesive dough. Check out the stages.

Underkneaded Dough: The dough still sticks to the sides of the bowl.

Perfectly Kneaded Dough: The dough clears the sides of the bowl (it will still stick to the bottom in most cases).

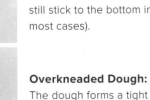

Overkneaded Dough: The dough forms a tight ball that lacks elasticity.

Mixed Dough Before Folding: Dough starts as a lumpy mass.

Dough Mid-Folding: Dough becomes cohesive.

Finished Dough: Dough becomes smooth and extensible.

ESSENTIAL EQUIPMENT FOR EVERYDAY BREAD

Many bread books and recipes call for such a list of equipment that it seems they assume bread baking is your only kitchen activity—the collection becomes expensive, takes up a lot of space, and is too niche to use for anything else. We've developed recipes to call for only a set of multiuse essentials.

SCALE

Weighing your ingredients—wet and dry—ensures consistent results. We prefer digital scales for their readability and precision. Look for one that has a large weight range and that can be "zeroed." The **OXO Good Grips 11 lb. Food Scale with Pull Out Display** has easy-to-read buttons, and its display can be pulled out from the platform when weighing bulky items.

LIQUID MEASURING CUP

It's helpful to have multiple sizes of liquid measuring cups for bread baking. Whisk together your liquid ingredients right in the cup before mixing. The industry-standard **Pyrex Measuring Cup** is unbeatable. We use the 2-cup, 4-cup, and 8-cup sizes in this book.

STAND MIXER

A stand mixer, with its hands-free operation, attachments, and strong mixing arm, is a must if you bake bread regularly. Heft matters, as does a motor that can handle stiff dough. Our favorite is the **KitchenAid Pro Line Series 7 Quart Stand Mixer**. Our best buy is the **KitchenAid Classic Plus Series 4.5-Quart Tilt-Head Stand Mixer**.

FOOD PROCESSOR

Though not necessary for loaves, a food processor brings together pizza dough in a flash. Look for a workbowl that has a capacity of at least 11 cups. With a powerful motor, responsive pulsing action, sharp blades, and a simple design, the **Cuisinart Custom 14 Food Processor** is our favorite.

BENCH SCRAPER

This basic tool is handy for transferring dough from one surface to another and for cutting dough into pieces. Our winner is the **Dexter-Russell Sani-Safe 6" x 3" Dough Cutter/Scraper**. It has a comfortable handle, and the deeply beveled edge cuts through dough quickly.

ROLLING PIN

We roll out sandwich bread dough, flatbreads, layered loaves like Prosciutto and Fig Pinwheel Bread (page 312), and shaped rolls like Crescent Rolls (page 106). We like French-style wood rolling pins without handles. These pins come straight and tapered. We tend to reach for straight, which makes achieving even dough thickness and rolling out larger disks easy. The **J.K. Adams Plain Maple Rolling Dowel** has a gentle weight and a slightly textured surface for less sticking.

PIZZA PEEL

A peel is a wide, paddle-like board or metal spatula with a long handle that's useful for sliding flatbreads into and out of a hot oven. Metal baking peels are easy to clean and store. If you don't have a pizza peel, you can shape flatbreads on an overturned baking sheet.

BAKING STEEL/STONE

Both steels and stones encourage the development of a crisp, browned crust by conducting heat and transferring it evenly and steadily to the bread. We've found that steels, when a recipe allows for them, perform better: The faster transfer of heat causes bread to rise higher and bake more quickly. We have two favorites: **The Original Baking Steel** and the **Nerd Chef Steel Stone, Standard ¼"**. A stone is more lightweight and generally has more surface area to accommodate long breads or a baking sheet. Look for one made of clay or stone like the **Old Stone Oven Pizza Baking Stone**. If you don't have either, use an overturned rimmed baking sheet in place of them.

WIRE RACK

Cooling loaves on a wire rack allows air to circulate so the bread dries properly and retains a crisp crust. The **Checkered Chef Cooling Rack** is an essential.

LOAF PAN

We prefer 8½ x 4½-inch loaf pans to 9 x 5-inch pans; they produce tall loaves with rounder tops. Our favorite for professional-quality results is the **USA Pan Loaf Pan, 1 lb Volume**.

13 BY 9-INCH BAKING DISH

Thick, tempered glass dishes retain heat to ensure deep, even browning on rolls. The **Pyrex Basics 3 Quart Glass Oblong Baking Dish** is sturdy, dishwasher-safe, and scratch-resistant.

BAKING PANS

Sweet treats won't stick to straight-sided nonstick pans. For a 13 by 9-inch rectangular pan and a 9-inch cake pan that browns breads evenly and releases them cleanly, choose the **Williams-Sonoma Goldtouch Nonstick** series.

MUFFIN TIN

The **OXO Good Grips Non-Stick Pro 12-Cup Muffin Pan** has an oversized rim for easy holding and turning.

CAST-IRON SKILLET

A cast-iron skillet creates crisp crusts on flatbreads and cornbread and beautiful browning and height on pull-apart dinner rolls and wreath-like loaves. You'll never replace the pre-seasoned **Lodge 12-inch Cast Iron Skillet**. Or you can go big with the **Smithey Ironware No. 12 Cast Iron Skillet**.

DUTCH OVEN

The humid environment created in a covered Dutch oven helps to produce a dramatically open crumb structure and a shiny, crisp crust on breads. The **Le Creuset 7¼-Quart Round French Oven** is the gold standard of Dutch ovens. We've found you can also produce a proper rustic loaf in a Dutch oven of 4½ quarts or greater. As a bonus, if you have an oval Dutch oven (8 quarts), you can shape our rustic breads into bâtards (see page 188).

RIMMED BAKING SHEET

We bake a number of free-form buns and flatbreads on a rimmed baking sheet. A light-colored surface heats and browns breads evenly. You'll want more than one thick, sturdy **Nordic Ware Baker's Half Sheet** on hand.

INSTANT-READ THERMOMETER

It's helpful to use a thermometer to check that breads are within a given temperature range before you pull them from the oven. Thermometers with long probes easily reach the center of a loaf. The **Thermo Works Thermapen Mk4** has every bell and whistle.

SERRATED KNIFE

You need a good knife to make it all the way through your loaves, from crust to crumb. The sharp, well-balanced **Mercer Culinary M23210 Millennia 10-inch Wide Wavy Edge Bread Knife** has a blade long enough to span large loaves and thick sandwiches.

OVEN THERMOMETER

It's common for ovens to run hot or cold. The most reliable way to know the exact temperature of your oven is to use a thermometer. The **CDN Pro Accurate Oven Thermometer** has a clear display and attaches to the oven rack securely.

PASTRY BRUSH

We use a pastry brush to paint loaves with egg wash before they enter the oven or to finish baked breads with melted butter. Our favorite pastry brush, the **Winco Flat Pastry and Basting Brush, 1½ Inch** has a thick head of bristles, allowing it to pick up and deposit the greatest volume of egg wash, oil, butter, or glaze in a single pass. The bristles feel agile and precise.

 ## THE CHALLENGER BREAD PAN

If you do a lot of bread baking and happen to have this popular pan, essentially an oblong cast-iron cloche (a stoneware vessel with a shallow base and domed lid that is used for baking bread), you can use it in our recipes calling for a Dutch oven. It works essentially the same way—heating well and evenly and enclosing the bread in a humid environment. Its shape accommodates boule and bâtard bread shapes. We made our breads in both Dutch ovens and the Challenger pan and saw little difference in the final product.

THE BAKER'S LARDER

FLOURS

Flours are distinguished by their protein content, their variety of wheat, and if they're refined or not. More protein leads to more gluten development, which, in turn, translates to chewier bread. For bread-baking flours, we prefer unbleached to bleached because bleached flour can carry off-flavors. You can store flour in an airtight container in your pantry for up to one year. Here are the flours we use again and again in this book. For information on other whole-grain varieties we use in our rustic breads, see page 34.

ALL-PURPOSE

All-purpose flour is the most versatile variety. It has a moderate protein content (10 to 11.7 percent, depending on the brand) and is good when you want a relatively tender, soft crumb, like for quick breads, rolls, and sweet breads. We use easy-to-find Gold Medal Unbleached All-Purpose Flour (10.5 percent protein). Pillsbury All-Purpose Unbleached Flour (also 10.5 percent protein) offers comparable results. If you use an AP flour with a higher protein content (such as King Arthur Unbleached All-Purpose Flour, with 11.7 percent protein) in moist, cakey recipes, the results may be drier and chewier.

BREAD

Bread flour has a high protein content (12 to 14 percent), which ensures strong gluten development. Because of its structure-building properties, we use it for most breads in this book. You cannot substitute all-purpose flour in these recipes; the bread will not be able to support an airy, chewy crumb. We use King Arthur Unbleached Bread Flour.

SEMOLINA

Semolina flour is a golden-colored flour that is made by coarsely grinding the endosperm of durum wheat. Using some of this Italian flour in our One-Hour Pizza (page 236) gives the dough more extensibility in less time because the gluten network semolina forms isn't as elastic as with other flours. The flour is high in protein but forms a dough that's easier to stretch and doesn't snap back. Its coarse texture makes it good for dusting a pizza peel.

DURUM

Durum flour is the by-product of semolina production. "Durum" means "hard" in Latin; it's very high in protein, but not in gluten-forming proteins. Like semolina flour, it's associated with pasta. Fine, powdery, and flavorful, the flour is high in beta-carotene and gives bread a golden hue. Be sure to use durum flour for our durum breads (pages 218 and 222); semolina flour gives it a gummy crumb.

WHOLE-WHEAT

Whole-wheat flour has a distinctive flavor and texture because it is made from the entire wheat berry, unlike white flours, which are ground solely from the endosperm. Whole-wheat flour has a high protein content (about 13 percent), but it behaves differently than white flour, and it can make breads dense (see page 34). We rely on a combination of white and whole-wheat flours. We use King Arthur Premium Whole Wheat Flour in the test kitchen. Whole-wheat flour contains more fat than refined flours and goes rancid more quickly; store it in the freezer and bring it to room temperature before using it.

CORNMEAL

Cornmeal comes in many different varieties and grind sizes and it's important to use what a recipe calls for. We prefer fine cornmeal in most of our baking recipes. While coarse stone-ground cornmeal has great texture and strong corn flavor, it doesn't soften and can make bread gritty.

LEAVENERS

Quick breads rise with chemical leaveners. There are two varieties— baking soda and baking powder—and they can be used alone or in combination. Other breads rise with yeast and time. Yeast comes in two forms: fresh and dry. We don't use fresh, as it is highly perishable. There are two types of dry yeast: active dry yeast and instant yeast. We prefer instant.

BAKING SODA

Baking soda is an alkali and therefore requires an acidic ingredient in the batter or dough, such as buttermilk, in order to produce carbon dioxide. The leavening action happens right after mixing, so you should bake right away. Baking soda also promotes browning. Once its container is opened, it will lose its effectiveness after six months.

BAKING POWDER

Baking powder is a mixture of baking soda, a dry acid, and double-dried cornstarch. The cornstarch absorbs moisture and prevents premature production of gas. Baking powder works twice—when it first comes in contact with a liquid, and again in response to heat. Baking powder also has a six-month shelf life.

YEAST

Active dry yeast is treated with heat, so it must be proofed, or dissolved in liquid with some sugar, before use. We use instant yeast in the test kitchen because it can be added directly to the dry ingredients—the result of undergoing a gentler drying process that does not destroy the outer cells. We have also found that it yields breads with a cleaner flavor than those made with active dry because it doesn't contain any dead yeast cells. (One exception: Kesra Rakhsis on page 274.) Yeast has a four-month shelf life. We like to store it in the freezer.

LIQUIDS

The type of liquid you use to bring a dough together affects the loaf's structure and, in some cases, richness.

WATER

Water is the default liquid in bread baking. When it mixes with flour, the proteins in the flour hydrate and begin to form gluten.

MILK

Milk features in a lot of our recipes. The fat in the milk tenderizes the crumb and can weaken the gluten structure; the proteins can contribute to browning.

BUTTERMILK

Buttermilk is a favorite in quick breads like biscuits. The acidic dairy can react with baking soda for a lighter crumb. It also provides breads like our Buttermilk Dill Bread (page 171) with a pleasant tang.

BEER

Beer is, in some ways, like liquid bread: The fermented flavor compounds in beer are similar to those in a bread dough starter. Therefore, its addition can give your bread the more complex flavor of one made with a starter. We use mild-flavored lager, like Budweiser; the fermentation process it goes through allows the bready flavors to come forward.

FATS

Fat isn't just for flavor. When you add fat in large enough amounts, it coats the flour proteins, making them less able to form a strong gluten network; that means tender, less open bread.

OIL

Oil is usually added in small quantities to add extensibility to doughs and to tenderize breads that don't need rich flavor. Neutral-tasting oil, such as vegetable oil, adds tenderness without changing the dough's flavor. For flatbreads that are baked at superhot temperatures, oil in dough can also result in a crisp crust: the oil essentially fries our Coques with Spinach, Raisins and Pinenuts (page 270) in the oven.

BUTTER

Butter is a must in most enriched bread recipes. We use unsalted butter. (The salt amount in different brands of butter varies; plus, salted butters have a higher water content.) Most unsalted butter contains 81 to 82 percent fat; some European-style butters contain 83 to 86 percent fat (and therefore less water). This difference isn't noticeable enough in most breads to warrant splurging on premium butter.

LARD

Lard is rendered pork fat and, unlike butter, contains no water that can turn to steam during baking. Without water, the lard fully coats flour particles without encouraging gluten formation so it produces very tender baked goods. We use it here for biscuits (see page 55).

EGGS

Typically used in sweet doughs, egg yolks give doughs richness, and egg whites contribute extra structure. We brush a lot of our breads with a mixture of egg and water (with a pinch of salt). The protein in the white browns the loaf's exterior, and the fat in the yolk makes the crust shiny. The salt doesn't just give the wash flavor; it denatures the proteins, making the wash more fluid and easier to brush over delicate doughs.

SALT

Unless otherwise stated, we use inexpensive table salt in our bread recipes because it is fine-grained and thus dissolves easily. Salt isn't just for flavor; it actually strengthens the gluten network in dough to help make chewy bread.

SUGAR

Many bread recipes call for adding a couple tablespoons of sugar to add subtle sweetness and to help with browning. The most common sugar choices in bread are granulated, for a cleaner flavor, and honey, for an earthier flavor. Note that liquid honey can contribute to the hydration level of the bread dough.

QUICK BREAD:

REAL BREAD WITHOUT YEAST, KNEADING, OR TIME

We're thrilled about the bountiful chapter of quick breads in this book (see page 38). "Quick bread" sounds like an oxymoron. Maybe that's why the term is used more often for sweet cakey loaves than for the large category of real multipurpose, savory breads it covers. Quick bread recipes might be the gateway to a lifestyle of turning out fresh bread in your kitchen every week. While they lower the bar of entry, they're also just fun to make and delicious in their own right.

These batters and soft doughs, leavened by baking powder and/or baking soda, aren't worked much; they don't need to sit aside to rise; and they're usually dropped on a baking sheet, in a muffin tin, or spread in a pan. They eschew a lot of the steps we reviewed in pages 2–9. That's what makes them quick. But to satisfy like yeasted breads do, they benefit from some test kitchen tricks. Let's take the fast track to bread.

RETHINK WHAT'S A ROLL

You'll find a chapter of rolls in this book (see page 96), but individual, hand-held, satisfying savory soup/stew/roast partners can come in quick bread forms too. You can enjoy biscuits with butter and jam or savor an impressive Gruyère and Herb Buttermilk Biscuit (page 52) all on its own. Or do more, like serving drop biscuits (see page 42) to accompany a roast ham or Cast Iron Orange-Herb Biscuits (page 50) to dunk into a creamy carrot soup. Muffins aren't just for mornings. Mop up the braising liquid from braised short ribs with Rosemary-Parmesan Polenta Muffins (page 64).

HAVE FUN WITH FLAVOR

Simple flavor additions not only make quick breads more interesting, they also give them savory notes you'd expect from regular bread. Sprinkle spices or seeds on biscuits (see page 43), stuff them with cheese (see page 44), or fill them with pork (see page 46). Stir spicy chorizo into a simple muffin (see page 67). Add briny feta and fresh dill to your garden zucchini bread (see page 73). Spread something simple like Three-Ingredient Bread (page 69) or Fresh Corn Muffins (page 63) with a flavored butter (see pages 94–95).

ALT-FLOUR ADVENTURE

Adding whole-wheat flour to date-nut bread (see page 74), sweet, earthy sorghum flour to skillet bread (see page 82), or rye and whole-wheat flour to Boston Brown Bread (page 92), or even binding nuts and seeds with psyllium husk in a flourless loaf (see page 70), gives flash-made breads the heartiness of all-day-affair recipes. These breads all stand up to a generous schmear.

BATTER UP

Don't associate a loaf pan with cake. We love some sweet, tender breads produced by the pan like glazed Pumpkin Bread (page 77), but we also achieve savory quick loaves that remind you of bakery bread by adjusting the consistency of the batter—we make it so thick it seems more like a dough. A drier batter (and therefore a thicker one) won't generate so much steam in the oven, and so it won't lighten so significantly as it bakes. Unlike with the sweet version, you can take a real bite out of Feta-Dill Zucchini Bread (page 73) and slather it with butter (see page 95). Cut Bacon-Onion Cheese Bread (page 78) into hearty meal-making slices.

CRACK OPEN A COLD ONE

You'll see us adding beer to recipes to up the yeasty, caramelized wheat flavors in baked breads, and the trick is particularly useful in breads that don't get the time to sit and ferment and create new flavor compounds. You can build a satisfying sandwich on our three-ingredient quick bread (see page 69) that's powered by beer.

✱ WHAT BISCUIT SHOULD YOU MAKE RIGHT NOW?

We've made the case for biscuits anytime. And we've provided enough recipes so that making biscuits often won't turn into a bore. So how do you choose?

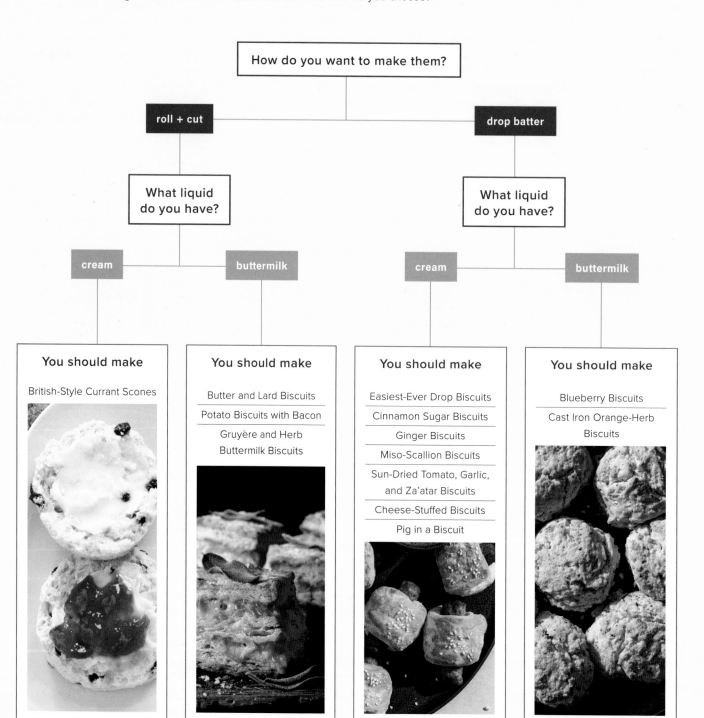

How do you want to make them?

roll + cut

drop batter

What liquid do you have?

What liquid do you have?

cream **buttermilk**

cream **buttermilk**

You should make

British-Style Currant Scones

You should make

Butter and Lard Biscuits

Potato Biscuits with Bacon

Gruyère and Herb Buttermilk Biscuits

You should make

Easiest-Ever Drop Biscuits

Cinnamon Sugar Biscuits

Ginger Biscuits

Miso-Scallion Biscuits

Sun-Dried Tomato, Garlic, and Za'atar Biscuits

Cheese-Stuffed Biscuits

Pig in a Biscuit

You should make

Blueberry Biscuits

Cast Iron Orange-Herb Biscuits

ROLLS DON'T NEED TO COME FROM A BAG

A roll is nice anytime, but it's often a special-occasion accompaniment. If you have too many dishes for your event that also need advance care—say, a long-cooking turkey or a dessert in the oven—the thought of preparing rolls so that they're warm, soft, and fresh at go-time could easily drive you to the supermarket version. But packaged sponges aren't worthy of a special meal. The rolls in this book are accessible to anyone, due in part to how you can manipulate the timeline for making them (see page 31), and in part to the easy-to-follow techniques we use for them.

HOT AND FRESH

Almost any roll in this book can be made, risen, and shaped—and then hidden away. Clear the scene for making supper, and refrigerate the dough until you want to bake. A room-temperature rise, usually an hour or so, is all rolls need before hitting the oven. For more information, see page 31.

STRESS-FREE SHAPING

No matter how intricate it might be, when you shape a loaf of bread, you're generally working on that technique one time—and then the loaf is ready for the oven. Rolls take more time to shape, and if the action is difficult, you probably won't enjoy doing it 12 or more times. With our doughs, shaping will never be a problem. Take our White Dinner Rolls (page 100), for example. We developed this dough to be ultraworkable—so workable that you can also make it into knots and crescents with ease. Using some shortening instead of all butter prevents the dough from being greasy and an egg makes it supple.

These fluffy, tight-crumbed rolls don't need to be so hydrated that they're too wet to work with. But wetter doughs that create a rustic, open crumb can be incredibly stressful to drag across the counter since they stick at every turn. Our solution for really wet doughs: Don't shape them at all. For our Rustic Dinner Rolls (page 130), we simply toss portions of dough back and forth in our floured hands and bake them in a cake pan to start so they take on a nice shape.

how-to
SHAPING ROLLS

TWO SIMPLE TOOLS TO MAKE SIMPLE ROLLS EVEN MORE SIMPLE

Dough balls of even size, cut cleanly from a log of dough, are key to well-shaped, evenly risen and baked rolls and you can achieve this with a basic kitchen ruler and a bench scraper (see page 10). Measure your dough log to make sure you've stretched it to the right length and then all you need to do is press down quickly and confidently at even intervals with one motion of the bench scraper. This creates less risk of dragging than cutting with a knife (of course, if you're more confident doing this with a knife, you can use a sharp chef's knife).

UP AND AWAY

Rolls are meant to be true rounds, not flying saucers. An easy way to achieve that even for beginners? Bake the shaped dough rounds in a vessel. It's fun to pull the finished rolls apart at a communal table. Dutch Oven Pull-Apart Rolls (page 102) are impressively lofty. Oatmeal Dinner Rolls (page 116) look attractive as a round of oat-sprinkled fluffy rolls; a traditional baking dish lets the rolls sit snug. Cast Iron Garlic-Herb Butter Rolls (page 123) get beautiful browned exteriors from the pan that shine through their garlic butter painting. Our Scoop-and-Bake Dinner Rolls (page 111) need only to be dropped into the cups of a muffin tin.

IT'S IN THE WRIST

It's important to cup and roll dough rounds until taut to set the gluten sheath (see page 6) and seal the bottom to achieve well-shaped rolls. The steps to shaping White Dinner Rolls on page 100 translate to a lot of rolls in this book and beyond. Check out exactly what the dough should look like when you're done rolling and how that translates to a better-than-from-the-bag roll once baked.

Loose Shaping

Misshapen Roll

Tight Shaping

Proper Roll

STORING ROLLS

The satisfaction a warm-from-the-oven roll delivers is up there with freshly baked chocolate chip cookies and hot-from-the-oil french fries. But if you want to store rolls, we can help you relive those minutes as best as you can after the fact.

Many rolls and buns are enriched—that is, they have some incorporated fat (butter, egg, or milk). These can taste good after being stored in a zipper-lock bag at room temperature for up to two days. Lean rolls are really best the day they're made or maybe the day after with a reheat if stored in a zipper-lock bag. Wrapped in foil before being placed in the bag, all rolls can be frozen for up to one month. To reheat rolls stored either way, wrap them (thawed if frozen) in aluminum foil, place them on a rimmed baking sheet, and bake them in a 350-degree oven for 10 minutes.

 PICKING THE RIGHT ROLL

There are a lot of rolls in chapter 2 of this book. Pick your desired outcome and learn what recipes are best for you to choose from.

SOFT

White Dinner Rolls

Fluffy Dinner Rolls

Potato Burger Buns

Brown-and-Serve
Dinner Rolls

Hawaiian Sweet Rolls

Oatmeal Dinner Rolls

RUSTIC

Rustic Dinner Rolls

No-Knead Rustic
Dinner Rolls

Olive Rolls with
Rosemary and Fennel

SANDWICH

Hoagie Rolls

Pretzel Buns

Potato Burger Buns

English Muffins

Brioche Burger Buns

RICH

Fluffy Dinner Rolls

Hawaiian Sweet Rolls

Cast Iron Garlic-Herb
Butter Rolls

Crescent Rolls

Thai Curry Butter
Fan Rolls

Porcini-Truffle
Crescent Rolls

Brioche Burger Buns

FUN SHAPES

Knotted Rolls

Crescent Rolls

Chive Spiral Rolls

Porcini-Truffle
Crescent Rolls

Thai Curry
Butter Fan Rolls

Lop Cheung Bao

QUICK

Scoop-and-Bake
Dinner Rolls

Brown-and-Serve
Dinner Rolls

Crumpets

SERVE SANDWICHES ON HOMEMADE BREAD EVERY DAY

There are on average 12 slices of bread in a loaf. If you make two sandwiches per day, that's three days of sandwiches per loaf. Once you learn how easy it is to make homemade sandwich bread, it will feel like a breeze to make two loaves per week—and fun to try a new kind each time. Nearly every sandwich loaf uses the same mixing and shaping techniques so your muscle memory will be strong. Learn the steps on page 159 and/or check out our how-to video. Be sure to roll the dough tightly, seal any seams, and tuck the ends of the dough as needed to fit into the loaf pan.

✳ BEST BREAD IN THE BREAK ROOM

"White or wheat," the sandwich shop usually asks (the latter a bit of a misnomer for whole-wheat). And despite all the breads at the supermarket, that's usually the extent of what you'll see for a homemade brown-bag lunch sandwich. But condiments aren't the only things that can liven up your deli ham sandwich. Make lunch special with:

- **sweet** (see page 160) **or spicy** (see page 162) **swirls**
- **crunchy seed** (see page 164) **or grain** (see page 180) **coatings**
- **rich crusts** (see page 159)
- **hits of freshness** (see page 171)
- **a wholesome oat finish** (see page 178)
- **a spice blend exterior** (see page 174)

STORING SANDWICH BREAD

Sandwich breads are great to have on hand for lunches for a few days. They generally don't have crisp crusts so you don't have to worry about the exteriors softening if you wrap them. Wrap loaves in a double layer of plastic wrap and store them at room temperature for up to three days. Wrapped in aluminum foil after the plastic, loaves can be frozen for up to one month. Sometimes we like to freeze half of a loaf for fresh bread for the second half of the week. You can also slice leftover bread and freeze the slices in a zipper-lock bag, thawing individual slices in the microwave: Place the slices on a plate (uncovered) and microwave them on high power for 15 to 25 seconds.

 how-to
SHAPING A SANDWICH LOAF

YOU REALLY CAN MAKE BAKERY LOAVES AT HOME

Those first diving into bread baking often start with the perceived achievable basics—buttery rolls, fluffy white sandwich breads, of course quick breads. It's understandable. Recipes that promise the browning, crackle, rise, and crumb of an artisan bakery–style bread usually call for much more than ingredients—equipment like a banneton, a couche, a lame, even lava rocks to transform your oven into a professional one—and these are far from kitchen standards. What if we said that all you need to make bakery-quality breads, as a beginner or an expert, are a hot oven and a Dutch oven? Our recipes show just how to produce a baker's shelf full of the very best breads, all using this method.

 ## WHAT MAKES A BREAD "RUSTIC"?

"Rustic" is an adjective that people use to describe so many things, from accommodations to furniture to food. These are the qualities that we think of as rustic in the bread world.

THE DOUGH

- little to no fat and lots of water
- lots of developed gluten
- a long fermentation time
- a moist baking environment

THE BREAD

- a moist, chewy interior
- a structure with some open holes
- a complex flavor
- a dark, crisp crust

 ## BOULE OR BÂTARD

We use the boule as the default shape in our chapter of no-knead breads, but you can make any of those breads into a bâtard if you own an oval Dutch oven (see page 11). The boule has an impressive round and tall shape for the dinner table and the center yields wide slices for loaded topped toasts; the torpedo-shaped bâtard has a more even width and is excellent for slicing for sandwiches. Learn how to shape both on pages 187 and 189 and/or check out our how-to videos.

 how-to
SHAPING A BOULE

 how-to
SHAPING A BÂTARD

ATK'S NEW AND IMPROVED NO-KNEAD LOAF

The idea of no-knead bread was once a breakthrough phenomenon in the bread world—a rustic boule stitched together with time and no manual work. The standard method replaces the typical kneading that develops gluten to give bread structure with a long 8- to 16-hour autolyse (see page 2). During autolyse, the flour hydrates and enzymes work to break up its proteins so that the dough requires only a brief hand-knead to develop gluten. The dough is then baked in a Dutch oven instead of on a hot baking stone that is common for this style of bread; the humid environment gives the loaf a dramatic open crumb and a crisp crust.

America's Test Kitchen had our version that adapted the accepted technique for years, the "Almost No-Knead Bread" (let's call it No-Knead Bread A)—"*almost*" because we found the loaf needed more structure and flavor. So in our version, we added less than a minute of kneading, and we introduced an acidic tang from vinegar and a shot of yeasty flavor from beer.

When we dusted off that recipe for this book and baked it, we thought that, with all of our gained bread knowledge since its development, we could do better. And we did, producing a loftier, moister, chewier, more impressive loaf, our No-Knead Rustic Loaf (page 186) (let's call it No-Knead Bread B).

Experimenting with incremental changes that didn't increase but actually *decreased* the difficulty of making this already-simple loaf resulted in a recipe for beginners that would satisfy the most discerning bread head. How did we do it?

No-Knead Bread A   No-Knead Bread B

STEP-BY-STEP

1. WETTER IS BETTER

Increasing the dough's hydration (see page 4) ups the ante on two desirable aspects of this bread: an airy, open crumb and great chew. No-Knead Bread A had a hydration level (weight of liquid relative to flour) of 67 percent. We brought that up to a more liberal 73 percent for No-Knead Bread B. As the bread bakes, the extra water turns to steam, leaving hollow pockets in the dough that expand and are supported by the inherently stronger gluten structure. Additionally, these pockets expand more readily since the wetter dough is looser.

If wetter is better, could we keep going, then? No. Higher hydration levels cause adverse effects in dough: All that water dilutes and weakens the gluten it would otherwise work so well to build, hindering the bread's ability to rise—it will bloat out but not rise up.

2. TECHNICALLY COMPLETELY NO-KNEAD

With this wet dough, the minute knead was out—the dough would be too sticky. But we needed the structure to encourage that upward-not-outward rise. This is an excellent example of where including a set of folds is incredibly useful (see page 9). These are folds of the simple variety: After letting the dough rest to hydrate and start coming together (autolyse), you fold and turn the dough eight times, let it rest for 15 minutes, and then shape it as normal. That's it—and that improves the loaf's structure dramatically.

3. FIXING THE FLOUR

No-Knead Bread A was made with all-purpose flour. A simple upgrade: switching to bread flour. With its higher protein content, bread flour automatically optimizes gluten development for all things good: structure, chew, rise.

4. PREHEAT THE POT

The humid environment of the Dutch oven does wonders for a bread's crumb structure and creates a shiny, crisp crust. Getting the pot good and hot before placing the loaf inside does even more wonders—it gets the water to vaporize rapidly to open the crumb and expand the loaf further. The immediate hit of heat really turns your common pot into a steam-injected oven.

5. UNCOVERING A MASTERPIECE

Just like a hot pot, naturally, a hot oven helps get the activity within your Dutch oven going. For our No-Knead Bread A, we baked the bread at 425 degrees. For our updated version we take a dual approach, putting the loaf, covered, in the 475-degree oven we had preheated the pot in for greater oven spring, and then immediately reducing the temperature to 425 degrees. After 30 minutes, we remove the lid to finish browning and crisping the bread.

TWO VESSELS THAT TURN YOUR HOME OVEN INTO A PROFESSIONAL ONE

Cast-Iron Skillet

If you want a pan to get good and hot and stay that way, employ cast iron. You know it will give your steak a good sear, but you might not think to fill your skillet with dough. Cast iron has impeccable heat retention and it distributes that heat from the oven evenly to achieve biscuits, rolls, and breads with a crisp bottom and nicely browned crust. You could never achieve the burnish on recipes like Cast Iron Cinnamon Swirl Bread (page 320) or Garlic-Herb Butter Rolls (page 123) in a cake pan. The cast iron eliminates the need to bring out the heavy baking stone for recipes other than pizza and by snuggling dough pieces together in it, it encourages an upward rise and creates a warm and satisfying pull-apart bread situation, ideal for communal enjoyment.

Dutch Oven

This enameled cast-iron pot is closer to a professional baker's oven than a hot home oven. A loaf baked in one can achieve the two elements of rustic bread perfection: a dramatic open-crumbed structure and a shatteringly crisp crust. How?

First, as the loaf heats, it gives off steam to create a very humid environment inside the pot. Since moist air transfers heat much more efficiently than dry, the loaf heats rapidly. This in turn causes air bubbles inside to expand much faster, leading to a more open crumb. As a test, we baked two loaves, one in a Dutch oven and the other on a preheated baking stone. After 1 minute, the surface temperature of the Dutch oven–baked loaf had risen past 200 degrees, while the other loaf had reached only 135 degrees. Second, as steam condenses on the dough, it causes the starches to form a sheath that eventually dries out, giving the finished loaf a shiny, crisp crust.

Many recipes suggest adding water or ice to the oven, but home ovens cannot retain moisture in the way a steam-injected one can. With its thick walls, small volume, and heavy lid, a Dutch oven is perfect for creating and trapping steam.

BREAD: IT'S WHAT'S FOR DINNER

Bread is often a vehicle for sandwich fillings, a splash of soup, a hunk of cheese, a sweet glaze, smashed or shingled avocado, or just a good spread of butter. But bread doesn't just accompany the meal—it can be the meal. Case in point: flatbreads. In every culture, satisfying meals are built on the foundation of flavorful flatbreads. If, as we hope, baking bread becomes a pleasure for you, our flatbread recipes can turn that pleasure into a weekly menu helper.

Flatbreads are particularly helpful because the dough often rests a long time—sometimes up to three days—in the refrigerator to ferment, which means you can plan ahead, make your dough when you have more time, and shape and bake it off quickly when you don't. The time is spent all in the making—baking in a hot oven takes no time for these breads and cooling isn't a factor. Just don't burn the roof of your mouth.

FLATBREADS, TIMED

With the vibrant roster of flatbreads in this book, it's likely you might choose by flavor. But, since you'll presumably want to try all the recipes at some point, we suggest making your decision based on how much time you have. Note that in most cases, you can also make dough and then freeze it, so you can bake any time you want after thawing.

WHEN YOU MAKE THE DOUGH:

• 1 to 3 days before you want to bake and eat:
These are the ultimate set-it-and-forget flatbreads. Make the dough, let it ferment for days, and then top and bake with ease after work at a later date—as a bonus, these doughs' toppings require little work.

- Thin-Crust Pizza
- Broccoli Rabe and Salami Stromboli

• 1 to 2 days before you want to bake and eat:
This is a great category for Sunday prep. Make it a leisure day activity and bake early in the week when you're back to reality with obligation-filled days.

- Lahmajun
- Pizza al Taglio with Potatoes and Soppressata
- Thin-Crust Whole-Wheat Pizza with Garlic Oil, Three Cheeses, and Basil

• 3 to 4 hours before you want to bake and eat:
If you work from home or have the day off, you can prepare these breads earlier in the day and bake them at dinnertime.

- Adjaruli Khachapuri
- Detroit-Style Pizza
- Mana'eesh Za'atar
- Mushroom Musakhan
- Stuffed Pizza

• 2 hours before you want to bake and eat:
If you get these started when you walk in the door after a long day, you can reward yourself with a comforting dinner.

- Pepperoni Sheet-Pan Pizza
- Caprese Sheet-Pan Pizza
- Sheet-Pan Pizza with 'Nduja, Ricotta, and Cherry Peppers

• 1 hour before you want to bake and eat:
In a rush? Walk in the door, prepare these recipes, mangia.

- Kesra Rakhsis
- One-Hour Pizza
- Piadine
- Socca with Sautéed Onions and Rosemary

ENRICHED BREADS AREN'T JUST FOR SPECIAL OCCASIONS

They're buttery, usually a shiny golden color, shaped in beautiful stacks and snails, and often filled or topped with something intriguing or sparkly and sweet: Enriched breads might seem like the Cadillac of breads, baked goods only the most nimble of pastry chefs can craft. That's because the most impressive recipes take the most work, right? That was certainly the case with enriched breads of the past. But this book scratches the record hard on that. In fact, with these recipes, we might go as far as to say we've revolutionized enriched bread.

SAY NO TO KNEADING—AGAIN

It all begins with our brioche technique—another no-knead success story. Kneading traditional brioche dough presents challenges beyond other bread doughs. Traditionally, pats of perfectly softened butter are gradually thrown into the stand mixer and mixed into the dough until it turns supple—but only after the base dough has been kneaded enough to have developed a strong gluten network. Without the initial knead, which is subject to the normal issues of kneading bread dough, the butter would heavily coat the flour particles, impeding the gluten development required to give this bread its crumb. Still, on the dough's road to richness, it can break from the influx of butter or overheat and turn greasy; not to mention, the process can take 20 minutes of stand mixer time.

With water, eggs, and even all that butter, brioche is a good candidate for the no-knead method, because it's plenty hydrated. No more softened butter science: We simply melt the butter and fold it (along with egg yolks, water, and sugar) into the dry ingredients to create a loose—soupy, even—dough. We give it a series of folds at 30-minute intervals to encourage gluten to develop. Then we give it an overnight refrigerator fermentation to further strengthen gluten without the risk of overproofing. Finally, a unique shaping method—dividing the dough and shaping it into two tight balls before placing them in the pan (for a loaf)—is enough extra manipulation to strengthen the dough a final time and ensure a fine crumb. These steps result in a dough with as much strength as one kneaded in a machine—but it is also foolproof. We call that revolutionary.

how-to
FOLDING NO-KNEAD BRIOCHE

WAKE UP WITH SOMETHING SWEET

A pan full of warm, squidgy cinnamon rolls or a plate of glazed doughnuts always seems like a good idea for a slowed-down weekend morning or a brunch with company, but it's not that enjoyable when you're sleep-deprived—these breads have a lot of steps that might mean waking at dawn to have something to eat by 10 a.m. With the relaxed timelines of our enriched bread recipes, you can schedule your preparation so that the morning steps are minimal.

Enriched breads by definition have a lot of butter, and butter is liquid at warm temperatures and soft-to-greasy at room temperature, which means enriched doughs can be hard to work with. Depending on the composition of the dough, we sometimes let the dough spend its first rise in the fridge for a good while—at least 16 hours—before shaping and baking. That means for breads like Chocolate Babka (page 314), you can plan to wake up at, say, 7:30 a.m. for a 10 a.m. serve time. For other sweet breads, often rolls, we let them spend their second rise in the refrigerator. This makes recipes like Sticky Buns (page 302) ideal: You can wake an hour or so before you want to bake, bring the buns to room temperature and then pop them in the oven.

THE SWEET AND SAVORY SIDE OF ENRICHED BREADS

Enriched breads, with their buttery flavor and exceptional workability, can be loaves and they can be rolls, but they can also be platforms for impressive flavor. You know sticky buns, you know babka, but we like to swap these iconic sweet fillings and coatings for savory ingredients on occasion.

No-Knead Brioche	→	Garlic-Thyme Pull-Apart Brioche
Sticky Buns	→	Sausage and Chive Pull-Apart Rolls
Chocolate Babka	→	Pizza Babka
Butter Fan Rolls	→	Thai Curry Butter Fan Rolls
Crescent Rolls	→	Porcini-Truffle Crescent Rolls

ONE DOUGH, MANY BREADS

Once you know your bread categories and how simple it can be to fashion all the beautiful breads in this book, you can finesse them as you like. Change up the shape or the filling or topping for a bread that is intimately appropriate for the occasion without learning how to make another dough. We make it explicitly clear how to do so.

In each chapter, we have a special feature devoted to "One Great Dough." These are your must-haves like white dinner rolls and brioche. Then, we provide variations that use those same doughs to shape or flavor them in a number of completely different ways. This exponentially grows the breads in your catalog: By mastering seven key bread recipes, you automatically become skilled at baking 34 unique breads.

DROP BISCUITS

Cheese-Stuffed Biscuits

Cinnamon Sugar Biscuits

Ginger Biscuits

Miso-Scallion Biscuits

Pig in a Biscuit

Sun-Dried Tomato, Garlic, and Za'atar Biscuits

THIN-CRUST PIZZA

Broccoli Rabe and Salami Stromboli

Shakshuka Breakfast Pizza

WHITE DINNER ROLLS

Chive Spiral Rolls

Crescent Rolls

Dutch Oven Pull-Apart Rolls

Knotted Rolls

MANA'EESH ZA'ATAR

Cheese Mana'eesh

Labneh Mana'eesh Za'atar

Tomato Mana'eesh

WHITE SANDWICH BREAD

Cinnamon Raisin Swirl Bread

Sandwich Bread with Everything Bagel Crust

Parmesan–Black Pepper Sandwich Bread

Zhoug Swirl Bread

NO-KNEAD BRIOCHE

Brioche Burger Buns

Brioche Cinnamon Buns

Garlic-Thyme Pull-Apart Brioche

Pumpkin Spice Brioche à Tête

NO-KNEAD RUSTIC LOAF

(Almost) No-Knead Rustic Flatbreads

No-Knead Rustic Rolls

No-Knead Rustic Bâtard

No-Knead Rustic Sandwich Loaf

RISE ON YOUR TIME

Convenience and bread baking may seem mutually exclusive to you. While there are alternating hands-on and hands-off steps and sometimes long periods of waiting that come along with yeasted doughs, this up and down time is what allows you to adapt bread recipes according to your own timetable. No matter the bread, no matter the steps, you can make bread work for you.

There are two points in the bread baking process that you can shorten or elongate depending on how much time you have to babysit your bread: the first rise (fermentation) and the second rise (proofing). Two factors controlling the activity of yeast are temperature and time (and time is the busy baker's friend). A room-temperature rise puts you on a faster track to bread, which could be convenient if you have a day without plans or you just want bread ASAP (although we can also suggest quick breads for that). But in many cases rising can take place in the refrigerator. Chilling things doesn't kill yeast or stunt its abilities, but it does slow down its activity, so rising to the appropriate level or fermenting adequately can take place over longer periods of time.

THE OVERNIGHT FIRST RISE

Once you've mixed the dough, some of our recipes offer the option to let the bulk dough rise for more than 8 hours in the refrigerator (normally, this would happen in 1 or 2 hours on the counter at room temperature). The upper limit could be 18 hours, as for our rustic loaves (see pages 186–223), or even up to three days, as for our Thin-Crust Pizza (page 228). You *could* finish the rustic loaf's first rise in 8 hours but you'd be baking before you go to sleep. You *could* let pizza rise in a day but maybe you want to prep in advance of working late all week. This elongated rise is ideal when you want to do just a little work at a time or you like to prep and plan for your week.

We should note that adding time to your bread's rise has benefits beyond convenience. A cold bulk ferment can make rich doughs, like the layered braids of Chocolate Babka (page 314) easier to shape as the refrigerator time firms up the butter. And the slower yeast activity translates to higher rises, nicely developed air bubbles, and more time for complex-tasting flavor compounds to develop. In our recipes, we'll spell out when a dough is suited to rising overnight in the refrigerator.

THE OVERNIGHT SECOND RISE

The second option for adjusting your bread recipe's timeline is to make it all the way through shaping (arguably the most consuming part) and then let the dough rise in the refrigerator before baking. This is great when the day you want bread is filled with activities or with other recipes to cook. You've already done the work; you just need to bake. This allows you the satisfaction of pulling apart a warm sticky bun (see page 302) early in the morning, of serving a hot pan of Cast Iron Garlic-Herb Butter Rolls (page 123) to a crowd for game-day snacks, of topping a potato, meat, and cheese pizza al taglio (see page 246) and popping it in the oven before a short bake to serve after work, or of offering fresh, warm rolls to your guests.

There is one hands-off step you may need to add if your bread proofs overnight—an hour or so sitting at room temperature to lighten and reach the proper height and internal temperature before baking. (Note that in some roll recipes, you may experience a slightly less tall rise in doughs that were refrigerated.)

EXPAND YOUR YEAST KNOWLEDGE

Yeast functions to consume sugars and starches within (in this case) dough and convert them into alcohol, releasing carbon dioxide as a by-product. In doing this, yeast both leavens bread and creates flavor. During fermentation, two enzymes present in yeast break the flour's starches into simple sugars. When feeding on these, the yeast releases carbon dioxide, which allows the loaf to lift and expand; alcohol, which gives the bread flavor; and a multitude of aromatic molecules, which contribute further to the flavor of the bread. Food sources are redistributed after shaping and so the yeast gets a second wind in the second rise.

MANIPULATING RISE

Below is an example standard timeline for baking a workaday bread—make the dough, let it rise for a couple hours, shape the dough, let it rise for another hour or so, bake it, and let it cool. Below that is one for adding time to the first rise and another for adding time to the second rise. Our individual recipes extend the rise that makes sense for the mechanics of that particular recipe. When you bake this way, you don't have to wait around the house for the dough to rise before you get it ready for yet another rise and the oven.

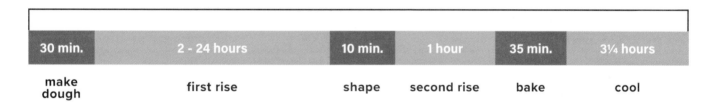

Work in one day: **total time** 7 hours

30 min.	1½ hours	10 min.	1 hour	35 min.	3¼ hours
make dough	first rise	shape	second rise	bake	cool

Work in two days, option 1:   **total time** 2 days

30 min.	2 - 24 hours	10 min.	1 hour	35 min.	3¼ hours
make dough	first rise	shape	second rise	bake	cool

Work in two days, option 2:   **total time** 2 days

30 min.	1½ hours	10 min.	8 - 16 hours	35 min.	3¼ hours
make dough	first rise	shape	second rise	bake	cool

In the above example, the first rise can slow down so you can make the bread in two days rather than in one very packed day that's devoted only to your bread. Or, the second rise can slow down, which means the hardest parts will be over the first day: You'll have kneaded and shaped the loaf, it'll likely rise while you sleep, and you just need to put the bread to bed and bake when you want it fresh for sandwiches. Let's look at some specific ways our approach could benefit your lifestyle.

WARM BUNS FOR BREAKFAST

While you could start baking at 6 a.m. to get Sticky Buns (page 302) on the brunch table at 10, you'd get more weekend rest (and have to do less intricate work while bleary-eyed) if you shaped the buns the day before, put them in the refrigerator and baked and served them when you want to eat them hot, fresh, and, well, sticky. You'll find this also applies to other morning treats in chapter 6.

EARLY RISE

make over 3¼ hours

6:30 a.m.	Make dough	1 hour
7:30 a.m.	First rise	40 min.
8:10 a.m.	Shape dough	10 min.
8:20 a.m.	Second rise	40 min.
9:00 a.m.	Bake	30 min.
9:30 a.m.	Cool	20 min.

WAKE AND BAKE

make over 11¾ hours to 17¾ hours

4:00 p.m.	Make dough	1 hour
5:00 p.m.	First rise	40 min.
5:40 p.m.	Shape dough	10 min.
5:50 p.m.	Second rise	8 to 14 hours, plus 1 hour at room temp
9:00 a.m.	Bake	30 min.
9:30 a.m.	Cool	20 min.

BREAD FOR DINNER

A pizza, flatbread, or stuffed loaf is a great choice for dinner (see pages 224–285). It's also generally made from a very flavorful dough, which achieves that flavor from a generous time fermenting in the refrigerator. A generous first rise for Thin-Crust Pizza (page 228), for example, means generous flexibility in getting bread on the dinner table. Plan to make pizza up to four days ahead and serving it will be, indeed, as easy as delivery.

BAKE A DAY AFTER MAKING

make over 2 days

Mon.	5:30 p.m.	Make dough	20 min.
Mon.	5:50 p.m.	Rise	24 hours
Tues.	5:50 p.m.	Shape	15 min.
Tues.	6:05 p.m.	Rest	1 hour
Tues.	7:05 p.m.	Bake	40 min.

BAKE UP TO 4 DAYS AFTER MAKING

make over 4 days

Mon.	5:30 p.m.	Make dough	20 min.
Mon.	5:50 p.m.	Rise	3 days
Thurs.	5:50 p.m.	Shape	15 min.
Thurs.	6:05 p.m.	Rest	1 hour
Thurs.	7:05 p.m.	Bake	40 min.

 ## DON'T LIKE IT HOT

At temperatures higher than room temperature, enzymes in the dough break down gluten, forcing the yeast to work harder and faster to make bread rise. Making bread rise faster by placing it in a warm oven or near a radiator, or by adding hot liquids to the dough, also sounds convenient, but we can't recommend this faster rise. In this situation, too much alcohol is produced for a boozy, tangy flavor because the yeast must digest much more sugar to create enough carbon dioxide to achieve a decent rise. Further, less available sugar means less surface browning and less flavor. There are better ways to get bread on the table. Making a recipe from our chapter of quick breads is a great one; following these suggested timelines is another.

BAKERY BREAD ALWAYS IN THE BOX

There's reason to have a rustic bread around anytime, whether for breakfast toast, hearty sandwiches, snacks, cheese boards, appetizers, or dinner accompaniments. Make it any time too: Our no-knead rustic doughs require a long rest so bake them over a (long) day or over up to two days. Have one dough bubbling while you're enjoying another—with so many varieties using so many different flours and mix-ins, having a boule available every day is far from boring.

WEEKEND-DAY AFFAIR

make over 1 day

Sun.	8:00 a.m.	Make dough	25 min.
Sun.	8:25 a.m.	First rise	8 hours
Sun.	4:25 p.m.	Fold and rest	25 min.
Sun.	4:50 p.m.	Shape dough	15 min.
Sun.	5:05 p.m.	Second rise	1 hour
Sun.	6:05 p.m.	Bake	40 min.
Sun.	6:45 p.m.	Cool	3 hours

TWO-DAY AFFAIR

make over 2 days

Sat.	6:00 p.m.	Make dough	25 min.
Sat.	6:25 p.m.	First rise	16 hours
Sun.	10:25 a.m.	Fold and rest	25 min.
Sun.	10:50 a.m.	Shape dough	15 min.
Sun.	11:05 a.m.	Second rise	1 hour
Sun.	12:05 p.m.	Bake	40 min.
Sun.	12:45 p.m.	Cool	3 hours

ROLLS FOR A CROWD

The usual bun in the oven for a dinner party or holiday meal is a roll. And while the roll might not be the most challenging item on your menu, it might be the one with the most tangible steps. You could tackle baking rolls while you have other dishes going for a warm addition to the dinner table, but if you're juggling too many things, we suggest you make and shape them the day before and bake before serving. But there's one more option yet. Some rolls can be refrigerated for a couple days with minimal depreciation or can be frozen and returned to just-baked freshness.

ALL AT ONCE

make over 4½ hours

Sat.	1:45 p.m.	Make dough	35 min.
Sat.	2:20 p.m.	First rise	1½ hours
Sat.	3:50 p.m.	Fold and rest	30 min.
Sat.	4:20 p.m.	Shape dough	15 min.
Sat.	4:35 p.m.	Second rise	1 hour
Sat.	5:35 p.m.	Bake	25 min.
Sat.	6:00 p.m.	Cool	15 min.

PREP A DAY AHEAD

make over 2 days

Fri.	6:45 p.m.	Make dough	35 min.
Fri.	7:20 p.m.	First rise	1½ hours
Fri.	8:50 p.m.	Fold and rest	30 min.
Fri.	9:20 p.m.	Shape dough	15 min.
Fri.	9:35 p.m.	Second rise	8 to 16 hours
Sat.	1:35 p.m.	Bake	25 min.
Sat.	2:00 p.m.	Cool	15 min.

BREAD TO IMPRESS

how-to
**PREPARING
TANGZHONG**

*Just because we've streamlined the bread baking process doesn't mean we've
dumbed it down. Bake your way through any part of this book and—even if you
opened it as a beginner—you'll earn the title of bread baker. There are ways to
build on your bread game, techniques used by professionals even, that are as
simple to incorporate as any other. Unlock these secrets to better bread.*

WORKING WITH WETTER DOUGHS

As we've covered (see page 21), there is beauty in well-hydrated bread if you're looking to achieve an airy, open loaf. And we've addressed the challenges of working with
wet doughs that are naturally looser and more sticky. Folding allows you to engage the
dough since it would just puddle in a stand mixer. And rising wet doughs in the refrigerator makes the dry ingredients hydrate fully, so the dough tightens enough to shape.
Baking wet doughs in a vessel forces the bread to rise up and not out.

Sandwich bread dough has a relatively low hydration level (around 60 percent) to yield
a loaf with an appropriately tight crumb. Rustic loaves are wetter (ours is 73 percent)
for large, irregular holes. We were curious what loaves would look like if we took them
to the extreme. Here, we've baked our No-Knead Rustic Loaf (page 186) at three
hydration levels (that is, with three different amounts of water added to the dough).

For the first bake, we lowered the hydration to 60 percent. For the second, we
increased the recipe's hydration to 80 percent. The 60 percent hydrated loaf had a
tight, fine crumb, was dense, and showed little spread or expansion. The 80 percent
hydrated loaf, on the other hand, hardly rose, spreading out instead of up, and it
featured a loose, open irregular crumb. Too much liquid in a recipe can actually dilute
and weaken the gluten it typically works so well to build, hindering a bread's ability
to rise. 73 percent is just right for this style of bread.

Too Dry (60 percent hydration)

Too Wet (80 percent hydration)

Just Right (73 percent hydration)

 ## WHY YOU SHOULD LEARN TANGZHONG

Tangzhong is a method traditionally used for Japanese milk bread that we frequently
employ to make wetter dough that isn't hard to work with. The tangzhong method
calls for briefly cooking a portion of the bread's flour and water to make a paste,
which is then combined with the rest of the ingredients. With this paste, you can
add more liquid to the dough without making it sticky, because flour can absorb
twice as much hot water as cold. The technique is great for rolled or braided
creations that need workability and for the fluffiest dinner rolls. The extra water
converts to steam in the oven, creating rise. The extra water also increases gluten
development, giving the bread the structure it needs to contain the steam rather
than let it escape. A final benefit: The shelf life of your bread is increased.

FLAVOR YOUR BREAD BETTER

We think the flavor additions to the breads in this book are far from the norm you'll find at the neighborhood bakery or in your average cookbook. The abundant flavors might make the breads seem fancy, but they in fact increase their accessibility—once you learn the motions it doesn't take know-how to add flavorings for a long roster of interesting breads. Well, it doesn't take *much* know-how. In our recipe testing, we discovered easy but important accommodations for additions like nuts and seeds, dried fruit, bacon, and different flours that result in the very best chockablock loaves.

• spice things up not down

You can change the flavor profile of dough by incorporating warmth through spices or citrusy aroma through zest. But we found from testing that both these ingredients impact rise if incorporated too soon because they interfere with yeast fermentation. You could just add more yeast, but we don't like that flavor. Instead, we learned that the answer is to add these ingredients to dough after its bulk fermentation (when the yeast is the most active) rather than the intuitive way—just mixing it in with the dry ingredients at the start of a recipe. Below is our Orange-Chocolate Durum Bread (page 222; chocolate omitted for illustrative purposes) made with orange zest mixed with the dry ingredients at the start (left) and made according to the recipe, with orange zest incorporated during the post-fermentation folding step (right). You can see a significant difference in openness and rise in the final bread.

Orange Zest Mixed in the Beginning

Orange Zest Incorporated in Folding

how-to
FOLDING MIX-INS

• thwart thirsty fruit

Dried fruits are an easy way to give breads fruity sweetness without adding hard-to-incorporate fresh fruits that could alter the hydration of your dough and make things soggy. But did you know dried fruit can actually do the opposite? As implied by the name, "dried" fruits seek rehydration and they plump in liquids. And so, these additions actually suck up the moisture from the bread dough, turning a well-hydrated dough too dry. To compensate, we add more moisture to (and thus increase the hydration of) breads such as Cranberry Walnut Bread (page 198) and Cocoa Cherry Rye Bread (page 216) that call for dried fruit, in some cases doubling the amount of water we'd normally use, to give the bread the proper structure.

• don't weigh down

A bite of earthy walnuts, tart dried cherries, or briny olives can add a lot of interest to your bread. But you work hard to create a delicate invisible matrix within the dough, and throwing in a load of heavy mix-ins before fermentation can really prevent proper rise and air bubble formation by interfering with the gluten structure. For wet rustic doughs, we fold items in after fermentation, once the dough already has structural integrity. For drier sandwich doughs, we make the items less obtrusive before they head to the mixer—like chopping the raisins for our Cinnamon Raisin Swirl Bread (page 160).

GET TO KNOW YOUR GRAINS

Through fermentation and baking, a loaf of white bread of any style really achieves great flavor and aroma. But you can augment those qualities or change their profile by experimenting with different grains. Whole-grain flours are healthful, hearty, and nutty. And while more robust flours may seem within the realm of artisan bakers, they're easier than ever to find without ordering and easy to incorporate with some flour-specific tricks.

What makes whole-wheat *whole-wheat*? It's ground from the whole wheat berry (the outer bran layer, the germ, and the endosperm) whereas white flour is ground just from the soft, starchy endosperm. It doesn't feel sharp in our hands, but on a microscopic level, the fiber of whole-wheat flour is sharp, so it tends to cut the gluten strands, weakening their bonds and making the dough less able to contain gases during rising and baking. The result is a squat, heavy, crumbly loaf.

Two rules apply to whole-grain flours in many bread recipes: The first is to cut the whole-grain flour with some bread flour. This is a quick, automatic boost in gluten-forming proteins. The second is to increase the dough's moisture. You soften the whole-grain flour's sharp bran by letting the bran absorb a lot of water in a highly hydrated dough. This will blunt the bran's sharp edges that cut through gluten strands. That said, whole-grain breads with long refrigerator rises often don't require modifications to hydration; the long fermentation period hydrates the flour and softens the bran.

The whole grains we use in this book each add unique flavor profiles to our breads. Try them all!

Whole-Wheat Flour is the most common addition to bread for which you want to increase nutrition and hearty flavor. It is easy to find and is nice and nutty. Find recipes using whole-wheat flour on pages 74, 91, 116, 177, 196, 244, 280, and more.

Oats add texture and sweet, wholesome flavor to recipes but they are thirsty for water and steal it from the dough's moisture. So we often make a porridge with the oats to hydrate them first like in our Oatmeal Sandwich Bread (page 172).

Sprouted Grains not only up the nutrition of your bread, they add exceptionally nutty flavor and welcome texture. Be sure to rinse and drain grains as directed before using them in our Sprouted Wheat Berry Bread on page 204.

Spelt Flour is an ancient grain with such a sweet, honeyed flavor that bread made with it is a treat that can be used for a variety of applications. Because of its high water solubility, spelt's nutrients are more quickly absorbed by the body, and it's full of fiber, protein, and vitamins. Approach Spelt Bread (page 206) as you would whole-wheat bread.

Rye Flour has an earthy, slightly tangy flavor. It comes in white or light, medium, whole grain, and pumpernickel, and each variety produces a different bread. The more bran that's left in rye after milling, the darker the flour. We use medium rye in this book.

IT'S SURPRISINGLY EASY TO EMBELLISH YOUR BREAD

You'll learn the mechanics of bread baking by heart as you make your way through the breads in this book, which gives you space to have some fun. And turning out a great-looking loaf will immediately boost your confidence. Here's how we give breads star power.

LIGHTS

Golden dough that gleams evokes richness and comfort. There are two easy ways to achieve this. The first is with an egg wash that you can brush on dinner rolls, enriched buns, and soft sandwich loaves before they go into the oven. We mix a little water and salt into the egg to loosen the proteins and make the wash more fluid and easier to brush evenly over the dough.

Another option for shiny bread is to brush with melted butter soon after the bread comes out of the oven. Warm, buttery rolls anyone?

how-to
SLASHING DOUGH

CAMERA

An option to beautify bread before it goes into the oven is coating it with seeds or spices. We make this riff on a lot of bread and it really has three benefits: appearance, taste, and texture. For sandwich loaves, first add half of your coating to the greased loaf pan that the dough will settle into, and mist the top of the loaf with water and sprinkle it with the remaining half for excellent even coverage (see page 165). For free-form loaves, add seeds to the parchment paper on which the shaped dough will rise and sprinkle the rest of the seeds on top (below).

ACTION

Just before transferring your bread to the oven, you often slash its top. This can beget beauty, but most importantly, the process cuts through the loaf's gluten sheath (see page 6), creating designated weak points that allow the loaf to expand evenly. Without the slashes, the loaf will expand wherever it finds a random weak spot, resulting in an odd shape. You can slash with a sharp knife or a single-edge razor blade. Slash quickly and decisively so the implement doesn't drag. It's better to go back and reinforce the slash before putting the loaf in the oven.

BAKE THE BREAD FOR YOU

As you make the recipes in this book, you'll notice that there are recurring themes; for each category of bread, certain ingredients and techniques are combined in a certain way to achieve results that are characteristic of that type. This chart lists the categories of breads in this book and shows you the ingredients and techniques that produce them.

	FLOUR	LIQUID	FAT	
Tender Breads (quick breads, soft rolls, sweet breads)	AP Flour - its lower protein content means less gluten development so the bread isn't tough	Milk, Buttermilk, Cream - rich liquids cause less gluten formation and tenderize the crumb	Melted Butter - adds rich flavor and is easy to incorporate Oil - keeps breads moist for a long time	
Moist, Fluffy Breads (milk breads, dinner rolls)	AP Flour - its lower protein content yields a soft result Bread Flour - provides more structure so rolls rise high or augments whole-wheat flour	Milk - impedes gluten formation and tenderizes the crumb	Butter - adds a rich flavor and tenderizes the crumb	
Sandwich Breads	Bread Flour - gives the loaves structure to rise evenly	Water, Buttermilk, Milk - what you use depends on how tender you want the crumb	Butter - a small amount may be used for a touch of richness	
Airy, Chewy Breads (rustic breads)	Bread Flour - provides the greatest gluten development for ultimate chew and air bubbles	Water - a large amount creates steam for an open crumb Beer - increases the fermented flavor of the dough	None	
Crispy Flatbreads	Bread Flour - provides bite and chew	Water - makes a lean, bubbly dough	Oil - creates an extensible dough and a crisp bread	
Rich, Plush Breads (brioche, challah, etc.)	AP Flour - makes tender, soft creations Bread Flour - adds structure to handle an influx of rich ingredients	Water - provides a cleaner taste Milk - gives sweet breads a richer crumb	Butter and Eggs - add golden color and make the crumb plush	

WORKING	RISING	SPECIAL TECHNIQUE
Whisk and Stir - aerates batters and incorporates ingredients	None	Gentle Mixing - brings ingredients together for just enough but not too much gluten development
Knead - gives rolls enough structure to rise up and not out	Second Rise - can take place in the refrigerator to extend the time	Tangzhong - combines extra moisture with optimal workability for bread with a feathery texture
Knead - adds structure and makes a relatively tight crumb	Standard	Roll Tight Cylinder - makes a taut loaf shape that rises without bursting the gluten network
Fold - gives highly hydrated breads the ultimate open crumb structure	First Rise - a long rise encourages gluten strands to link into a structured matrix	Bake in Preheated Dutch Oven - enables oven spring and a moist environment to support an open crumb and thick, crisp crust
Knead or Fold - adds just enough structure for a bubbly crumb (some more than others)	First Rise - a long rise provides great flavor and an airy crumb	Rests as Needed - relaxes the dough for stretching and rolling
Knead (drier doughs) or Fold (wetter doughs) - provides adequate structure to support heavy, rich ingredients	First Rise - can be extended to firm up butter for easier shaping Second Rise - can be extended for buns in a pan that can be baked and served warm	No-Knead Method - prevents really rich doughs from turning greasy or breaking Melted Butter - is easier and faster to incorporate than softened butter

CHAPTER ONE

quick breads

DROP BISCUITS

Quick breads as we define them (see page 14) aren't just cakey breads made in a loaf pan. Biscuits also fall into this category and they can make a number of comforting meals (think biscuits and gravy, biscuit sandwiches, biscuits and jam) or accessorize them (think biscuits with chowder, a salad, or a roast).

Drop biscuits are simple because they don't involve kneading or folding dough—just mixing wet ingredients with dry ones and "dropping" portions of the dough on a baking sheet to bake. That's why we wanted a core version that we could easily gussy up a few ways. This cream biscuit recipe is as delicious as it is easy—it has a crisp outer crust and a tender, cake-like, and subtly layered crumb. The dough is wet enough that when it's baked it has a high rise and fluffy texture but it's workable enough that we can stuff it with cheese or wrap it around sausage links for two supersavory anytime biscuit twists.

EASIEST-EVER DROP BISCUITS

makes 10 biscuits

3 cups (15 ounces)
all-purpose flour

4 teaspoons sugar

1 tablespoon baking powder

¼ teaspoon baking soda

1¼ teaspoons table salt

2 cups (16 ounces) heavy cream

2 tablespoons unsalted butter,
melted (optional)

These cream biscuits also go by the name "dream biscuits" because they come together like one, and they taste simply heavenly—rich and ultratender with no rolling involved. The key to these biscuits is using cream instead of butter, of course. Adding enough cream to achieve a droppable consistency resulted in greasy, spread-out biscuits, however. To solve this, we use less cream and we heat it. This liquefies the cream's fat particles, allowing them to thoroughly incorporate with the dry ingredients, effectively stretching the cream. These biscuits come together very quickly—just stir the warm cream into the dry ingredients—so in the interest of efficiency, start heating your oven before gathering your ingredients. They're a blank canvas for flavors both slightly sweet and deeply savory and for stuffing with rich fillings, as you'll see.

1   Adjust oven rack to upper-middle position and heat oven to 450 degrees. Line rimmed baking sheet with parchment paper.

2   make dough   Whisk flour, sugar, baking powder, baking soda, and salt together in medium bowl. Microwave cream until just warmed to body temperature (95 to 100 degrees), 60 to 90 seconds, stirring halfway through microwaving. Stir cream into flour mixture until soft, uniform dough forms.

3   shape dough   Spray ⅓-cup dry measuring cup with vegetable oil spray. Drop level scoops of dough 2 inches apart on prepared sheet (biscuits should measure about 2½ inches wide and 1¼ inches tall). Respray measuring cup after every 3 or 4 scoops. If portions are misshapen, use your fingertips to gently reshape dough into level cylinders.

4   bake   Bake until tops are light golden brown, 10 to 12 minutes, rotating sheet halfway through baking. Transfer sheet to wire rack, brush hot biscuits with melted butter, if using, and let cool for 5 minutes. Serve warm. (Biscuits can be stored in zipper-lock bag at room temperature for up to 24 hours. Reheat biscuits in 300-degree oven for 10 minutes.)

total time 35 minutes

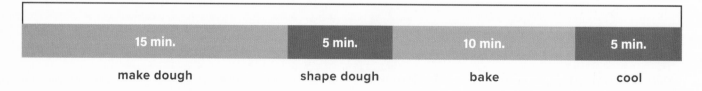

15 min.	5 min.	10 min.	5 min.
make dough	**shape dough**	**bake**	**cool**

CINNAMON SUGAR BISCUITS

For a spicy-sweet biscuit, bloom ¾ teaspoon ground cayenne in melted butter before coating the biscuits.

Combine ½ cup granulated sugar and 1 teaspoon ground cinnamon in medium bowl; set aside. Once baked biscuits are cool enough to handle, brush all over with 5 tablespoons melted unsalted butter, then coat in reserved sugar mixture.

GINGER BISCUITS

Increase sugar to ¼ cup. Add ¾ cup chopped crystallized ginger and 1½ teaspoons ground ginger to flour mixture in step 2.

MISO-SCALLION BISCUITS

Add 8 thinly sliced scallions to flour mixture in step 2. Whisk 1 tablespoon white miso with 1½ teaspoons water until smooth; brush tops and sides of biscuits with miso mixture and sprinkle with 2 teaspoons sesame seeds before baking.

SUN-DRIED TOMATO, GARLIC, AND ZA'ATAR BISCUITS

See our recipe for Za'atar (page 147) or use store-bought.

Reduce sugar to 2 teaspoons. Add ½ teaspoon pepper to flour mixture in step 2. Add 3 minced garlic cloves to cream before microwaving. Gently fold 1 cup rinsed, patted dry, and finely chopped oil-packed sun-dried tomatoes into flour mixture along with cream mixture in step 2. Brush tops of biscuits with 4 teaspoons sun-dried tomato oil and sprinkle with 3 teaspoons za'atar before baking.

Stir until soft, uniform dough forms.

Drop level scoops of dough on sheet with measuring cup.

CHEESE-STUFFED BISCUITS

makes 10 biscuits

1 (8-ounce) block pepper
Jack cheese

1 recipe Easiest-Ever Drop
Biscuits, made through step 3

Creating a base biscuit with a scoopable but not sticky consistency is great for leveling up. Cheesy biscuits are a Southern specialty that are made quickly with our Easiest-Ever Drop Biscuits dough. We simply press a piece of cheese into each mound of biscuit dough and then bring up the dough sides to seal around it. Once baked, a gooey, molten center is perfectly contained until you rip the biscuits apart. You can use your favorite flavorful cheese that melts well in this recipe: In addition to pepper Jack, we like smoked gouda, Gruyère, and herbed or other flavored goat cheese.

1   Cut ten 1-inch pieces of pepper Jack cheese from block; set pieces aside and reserve remaining cheese for another use. (For softer cheeses like goat cheese, working with 1 tablespoon cheese at a time, pack ten 1-inch balls and refrigerate until firm, about 15 minutes before using).

2   Using your fingers, press 1-inch-wide divot into center of dough, being sure not to press through biscuit into sheet below. Place 1 piece of cheese inside hole in each biscuit, then bring sides of biscuit dough up around cheese and pinch at top to seal.

3   Bake until tops are light golden brown, 10 to 12 minutes, rotating sheet halfway through baking. Transfer sheet to wire rack, brush hot biscuits with melted butter, if using, and let cool for 5 minutes. Serve warm.

Press divot in each portion of dough.

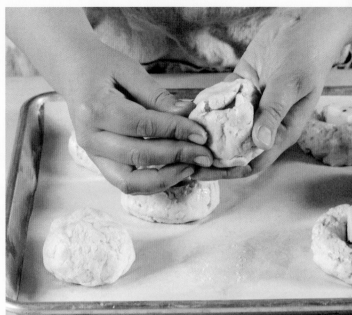

Place cheese inside divots and wrap with dough.

PIG IN A BISCUIT

makes 26 biscuits

26 precooked breakfast
sausage links

1 recipe Easiest-Ever Drop
Biscuits, made through step 2,
with 2 baking sheets prepared

1 large egg beaten with
1 tablespoon water and
pinch table salt

2 teaspoons sesame seeds

Popping a can of biscuit dough to wrap around a cocktail wiener is like throwing a wet (or in this case, dry) blanket on an appetizer. Why bother? Making our delightfully fluffy, moist biscuit dough for the wrapper is almost as fast and you have a really great appetizer, or even a savory breakfast bite (we like sausages better than hot dogs). Prepare two baking sheets for this recipe. We prefer precooked breakfast sausage links in this recipe, but you can also use cocktail franks or smoked sausages, kielbasa (cut into 3-inch lengths and quartered lengthwise), or hot dogs (cut into 3-inch lengths and halved lengthwise). Do not use uncooked sausage. Thaw frozen sausage before using. You can serve the biscuits with the mustard of your choice or even maple syrup.

1 Pat sausage links dry with paper towels; set aside.

2 Spray ¼-cup dry measuring cup with vegetable oil spray. Drop level scoop of dough onto lightly floured counter. Using knife or bench scraper, divide piece of dough in half, then press each half into rough 3½-inch-long by 1½-inch-wide oval.

3 Place 1 sausage link at 1 narrow end of each oval, then roll dough around link, overlapping dough. Transfer sausage rolls seam side down to prepared sheet. Repeat with remaining dough and remaining 25 sausage links, respraying measuring cup as needed.

4 Brush biscuits with egg wash, then sprinkle with sesame seeds. Bake until light golden brown, 10 to 12 minutes, switching and rotating sheets halfway through baking. Transfer sheet to wire rack and let cool for 5 minutes. Serve warm.

Divide 1 portion of dough in half.

Press dough into oval.

Roll dough around sausage link.

Brush with egg wash; sprinkle with sesame seeds.

POTATO BISCUITS WITH BACON

makes 12 biscuits

6 slices bacon

2½ cups (12½ ounces) all-purpose flour

¾ cup (1¾ ounces) plain instant mashed potato flakes

4 teaspoons baking powder

½ teaspoon baking soda

1 tablespoon sugar

1 teaspoon table salt

8 tablespoons unsalted butter, cut into ½-inch pieces and chilled, plus 2 tablespoons melted

4 tablespoons vegetable shortening, cut into ½-inch pieces and chilled

1¼ cups (10 ounces) buttermilk, chilled

why this recipe works Potato biscuits, potato bread, potato rolls—these baked goods pack in potato not so much for flavor but for texture. Potato can produce an extra-tender texture by interrupting the matrix that forms when the proteins in wheat flour mix with liquid and link together. But adding homemade mashed potato to dough introduces more moisture that throws off the recipe's ratio. We use instant mashed potato flakes for all the starch without the water of fresh spuds. To compensate for the fact that potato starch has no gluten, we add a little more baking powder, which helps these rolled-and-stamped biscuits rise tender and tall. The mix-ins are classic potato flavor partners. We like the texture of these savory biscuits when they're made with both butter and shortening, but if you prefer to use all butter, omit the shortening and use 12 tablespoons of chilled butter in step 2. These would be particularly great for a fried egg sandwich.

1 Adjust oven rack to middle position and heat oven to 450 degrees. Line rimmed baking sheet with parchment paper. Cook bacon in 12-inch skillet over medium heat until crispy, 7 to 9 minutes; transfer to paper towel–lined plate to cool. Once bacon is cool enough to handle, break into 1-inch pieces.

2 make dough Process flour, potato flakes, baking powder, baking soda, sugar, salt, and cooled bacon in food processor until combined, about 15 seconds. Add butter and shortening and pulse until mixture resembles coarse crumbs, 7 to 9 pulses. Transfer flour mixture to large bowl. Using rubber spatula, stir in buttermilk, turning and pressing dough until no dry flour remains.

3 shape dough Transfer dough to lightly floured counter and knead briefly to form smooth, cohesive ball, 8 to 10 turns. Roll out dough into 9-inch circle, about ¾ inch thick. Using floured 2½-inch round cutter, stamp out 8 or 9 biscuits and arrange upside down on prepared sheet. Gather dough scraps and ge1ntly pat into ¾-inch-thick circle. Stamp out 3 or 4 biscuits and transfer to sheet.

4 bake Bake until biscuits begin to rise, about 5 minutes, then rotate sheet and reduce oven temperature to 400 degrees. Continue to bake until golden brown, 10 to 12 minutes. Brush hot biscuits with melted butter and transfer to wire rack to cool for 5 minutes. Serve warm.

total time 55 minutes

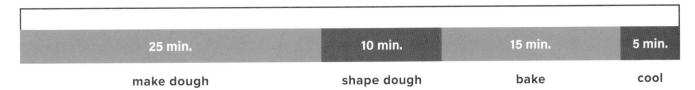

25 min.	10 min.	15 min.	5 min.
make dough	shape dough	bake	cool

CAST IRON ORANGE-HERB BISCUITS

makes 8 biscuits

3 cups (15 ounces)
  all-purpose flour

⅓ cup minced fresh tarragon

1 tablespoon grated orange zest

1 tablespoon baking powder

½ teaspoon baking soda

1 teaspoon table salt

8 tablespoons unsalted butter, cut
  into ½-inch pieces and softened, plus 1 tablespoon melted

4 tablespoons vegetable shortening, cut into ½-inch pieces

1¼ cups (10 ounces) buttermilk

why this recipe works Immediately out of the oven, the initial appeal of these biscuits is their beautiful aroma of citrus and herbs. With these flavors, they hold their own alongside any meal. But they're also free from fuss (you can make them right before you want to serve that meal), which is just as great a draw to us. The dough goes from one bowl to one pan—no rolling or cutting required. Oh, and we make the biscuits big with an ultrafluffy crumb derived from a combination of butter and shortening. We drop the biscuits right into a greased cast-iron skillet, which distributes the heat of the oven evenly to ensure a crisp bottom and nicely browned crust. You can flavor the biscuits with the same amounts of dill and lemon zest, if desired.

1 Adjust oven rack to upper-middle position and heat oven to 425 degrees. Grease 12-inch cast-iron skillet.

2 make dough Whisk flour, tarragon, orange zest, baking powder, baking soda, and salt together in large bowl. Using your hands, rub butter and shortening into flour until mixture resembles coarse meal. Stir buttermilk into flour mixture until just combined.

3 shape dough Spray ⅓-cup dry measuring cup with vegetable oil spray. Drop level scoops of dough evenly into prepared skillet. Brush tops with melted butter.

4 bake Bake until biscuits are puffed and golden brown, 20 to 25 minutes, rotating skillet halfway through baking. Being careful of hot skillet handle, transfer skillet to wire rack and let biscuits cool for at least 15 minutes in skillet before serving.

total time 55 minutes

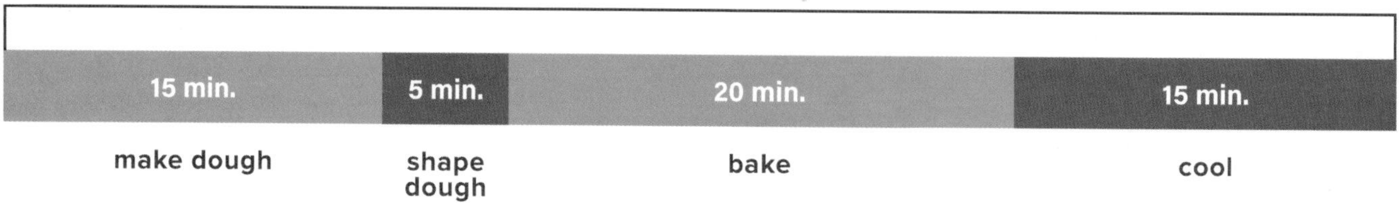

15 min.	5 min.	20 min.	15 min.
make dough	shape dough	bake	cool

GRUYÈRE AND HERB BUTTERMILK BISCUITS

makes 9 biscuits

3 **cups (15 ounces) all-purpose flour**

2 **tablespoons sugar**

2 **tablespoons minced fresh parsley**

2 **tablespoons minced fresh chives**

4 **teaspoons baking powder**

½ **teaspoon baking soda**

1 **tablespoon minced fresh sage, plus 9 whole leaves**

¾ **teaspoon table salt**

16 **tablespoons (2 sticks) unsalted butter, frozen for 30 minutes**

1¼ **cups (10 ounces) buttermilk, chilled**

4 **ounces Gruyère cheese, shredded (1⅓ cups), room temperature**

why this recipe works Crisp and crunchy on the outside, tender and as light as air on the inside, with hundreds of flaky layers flavored with cheese and fresh herbs, these are the most indulgent biscuits you'll ever eat. They rise up tall and true with strata that peel apart like sheets of buttery paper, thanks to our simplified lamination process in which we grate frozen butter sticks directly into the flour. After adding buttermilk, we take the dough through a sequence of rolling and folding, which spreads the butter and flour into a multitude of layers. We use just butter (rather than incorporating shortening). Butter contains water, whereas shortening does not, and a more hydrated dough means a better gluten structure—the better to support all those layers. We prefer King Arthur brand all-purpose flour, but other brands will work. Use sticks of butter. In hot or humid environments, chill the flour mixture, grater, and bowl before use. The dough will start out very crumbly and dry in pockets but will be smooth by the end of the folding process, so don't be tempted to add extra buttermilk. Flour the counter and the top of the dough as needed to prevent sticking, but be careful not to incorporate large pockets of flour into the dough when folding. You can use cheddar cheese in place of the Gruyère, if you prefer.

1 make dough Line rimmed baking sheet with parchment paper. Whisk flour, sugar, parsley, chives, baking powder, baking soda, minced sage, and table salt together in large bowl. Coat sticks of butter in flour mixture, then grate 7 tablespoons from each stick on large holes of box grater directly into flour mixture. Toss gently to combine. Set aside remaining 2 tablespoons butter. Using rubber spatula, gently fold buttermilk into flour mixture until just combined (dough will look dry).

2 shape dough Transfer dough to liberally floured counter. Dust surface of dough with flour; using your floured hands, press dough into rough 7-inch square. Roll dough into 12 by 9-inch rectangle with short side parallel to counter edge. Starting at bottom of dough, fold into thirds like business letter, using bench scraper or metal spatula to release dough from counter. Press top of dough firmly to seal folds.

3 Using bench scraper, turn dough 90 degrees clockwise. Repeat rolling into 12 by 9-inch rectangle, folding into thirds, and turning clockwise 3 more times, for a total of 4 sets of folds, sprinkling with extra flour as needed.

total time 2 hours

30 min.	20 min.	30 min.	22 min.	15 min.
make dough	shape dough	rest	bake	cool

4 Roll out dough into 12 by 9-inch rectangle, then sprinkle with Gruyère, leaving bottom 4 inches and ½-inch border around top and sides free from cheese. Using bench scraper, fold cheese-free bottom third of dough up over center, then fold center up over top, tucking any cheese that may have escaped back underneath top fold. Press to seal, then roll dough into 8½-inch square, about 1 inch thick.

5 rest Transfer dough to prepared sheet, cover with plastic wrap, and refrigerate for 30 minutes.

6 Adjust oven rack to upper-middle position and heat oven to 400 degrees. Transfer dough to lightly floured cutting board. Using sharp, floured chef's knife, trim ¼ inch of dough from each side of square; discard. Cut remaining dough into 9 squares, flouring knife after each cut. Arrange biscuits at least 1 inch apart on now-empty sheet and place 1 sage leaf on top of each biscuit. Melt reserved 2 tablespoons butter, then brush sage leaves and tops of biscuits with melted butter.

7 bake Bake until tops are golden brown, 22 to 25 minutes, rotating sheet halfway through baking. Transfer biscuits to wire rack, sprinkle with flake sea salt, and let cool for 15 minutes before serving.

Sprinkle with Gruyère.

Fold into thirds.

Roll dough into 8½-inch square.

Cut dough into 9 squares.

BUTTER AND LARD BISCUITS

makes 9 biscuits

4½ cups (22½ ounces) all-purpose flour

1½ tablespoons sugar

1½ tablespoons baking powder

¾ teaspoon baking soda

1½ teaspoons table salt

6 ounces lard, cut into ½-inch pieces and frozen for 30 minutes

12 tablespoons unsalted butter, cut into ½-inch pieces and frozen for 30 minutes

1¼ cups (10 ounces) buttermilk

why this recipe works   Two fats translate to twice as much richness and tenderness in these archetypal flaky, mouthwatering biscuits. Like shortening, lard doesn't contain water so it doesn't encourage gluten development when worked into the dough—and the resulting biscuits have a supersavory flavor on top of their tender texture. Buttermilk hydrates the mixture. We start the biscuits in a 450-degree oven and then lower the temperature. While baking, the butter (which contains water) melts, and steam fills the small spaces left behind, creating flaky layers. Rolling the dough into a square and trimming ¼ inch off the edges ensures that the biscuits rise unimpeded in the oven. Cutting the dough into nine squares makes even-size biscuits and avoids any wasted scraps (or tough rerolls).

1 make dough   Line rimmed baking sheet with parchment paper. Process flour, sugar, baking powder, baking soda, and salt in food processor until combined, about 3 seconds. Scatter frozen lard and butter over top and pulse until mixture resembles coarse crumbs with visible pea-size pieces, about 14 pulses. Transfer flour mixture to large bowl. Stir in buttermilk until very shaggy dough forms and some bits of dry flour remain.

2 shape dough   Transfer dough to lightly floured counter and knead briefly until dough comes together, 4 to 6 turns. Using your floured hands and bench scraper, shape dough into 8-inch square, about 1½ inches thick. (Dough may be sticky; re-flour your hands as needed.) Using sharp, floured chef's knife, trim ¼ inch of dough from each side of square; discard. Cut remaining dough into 9 squares, flouring knife after each cut. Arrange biscuits at least 1 inch apart on prepared sheet and cover with plastic wrap.

3 rest   Refrigerate biscuits for 30 minutes.

4 bake   Adjust oven rack to upper-middle position and heat oven to 450 degrees. Bake until biscuits begin to rise, about 5 minutes. Rotate sheet and reduce oven temperature to 400 degrees. Bake until biscuits are golden brown, 12 to 14 minutes. Transfer sheet to wire rack and let biscuits cool for 5 minutes. Serve warm.

total time 1½ hours

35 min.	5 min.	30 min.	17 min.	5 min.
make dough	shape dough	rest	bake	cool

» **Take your time** To make the next day, refrigerate biscuits for up to 24 hours in step 3.

BLUEBERRY BISCUITS

makes 9 biscuits

dough

- 3 cups (15 ounces) all-purpose flour
- ½ cup (3½ ounces) sugar
- 2 teaspoons baking powder
- ½ teaspoon baking soda
- 1¼ teaspoons table salt
- 10 tablespoons unsalted butter, cut into ½-inch pieces and chilled
- 7½ ounces (1½ cups) blueberries
- 1⅔ cups (13⅓ ounces) buttermilk, chilled

honey butter

- 2 tablespoons unsalted butter, melted
- 1 tablespoon honey
- Pinch table salt

why this recipe works   Inspired by the sweet, slightly salty Bo-Berry Biscuits at Bojangles, the Southern fast-food chain, we set out to create our own blueberry biscuits, a dream breakfast treat. We took care to keep their sweetness in check—they should be flaky and not eat like a cake or a muffin. We start by mixing together all-purpose flour, a little sugar, baking powder, baking soda, and salt. Then we work in some chilled butter with our fingertips, a step that gives the biscuits their flaky interior crumb. Finally, we fold in tangy buttermilk and plenty of fresh blueberries. Shaping couldn't be easier: To avoid rolling and stamping out biscuits, we pat the dough right into the pan and score it into squares. A brush of lightly salty-sweet butter on the hot biscuits is an irresistible pairing with the sweet berries. We prefer fresh blueberries here, but you can also use 7½ ounces (1½ cups) of frozen blueberries that have been thawed, drained, and then patted dry with paper towels.

1   Adjust oven rack to middle position and heat oven to 425 degrees. Grease 8-inch square baking pan.

2   **make dough**   Whisk flour, sugar, baking powder, baking soda, and salt together in large bowl. Using your hands, rub butter into flour into flat, irregular pieces. Add blueberries and toss with flour mixture. Gently stir in buttermilk until no dry pockets of flour remain. Transfer dough to prepared pan and spread into even layer. Using bench scraper sprayed with vegetable oil spray, cut dough into 9 equal squares, but do not separate.

3   **bake**   Bake until browned on top and paring knife inserted into center biscuit comes out clean, 35 to 45 minutes.

4   **make honey butter**   Meanwhile, combine melted butter, honey, and salt in small bowl and stir to combine; set aside.

5   Remove pan from oven and let biscuits cool in pan for 5 minutes. Turn biscuits out onto baking sheet, then reinvert biscuits onto wire rack. Brush tops of biscuits with honey butter (use all of it) and let cool for 10 minutes longer. Using serrated knife, cut biscuits along scored marks and serve warm.

total time 1¼ hours

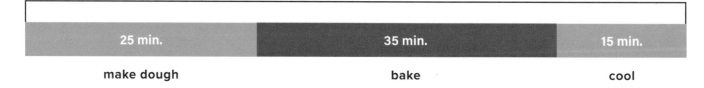

25 min.	35 min.	15 min.
make dough	bake	cool

BRITISH-STYLE CURRANT SCONES

makes 12 scones

- 3 cups (15 ounces) all-purpose flour
- ⅓ cup (2⅓ ounces) sugar
- 2 tablespoons baking powder
- ½ teaspoon table salt
- 8 tablespoons unsalted butter, cut into ½-inch pieces and softened
- ¾ cup dried currants
- 1 cup (8 ounces) whole milk
- 2 large eggs

why this recipe works   Compared to American scones, British scones are lighter, fluffier, and less sweet—perfect for serving with butter and jam. We thoroughly work softened butter into the flour. This protects some of the granules from moisture, limiting gluten development so the crumb is tender and cakey. For a high rise, we add a liberal amount of leavening and start the scones in a 500-degree oven to jump-start their lift. We prefer whole milk in this recipe, but low-fat milk can be used. The dough will be quite soft and wet; dust the counter and your hands liberally with flour. These scones are best served fresh, but leftover scones may be stored in the freezer and reheated in a 300-degree oven for 15 minutes before serving. Serve with jam as well as salted butter or clotted cream.

1   make dough   Adjust oven rack to upper-middle position and heat oven to 500 degrees. Line rimmed baking sheet with parchment paper. Pulse flour, sugar, baking powder, and salt in food processor until combined, about 5 pulses. Add butter and pulse until fully incorporated and mixture resembles very fine crumbs with no butter visible, about 20 pulses. Transfer mixture to large bowl and stir in currants. Whisk milk and eggs together in second bowl; set aside 2 tablespoons milk mixture. Stir remaining milk mixture into flour mixture until almost no dry bits of flour remain.

2   shape dough   Turn out dough onto well-floured counter and gather into ball. Using your floured hands, knead until surface is smooth and free of cracks, 25 to 30 turns. Press gently to form disk then, using floured rolling pin, roll disk into 9-inch round, about 1 inch thick. Using floured 2½-inch round cutter, stamp out 8 scones and arrange on prepared sheet. Gather dough scraps, form into ball, and knead gently until surface is smooth. Roll dough to 1-inch thickness, stamp out 4 scones, and transfer to sheet. Discard remaining dough.

3   bake   Brush tops of scones with reserved milk mixture. Reduce oven temperature to 425 degrees and bake scones until risen and golden brown, 10 to 12 minutes, rotating sheet halfway through baking. Transfer scones to wire rack and let cool for at least 10 minutes. Serve warm or at room temperature.

total time 1 hour

30 min.	10 min.	10 min.	10 min.
make dough	shape dough	bake	cool

JALAPEÑO-CHEDDAR CORNBREAD

makes 1 loaf

- 1½ cups (7½ ounces) cornmeal
- 1 cup (5 ounces) all-purpose flour
- 2 tablespoons sugar
- 1½ teaspoons baking powder
- ½ teaspoon baking soda
- 1½ teaspoons table salt
- 1¼ cups (10 ounces) whole milk
- 2 large eggs
- 6 tablespoons unsalted butter, melted
- 6 ounces extra-sharp cheddar cheese, shredded (1½ cups), divided
- 4 jalapeño chiles, stemmed, seeded, and minced (¾ cup)

why this recipe works   With a foolproof recipe for cornbread in hand, you can easily add a vast world of flavors to the sweet corn, like enlivening chiles and rich cheese. For this recipe, we use a ratio of 1½ cups cornmeal to 1 cup flour so the bread is tender yet sturdy enough to hold the add-ins. Just 2 tablespoons of sugar enhances the cornmeal's subtly sweet flavor. We add four minced jalapeños to the batter, removing the ribs and seeds for a vibrant yet controlled jalapeño kick. Extra-sharp cheddar lends savory, cheesy tang, and we reserve ½ cup to sprinkle over the top, where it bakes into a beautiful cheesy crust. We developed this recipe using Quaker Yellow Corn Meal. Do not use coarse-ground cornmeal. Do not use mild or regular sharp cheddar cheese in this recipe, as its flavor doesn't stand out.

1   Adjust oven rack to middle position and heat oven to 400 degrees. Grease 9-inch round cake pan, line with parchment paper, and grease parchment.

2   make batter   Whisk cornmeal, flour, sugar, baking powder, baking soda, and salt together in large bowl. Whisk milk, eggs, and melted butter together in second bowl. Stir milk mixture into cornmeal mixture until just combined. Stir in 1 cup cheddar and jalapeños until just combined. Transfer batter to prepared pan, smooth top with spatula, and sprinkle with remaining ½ cup cheddar.

3   bake   Bake until cornbread is deep golden brown, top is firm to touch, and paring knife inserted in center comes out clean, 35 to 40 minutes, rotating pan halfway through baking. Let cornbread cool in pan on wire rack for 10 minutes. Remove cornbread from pan, discarding parchment, and let cool completely, about 1 hour. Serve.

total time 2¼ hours

20 min.	35 min.	1¼ hours
make batter	bake	cool

FRESH CORN MUFFINS WITH CARDAMOM–BROWN SUGAR BUTTER

makes 12 muffins

1½ cups (7½ ounces) all-purpose flour

1½ cups (7½ ounces) cornmeal, divided

1 cup (7 ounces) sugar

1½ teaspoons table salt

1½ teaspoons baking powder

1 teaspoon baking soda

1 cup (8 ounces) whole milk

½ cup (4 ounces) sour cream

8 tablespoons unsalted butter, melted

2 large eggs

2 cups corn kernels

1 recipe Cardamom–Brown Sugar Butter (page 94)

why this recipe works   When corn is in season, we desire buttery, golden, sweet corn muffins that showcase not just cornmeal but the fresh vegetable. For a tender corn muffin, recipes often call for more flour than cornmeal, but we use an equal amount: We microwave cornmeal with milk until the mixture thickens to a paste-like consistency. This step hydrates and gels the starch in the cornmeal for a tender crumb with no flavor sacrifices. Two cups of fresh corn kernels add nice pops of sweetness in each bite. To take the muffins over the top, we serve them with our Cardamom–Brown Sugar Butter (page 94), inspired by Asha Gomez's cardamom cornbread in her cookbook *My Two Souths: Blending the Flavors of India into a Southern Kitchen* (2016). The warm flavor of cardamom and sweet corn make a delicious, distinct pairing. We developed this recipe using Quaker Yellow Corn Meal. Do not use coarse-ground cornmeal. Three medium ears of corn should yield at least 2 cups of corn kernels. You can use thawed, frozen corn in a pinch, but the flavor will be duller.

1   Adjust oven rack to middle position and heat oven to 400 degrees. Generously spray 12-cup muffin tin, including top, with vegetable oil spray.

2 make batter   Whisk flour, 1 cup cornmeal, sugar, salt, baking powder, and baking soda together in large bowl; set aside. Whisk milk and remaining ½ cup cornmeal together in medium bowl. Microwave until mixture begins to thicken to paste-like consistency, 1 to 3 minutes, whisking frequently. Whisk sour cream and melted butter into cornmeal paste. Whisk in eggs. Stir cornmeal mixture and corn kernels into flour mixture until just combined. Using ice cream scoop or large spoon, divide batter evenly among prepared muffin cups (cups will be full).

3 bake   Bake until muffins are golden brown and toothpick inserted in center comes out with few crumbs attached, 20 to 24 minutes. Let muffins cool in muffin tin on wire rack for 5 minutes. Remove muffins from muffin tin and let cool on rack for 15 minutes. Serve warm.

total time 1¼ hours

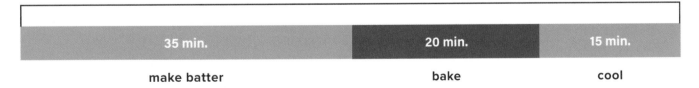

35 min.	20 min.	15 min.
make batter	bake	cool

ROSEMARY-PARMESAN POLENTA MUFFINS

makes 12 muffins

2 cups (10 ounces)
all-purpose flour

1 cup (5 ounces) coarsely
ground polenta

2 teaspoons minced
fresh rosemary

1½ teaspoons baking powder

1 teaspoon baking soda

¾ teaspoon pepper

½ teaspoon table salt

½ teaspoon garlic powder

4½ ounces Parmesan cheese,
shredded (1½ cups), divided

¾ cup (6 ounces) sour cream

¾ cup (6 ounces) whole milk

6 tablespoons extra-virgin olive oil

¼ cup (1¾ ounces) sugar

2 large eggs

why this recipe works   The flavor of polenta, especially when enhanced with cheese and herbs, is perfect for a corn-based muffin that's decidedly savory—one you'll want to eat with a variety of warming dinners. Choosing coarsely ground polenta instead of regular cornmeal gives the crumb a real heartiness, but it's still tender from plenty of all-purpose flour. Two teaspoons of minced fresh rosemary is the perfect amount to scent the muffins without making them taste piney, and using 4½ ounces of Parmesan ensures salty savor throughout. You can substitute cornmeal for the polenta here if necessary; however, the texture of the muffin will be finer and more cake-like. Use the large holes of a box grater to shred the Parmesan. Be sure to generously spray the top and sides of the muffin tin with vegetable oil spray to prevent the cheese from sticking to the tin; if the muffins do stick, run a paring knife around them to loosen before removing.

1   Adjust oven rack to middle position and heat oven to 400 degrees. Generously spray 12-cup muffin tin, including top, with vegetable oil spray.

2   make batter   Whisk flour, polenta, rosemary, baking powder, baking soda, pepper, salt, and garlic powder together in large bowl. Stir in 1 cup Parmesan, breaking up any clumps, until coated with flour. Whisk sour cream, milk, oil, sugar, and eggs in second bowl until smooth. Gently fold sour cream mixture into flour mixture with until just combined. Using ice cream scoop or large spoon, divide batter evenly among prepared muffin cups. Sprinkle remaining ½ cup Parmesan over top of muffins.

3   bake   Bake until golden brown and toothpick inserted into center comes out clean, 15 to 20 minutes, rotating pan halfway through baking. Let muffins cool in muffin tin on wire rack for 5 minutes. Serve warm or at room temperature.

total time 45 minutes

25 min.	15 min.	5 min.
make batter	bake	cool

MANCHEGO AND CHORIZO MUFFINS

makes 12 muffins

4 ounces Spanish-style chorizo
sausage, cut into ¼-inch pieces

3 cups (15 ounces)
all-purpose flour

1 tablespoon baking powder

1 teaspoon table salt

¼ teaspoon pepper

¼ teaspoon cayenne pepper

4 ounces Manchego cheese, cut
into ¼-inch pieces

⅓ cup finely chopped jarred
roasted red peppers, patted dry

1¼ cups (10 ounces) whole milk

¾ cup (6 ounces) sour cream

¼ cup minced fresh parsley

3 tablespoons unsalted butter,
melted and cooled slightly

1 large egg

1 large egg beaten with 1 tablespoon water and pinch salt

why this recipe works Who says muffins have to be sweet—or reserved only for breakfast? These savory beauties, studded with chunks of smoky Spanish-style chorizo, nutty Manchego cheese, and bright and sweet roasted red peppers, pair just as perfectly with a green salad for lunch as they do with a stew at dinnertime. Parcooking the chorizo in the microwave is an easy way to remove some of its fat, preventing orange streaks in the muffins, and patting extra moisture from the roasted red peppers keeps them from weighing down the fluffy and tender crumb. A generous amount of minced parsley adds grassy, fresh flavors and pops of contrasting color, and a quick brush with egg wash before baking gives the tops of the muffins extra golden color and sheen. The texture of these muffins improves as they cool, so (try to) resist the urge to eat them while they're piping hot. Leftover muffins are excellent toasted; toast halved muffins in a toaster oven or on a baking sheet in a 425-degree oven for 5 to 10 minutes. You can substitute 2 percent low-fat milk for the whole milk, but don't use skim milk.

1 Adjust oven rack to middle position and heat oven to 375 degrees. Spray 12-cup muffin tin with vegetable oil spray.

2 make batter Microwave chorizo on paper towel–lined plate until chorizo starts to release fat, 30 to 60 seconds. Transfer chorizo to clean paper towels and press with paper towels to absorb excess oil.

3 Whisk flour, baking powder, salt, pepper, and cayenne together in large bowl. Using rubber spatula, stir in chorizo, Manchego, and red peppers until coated with flour mixture. Whisk milk, sour cream, parsley, melted butter, and whole egg together in second bowl. Using rubber spatula, gently fold milk mixture into flour mixture until just combined (batter will be heavy and thick). Using ice cream scoop or large spoon, divide batter evenly among prepared muffin cups and smooth tops. Brush muffin tops with egg wash.

4 bake Bake until muffins are light golden brown and toothpick inserted in center comes out clean, about 20 minutes, rotating muffin tin halfway through baking. Let muffins cool in muffin tin on wire rack for 5 minutes. Remove muffins from muffin tin and let cool for 30 minutes. Serve.

total time 1¼ hours

25 min.	20 min.	35 min.
make batter	bake	cool

THREE-INGREDIENT BREAD

makes 1 loaf

3 cups (14¼ ounces)
self-rising flour

3 tablespoons sugar

¾ cup (6 ounces) beer

why this recipe works   You can slice this hearty bread like a loaf and it's delicious dunked into a savory stew, slathered in honey butter, or slicked with jam. This multiuse loaf's secrets? It includes only three ingredients and it's out of the oven in under an hour. There's no yeast, no baking powder, no baking soda, and almost no time involved. That's because self-rising flour is three ingredients in one: The low-protein flour already has salt and leavener mixed in. The clever addition of beer gives this loaf the mild fermented flavor of yeasted and risen bread. The liquid brings the bread together so all it needs is a bit of sugar to balance its tanginess. Do not substitute all-purpose flour for the self-rising flour, or your bread won't rise. Use a mild-flavored lager, such as Budweiser (mild nonalcoholic lager also works). The test kitchen's preferred loaf pan measures 8½ by 4½ inches; if you use a 9 by 5-inch loaf pan, start checking for doneness 5 minutes earlier than advised in the recipe.

1   Adjust oven rack to middle position and heat oven to 400 degrees. Grease 8½ by 4½-inch loaf pan.

2   make batter   Stir flour and sugar together in large bowl. Stir in beer until combined. Transfer batter to prepared pan and smooth top.

3   bake   Bake until toothpick inserted in center of loaf comes out with no crumbs attached and top is light golden brown, 35 to 40 minutes. Transfer pan to wire rack and let cool for 5 minutes. Remove loaf from pan and let cool completely on wire rack, about 2 hours. Serve.

total time 2¾ hours

10 min.	35 min.	2 hours
make batter	bake	cool

FLOURLESS NUT AND SEED LOAF

makes 1 loaf

1 cup raw sunflower seeds

1 cup sliced almonds

½ cup raw unsalted pepitas

1¾ cups (5¼ ounces) old-fashioned rolled oats

¼ cup whole flaxseeds

3 tablespoons powdered psyllium husk

1½ cups (12 ounces) water

3 tablespoons refined coconut oil, melted

2 tablespoons maple syrup

¾ teaspoon table salt

why this recipe works Flourless nut and seed loaves have gained popularity for a reason: They're high in protein and all-around nutritious with a hearty flavor. A slice of this bread, toasted and slathered with butter and good jam, is all you need for breakfast. To start, we toast the nuts and seeds—a combination of sunflower seeds, sliced almonds, and pepitas—to enhance their flavor. To bind them, we make a porridge of oats plus flaxseeds and powdered psyllium husk, which, when hydrated, create a gel with strong binding properties. Maple syrup adds a subtle sweetness. To ensure that the bread stays together, we let everything hydrate for a few hours in the loaf pan before baking. Fully baking this bread in the pan leads to a wet loaf. To fix this, we bake the loaf for 20 minutes to allow the outside to set and then turn it out to bake free-form for 35 to 45 minutes. The test kitchen's preferred loaf pan measures 8½ by 4½ inches; if you use a 9 by 5-inch loaf pan, start checking for doneness 5 minutes earlier than advised in the recipe.

1 Adjust oven rack to middle position and heat oven to 350 degrees. Line bottom of 8½ by 4½-inch loaf pan with parchment paper and spray with vegetable oil spray.

2 make dough Combine sunflower seeds, almonds, and pepitas on rimmed baking sheet and bake, stirring occasionally, until lightly browned, 10 to 12 minutes. Transfer to bowl and let cool slightly, about 5 minutes.

3 Stir oats, flaxseeds, and psyllium into bowl with toasted seed-nut mixture. Whisk water, coconut oil, maple syrup, and salt in second bowl until well combined. Using rubber spatula, stir water mixture into nut-seed mixture, then transfer to prepared pan. Using your wet hands, press dough into corners of pan and smooth top.

4 rest Cover loosely with plastic wrap and let sit at room temperature until mixture is fully hydrated and cohesive, about 2 hours.

5 bake Remove plastic and bake loaf for 20 minutes. Invert loaf onto wire rack set in rimmed baking sheet. Remove loaf pan and discard parchment. Bake loaf (still inverted) until deep golden brown and loaf sounds hollow when tapped, 35 to 45 minutes. Let loaf cool completely on wire rack, about 2 hours. Serve.

total time 5½ hours

25 min.	2 hours	1 hour	2 hours
make dough	rest	bake	cool

FETA-DILL ZUCCHINI BREAD

makes 1 loaf

1 pound zucchini, shredded

2 cups (10 ounces) all-purpose flour

½ cup (2¾ ounces) whole-wheat flour

2 teaspoons baking powder

1 teaspoon baking soda

¾ teaspoon pepper

½ teaspoon table salt

3 large eggs

7 tablespoons unsalted butter, melted, divided

6 ounces feta cheese, crumbled (1½ cups)

⅓ cup chopped fresh dill

why this recipe works   Anyone lucky enough to have a vegetable garden is always looking for new ways to use up surplus zucchini. But there's no reason why the squash's flavor should be hidden behind lots of sugar in a sweet bread. In this savory spin, the zucchini flavor really shines, and it's complemented by assertively briny feta cheese, grassy fresh dill, and a touch of nutty whole-wheat flour mixed in with the all-purpose flour. You may know that zucchini releases lots of moisture, so you must squeeze the shredded squash in a dish towel before incorporating it. But the unique consistency of this quick-bread batter also helps control moisture: When the zucchini releases moisture during baking it turns what starts out as a stiff, dry dough into a perfectly tender loaf. Brushing the top with melted butter before baking creates a craggy, crunchy crust. We like to slather slices with rich Feta Butter (page 95); you could go further and top it with seasonal tomato slices for a summer snack, or serve alongside soup or salad. The test kitchen's preferred loaf pan measures 8½ by 4½ inches; if you use a 9 by 5-inch loaf pan, start checking for doneness 5 minutes earlier than advised in the recipe.

1   Adjust oven rack to middle position and heat oven to 350 degrees. Grease 8½ by 4½-inch loaf pan.

2   make batter   Place zucchini in dish towel. Gather ends together and twist tightly over sink to drain as much liquid as possible.

3   Whisk all-purpose flour, whole-wheat flour, baking powder, baking soda, pepper, and salt together in large bowl. Whisk eggs and 6 tablespoons melted butter together in medium bowl, then stir in zucchini, feta, and dill. Using rubber spatula, gently fold zucchini mixture into flour mixture, then lightly knead batter with your oiled hands or bowl scraper until no dry spots remain (batter will be very thick). Transfer batter to prepared pan, smooth top with rubber spatula, and brush with remaining 1 tablespoon melted butter.

4   bake   Bake until toothpick inserted in center of loaf comes out with few moist crumbs attached, 1 hour 5 minutes to 1¼ hours, rotating pan halfway through baking. Let bread cool in pan on wire rack for 30 minutes. Remove bread from pan and let cool completely on wire rack, about 1½ hours. Slice and serve.

total time 3½ hours

25 min.	1 hour 5 min.	2 hours
make batter	bake	cool

WHOLE-WHEAT DATE-NUT BREAD

makes 1 loaf

10 ounces pitted dates, chopped coarse (1⅔ cups)

1 cup (8 ounces) boiling water

1 teaspoon baking soda

1½ cups (8¼ ounces) whole-wheat flour

½ cup (2½ ounces) all-purpose flour

1 teaspoon baking powder

½ teaspoon table salt

⅔ cup (5⅓ ounces) buttermilk

⅓ cup packed (2⅓ ounces) dark brown sugar

¼ cup vegetable oil

1 large egg

1 cup walnuts, toasted and chopped coarse

why this recipe works   Although date-nut bread is a classic, it often suffers from unmitigated sweetness and hard, chewy dates. We wanted a more wholesome loaf full of soft, sweet dates and toasty nuts suspended in a tender, not-too-sweet crumb. To soften the fibrous dates we soak them in an alkaline mix of hot water and baking soda; both the softened dates and their flavorful soaking liquid go into the batter. With the dates and their liquid in play, just ⅓ cup of dark brown sugar gives the batter all the sweetness it needs. Nutty whole-wheat flour is a natural choice for this heartier, fruit-studded loaf; we use 75 percent whole-wheat flour, with just a bit of all-purpose flour providing structure and lift. For an accurate measurement of boiling water, bring a full kettle of water to a boil and then measure out the desired amount. The test kitchen's preferred loaf pan measures 8½ by 4½ inches; if you use a 9 by 5-inch loaf pan, start checking for doneness 5 minutes earlier than advised in the recipe.

1   Adjust oven rack to middle position and heat oven to 350 degrees. Grease 8½ by 4½-inch loaf pan. Combine dates, boiling water, and baking soda in medium bowl, cover, and let sit until dates have softened, about 30 minutes.

2   make batter   Whisk whole-wheat flour, all-purpose flour, baking powder, and salt together in large bowl. Whisk buttermilk, sugar, oil, and egg in second bowl until smooth, then stir in dates and their soaking liquid until combined. Using rubber spatula, gently fold buttermilk mixture into flour mixture until just combined. Gently fold in walnuts. Transfer batter to prepared pan and smooth top.

3   bake   Bake until golden and skewer inserted in center comes out clean, 55 minutes to 1 hour, rotating pan halfway through baking. Let bread cool in pan on wire rack for 10 minutes. Remove bread from pan and let cool completely on wire rack, about 2 hours. Serve.

total time   4 hours

45 min.	55 min.	2¼ hours
make batter	bake	cool

PUMPKIN BREAD

makes 1 loaf

- 1¼ cups (6¼ ounces) all-purpose flour
- 1 teaspoon baking powder
- 1 teaspoon baking soda
- ¾ cup plus 1 tablespoon canned unsweetened pumpkin puree, divided
- 2 teaspoons pumpkin pie spice, divided
- ½ teaspoon plus pinch table salt, divided
- ½ cup (3½ ounces) granulated sugar
- ½ cup packed (3½ ounces) light brown sugar
- ½ cup vegetable oil
- 2 large eggs
- 3 tablespoons plus 1 teaspoon milk, divided
- 1 cup (4 ounces) confectioners' sugar
- 2 tablespoons roasted pepitas

why this recipe works When pumpkin spice season hits (or whenever a craving strikes, break out this recipe for a quick bread with plenty of pumpkin and plenty of spice. We start by cooking canned pumpkin on the stove along with a generous blend of cinnamon, ginger, nutmeg, and allspice; this blooms the spices and increases their intensity as the pumpkin loses its raw, canned flavor. To top off an otherwise plain-looking loaf, we make a simple confectioners' sugar glaze with a bit more canned pumpkin (giving it a beautiful orange hue) and more pumpkin pie spice, and we spread it attractively over the cooled bread. A sprinkle of roasted pepitas adds crunch. The test kitchen's preferred loaf pan measures 8½ by 4½ inches; if you use a 9 by 5-inch loaf pan, start checking for doneness 5 minutes earlier than advised in the recipe.

1 Adjust oven rack to middle position and heat oven to 350 degrees. Grease 8½ by 4½-inch loaf pan.

2 make batter Whisk flour, baking powder, and baking soda together in bowl; set aside. Combine ¾ cup pumpkin, 1½ teaspoons pumpkin pie spice, and ½ teaspoon salt in large saucepan. Cook over medium heat, stirring constantly with rubber spatula, until mixture just begins to bubble, 4 to 6 minutes. Off heat, add granulated sugar, brown sugar, and oil to pumpkin mixture and whisk until combined. Let mixture cool for 10 minutes. Add eggs and 2 tablespoons milk to pumpkin mixture and whisk until smooth. Add flour mixture and use rubber spatula to stir until just combined and no dry flour is visible. Transfer batter into prepared pan and smooth top.

3 bake Bake until toothpick inserted in center of pumpkin bread comes out clean, 40 to 50 minutes, rotating pan halfway through baking. Let bread cool in pan on wire rack for 15 minutes. Remove bread from pan and let cool for 1 hour.

4 Meanwhile, whisk confectioners' sugar, remaining 1 tablespoon pumpkin, remaining ½ teaspoon pumpkin pie spice, remaining pinch salt, and remaining 4 teaspoons milk, together in bowl until smooth; set aside. Whisk glaze to recombine, then spread over top of bread (it will run down sides) and sprinkle with pepitas. Let glaze set for 15 minutes before serving.

total time 2½ hours

35 min.	40 min.	1¼ hours
make batter	bake	cool

BACON-ONION CHEESE BREAD

makes 1 loaf

3 ounces Parmesan cheese, shredded (1 cup), divided

5 slices bacon, cut into ½-inch pieces

½ cup finely chopped onion

2½ cups (12½ ounces) all-purpose flour

1 tablespoon baking powder

1 teaspoon table salt

⅛ teaspoon pepper

⅛ teaspoon cayenne pepper

4 ounces Gruyère cheese, cut into ½-inch pieces (1 cup)

1 cup (8 ounces) whole milk

½ cup (4 ounces) sour cream

1 large egg

why this recipe works   This might be the most savory quick bread you ever try—perfect to serve guests before dinner or with a pot of chili any night of the week. It's moist, rich, and hearty, with a bold, cheesy crust. We cook bacon until crisp and then sauté onion in some of the rendered fat. We mix small chunks of Gruyère (rather than shreds) into the dough to create pockets of rich, salty flavor throughout. And we coat the pan and top the loaf with shredded Parmesan which browns and crisps the exterior. The test kitchen's preferred loaf pan measures 8½ by 4½ inches; if you use a 9 by 5-inch loaf pan, start checking for doneness 5 minutes earlier than advised in the recipe. Use the large holes of a box grater to shred the Parmesan. If, when testing the bread for doneness, the skewer comes out with what looks like uncooked batter clinging to it, try again in a different, but still central, spot. (A skewer hitting a pocket of cheese may give a false indication.) The texture of the bread improves as it cools, so resist the urge to slice the loaf when it's still warm.

1   Adjust oven rack to middle position and heat oven to 350 degrees. Grease 8½ by 4½-inch loaf pan, then sprinkle ½ cup Parmesan evenly in bottom of pan.

2   make batter   Cook bacon in 10-inch nonstick skillet over medium heat until crispy, 5 to 7 minutes. Using slotted spoon, transfer bacon to paper towel–lined plate. Pour off all but 3 tablespoons fat from skillet. Add onion to fat left in skillet and cook until softened, about 3 minutes; set aside.

3   Whisk flour, baking powder, salt, pepper, and cayenne together in large bowl. Stir in Gruyère and bacon, breaking up clumps, until stir-ins are coated with flour. Whisk milk, sour cream, and egg together in second bowl. Whisk onion into milk mixture. Using rubber spatula, gently fold milk mixture into flour mixture until just combined (batter will be heavy and thick). Transfer batter to prepared pan and smooth top. Sprinkle remaining ½ cup Parmesan evenly over top.

4   bake   Bake loaf until golden brown and skewer inserted in center comes out clean, 45 to 50 minutes, rotating pan halfway through baking. Let loaf cool in pan for 15 minutes. Remove loaf from pan and let cool completely on wire rack, about 3 hours, before serving.

total time 4½ hours

30 min.	45 min.	3¼ hours
make batter	bake	cool

DOUBLE-CHOCOLATE BANANA BREAD

makes 1 loaf

1¼ cups (6¼ ounces) all-purpose flour

¼ cup (¾ ounce) Dutch-processed cocoa powder

1¼ teaspoons baking soda

¾ teaspoon table salt

2 cups mashed very ripe bananas (about 4 bananas)

1 cup packed (7 ounces) dark brown sugar

10 tablespoons unsalted butter, melted and cooled slightly

2 large eggs

4 ounces bittersweet chocolate, chopped

2 tablespoons granulated sugar

why this recipe works Banana bread recipes go to great lengths to crack the code to ultimate banana flavor. This dead-simple version does that and more, counting in chocolate as well for tender, moist, buttery slices with just the right amount of sweetness. After extensive testing, we arrived at a recipe that calls for more than a pound of sweet, very ripe bananas (which also makes this one of the moistest loaves we've had) and two types of chocolate (cocoa powder and chopped bittersweet chocolate). Plus, it's as easy as mixing the wet and dry ingredients together in a bowl. Be sure to use very ripe, heavily speckled (or even black) bananas in this recipe. Use a potato masher to thoroughly mash the bananas. The test kitchen's preferred loaf pan measures 8½ by 4½ inches; if you use a 9 by 5-inch loaf pan, start checking for doneness 5 minutes earlier than advised in the recipe. We place the loaf pan on a rimmed baking sheet in case the batter overflows in the oven.

1 Adjust oven rack to middle position and heat oven to 350 degrees. Grease 8½ by 4½-inch loaf pan.

2 **make batter** Whisk flour, cocoa, baking soda, and salt together in bowl. Whisk bananas, brown sugar, melted butter, and eggs in large bowl until thoroughly combined, making sure to break up any clumps of brown sugar with whisk. Add flour mixture to banana mixture and whisk gently until just combined (batter will be lumpy). Fold in chocolate.

3 Place prepared pan on rimmed baking sheet. Transfer batter to prepared pan and sprinkle with granulated sugar.

4 **bake** Bake until toothpick inserted in center comes out clean, about 1 hour 10 minutes. Let bread cool in pan on wire rack for 30 minutes. Remove loaf from pan and let cool for at least 30 minutes longer. Serve warm or at room temperature.

total time 2½ hours

20 min.	1 hour 10 min.	1 hour
make batter	bake	cool

MAPLE-SORGHUM SKILLET BREAD

makes 1 loaf

¼ cup vegetable oil

6 ounces (1⅓ cups) sorghum flour

3¾ ounces (¾ cup) cornmeal

1¼ cups (10 ounces) sour cream

½ cup (4 ounces) whole milk

½ cup maple syrup

4 tablespoons unsalted butter

1 teaspoon baking powder

½ teaspoon baking soda

¾ teaspoon table salt

2 large eggs

why this recipe works Sorghum cornbread has a unique nutty flavor; a tender, dense crumb; and a rough-textured, thick crust. It's a delicious bread that tastes great served alongside chili or barbecue. And it also happens to be gluten-free. The sorghum flour produces just enough fluffiness to keep this Southern-style cornbread from being too dense. We add a generous amount of maple syrup to the batter, as it further enhances the nutty flavor of the sorghum and contributes to a nicely browned crust. Baking the bread in a greased preheated cast-iron skillet gives that crust some crunch. We use a combination of oil and butter for greasing the skillet; the butter adds flavor while the oil raises the smoke point so the butter doesn't burn. We prefer to use a cast-iron skillet here because it makes the best crust; however, any 10-inch ovensafe skillet will work for this recipe. This bread is best served warm.

1 Adjust oven rack to middle position and heat oven to 450 degrees. When oven has reached 450 degrees, place 10-inch cast-iron skillet on rack and let heat for 10 minutes. Add oil and continue to heat skillet until just smoking, about 5 minutes.

2 make batter Meanwhile, whisk sorghum flour, cornmeal, sour cream, milk, and maple syrup together in medium bowl (batter will be thick). Being careful of hot skillet handle, remove skillet from oven. Add butter and gently swirl to incorporate. Pour hot oil-butter mixture into sorghum mixture and whisk to incorporate. Whisk in baking powder, baking soda, and salt, followed by eggs. Quickly scrape batter into hot skillet and smooth top.

3 bake Bake until top begins to crack, edges are golden brown, and toothpick inserted in center comes out clean, 20 to 24 minutes, rotating skillet halfway through baking. Being careful of hot skillet handle, remove skillet from oven. Let bread cool in skillet for 5 minutes, then transfer to wire rack and let cool for 20 minutes before serving.

total time 1¼ hours

35 min.	20 min.	25 min.
make batter	bake	cool

SWEET POTATO CORNBREAD

makes 1 loaf

1½ pounds sweet potatoes, unpeeled

½ cup (4 ounces) whole milk

8 tablespoons unsalted butter, melted, plus 1 tablespoon unsalted butter

4 large eggs

1½ cups (7½ ounces) cornmeal

½ cup (2½ ounces) all-purpose flour

¼ cup packed (1¾ ounces) brown sugar

1 tablespoon baking powder

½ teaspoon baking soda

1¾ teaspoons table salt

why this recipe works   Sweet potato cornbread marries two favorite Southern ingredients to take bread in a colorful and flavorful direction. This rendition, with its browned crust and brilliant orange-gold interior, is in a league of its own. As you might expect, introducing dense, moist sweet potatoes to cornbread affects the bread's texture, so the potatoes need to be handled properly to keep the bread light. Precooking and mashing the potatoes is a must, of course. Unlike with boiling, a drier cooking method helps keep the potatoes' moisture under control while intensifying the vegetable's flavor, and microwaving is the easiest way to achieve this. For corn flavor that stands up to the spuds, we use 1½ cups cornmeal to just ½ cup all-purpose flour. The ¼ cup of brown sugar helps the bread develop deeper color and enhances the delicate sweet potato flavor without making the bread too sweet.

1   Adjust oven rack to middle position and heat oven to 425 degrees.

2   make batter   Prick potatoes all over with fork. Microwave on large plate until potatoes are very soft and surfaces are slightly wet, 10 to 15 minutes, flipping every 5 minutes. Immediately slice potatoes in half to release steam. When potatoes are cool enough to handle, scoop flesh into bowl and mash until smooth (you should have about 1¾ cups); discard skins. Whisk in milk, melted butter, and eggs. Whisk cornmeal, flour, sugar, baking powder, baking soda, and salt together in second large bowl. Using rubber spatula, gently fold potato mixture into cornmeal mixture until just combined.

3   bake   Melt remaining 1 tablespoon butter in 10-inch cast-iron skillet over medium heat. Scrape batter into hot skillet and spread into even layer. Transfer skillet to oven and bake until cornbread is golden brown and toothpick inserted in center comes out clean, 25 to 30 minutes. Being careful of hot skillet handle, transfer skillet to wire rack and let cornbread cool for 1 hour. Slide cornbread onto cutting board and cut into wedges. Serve.

total time 2 hours

30 min.	30 min.	1 hour
make batter	bake	cool

BHATURE

makes 8 breads

½ cup (4 ounces) plain yogurt

¼ cup (2 ounces) water

3 tablespoons vegetable oil

2 cups (10 ounces)
  all-purpose flour

1 teaspoon sugar

¾ teaspoon table salt

¾ teaspoon baking powder

¼ teaspoon baking soda

2 quarts vegetable oil for frying

why this recipe works   Bhature are rich and tender fried breads that are a common accompaniment to chana masala (together, the dish is called chole bhature), but they're a marvel no matter how you eat them: The slim disks of dough balloon dramatically when cooked in hot oil. Though bhature are sometimes leavened with yeast, we opt for the simpler combination of baking powder and baking soda. The flour-and-yogurt dough comes together quickly in the food processor, but we also knead it by hand to build the gluten necessary for optimum inflation. When the dough is fried, the hot oil quickly seals the outermost layer, forming a thin skin. Simultaneously, water in the dough turns to steam, pushing outward. The skin stretches and expands—small bubbles first form around the edge and eventually merge into a single large balloon. Stir the yogurt well before measuring it. Use a Dutch oven that holds 6 quarts or more for frying. Each bhatura takes less than a minute to cook, so make sure that you have everything in place before you start to fry.

1   make dough   Whisk yogurt, water, and oil in small bowl until smooth. Pulse flour, sugar, salt, baking powder, and baking soda in food processor until combined, about 2 pulses. With processor running, add yogurt mixture and process until mixture forms smooth ball, about 30 seconds. Using your lightly oiled hands, transfer dough to lightly oiled counter. Knead until dough is smooth and springy, about 5 minutes. Form dough into ball and transfer to lightly greased bowl.

2   rest   Place plastic wrap or damp dish towel on surface of dough and let rest for at least 1 hour or up to 3 hours.

3   Add 2 quarts oil to large Dutch oven until it measures about 1½ inches deep and heat over medium-high heat to 390 degrees. Set wire rack in rimmed baking sheet and line with double layer of paper towels.

4   shape dough   While oil is heating, transfer dough to clean counter, divide into 8 equal pieces, and cover loosely with plastic. Working with 1 piece of dough at a time (keep remaining pieces covered), form each piece into rough ball by stretching dough around your thumb and pinching edges together so that top is smooth. Place ball seam side down on clean counter and, using your cupped hand, drag in small circles until dough feels taut and round. Coat lightly with oil and cover with plastic. Again working with 1 piece at a time, use heel of your hand to press dough ball into 3-inch round. Using rolling pin, gently roll into 6-inch round of even thickness, adding extra oil to counter as necessary to prevent sticking. Roll slowly and gently to prevent creasing. Cover rounds with plastic or damp dish towel.

5   cook   Carefully place 1 dough round in hot oil. Press gently with back of spider skimmer to keep dough submerged until it begins to puff. As bread begins to puff on 1 side, gently press unpuffed side into oil until bread is evenly inflated, about 20 seconds. Continue to cook until bottom is light golden brown, about 10 seconds longer. Flip bread and cook on second side, lightly pressing both sides into oil to ensure even browning, about 20 seconds. Lift bhatura with spider skimmer and let drain briefly over pot before transferring to prepared rack. Repeat with remaining dough rounds, adjusting burner, if necessary, to maintain oil temperature between 380 and 400 degrees. Serve.

total time 2¼ hours

20 min.	1 hour	25 min.	25 min.
make dough	rest	shape dough	cook

APPLE CIDER DOUGHNUTS

makes 12 doughnuts and 12 doughnut holes

coating

- ½ cup (3½ ounces) sugar
- ⅛ teaspoon ground cinnamon
- Pinch table salt

dough

- 2½ cups (12½ ounces) all-purpose flour
- 1 teaspoon baking powder
- ½ teaspoon baking soda
- ½ teaspoon ground cinnamon
- ¼ teaspoon ground nutmeg
- ¼ teaspoon table salt
- ½ cup thawed apple juice concentrate
- ⅓ cup (2⅓ ounces) sugar
- ¼ cup (2 ounces) buttermilk
- 4 tablespoons unsalted butter, melted and cooled
- 1 large egg
- 2 quarts vegetable oil for frying

why this recipe works   These sweet treats are a must-have when visiting apple orchards in the fall, but despite their name and provenance, we often find ourselves searching for the apple flavor. Boiling down apple cider concentrates its flavor but we found a more surefire way to flavor: We simply stir tart, intensely flavorful apple juice concentrate right into the dough. Using acidic buttermilk activates the leaveners in the batter and gives the doughnuts extra lift and lightness. A bit of cinnamon and nutmeg complements the doughnuts' sweetness. After frying them, we give our old-fashioned doughnuts a quick toss in cinnamon sugar seasoned with a touch of salt to add a layer of flavor and a sugary crunch that might just be your favorite part. Use a Dutch oven that holds 6 quarts or more for this recipe.

1 make coating   Whisk all ingredients together in medium bowl; set aside.

2 make dough   Whisk flour, baking powder, baking soda, cinnamon, nutmeg, and salt together in bowl. Whisk apple juice concentrate, sugar, buttermilk, melted butter, and egg together in large bowl. Whisk half of flour mixture into apple juice concentrate mixture until smooth. Add remaining flour mixture; using rubber spatula, use folding motion to mix and press dough until all flour is hydrated and no dry bits remain. (Dough can be covered with plastic wrap and refrigerated for up to 24 hours.)

3 shape dough   Dust counter heavily with flour. Turn out dough onto floured counter, then dust top of dough with additional flour. Using your floured hands, gently pat dough into ⅓-inch-thick round, 10 to 11 inches in diameter. Using floured 3-inch round cutter, stamp out 9 or 10 doughnut rounds. Using 1-inch round cutter, cut hole in center of each round. Lightly dust rimmed baking sheet with flour. Transfer doughnut rounds and holes to prepared sheet. Combine dough scraps, then knead into cohesive ball and pat into ⅓-inch-thick round. Stamp out 2 or 3 more doughnut rounds and holes (you should have 12 of each). Transfer to sheet and refrigerate while heating oil.

4 cook   Set wire rack in second rimmed baking sheet and line half of rack with triple layer of paper towels. Add oil to large Dutch oven until it measures about 1½ inches deep and heat over medium-high heat to 350 degrees. Add 6 doughnut rounds and cook, flipping every 30 seconds, until deep golden brown, about 2 minutes. Adjust burner as needed to maintain oil temperature between 325 and 350 degrees. Using spider skimmer or slotted spoon, transfer doughnuts to paper towel–lined side of prepared rack and let sit while frying remaining doughnut rounds. Return oil to 350 degrees and repeat with remaining doughnut rounds.

5   Return oil to 350 degrees and, using spider skimmer or slotted spoon, carefully add doughnut holes to hot oil. Cook, stirring often, until deep golden brown, about 2 minutes. Transfer to paper towel–lined side of wire rack. Lightly toss doughnuts and doughnut holes in reserved coating and transfer to unlined side of wire rack. Serve.

total time 1¼ hours

20 min.	15 min.	30 min.
make dough	shape dough	cook

SODA BREAD WITH NUTS AND CACAO NIBS

makes 1 loaf

2 cups (11 ounces) whole-wheat flour

1 cup (5 ounces) all-purpose flour

1 cup wheat bran

¼ cup wheat germ

2 teaspoons sugar

1½ teaspoons baking powder

1½ teaspoons baking soda

1 teaspoon table salt

2 cups (16 ounces) buttermilk

1 cup walnuts, toasted and chopped

6 tablespoons cacao nibs

why this recipe works   What you usually find in the United States under the moniker "Irish soda bread" is a fairly sweet white bread made with butter, eggs, raisins, and caraway seeds. While delicious, it's not actually Irish. Traditional Irish soda bread, made with whole-wheat flour and without raisins, butter, or eggs, is the simple, savory counterpart to its sweeter Americanized cousin. It's craggy, hearty, and nutty, perfect for slathering with salted butter and enjoying alongside a cup of tea or pairing with soup or a wedge of cheese. Our rendition is true to this whole-wheat, not-sweet Irish ethos. Adding both wheat bran and wheat germ to the flour mixture creates complex flavor and a rustic, coarse texture. We still take some decidedly nontraditional liberties with the mix-ins, though, studding the bread with rich toasted walnuts and crunchy cacao nibs. The cacao nibs provide the intense flavor of chocolate without any sweetness. The dough comes together in just one bowl and requires a bare minimum of shaping.

1   Adjust oven rack to middle position and heat oven to 375 degrees. Lightly grease 8-inch round cake pan.

2   make dough   Whisk whole-wheat flour, all-purpose flour, wheat bran, wheat germ, sugar, baking powder, baking soda, and salt together in large bowl. Stir in buttermilk, walnuts, and cacao nibs until all flour is moistened and dough forms soft, ragged mass.

3   shape dough   Transfer dough to counter and gently shape into 6-inch round (surface will be craggy). Using serrated knife, cut ½-inch-deep cross about 5 inches long on top of loaf. Transfer to prepared pan.

4   bake   Bake until loaf is lightly browned and center registers 185 degrees, 50 minutes to 1 hour, rotating pan halfway through baking. Remove bread from pan and let cool on wire rack for at least 1 hour. Slice and serve.

total time 2¼ hours

20 min.	5 min.	50 min.	1 hour
make dough	shape dough	bake	cool

BOSTON BROWN BREAD

makes 2 small loaves

¾ cup (4⅛ ounces) rye flour

¾ cup (4⅛ ounces) whole-wheat flour

¾ cup (3¾ ounces) fine white cornmeal

1¾ teaspoons baking soda

½ teaspoon baking powder

1 teaspoon table salt

1⅔ cups (13⅓ ounces) buttermilk

½ cup molasses

3 tablespoons butter, melted and cooled slightly

¾ cup raisins

why this recipe works New Englanders know the appeal of Boston brown bread: It's deeply, darkly delicious—cakey and rich with molasses, raisins, and the complex flavors (and nutrition) of whole grains. The bread is steamed on the stovetop, traditionally in a 1-pound coffee can. We call for whole-wheat flour, rye flour, and finely ground cornmeal in equal amounts. Baking soda and baking powder react with the acid in the batter to lighten the bread, and melted butter gives the lean loaves some richness. Two empty BPA-free 28-ounce tomato cans are a good substitute for traditional (but increasingly uncommon) coffee cans. We prefer Quaker white cornmeal in this recipe, though other types will work; do not use coarse grits. Any style of molasses will work except for blackstrap. This recipe requires a 10-quart or larger stockpot that is at least 7 inches deep. Brown bread is traditionally served with baked beans but is also good toasted and buttered.

1 Bring 3 quarts water to simmer in large stockpot over high heat. Fold two 16 by 12-inch pieces of aluminum foil in half to yield two rectangles that measure 8 by 12 inches. Spray 4-inch circle in center of each rectangle with vegetable oil spray. Spray insides of two clean 28-ounce cans with vegetable oil spray.

2 make batter Whisk rye flour, whole-wheat flour, cornmeal, baking soda, baking powder, and salt together in large bowl. Whisk buttermilk, molasses, and melted butter together in second bowl. Stir raisins into buttermilk mixture. Add buttermilk mixture to flour mixture and stir until combined and no dry flour remains. Evenly divide batter between cans. Wrap tops of cans tightly with prepared foil, positioning sprayed side of foil over can openings.

3 cook Place cans in stockpot (water should come about halfway up sides of cans). Cover pot and cook, maintaining gentle simmer, until skewer inserted in center of loaves comes out clean, about 2 hours. Check pot occasionally and add hot water as needed to maintain water level. Using jar lifter, carefully transfer cans to wire rack set in rimmed baking sheet and let cool for 20 minutes. Slide loaves from cans onto rack and let cool completely, about 1 hour. Slice and serve.

total time 3¾ hours

30 min.	2 hours	1¼ hours
make batter	cook	cool

FLAVORED BUTTERS

Bread and butter are such a natural pair, they're a fundamental idiom in the English lexicon. A warm biscuit dribbling with melting butter or a slice of hearty rustic bread with a flavorful schmear served with soup is a nice comforting extra for some and a no-brainer for others. No matter how elaborate you like to get with your bread-topping pairings, we have a butter that will work.

TO MAKE FLAVORED BUTTER

Using fork, mash 8 tablespoons softened butter with any of the following combinations in bowl until combined. Cover with plastic wrap and let rest for 10 minutes, or roll into log and refrigerate in airtight container for up to 1 week or freeze for up to 2 months. Let come to room temperature before serving.

GINGER-MOLASSES BUTTER

makes about ½ cup

Do not use blackstrap molasses; its intense flavor will overwhelm the other flavors. We like to highlight the flavor of molasses in our Boston Brown Bread (page 92) with this unexpected butter. It's also nice with our Whole-Wheat Date-Nut Bread (page 74) or Anadama Bread (page 212).

- **2 teaspoons molasses**
- **1 teaspoon grated fresh ginger**
- **⅛ teaspoon table salt**

CARDAMOM-BROWN SUGAR BUTTER

makes about ⅔ cup

This butter was developed to accompany our sweet Fresh Corn Muffins (page 63), but it's also nice with more savory recipes like Sweet Potato Cornbread (page 85) and Flourless Nut and Seed Loaf (page 70).

- **¼ cup packed (1¾ ounces) light brown sugar**
- **¾ teaspoon ground cardamom**
- **½ teaspoon table salt**

HONEY BUTTER

makes about ⅔ cup

Honey butter is great to have around: There isn't really a bread it doesn't go with, sweet or savory, but biscuits are a favorite. Add some cayenne for heat, if desired.

- ¼ **cup honey**
- ½ **teaspoon table salt**
- ⅛ **teaspoon ground cayenne pepper (optional)**

FETA BUTTER

makes about ¾ cup

We developed this butter to go with our Feta-Dill Zucchini Bread (page 73), but it's great with a number of breads of any style. Don't be afraid to try it with Whole-Wheat Date-Nut Bread (page 74).

- 4 **ounces feta cheese, crumbled (1 cup)**

RADISH BUTTER

makes 1 cup

When broken down in the food processor, radishes give the butter a sweet-spicy profile that's perfect with Rye Bread (page 214) or simple Three-Ingredient Bread (page 69). If your radishes have the greens attached, buy one small (9- to 10-ounce) bunch.

- 6 **ounces radishes, trimmed and quartered**
- 2 **teaspoons distilled white vinegar**
- 4 **tablespoons unsalted butter, softened**
- 1–2 **teaspoons prepared horseradish**
- ¼ **teaspoon table salt**

1 Pulse radishes and vinegar in food processor until finely chopped, 10 to 15 pulses, scraping down sides of bowl as needed. Let stand for 10 minutes. Transfer radishes to large plate lined with triple layer of paper towels and spread into even layer. Top with another layer of paper towels and press gently. Let stand for 5 minutes.

2 Combine butter, 1 teaspoon horseradish, and salt in bowl. Stir in radishes until well combined. Season with salt and up to 1 teaspoon additional horseradish to taste. Serve.

NORI BUTTER

makes about ½ cup

Nori adds tons of savory depth but is mild enough that this butter remains incredibly versatile.

- 2 **teaspoons nori powder**
- ¼ **teaspoon table salt**

CHAPTER TWO

rolls and more

DINNER ROLLS

A bread basket of dinner rolls is the ideal finishing touch to a dinner party, holiday meal, even a winter Tuesday night—but, accordingly, the rolls typically get the last thought. That's too bad, because soft homemade rolls beat plastic-wrapped store-bought versions any day. We developed a core dinner roll dough anyone could feel confident making—one with a basic kneading technique and a gorgeous texture that bakes up fluffy and rich. Then, we manipulated this multipurpose dough into a number of shapes—from comforting crescent rolls to elegant S-shaped snails filled with fresh chives. It's perfect for these kinds of adaptations; it's enriched but not sticky, it's moderately hydrated, and it's gorgeously supple from the egg.

White, light, and fluffy rolls are just one kind, and when you make other breads in this chapter—whether you like crusty rolls with a chewy crumb for rustic dinners or a butter-soaked English muffin for breakfast—you'll be nearly fluent in the procedure. The dance of dividing the dough into portions, then rolling the dough portions into balls and dragging them across the counter to ensure tight, sealed rounds (see page 101) applies to nearly every roll recipe there is. No day has to go without bread on the side.

WHITE DINNER ROLLS

makes 15 rolls

how-to

Ingredients

5 cups (25 ounces) all-purpose flour

2¼ teaspoons instant or rapid-rise yeast

2 teaspoons table salt

1½ cups (12 ounces) whole milk, room temperature

⅓ cup honey

1 large egg, room temperature

4 tablespoons vegetable shortening, melted

3 tablespoons unsalted butter, melted

1 large egg, beaten with 1 tablespoon water and pinch table salt

Sure, a whole chapter of rolls follows, but this is the one you'll turn to again and again for its ease, its adaptability, and its soft, comforting familiarity. A basic white dinner roll should be buttery, but butter alone can yield a heavy (or greasy) product. Substituting vegetable shortening for a portion of the butter delivers a soft crumb. (Shortening coats the gluten strands in the flour more effectively than butter, creating tenderness.) Shortening also prevents the rolls from drying out. Whole milk provides our rolls with just the right level of moisture and richness, and one egg contributes structure and flavor. As a bonus, this dough can be refrigerated overnight after shaping into rolls, making it easy and convenient to serve for a special meal.

1 make dough Whisk flour, yeast, and salt together in bowl of stand mixer. Whisk milk, honey, egg, melted shortening, and melted butter in 4-cup liquid measuring cup until honey has dissolved.

2 Using dough hook on low speed, slowly add milk mixture to flour mixture and mix until cohesive dough starts to form and no dry flour remains, about 2 minutes, scraping down bowl as needed. Increase speed to medium-low and knead until dough is smooth and elastic and clears sides of bowl, about 8 minutes. Transfer dough to lightly floured counter and knead by hand to form smooth, round ball, about 30 seconds.

3 first rise Place dough seam side down in lightly greased large bowl or container, cover with plastic wrap, and let dough rise until doubled in volume, 1½ to 2 hours.

4 Make foil sling for 13 by 9-inch baking dish by folding 2 long sheets of aluminum foil; first sheet should be 13 inches wide and second sheet should be 9 inches wide. Lay sheets of foil in dish perpendicular to each other, with extra foil hanging over edges of dish. Push foil into corners and up sides of dish, smoothing foil flush to dish, then spray foil with vegetable oil spray.

5 shape dough Press down on dough to deflate. Transfer dough to clean counter and stretch into even 15-inch log. Cut log into 15 equal pieces and cover loosely with greased plastic. Working with 1 piece of dough at a time (keep remaining pieces covered), form into rough ball by stretching dough around your thumb and pinching edges together so that top is smooth. Place ball seam side down on clean counter and, using your cupped hand, drag in small circles until dough feels taut and round. Arrange dough balls seam side down into 5 rows of 3 balls in prepared dish and cover loosely with greased plastic.

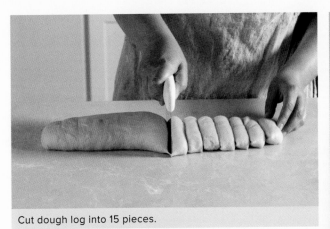
Cut dough log into 15 pieces.

Drag balls in small circles until taut and round.

Stretch dough around your thumb and pinch into ball.

6a second rise Let rolls rise until nearly doubled in size and dough springs back minimally when poked gently with your finger, 1 to 1½ hours.

6b for an overnight rise Refrigerate rolls for at least 8 hours or up to 16 hours; let rolls sit at room temperature for 1 hour before baking.

7 bake Adjust oven rack to lower-middle position and heat oven to 350 degrees. Gently brush rolls with egg wash and bake until golden brown, 25 to 30 minutes, rotating dish halfway through baking. Let rolls cool in dish for 15 minutes. Using foil overhang, transfer rolls to wire rack. Serve warm or at room temperature. (Rolls can be refrigerated for up to 2 days or frozen for up to 1 month. Place on rimmed baking sheet, cover with foil, and heat in a 350-degree oven for 12 minutes.)

total time 4½ hours

35 min.	1½ hours	35 min.	1 hour	25 min.	15 min.
make dough	**first rise**	**shape dough**	**second rise**	**bake**	**cool**

» **Take your time** To bake the next day, refrigerate rolls for at least 8 hours or up to 16 hours in step 6.

DUTCH OVEN PULL-APART ROLLS

makes 15 rolls

1 recipe White Dinner Rolls, made through step 5, omitting baking dish

The interactive nature of pull-apart rolls is perfect for the communal mood you want at a dinner party or gathering. Instead of placing the shaped rolls in a baking dish, we bake them, still in a foil sling, in a Dutch oven, which adequately compresses the rolls while giving them support for impressive height. When making the dough, do not prepare the baking dish in step 4.

1   Make foil sling for Dutch oven by folding 2 long sheets of aluminum foil so each is 7 inches wide. Lay sheets of foil in pot perpendicular to each other, with extra foil hanging over edges of pot. Push foil into bottom and up sides of pot, smoothing foil flush to bottom of pot, then spray with vegetable oil spray.

2a   second rise   Evenly space 10 dough balls, seam side down, around edge of pot. Place remaining 5 balls in center, staggering them between seams of balls around edge, and cover. Let rolls rise until nearly doubled in size and dough springs back minimally when poked gently with your finger, 1 to 1½ hours.

2b   for an overnight rise   Place dough balls on parchment paper–lined rimmed baking sheet, cover with plastic wrap, and refrigerate for at least 8 hours or up to 16 hours. Evenly space 10 dough balls, seam side down, around edge of Dutch oven. Place remaining 5 balls in center, staggering them between seams of balls around edge. Cover and let sit at room temperature for 1 hour.

3   bake   Adjust oven rack to lower-middle position and heat oven to 350 degrees. Gently brush rolls with egg wash. Transfer pot to oven and bake, uncovered, until rolls are golden brown, 35 to 40 minutes, rotating pot halfway through baking. Let rolls cool in pot for 15 minutes; then, using foil overhang, transfer rolls to wire rack. Serve warm or at room temperature.

KNOTTED ROLLS

makes 24 rolls

how-to

1 recipe White Dinner Rolls, made through step 3

The dough for our White Dinner Rolls is so versatile it can be twisted and tied into these intricate looking (but easy) knotted rolls without rips, tears, sticking, or snagging. After the first rise, we divide the dough into halves, stretch them into simple rectangles, and slice the rectangles into strips before knotting. Have fun with shaping.

1   Line 2 rimmed baking sheets with parchment paper.

2   shape   Press down on dough to deflate. Transfer dough to clean counter and divide dough in half. Working with 1 piece of dough at a time, press and stretch dough into 12 by 6-inch rectangle. Using pizza cutter or chef's knife, cut dough into 12 (6 by 1-inch) strips and cover loosely with greased plastic. Repeat with remaining dough.

3   Working with 1 strip of dough at a time (keep remaining pieces covered), stretch and roll into 10-inch rope. Tie knot into center of rope, tucking tails underneath roll. Space knots evenly over prepared sheets and reshape as needed. Cover loosely with greased plastic wrap.

4a   second rise   Let rise until nearly doubled in size and dough springs back minimally when poked gently with your finger, 1 to 1½ hours.

4b   for an overnight rise   Refrigerate roll for at least 8 hours or up to 16 hours. Let sit at room temperature for 1 hour.

5   bake   Adjust oven racks to upper-middle and lower-middle positions and heat oven to 350 degrees. Gently brush rolls with egg wash and bake until golden brown, about 20 minutes, switching and rotating sheets halfway through baking. Let rolls cool on sheet on wire rack for 15 minutes. Serve warm or at room temperature.

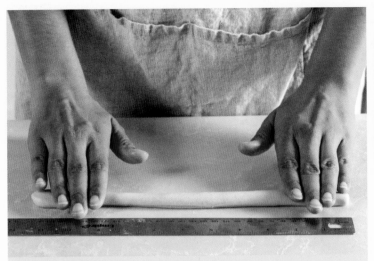

Stretch and roll dough into 10-inch rope.

Tie knot in center of dough ropes, tucking tails.

CRESCENT ROLLS

makes 16 rolls

1 recipe White Dinner Rolls, made through step 2

There's no excuse for popping a tube of crescent rolls if you know how to make our White Dinner Rolls. Making the iconic horns from that simple dough is a breeze. We divide the kneaded dough into halves before it's left to rise; that way, when we're ready to shape, we can simply press the risen dough rounds into the perfect size circle for cutting our wedges. Finally, we roll the wedges into the trademark shape.

1 Line rimmed baking sheet with parchment paper and spray with vegetable oil spray.

2 first rise Transfer dough to lightly floured counter and divide in half. Knead each dough ball by hand to form smooth, round ball, about 30 seconds each. Place dough balls seam side down on prepared sheet, spaced about 6 inches apart. Cover loosely with greased plastic wrap and let rise until doubled in volume, 1½ to 2 hours.

3 shape dough Line second sheet with parchment. Working with 1 dough ball at a time (keep remaining dough ball covered), press down on dough to deflate and transfer to clean counter. Press and roll dough into 12-inch circle. Using pizza cutter or chef's knife, cut circle into 8 even wedges. Starting at wide end, gently roll up each dough wedge, ending with pointed tip on bottom. Push ends toward each other to form crescent shape. Arrange crescent rolls evenly over prepared sheets and reshape as needed. Cover loosely with greased plastic.

4a second rise Let rolls rise until nearly doubled in size and dough springs back minimally when poked gently with your finger, 1 to 1½ hours.

4b for an overnight rise Refrigerate rolls for at least 8 hours or up to 16 hours. Let sit at room temperature for 1 hour.

5 bake Adjust oven racks to upper-middle and lower-middle positions and heat oven to 350 degrees. Gently brush rolls with egg wash and bake until golden brown, about 20 minutes, switching and rotating sheets halfway through baking. Let rolls cool on sheet on wire rack for 15 minutes. Serve warm or at room temperature.

Cut dough into 8 wedges.

Roll up each wedge.

Push ends toward each other to form crescent.

CHIVE SPIRAL ROLLS

makes 24 rolls

1 recipe White Dinner Rolls, made through step 3, adding ½ cup minced chives to flour mixture in step 1

3 tablespoons unsalted butter, melted

¾ teaspoon flake sea salt

Swirl some flavor into these rolls: Chives, amplified with some finishing flaky salt, freshen up the rich rolls and go with just about everything. The chives enter the mix right away; whisking them into the flour mixture before kneading ensures that their presence and aroma are distributed throughout the dough. The fancy snail shape ups the elegance on this twist.

1   Line 2 rimmed baking sheets with parchment paper.

2   shape dough   Press down on dough to deflate. Transfer dough to clean counter and divide dough in half. Working with 1 piece at a time, press and stretch dough into 12 by 6-inch rectangle. Using pizza cutter or chef's knife, cut dough into twelve 6 by 1-inch strips and cover loosely with greased plastic. Repeat with remaining dough.

3   Working with 1 strip of dough at a time (keep remaining pieces covered), stretch and roll into 12-inch rope. Coil ends of rope in opposite directions to form tight S shape. Arrange buns evenly on prepared sheets and reshape as needed. Cover loosely with greased plastic.

4   second rise   Let rolls rise until nearly doubled in size and dough springs back minimally when poked gently with your finger, 1 to 1½ hours.

5   bake   Adjust oven racks to upper-middle and lower-middle positions and heat oven to 350 degrees. Gently brush rolls with egg wash and bake until golden brown, about 20 minutes, switching and rotating sheets halfway through baking. Let rolls cool on sheet on wire rack for 10 minutes, then brush with melted butter and sprinkle with sea salt. Serve warm or at room temperature.

Stretch and roll dough into 12-inch rope.

Coil ends of ropes in opposite directions to form tight S.

SCOOP-AND-BAKE DINNER ROLLS

makes 12 rolls

2¼ cups (11¼ ounces) all-purpose flour, divided

¼ cup (1¾ ounces) sugar

2¼ teaspoons instant or rapid-rise yeast

1 teaspoon table salt

1 cup (8 ounces) warm water

6 tablespoons unsalted butter, melted

1 large egg, room temperature

why this recipe works Even with the ease of our collection of rolls, we understand that baking anything might seem out of the question if you're preparing a full meal and a dessert. Here's how we bring it back into the equation: Avoid mixing, kneading, and shaping altogether. We stir together the ingredients for our scoop-and-bake roll recipe, briefly allow the loose dough to rise in the same bowl, and scoop it into a muffin tin without it ever touching our hands or the counter. One issue: The quick rise doesn't give yeast time to mellow. Using rich butter in the rolls tempers the stronger yeasty flavor. Beating the batter with a whisk gives our dinner rolls extra lift, making them tall and light like a kneaded dough.

1 make batter Whisk 1¼ cups flour, sugar, yeast, and salt together in large bowl. Whisk water, melted butter, and egg in 4-cup liquid measuring cup until combined, then add to flour mixture and whisk until very smooth. Gently stir in remaining 1 cup flour until just combined.

2 first rise Cover bowl with plastic wrap and let rise until batter has doubled in volume, about 40 minutes.

3 divide batter Spray 12-cup muffin tin with vegetable oil spray. Adjust oven rack to middle position and heat oven to 375 degrees. Press down on dough to deflate. Using greased ¼-cup dry measuring cup, divide batter equally among prepared muffin cups, respraying measuring cup as needed. Cover with greased plastic.

4a second rise Let batter rise until nearly doubled in size, 15 to 30 minutes.

4b for an overnight rise Refrigerate rolls for up to 24 hours. Let sit at room temperature for 30 minutes before baking.

5 bake Bake until rolls are golden brown, 14 to 18 minutes, rotating muffin tin halfway through baking. Let rolls cool in muffin tin on wire rack for 5 minutes. Serve warm or at room temperature.

total time 1¾ hours

25 min.	40 min.	15 min.	15 min.	5 min.
make batter	first rise	second rise	bake	cool

» **Take your time** To bake the next day, refrigerate rolls for up to 24 hours in step 4.

FLUFFY DINNER ROLLS

makes 12 rolls

flour paste

- ½ **cup (4 ounces) water**
- 3 **tablespoons bread flour**

dough

- ½ **cup (4 ounces) cold milk**
- 1 **large egg**
- 2 **cups (11 ounces) bread flour**
- 1½ **teaspoons instant or rapid-rise yeast**
- 2 **tablespoons sugar**
- 1 **teaspoon table salt**
- 4 **tablespoons unsalted butter, cut into 4 pieces and softened, plus ½ tablespoon melted**

why this recipe works These dinner rolls might take a little more work than the basic but they have a lot going for them: In addition to being our most luxurious roll offering—superlatively fluffy and made up of delicate, almost croissant-like sheets—they also taste fresh even after more than a day. So while sometimes you might want to proof a bread overnight and bake before serving, you can bake these rolls fully in advance. We use a bread-making technique known as tangzhong, in which extra moisture is added to the dough in the form of a flour paste (see page 32 for more information). To support the weight of the extra moisture, we build a strong gluten structure by adding a resting period during which gluten strands form and by withholding the butter until the gluten network is firmly established. The shaping method, inspired by Japanese milk bread, is also important. Flattening each portion of dough and rolling it up in a spiral organizes the gluten strands into coiled layers, which baked up into feathery pull-apart sheets.

1 make flour paste Whisk water and flour in small bowl until smooth. Microwave, whisking every 20 seconds, until mixture thickens to stiff, smooth, pudding-like consistency that forms mound when dropped from end of whisk into bowl, 40 to 80 seconds.

2 make dough Whisk flour paste and milk together in bowl of stand mixer. Whisk in egg. Add flour and yeast. Using dough hook on low speed, mix until flour is moistened, about 1 minute. Let sit for 15 minutes.

3 Add sugar and salt and mix on medium-low speed for 5 minutes. With mixer running, add softened butter, 1 piece at a time. Continue to mix on medium-low speed for 5 minutes, scraping down dough hook and sides of bowl occasionally (dough will stick to bottom of bowl). Transfer dough to lightly floured counter and knead by hand to form smooth, round ball, about 30 seconds.

4 first rise Place dough seam side down in lightly greased large bowl or container and lightly coat surface of dough with oil spray. Cover with plastic wrap and let rise until doubled in volume, about 1 hour.

5 shape dough Grease 9-inch round cake pan. Press down on dough to deflate. Transfer dough to clean counter and press and stretch into 8 by 9-inch rectangle with short side facing you. Cut dough lengthwise into 4 equal strips and cut each strip crosswise into 3 equal pieces. Working with 1 piece at a time, gently press and stretch dough into 8 by 2-inch strips. Starting on short side, roll dough to form snug cylinder. Arrange shaped rolls seam side down in prepared pan, placing 10 rolls around edge of pan, pointing inward, and remaining 2 rolls in center.

6 second rise Cover loosely with plastic and let rise until doubled in size and dough springs back minimally when poked gently with your finger, 45 minutes to 1 hour.

7 bake Adjust oven rack to lowest position and heat oven to 375 degrees. Bake rolls until deep golden brown, 25 to 30 minutes. Let rolls cool in pan on wire rack for 3 minutes; invert rolls onto rack, then reinvert. Brush tops and sides of rolls with melted butter and let rolls cool for 20 minutes. Serve warm or at room temperature.

Microwave flour mixture.

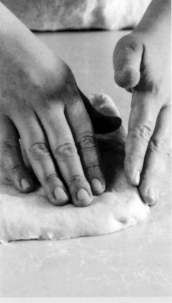

Press dough into rectangle.

Cut lengthwise into 4 strips; cut crosswise into 3 pieces.

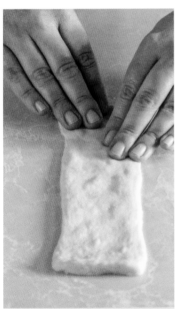

Press dough into strips.

Roll dough to form snug cylinder.

Arrange rolls in pan.

total time 3¼ hours

50 min.	1 hour	45 min.	25 min.	20 min.
make dough	first rise	second rise	bake	cool

fluffy dinner rolls (page 112)

oatmeal dinner rolls (page 116)

OATMEAL DINNER ROLLS

makes 12 rolls

- ¾ cup (2¼ ounces) old-fashioned rolled oats, plus 4 teaspoons for sprinkling
- ⅔ cup (5⅓ ounces) boiling water, plus ½ cup cold water
- 2 tablespoons unsalted butter, cut into 4 pieces
- 1½ cups (8¼ ounces) bread flour
- ¾ cup (4⅛ ounces) whole-wheat flour
- ¼ cup molasses
- 1½ teaspoons instant or rapid-rise yeast
- 1 teaspoon table salt
- 1 large egg, beaten with 1 tablespoon water and pinch table salt

why this recipe works   These delightfully homey rolls avoid the dense, dry texture that both whole-wheat flour and oats can cause. We start by soaking old-fashioned rolled oats in hot water. During a short rest the oats absorb most of the water (and turn to meal), effectively hiding extra moisture in this dough, which turns to steam in the oven, so the re-sulting rolls are unexpectedly fluffy, plush, and light. Sound familiar? This strategy is similar to the tangzhong method (see page 32), but the oats do the absorption rather than the flour. Further, the high hydration of the dough and moisture-holding capabilities of whole grains extend the rolls' shelf life, so they can be enjoyed for a few days. We supplement the whole-wheat flour in the dough with white bread flour for structure and add molasses for its complexity and sweetness. Nestling the dough balls close together in a round cake pan ensures that they support each other in upward, rather than outward, expansion. For an accurate measurement of boiling water, bring a kettle of water to a boil and then measure out the desired amount. Avoid blackstrap molasses here, as it's too bitter.

1   make dough   Stir ¾ cup oats, boiling water, and butter together in bowl of stand mixer and let sit until butter is melted and most of water has been absorbed, about 10 minutes.

2   Add bread flour, whole-wheat flour, cold water, molasses, yeast, and salt. Using dough hook on low speed, mix until flour is moistened, about 1 minute (dough may look dry). Increase speed to medium-low and mix until dough clears sides of bowl (it will still stick to bottom), about 8 minutes, scraping down dough hook halfway through mixing (dough will be sticky). Transfer dough to clean counter and knead by hand to form smooth, round ball, about 30 seconds.

3   first rise   Place dough seam side down in lightly greased large bowl or container, cover with plastic wrap, and let rise until doubled in volume, 1 to 1¼ hours.

total time 3½ hours

40 min.	1 hour	45 min.	25 min.	20 min.
make dough	first rise	second rise	bake	cool

4 shape dough Grease 9-inch round cake pan. Press down on dough to deflate. Transfer dough to lightly floured counter and pat dough gently into 8-inch square. Cut dough into 12 equal pieces and cover loosely with plastic. Working with 1 piece of dough at a time (keep remaining pieces covered), form each piece into rough ball by stretching dough around your thumb and pinching edges together so that top is smooth. Place ball seam side down on clean counter and, using your cupped hand, drag in small circles until dough feels taut and round. Arrange dough balls seam side down in prepared pan, placing 9 dough balls around edge of pan and remaining 3 dough balls in center.

5 second rise Cover with plastic and let rise until doubled in size, no gaps are visible between rolls, and dough springs back minimally when poked gently with your finger, 45 minutes to 1 hour.

6 bake Adjust oven rack to lower-middle position and heat oven to 375 degrees. Gently brush rolls with egg wash and sprinkle with remaining 4 teaspoons oats. Bake until rolls are deep brown and register at least 195 degrees, 25 to 30 minutes. Let rolls cool in pan on wire rack for 3 minutes; invert rolls onto rack, then reinvert. Let rolls cool for 20 minutes. Serve warm or at room temperature.

Hydrate oat mixture.

Mix ingredients.

Knead dough until it clears sides of bowl.

BROWN-AND-SERVE DINNER ROLLS

makes 16 rolls

flour paste

½ cup water

3 tablespoons bread flour

dough

¾ cup (6 ounces) cold milk

2⅔ cups (14⅔ ounces) bread flour

1 large egg

2 teaspoons instant or
rapid-rise yeast

2 tablespoons sugar

1¼ teaspoons table salt

2 tablespoons unsalted
butter, softened

why this recipe works Brown-and-serve rolls are the most make-ahead you can get if you're looking to serve rolls hot from the oven. Maybe you are preparing for a multicourse dinner party, or maybe you want the ability to bake up just a roll or two to serve alongside your weeknight dinner. These rolls are the answer—they're parbaked and can go from the freezer to the oven to the plate in less than 15 minutes. Our brown-and-serve rolls are an improvement over traditional recipes because we include tangzhong for especially moist and light rolls. We bake the rolls at 300 degrees until they rise and set but have no color at all. Because they're very delicate in their freshly parbaked state, we cool them and then freeze them still on their baking sheet. Once they're firm, they go into a zipper-lock bag to be frozen for up to six weeks. To serve, we simply place the desired number of frozen rolls on a baking sheet and bake them in a very hot oven (or a toaster oven), where the insides of the rolls thaw and soften while the outsides brown, providing all the flavor, texture, and aroma of freshly baked bread. The parbaked rolls are quite delicate so do not handle them until they're fully frozen.

1 make flour paste Whisk water and flour together in small bowl until no lumps remain. Microwave, whisking every 20 seconds, until mixture thickens to stiff, pasty consistency, 40 to 80 seconds.

2 make dough Whisk flour paste and milk together in bowl of stand mixer. Add flour, egg, and yeast. Using dough hook on low speed, mix until all flour is moistened, about 1 minute. Let sit for 15 minutes.

3 Add sugar and salt and mix on medium-low speed for 5 minutes. With mixer running, add softened butter, 1 tablespoon at a time. Continue to mix on medium-low speed until dough is smooth and elastic, about 5 minutes longer. Transfer dough to lightly floured counter and knead by hand to form smooth, round ball, about 30 seconds.

4 first rise Place dough seam side down in lightly greased large bowl or container and lightly coat surface of dough with oil spray. Cover with plastic wrap. Let rise until doubled in volume, about 1 hour.

5 shape dough Line rimmed baking sheet with parchment paper. Press down on dough to deflate. Transfer dough to clean counter and pat dough gently into 8-inch square. Cut dough into 16 equal pieces and cover loosely with plastic wrap. Working with 1 piece of dough at a time (keep remaining pieces covered), form each piece into rough ball by stretching dough around your thumb and pinching edges together so that top is smooth. Place ball seam side down on clean counter and, using your cupped hand, drag in small circles until dough feels taut and round. Arrange dough balls seam side down on prepared sheet, spacing them evenly.

6 second rise Cover with plastic and let rise until nearly doubled in size and dough springs back minimally when poked gently with your finger, 45 minutes to 1 hour.

7 bake Adjust oven rack to middle position and heat oven to 300 degrees. Bake until rolls are risen and register 170 to 175 degrees, 15 to 17 minutes (they will have little to no color). Transfer baking sheet to wire rack and let cool completely, 30 to 45 minutes.

8 to freeze Transfer sheet with rolls to freezer and freeze rolls until completely solid, 30 minutes to 1 hour. Transfer frozen rolls to zipper-lock bag and freeze for up to 6 weeks.

9 to serve Adjust oven rack to middle position and heat oven to 425 degrees. Bake rolls until deep golden brown, 8 to 10 minutes. Transfer rolls to wire rack and cool for at least 5 minutes before serving.

total time 3¾ hours

50 min.	1 hour	10 min.	45 min.	15 min.	30 min.	15 min.
make dough	first rise	shape dough	second rise	bake	cool	to serve

HAWAIIAN SWEET ROLLS

makes 18 rolls

5½ cups (27½ ounces) all-purpose flour

1 tablespoon instant or rapid-rise yeast

2½ teaspoons table salt

1 cup (8 ounces) pineapple juice

½ cup (4 ounces) whole milk

6 tablespoons unsalted butter, melted, plus 2 tablespoons softened

⅓ cup honey

1 large egg, room temperature

2 teaspoons distilled white vinegar

2 teaspoons vanilla extract

why this recipe works   Hawaiian sweet rolls, most famously made by King's Hawaiian bakery in Hilo, Hawaii, are soft and fluffy—not as eggy as challah, not as buttery as brioche. Similar to Portuguese sweet rolls, they're sweet but not cloying, and their flavor is distinct but elusive: tangy, fruity, almost earthy. Ours get sweetness from an ingredient that's not in the King's version: pineapple juice (and some honey for earthy sweetness). But they were missing the appropriate balancing tang. Instead of upping the pineapple and throwing off our formula, we simply incorporated a couple teaspoons of white vinegar. Additional ingredients include an egg for structure and butter for richness, 6 tablespoons in the dough and 2 more tablespoons brushed on the just-baked rolls. Use a mild-flavored honey (like clover honey) and not an assertive one (like buckwheat honey) in this recipe. These rolls are best eaten warm the day they are baked. You can eat them like any dinner roll, but they're also great sliced in half and used for ham and cheese sliders.

1   make dough   Whisk flour, yeast, and salt together in bowl of stand mixer. Combine pineapple juice, milk, melted butter, and honey in 4-cup liquid measuring cup and microwave until mixture registers 110 degrees, about 1 minute. (Mixture may appear curdled.)

2   Using dough hook on low speed, slowly add pineapple juice mixture, followed by egg, vinegar, and vanilla, to flour mixture and knead until cohesive dough starts to form, about 2 minutes, scraping down sides of bowl as needed. Increase speed to medium-low and knead until dough is smooth and elastic and clears sides of bowl (it will stick to bottom), 5 to 7 minutes. Transfer dough to lightly floured counter and knead by hand to form smooth, round ball, about 30 seconds.

3   first rise   Place dough seam side down in lightly greased large bowl or container and lightly coat surface of dough with oil spray. Cover with plastic wrap and let rise until almost doubled in volume, 1 to 1½ hours.

4   shape dough   Grease 13 by 9-inch baking dish. Press down on dough to deflate. Transfer dough to clean counter and divide into thirds. Cut each third into 6 equal pieces and cover loosely with plastic. Working with 1 piece of dough at a time (keep remaining pieces covered), form each piece into rough ball by stretching dough around your thumb and pinching edges together so that top is smooth. Place ball seam side down on clean counter and, using your cupped hand, drag in small circles until dough feels taut and round. Repeat with remaining dough pieces. Arrange dough balls seam side down into 6 rows of 3 balls in prepared dish and cover loosely with plastic.

5a **second rise** Let rolls rise at room temperature until doubled in size and dough springs back minimally when poked gently with your finger, 1 to 1½ hours (rolls should almost reach top of dish and edges should be touching).

5b **for an overnight rise** Refrigerate rolls for at least 8 hours or up to 16 hours. Let rolls sit at room temperature for 1 hour before baking.

6 **bake** Adjust oven rack to lower-middle position and heat oven to 375 degrees. Bake until golden brown and rolls register at least 190 degrees, 20 to 23 minutes, rotating dish halfway through baking. Let rolls cool in dish on wire rack for 10 minutes, then transfer rolls to wire rack, brush with softened butter, and let cool for 20 minutes. Serve warm.

total time 3¾ hours

30 min.	1 hour	30 min.	1 hour	20 min.	30 min.
make dough	first rise	shape dough	second rise	bake	cool

» **Take your time** To bake the next day, refrigerate the rolls for at least 8 hours or up to 16 hours in step 5.

total time 3½ hours

50 min.	1 hour	15 min.	30 min.	30 min.	20 min.
make dough	first rise	shape dough	second rise	bake	cool

» **Take your time** To bake the next day, refrigerate dough for at least 8 hours or up to 24 hours in step 4.

CAST IRON GARLIC-HERB BUTTER ROLLS

makes 12 rolls

dough

- ¾ cup (6 ounces) whole milk, room temperature
- 4 tablespoons unsalted butter, melted, plus 1 tablespoon softened
- 1 large egg, room temperature
- 2 cups (10 ounces) all-purpose flour
- 2¼ teaspoons instant or rapid-rise yeast
- 2 tablespoons sugar
- 1 teaspoon table salt

- 1 large egg, beaten with 1 tablespoon water and pinch table salt

garlic-herb butter

- 4 tablespoons unsalted butter
- 3 garlic cloves, minced
- ¼ teaspoon table salt
- 1 tablespoon minced fresh parsley

why this recipe works   Their reflective buttery sheen and lavish amounts of garlic and herbs are enough to make these rolls unique, but on top of these qualities, they're baked in a cast-iron skillet for a chewy, beautifully burnished crust and soft, fluffy interiors without additional effort. The flavor of these plush rolls reminds us of pizzeria garlic knots but they're sophisticated enough for a Sunday dinner table. Brushing them with the butter just before serving makes pulling a roll from the lot an irresistible treat—there's nothing like a warm buttered roll.

1   make dough   Whisk milk, melted butter, and egg together in bowl of stand mixer. Add flour and yeast. Using dough hook on medium speed, mix until cohesive dough starts to form and no dry flour remains, about 2 minutes, scraping down bowl as needed. Cover bowl with plastic wrap and let dough rest for 15 minutes. Add sugar and salt and knead on medium speed until dough begins to pull away from sides and bottom of bowl (dough will be sticky), 8 to 12 minutes.

2   first rise   Transfer dough to lightly greased large bowl or container, cover with plastic, and let rise until doubled in volume, about 1 hour.

3   shape dough   Grease 10-inch cast-iron skillet with softened butter. Press down on dough to deflate. Transfer dough to clean counter, divide into 12 equal pieces, and cover loosely with plastic. Working with 1 piece of dough at a time (keep remaining pieces covered), form each piece into rough ball by stretching dough around your thumb and pinching edges together so that top is smooth. Place ball seam side down on clean counter and, using your cupped hand, drag in small circles until dough feels taut and round.

4a   second rise   Arrange dough balls seam side down in prepared skillet, placing 9 balls around edge and remaining 3 balls in center. Cover with plastic and let rise until doubled in size and dough springs back minimally when poked gently with your finger, about 30 minutes.

4b   for an overnight rise   Arrange dough balls in greased cake pan and refrigerate for at least 8 hours or up to 24 hours. Arrange dough balls in prepared skillet. Let dough sit at room temperature for 30 minutes before baking.

5   bake   Adjust oven rack to middle position and heat oven to 350 degrees. Gently brush rolls with egg wash and bake until deep golden brown, about 30 minutes, rotating skillet halfway through baking.

6   make garlic-herb butter   Meanwhile, melt butter in small saucepan over medium heat. Add garlic and salt and cook until just fragrant, about 1 minute. Off heat, stir in parsley.

7   Let rolls cool in skillet on wire rack for 5 minutes. Slide rolls out of skillet onto wire rack and let cool for 15 minutes then brush tops and sides of rolls with garlic-herb butter. Serve warm.

PORCINI-TRUFFLE CRESCENT ROLLS

makes 12 rolls

2½ cups (12½ ounces) all-purpose flour

1 ounce dried porcini mushrooms, rinsed and minced

4 teaspoons minced fresh thyme

1 teaspoon instant or rapid-rise yeast

1 teaspoon table salt

½ cup (4 ounces) half-and-half, room temperature

7 tablespoons unsalted butter, melted and cooled slightly

1 large egg plus 1 large yolk, room temperature

¼ cup (1¾ ounces) sugar

5 teaspoons truffle oil, divided

1 large egg, beaten with 1 tablespoon water and pinch table salt

why this recipe works Crescent Rolls (page 106) are already divine with their rich flavor, charming shape, and golden egg-painted exteriors. These little rolls have even more flavor potential, however. Traditional versions can be laborious but our method is supersimple and yields rolls just as buttery. We simply stir melted butter into the liquid ingredients and then combine that mixture with the dry ingredients in a stand mixer. For the over-the-top sophisticated flavor that makes these rolls a must-have anytime you're having people over, we add minced dried porcini mushrooms to the dough and brush on fragrant truffle oil twice: once over the circle of dough before cutting and shaping the rolls and then again over the golden crescents when they emerge from the oven.

1 make dough Whisk flour, mushrooms, thyme, yeast, and salt together in bowl of stand mixer. Whisk half-and-half, melted butter, egg and yolk, and sugar in 4-cup liquid measuring cup until sugar has dissolved.

2 Using dough hook on low speed, slowly add half-and-half mixture to flour mixture and mix until cohesive dough starts to form and no dry flour remains, about 2 minutes, scraping down bowl as needed. Increase speed to medium-low and knead until dough is smooth and elastic and clears sides of bowl (it will stick to bottom), about 8 minutes. Transfer dough to lightly floured counter and knead by hand to form smooth, round ball, about 30 seconds.

3 first rise Place dough seam side down to lightly greased large bowl or container, cover with plastic wrap, and let rise until doubled in volume, 1 to 1½ hours.

4 shape dough Line rimmed baking sheet with parchment paper. Press down on dough to deflate, then transfer to lightly floured counter. Press and roll dough into 15-inch circle, then brush top of dough with 1 tablespoon truffle oil. Using pizza cutter or chef's knife, cut circle into 12 even wedges. Starting at wide end, gently roll up each dough wedge, ending with pointed tip on bottom. Push ends toward each other to form crescent shape. Transfer to prepared sheet, spacing evenly over sheet and reshaping as needed. Repeat with remaining wedges. Cover loosely with greased plastic.

5a second rise Let rolls rise until nearly doubled in size and dough springs back minimally when poked gently with your finger, 1 to 1½ hours.

5b for an overnight rise Refrigerate rolls for at least 8 hours or up to 16 hours. Let rolls sit at room temperature for 1 hour before baking.

6 bake Adjust oven rack to middle position and heat oven to 350 degrees. Gently brush rolls with egg wash and bake until golden brown, 20 to 25 minutes, rotating sheet halfway through baking. Transfer sheet to wire rack, brush with remaining 2 teaspoons truffle oil, and let cool for 15 minutes. Serve warm.

total time 3½ hours

15 min.	1 hour	15 min.	1 hour	20 min.	15 min.
make dough	first rise	shape dough	second rise	bake	cool

» **Take your time** To bake the next day, refrigerate rolls for at least 8 hours or up to 16 hours in step 5.

THAI CURRY BUTTER FAN ROLLS

makes 12 rolls

3½ cups (17½ ounces)
    all-purpose flour

  1 tablespoon instant or
    rapid-rise yeast

  2 teaspoons table salt

¾ cup (6 ounces) whole milk,
    room temperature

12 tablespoons unsalted butter,
    melted, divided

¼ cup (1¾ ounces) sugar

  1 large egg plus 1 large yolk,
    room temperature

  4 scallions, minced

¼ cup Thai red curry paste

½ cup chopped fresh
    cilantro, divided

why this recipe works   If ever a roll was aptly named, it's the butter fan roll: layers of yeasty bread brushed with melted butter that fan out while baking to form rolls that are soft and tender, with faintly crisp tips. Stirring Thai red curry paste into the melted butter adds bold flavor and color, and adding scallions to the dough and sprinkling cilantro between the layers elevates these into restaurant-quality rolls that taste as amazing as they look. The rolls might look intricate, but the dough isn't harder than any other to make. The basic method goes like this: Mix and knead the dough and let it rise. Then punch down the dough, roll it out, cut it into strips, butter and stack the strips, cut the strips into roll-size portions, and nestle them into muffin tins. Let the dough rise again, and then bake the rolls on the upper-middle rack (which fosters the crisp-but-not-crunchy edges). The resulting layers are both impressive-looking and fun to pull apart when eating.

1 make dough   Whisk flour, yeast, and salt together in bowl of stand mixer. Whisk milk, 8 tablespoons melted butter, sugar, egg and yolk, and scallions in 4-cup liquid measuring cup until sugar has dissolved. Using dough hook on low speed, slowly add milk mixture to flour mixture and mix until cohesive dough starts to form and no dry flour remains, about 2 minutes. Increase speed to medium-low and knead until dough is smooth and clears sides of bowl, about 6 minutes, scraping down bowl as needed. Transfer dough to lightly floured counter and knead by hand to form smooth, round ball, about 30 seconds.

2 first rise   Place dough seam side down in lightly greased large bowl or container, cover with plastic wrap, and let rise until doubled in volume, 1½ to 2 hours.

3 shape dough   Grease 12-cup muffin tin. Press down on dough to deflate. Transfer dough to lightly floured counter, divide in half, and cover loosely with greased plastic. Press and roll 1 piece of dough (keep remaining piece covered) into 15 by 12-inch rectangle, with long side parallel to counter edge.

total time 4 hours

30 min.	1½ hours	10 min.	1½ hours	20 min.	5 min.
make dough	first rise	shape dough	second rise	bake	cool

» **Take your time** To bake the next day, refrigerate rolls for at least 8 hours or up to 16 hours in step 5.

4 Combine 3 tablespoons melted butter and curry paste in small bowl. Using pizza cutter or chef's knife, square off edges of rectangle, then cut dough vertically into six 2½-inch by 12-inch strips. Brush tops of 5 strips evenly with half of butter–curry paste mixture, leaving 1 strip unbuttered. Sprinkle ¼ cup cilantro over brushed dough strips. Stack strips on top of each other, buttered side to unbuttered side, finishing with unbuttered strip on top; cut into 6 stacks. Place stacks cut side up in prepared muffin cups. Repeat with remaining dough, remaining butter–curry paste mixture, and remaining ¼ cup cilantro. Cover muffin tin loosely with greased plastic.

5a second rise Let rolls rise until nearly doubled in size, 1½ to 2 hours.

5b for an overnight rise Refrigerate rolls for at least 8 hours or up to 16 hours. Let sit at room temperature for 1 hour.

6 bake Adjust oven rack to upper-middle position and heat oven to 350 degrees. Bake rolls until golden brown, 20 to 25 minutes, rotating muffin tin halfway through baking. Let rolls cool in muffin tin for 5 minutes, brush with remaining 1 tablespoon melted butter, and serve warm.

Cut dough vertically into 6 strips.

Stack buttered strips; finish with unbuttered strip.

Cut into 6 stacks and place in muffin tin.

thai curry butter fan rolls (page 126)

rustic dinner rolls (page 130)

RUSTIC DINNER ROLLS

makes 16 rolls

3 cups (16½ ounces) bread flour

3 tablespoons whole-wheat flour

1½ teaspoons instant or rapid-rise yeast

1½ cups (12 ounces) plus 1 tablespoon water, room temperature

2 teaspoons honey

1½ teaspoons table salt

why this recipe works   European-style dinner rolls are different from their rich, tender American cousins. The dough for these rustic rolls is lean and the crumb is open, with a yeasty, savory flavor. But the best part might be their crust—so crisp it practically shatters when you bite into it. It is this crust that keeps European-style dinner rolls in the domain of professionals, who use steam-injected ovens to expose the developing crust to moisture. We find success at home with barely any shaping. The crumb structure of artisan-style loaves is achieved with a wet dough, so we hydrate the dough more than many rolls. The water creates steam during baking, opening up the crumb and making it airier. For an ultracrisp crust, we turn to a two-step process that mimics a steam-injected oven: First, we mist the rolls with water before starting them in a cake pan at a high temperature to help set their shape. Next, we lower the temperature, pull the rolls apart, and return them to the oven on a baking sheet until they're golden on all sides.

1   make dough   Whisk bread flour, whole-wheat flour, and yeast together in bowl of stand mixer. Whisk water and honey in 4-cup liquid measuring cup until honey has dissolved. Using dough hook on low speed, slowly add water mixture to flour mixture and mix until cohesive dough starts to form and no dry flour remains, about 2 minutes, scraping down bowl and hook as needed. Cover bowl with plastic wrap and let dough rest for 30 minutes.

2   Add salt to dough and mix on low speed for 5 minutes. Increase speed to medium and knead until dough is smooth and slightly sticky, about 1 minute (dough will clear sides but stick to bottom).

3   first rise   Transfer dough to lightly greased large bowl or container, cover with plastic, and let rise until doubled in volume, 1 to 1½ hours.

4   fold and rest   Using greased bowl scraper (or your wet fingertips), fold dough over itself by gently lifting and folding edge of dough toward middle. Turn bowl 90 degrees and fold dough again; repeat turning bowl and folding dough 2 more times (total of 4 folds). Cover with plastic. Let dough rest for 30 minutes. Repeat folding, then cover bowl with plastic and let dough rise until doubled in size, about 30 minutes.

total time 5 hours

1 hour	1 hour	1 hour	10 min.	30 min.	20 min.	1 hour
make dough	first rise	fold + rest	shape dough	second rise	bake	cool

» **Take your time** To bake the next day, refrigerate rolls for at least 8 hours or up to 16 hours in step 6.

Stretch dough halves into log.

Coat dough pieces with flour.

Arrange rolls and let rise until doubled in size.

Bake until tops are brown.

Invert rolls out of pan, pull apart, and finish baking.

5 shape dough Grease two 9-inch round cake pans. Press down on dough to deflate. Transfer dough to well-floured counter, sprinkle lightly with flour, and divide in half. Stretch each half into even 16-inch log and cut into 8 equal pieces. Using your well-floured hands, gently pick up each piece and roll in your palms to coat with flour, shaking off excess. Arrange rolls in prepared pans, placing seven around edges and one in center, with cut side facing up and long side of each piece running from center to edge of pan. Cover loosely with greased plastic.

6a second rise Let rolls rise until nearly doubled in size and dough springs back minimally when poked gently with your finger, about 30 minutes.

6b for an overnight rise Refrigerate rolls for at least 8 hours or up to 16 hours. Let rolls sit at room temperature for 1½ hours before baking.

7 bake Adjust oven rack to middle position and heat oven to 500 degrees. Mist rolls with water and bake until tops are brown, about 10 minutes. Remove rolls from oven and reduce oven temperature to 400 degrees. Carefully invert rolls out of pans onto rimmed baking sheet. Turn hot rolls right side up, pull apart, and arrange evenly on sheet. Continue to bake until deep golden brown, 10 to 15 minutes, rotating sheet halfway through baking. Transfer rolls to wire rack and let cool completely, about 1 hour, before serving.

OLIVE ROLLS WITH ROSEMARY AND FENNEL

makes 12 rolls

3 cups (16 ½ ounces) bread flour

3 tablespoons whole-wheat flour

1½ teaspoons instant or
rapid-rise yeast

1½ cups plus 1 tablespoon water,
room temperature

2 teaspoons honey

1 cup pitted olives, patted dry, and
chopped coarse

1 tablespoon minced
fresh rosemary

2 teaspoons fennel seeds, toasted

1½ teaspoons table salt

2 tablespoons extra-virgin olive oil

why this recipe works   These might be the most fragrant dinner rolls you've ever had; our rustic rolls become savory and salty from a stir-in of chopped olives, aromatic from complementary rosemary, a little sweet and floral from toasted fennel seeds, and pleasingly rich from a brushing of extra-virgin olive oil. Whatever you serve these rolls with will be instantly elevated. Toast the fennel seeds in a dry skillet over medium heat until fragrant (1 to 2 minutes), and then remove the skillet from the heat so the fennel seeds don't scorch. You can use just about any variety of olive (or a mix) in this recipe, but avoid oil-cured olives as their flavor will be too intense.

1   make dough   Whisk bread flour, whole-wheat flour, and yeast together in bowl of stand mixer. Whisk water and honey in 4-cup liquid measuring cup until honey has dissolved. Using dough hook on low speed, slowly add water mixture to flour mixture and mix until cohesive dough starts to form and no dry flour remains, about 2 minutes, scraping down bowl and hook as needed. Cover bowl with plastic wrap and let dough rest for 30 minutes.

2   Add olives, rosemary, fennel seeds, and salt to dough and mix on low speed for 5 minutes. Increase speed to medium and knead until dough is smooth and slightly sticky, about 1 minute (dough will clear sides but stick to bottom).

3   first rise   Transfer dough to lightly greased large bowl or container, cover with plastic, and let rise until doubled in volume, 1 to 1½ hours.

4   fold and rest   Using greased bowl scraper (or your wet fingertips), fold dough over itself by gently lifting and folding edge of dough toward middle. Turn bowl 90 degrees and fold dough again; repeat turning bowl and folding dough 2 more times (total of 4 folds). Cover with plastic and let rise for 30 minutes. Repeat folding, then cover bowl with plastic and let dough rise until doubled in size and dough springs back minimally when poked gently with your finger, about 30 minutes.

5   shape dough   Grease two 9-inch round cake pans. Press down on dough to deflate. Transfer dough to well-floured counter and sprinkle lightly with flour. Divide dough into 12 equal pieces and cover loosely with plastic. Working with 1 piece of dough at a time (keep remaining pieces covered), form each piece into rough ball by stretching dough around your thumb and pinching edges together so that top is smooth. Arrange rolls seam side down in prepared pans, placing 5 around edges and 1 in center. Cover loosely with plastic.

6a second rise Let rolls rise until nearly doubled in size and dough springs back minimally when poked gently with your finger, about 30 minutes.

6b for an overnight rise Refrigerate rolls for at least 8 hours or up to 16 hours. Let sit at room temperature for 1½ hours before baking.

7 bake Adjust oven rack to middle position and heat oven to 500 degrees. Gently brush rolls with oil and bake until tops are just starting to brown, about 10 minutes. Remove rolls from oven and reduce oven temperature to 400 degrees. Carefully invert rolls out of pans onto rimmed baking sheet. Turn hot rolls right side up, pull apart, and arrange evenly on sheet. Continue to bake until deep golden brown, 10 to 15 minutes, rotating sheet halfway through baking. Transfer rolls to wire rack and let cool completely, about 1 hour, before serving.

total time 5 hours

1 hour	1 hour	1 hour	10 min.	30 min.	20 min.	1 hour
make dough	first rise	fold + rest	shape dough	second rise	bake	cool

» **Take your time** To bake the next day, refrigerate rolls for at least 8 hours or up to 16 hours in step 6.

HOAGIE ROLLS

makes 8 rolls

5 cups (27½ ounces) bread flour

4 teaspoons instant or rapid-rise yeast

1 tablespoon table salt

2 cups (16 ounces) water, room temperature

3 tablespoons vegetable oil

1 large egg, room temperature

4 teaspoons sugar

why this recipe works   Sandwich lovers get into battles over the name of the long white rolls that are stuffed with meats, cheeses, and relishes at corner delis. Whether you call them hoagie, hero, grinder, or submarine rolls, they make for one delicious sandwich bread. We created a version big enough to hold tons of hearty fillings and soft enough to sink our teeth into. And it's simple enough to make frequently so you can serve sandwiches anytime. We use higher-protein bread flour to achieve a roll that's tender yet can support mounds of deli meat. An egg and a bit of oil add the appropriate amount of richness. We treat each portion as a small baguette, folding the dough multiple times before forming it into a taut roll. This ensures a roll with no visible seams and a consistent shape. Scoring the rolls ¼ inch deep allows them to expand evenly while baking.

1 make dough   Whisk flour, yeast, and salt together in bowl of stand mixer. Whisk water, oil, egg, and sugar in 4-cup liquid measuring cup until sugar has dissolved. Using dough hook on low speed, slowly add water mixture to flour mixture and mix until cohesive dough starts to form and no dry flour remains, about 2 minutes, scraping down bowl as needed. Increase speed to medium-low and knead until dough is smooth and elastic and clears sides of bowl (it will stick to bottom), about 8 minutes. Transfer dough to lightly floured counter and knead by hand to form smooth, round ball, about 30 seconds.

2 first rise   Place dough seam side down in lightly greased large bowl or container, cover with plastic wrap, and let rise until doubled in volume, 1 to 1½ hours.

3 shape dough   Line 2 rimmed baking sheets with parchment paper. Press down on dough to deflate. Transfer dough to floured counter and divide into quarters, then cut each quarter into halves and cover loosely with greased plastic. Working with 1 piece of dough at a time (keep remaining pieces covered), press into 4-inch square. Fold top corners of dough diagonally into center of square and press gently to seal. Stretch and fold top of dough toward center and press to seal. Fold top half down to meet bottom and pinch to seal. Stretch and roll into 8-inch cylinder. Arrange rolls seam side down over prepared sheets, spaced evenly apart. Cover loosely with greased plastic.

total time 4 hours

35 min.	1 hour	30 min.	30 min.	30 min.	1 hour
make dough	first rise	shape dough	second rise	bake	cool

» **Take your time**   To bake the next day, refrigerate rolls for at least 8 hours or up to 16 hours in step 4.

Fold top corners in diagonally.

Stretch and fold toward center.

Fold top down to meet bottom.

Roll into 8-inch cylinder.

4a **second rise** Let rolls rise until nearly doubled in size and dough springs back minimally when poked gently with your finger, 30 minutes to 1 hour.

4b **for an overnight rise** Refrigerate for at least 8 hours or up to 16 hours. Let rolls sit at room temperature for 1 hour before baking.

5 **bake** Adjust oven racks to upper-middle and lower-middle positions and heat oven to 350 degrees. Using sharp paring knife or single-edge razor blade, make one ¼-inch-deep slash with swift, fluid motion lengthwise along top of rolls, starting and stopping about ½ inch from ends. Bake rolls until golden brown, 30 to 35 minutes, switching and rotating sheets halfway through baking. Transfer rolls to wire racks and let cool completely, about 1 hour, before serving.

PRETZEL BUNS

makes 8 buns

3¾ cups (20⅔ ounces) bread flour

2 teaspoons table salt

2 teaspoons instant or rapid-rise yeast

1½ cups (12 ounces) water, room temperature

2 tablespoons vegetable oil

2 tablespoons packed dark brown sugar

¼ cup baking soda

1 large egg, beaten with 1 tablespoon water and pinch table salt

1 teaspoon pretzel or kosher salt

why this recipe works With their mahogany-brown crusts, tender interiors, and salty bite, these buns are a great home for juicy burgers or a stacked ham-and-cheese. Bread flour helps achieve a proper soft yet chewy pretzel texture. Without the food-grade lye professional bakers use to create the dark, distinctly flavored crust unique to soft pretzels, we give the buns a dip in a solution of baking soda and boiling water to help create their chewy exterior. (A little brown sugar helps with coloring, too.) Then we bake them like normal rolls. Do not use pretzel salt in the dough. If you don't plan on serving these buns immediately, skip sprinkling them with pretzel salt until you are ready to reheat and serve; over time the salt crystals dissolve and can create a soggy exterior.

1 make dough Whisk flour, table salt, and yeast together in bowl of stand mixer. Whisk water, oil, and sugar in 4-cup liquid measuring cup until sugar has dissolved. Using dough hook on low speed, slowly add water mixture to flour mixture and mix until cohesive dough starts to form and no dry flour remains, about 2 minutes, scraping down bowl as needed. Increase speed to medium-low and knead until dough is smooth and elastic and clears sides of bowl, about 8 minutes. Transfer dough to lightly floured counter and knead by hand to form smooth, round ball, about 30 seconds.

2 first rise Place dough seam side down in lightly greased large bowl or container, cover with plastic wrap, and let rise until doubled in volume, 1 to 1½ hours.

3 shape dough Lightly flour 2 rimmed baking sheets. Press down on dough to deflate. Transfer dough to clean counter and stretch and roll into even 12-inch log. Cut log into 8 equal pieces and cover loosely with greased plastic. Working with 1 piece of dough at a time (keep remaining pieces covered), pat into 4-inch disk. Working around circumference of dough, fold edges of dough toward center until ball forms. Flip dough ball seam side down and, using your cupped hand, drag in small circles until dough feels taut and round and all seams are secured on underside of ball. Cover loosely with greased plastic and let rest for 15 minutes. Arrange dough balls seam side down on prepared sheets, spaced evenly apart. Cover loosely with greased plastic.

4a second rise Let rolls rise until nearly doubled in size and dough springs back minimally when poked gently with your finger, about 30 minutes.

4b for an overnight rise Refrigerate rolls for at least 8 hours or up to 16 hours. Let rolls sit at room temperature for 1 hour before cooking.

5 cook Adjust oven racks to upper-middle and lower-middle positions and heat oven to 425 degrees. Dissolve baking soda in 4 cups water in Dutch oven and bring to boil over medium-high heat. Using slotted spatula, transfer 4 buns seam side up to boiling water and cook for 30 seconds, flipping halfway through cooking. Transfer buns seam side down to wire rack and repeat with remaining 4 buns. Let rest for 5 minutes.

6 Line now-empty sheets with parchment paper and lightly spray with vegetable oil spray. Transfer buns seam side down to prepared sheets, spaced evenly apart. Gently brush buns with egg wash. Using sharp paring knife or single-edge razor blade, make two 2-inch long slashes along top of each bun to form cross. Sprinkle each bun with ⅛ teaspoon pretzel salt. Bake buns until mahogany brown, 16 to 20 minutes, switching and rotating sheets halfway through baking. Transfer buns to wire rack and let cool completely, about 1 hour, before serving.

total time 4¼ hours

35 min.	1 hour	30 min.	30 min.	30 min.	1 hour
make dough	first rise	shape dough	second rise	cook	cool

» **Take your time** To cook the next day, refrigerate buns for at least 8 hours or up to 16 hours in step 4.

POTATO BURGER BUNS

makes 9 buns

---

1 pound russet potatoes, peeled and cut into 1-inch pieces

2 tablespoons unsalted butter, cut into 4 pieces

2¼ cups (12⅓ ounces) bread flour

2 teaspoons instant or rapid-rise yeast

1 teaspoon table salt

1 large egg, room temperature

1 tablespoon sugar

1 large egg, lightly beaten with 1 tablespoon water and pinch table salt

1 tablespoon sesame seeds (optional)

why this recipe works   Mashed potatoes are hefty and substantial, but in recipes for potato rolls, they give the crumb a light, tender, moist texture. That's because the starches in potatoes dilute the gluten-forming proteins in flour, which weakens the structural network of the dough and makes it softer, moister, and more tender. For the lightest, airiest potato rolls, we combine ½ pound of mashed russet potatoes (russets absorb the most water for a moister crumb) with high-protein bread flour (for stable structure). You may have never thought of making your own buns for burgers, but these come together with convenience. They rise fast because the potassium in potatoes activates yeast. That said, you can also slow down the process by letting them rise in the refrigerator. Don't salt the cooking water for the potatoes. A pound of russet potatoes should yield just over 1 very firmly packed cup (½ pound) of mash. To ensure the optimum rise, your dough should be warm; if your potatoes or potato water are too hot to touch, let cool before proceeding with the recipe. This dough looks very dry when mixing begins but will soften as mixing progresses.

1   make dough   Place potatoes in medium saucepan and add water to just cover. Bring to boil over high heat, then reduce to simmer and cook until potatoes are just tender (paring knife can be slipped in and out of potato with little resistance), 8 to 10 minutes.

2   Transfer 5 tablespoons potato cooking water to 4-cup liquid measuring cup and let cool completely; drain potatoes. Return potatoes to now-empty saucepan and place over low heat. Cook, shaking saucepan occasionally, until any surface moisture has evaporated, about 30 seconds. Off heat, process potatoes through ricer or food mill or mash well with potato masher. Measure 1 cup very firmly packed potatoes (8 ounces) and transfer to bowl. Stir in butter until melted and let cool completely before using. Reserve any remaining potatoes for another use.

3   Whisk flour, yeast, and salt together in bowl of stand mixer. Whisk egg and sugar into reserved potato cooking water until sugar has dissolved. Add mashed potato mixture to flour mixture and mix with your hands until combined (some large lumps are OK). Using dough hook on low speed, slowly add cooking water mixture to flour mixture and mix until cohesive dough starts to form and no dry flour remains, about 2 minutes, scraping down bowl as needed. Increase speed to medium-low and knead until dough is smooth and elastic and clears sides of bowl but sticks to bottom, about 8 minutes. Transfer dough to lightly floured counter and knead by hand to form smooth, round ball, about 30 seconds.

4   first rise   Place dough seam side down in lightly greased large bowl or container, cover with plastic wrap, and let rise until doubled in volume, 30 minutes to 1 hour.

5   shape dough   Line 2 rimmed baking sheets with parchment paper. Press down on dough to deflate. Transfer dough to clean counter and divide into 9 equal pieces and cover loosely with plastic. Working with 1 piece of dough at a time (keep remaining pieces covered), form each piece into rough ball by stretching dough around your thumb and pinching edges together so that top is smooth. Place ball seam side down on clean counter and, using your cupped hand, drag in small circles until dough feels taut and round. Let rounds rest for 15 minutes, then press into 3½-inch disks of even thickness. Arrange disks on prepared sheets, evenly spaced. Cover loosely with greased plastic.

6a second rise Let rolls rise until nearly doubled in size and dough springs back minimally when poked gently with your finger, 30 minutes to 1 hour.

6b for an overnight rise
Refrigerate rolls for at least 8 hours or up to 16 hours. Let sit at room temperature for 1 hour before baking.

7 bake Adjust oven racks to upper-middle and middle positions and heat oven to 425 degrees. Gently brush rolls with egg wash and sprinkle with sesame seeds, if using. Bake rolls until deep golden brown, 15 to 18 minutes, switching and rotating sheets halfway through baking. Transfer buns to wire rack and let cool for 1 hour before serving.

total time 4 hours

1 hour 20 min.	30 min.	30 min.	30 min.	15 min.	1 hour
make dough	first rise	shape dough	second rise	bake	cool

» **Take your time** To bake the next day, refrigerate rolls for at least 8 hours or up to 16 hours in step 6.

total time 3 hours

10 min.	1 hour	10 min.	1 hour	18 min.	20 min.
make dough	first rise	shape dough	second rise	cook	cool

» **Take your time** To make over 2 or 3 days, refrigerate rolls for at least 12 hours or up to 48 hours in step 4.

ENGLISH MUFFINS

makes 8 muffins

2¾ cups (15⅛ ounces) bread flour

1 tablespoon instant or
rapid-rise yeast

1¼ teaspoons table salt

1 cup plus 6 tablespoons
(11 ounces) warm whole milk

2 tablespoons honey

5 tablespoons cornmeal, divided

2 tablespoons unsalted butter,
cut into 2 pieces, divided

why this recipe works   Time to bust a myth: English muffins are not hard to make at home. You don't need special equipment or even much time to turn out English muffins that are fresher and better than any you'd buy at the supermarket. We came up with a few tricks to make the fast route to satisfying nooks and crannies possible. First, we use honey and warm milk in the dough; the sugar helps jump-start the yeast, speeding up the rising process, and the duo provides flavor and richness to make up for the speed. Bread flour provides some extra protein, resulting in chewier muffins. We sear the muffins on both sides in a skillet before finishing them in the oven. And while these muffins are on the fast track, you can also slow down their rise in the fridge so you can have freshly made muffins first thing in the morning. For the best texture, use a fork to split the muffins.

1   make dough   Whisk flour, yeast, and salt together in large bowl. Whisk warm milk and honey together in separate bowl. Add milk mixture to flour mixture and stir until no pockets of dry flour remain.

2   first rise   Cover bowl with plastic wrap. Let dough rise until doubled in volume, about 1 hour.

3   shape dough   Line rimmed baking sheet with parchment paper and spray with vegetable oil spray. Sprinkle prepared sheet with 4 tablespoons cornmeal. Using greased ¼-cup dry measuring cup, divide dough into 8 heaping ¼-cup portions. Using your lightly greased hands, gently shape each dough portion into 2- to 2½-inch-wide round about 1 inch tall and place on prepared sheet. Sprinkle tops of rounds with remaining 1 tablespoon cornmeal. Cover sheet loosely with greased plastic.

4a   second rise   Let rounds rise until nearly doubled in size, about 1 hour.

4b   for an overnight rise   Refrigerate rounds for at least 12 hours or up to 48 hours.

5   cook   Adjust oven rack to middle position and heat oven to 350 degrees. Melt 1 tablespoon butter in 12-inch nonstick skillet over medium heat. Add 4 dough rounds and cook until deep golden brown on first side, about 2 minutes, moving rounds as needed for even browning. Flip muffins and cook until deep golden brown on second side, about 2 minutes, pressing down lightly with spatula if muffins begin to rise unevenly. Transfer muffins to clean rimmed baking sheet. Wipe skillet clean with paper towels and repeat with remaining 1 tablespoon butter and remaining 4 dough rounds. Bake until muffins register at least 205 degrees, 10 to 12 minutes. Let muffins cool on wire rack for 20 minutes. Using fork, split muffins. Toast and serve.

CRUMPETS

makes 3 large crumpets

- **1 cup (5 ounces) all-purpose flour**
- **1 cup (4 ounces) bleached cake flour**
- **2 teaspoons instant or rapid-rise yeast**
- **¾ teaspoon baking powder**
- **½ teaspoon table salt**
- **1½ cups (12 ounces) warm water (105 to 110 degrees), divided**
- **½ teaspoon vegetable oil**
- **Salted butter and jam or creamed honey**

why this recipe works   Crumpets—thick, yeasted rounds with moist, slightly elastic, honeycombed interiors that drink up butter and jam—can be hard to find in the United States. We made our own in a nonstick skillet and cut them into wedges since most don't own crumpet rings to corral the batter. A blast of high heat converts the water in the batter to steam; this expands air bubbles, producing the proper holes. Lifting a small amount of batter off the top before flipping the crumpets preserves the holes. These are quick to serve, as the batter requires just one rise. We developed this recipe on a responsive gas stovetop. If you're using electric, heat the skillet on one burner set to low for 5 minutes, and then increase the heat to medium for 1 minute before adding the batter and set the second burner to high. Move the skillet between the medium and high burners for the appropriate heat level.

1   make batter   Whisk all-purpose flour, cake flour, yeast, baking powder, and salt together in 8-cup liquid measuring cup. Add 1¼ cups warm water and whisk until smooth.

2   rise   Cover and let rise in warm place until doubled in volume, about 40 minutes.

3   cook   Heat oil in 8-inch nonstick skillet over low heat for at least 5 minutes. While skillet heats, add remaining ¼ cup warm water to batter and whisk until smooth. Increase heat to medium and heat skillet for 1 minute. Using paper towel, wipe out skillet, leaving thin film of oil on bottom and sides. Pour one-third of batter into skillet and increase heat to high. Cook for 45 seconds (bubbles will be visible just under surface of entire crumpet). Reduce heat to medium-low and continue to cook until edges are risen, set, and beginning to dry out, about 4 minutes longer. (Gently lift edge and peek at underside of crumpet occasionally; reduce heat if underside is getting too dark and increase heat if underside doesn't appear to be browning.)

4   Off heat, place dry, flat spatula on top of crumpet and pull up sharply to remove excess batter and reveal holes. Scrape excess batter from spatula back into measuring cup. Repeat procedure until holes are exposed over entire surface. Flip crumpet, return skillet to burner, increase heat to high, and cook until edges of second side are lightly browned, 1 to 2 minutes. Invert crumpet onto wire rack. Immediately add half of remaining batter to skillet. Return skillet to high heat and repeat cooking process (omitting 5-minute preheat). Repeat with remaining batter.

5   Let crumpets cool for 20 minutes. To serve, cut each crumpet into 4 wedges and toast until crumpets are heated through and exteriors are crisp. Spread crumpets generously with butter and jam or honey and serve.

total time 1¾ hours

15 min.	40 min.	30 min.	20 min.
make batter	rise	cook	cool

total time 3¼ hours

25 min.	2 hours	10 min.	40 min.	5 min.
make dough	rest	shape dough	bake	cool

» **Take your time** To bake the next day, refrigerate dough for up to 24 hours in step 2.

PÃO DE QUEIJO

makes 8 rolls

3 cups (11¾ ounces) tapioca starch

1 teaspoon table salt

¼ teaspoon baking powder

⅔ cup (5⅓ ounces) plus 2 table-spoons whole milk

½ cup vegetable oil

1½ tablespoons unsalted butter

2 large eggs

3½ ounces Parmesan cheese, grated fine (1¾ cups)

3½ ounces Pecorino Romano cheese, grated fine (1¾ cups)

1 large egg, beaten with 1 tablespoon water and pinch table salt

why this recipe works   Crackly and crunchy on the outside, bready just under the crust, and gooey in the center, these little baked cheese buns are a favorite break-fast food and snack in Brazil. (They would also be great dunked in tomato sauce, stuffed with ham, or split open for a quick sandwich.) They happen to be naturally gluten-free, because they are made with tapioca starch rather than wheat flour. Tapioca starch (also called tapioca flour) has several unique qualities that make it a great substitute for wheat flour. For one, it's low in amylose—one of the types of polysaccharides that make up starch—and therefore forms a high-viscosity paste that can trap air for light baked goods. The dough is similar to a classic French pate a choux (this is what is used for gougères and profiteroles) and relies primarily on steam rather than chemical leavening agents to create rise. This version has a little less moisture in the dough than is typical, which ensures the pão de queijo have just the right balance of crackle and soft cheesiness.

1 make dough   Whisk tapioca starch, salt, and baking powder together in bowl of stand mixer. Combine milk, oil, and butter in medium saucepan and bring to boil over high heat. Using paddle on low speed, working quickly, add milk mixture to tapioca mixture and mix until all ingredients are incorporated, about 3 minutes. Add eggs and mix on low speed until dough turns shiny and sticky and clings to sides of bowl, about 8 minutes, scraping down paddle and bowl halfway through mixing. Add Parmesan and Pecorino and mix on low speed until cheeses are incorporated, 30 to 60 seconds. Give dough final stir by hand to ensure mixture is fully incorporated.

2 rest   Press plastic wrap directly onto surface of dough in bowl and refrigerate for at least 2 hours or up to 24 hours.

3 shape dough   Adjust oven rack to middle position and heat oven to 450 degrees. Stack 2 rimmed baking sheets and line top sheet with parchment paper. Divide dough into 8 equal pieces. Working with 1 piece of dough at a time, roll dough between your damp palms until smooth and rounded. Evenly space rolls on prepared sheet.

4 bake   Gently brush rolls with egg wash. Place rolls in oven and immediately reduce oven temperature to 375 degrees. Bake until rolls are deep golden brown and outer crusts are dry and crunchy, about 40 minutes, rotating sheet halfway through baking. Transfer rolls to wire rack and let cool for 5 minutes. Serve.

ZA'ATAR MONKEY BREAD

serves 4 to 6

1½ cups (8¼ ounces) bread flour

1 teaspoon sugar

¼ teaspoon instant or rapid-rise yeast

⅔ cup (5⅓ ounces) ice water

1½ teaspoons plus ¼ cup extra-virgin olive oil, divided

¾ teaspoon table salt

¼ cup extra-virgin olive oil, divided

3 garlic cloves, minced

3 tablespoons za'atar (recipe follows), divided

Flake sea salt

why this recipe works Monkey bread—consisting of lots of little rolls of dough baked into a ring-shaped loaf meant for pulling apart and eating with your hands—may be a favorite with kids, but that doesn't mean it has to be sticky and tooth-achingly sweet. This version is good for any time of day: It replaces the sweet stuff with the aromatic, potent spice mixture za'atar. We start with a simple pizza dough and divide it evenly into individual portions, roll the portions into balls, and arrange them in a round cake pan. We sprinkle the za'atar over the top and let the dough rise. When the bread comes out of the oven looking beautifully golden brown, we brush on some toasted garlic oil and add a final sprinkle of za'atar and flake sea salt for the most sophisticated take on monkey bread you've ever had. See our recipe for Za'atar, or use a store-bought blend.

1 make dough Pulse flour, sugar, and yeast in food processor until combined, about 5 pulses. With processor running, slowly add ice water and process until dough is just combined and no dry flour remains, about 10 seconds. Let dough rest for 10 minutes. Add 1½ teaspoons oil and table salt to dough and process until dough forms satiny, sticky ball that clears sides of bowl, 30 to 60 seconds. Transfer dough to lightly floured counter and knead by hand to form smooth, round ball, about 30 seconds.

2 first rise Place dough seam side down in lightly greased large bowl or container and cover tightly with plastic wrap. Refrigerate dough for at least 24 hours or up to 3 days. (To freeze dough, refrigerate it for 24 hours. Place on baking sheet or plate lined with parchment paper, cover loosely with plastic wrap, and freeze until firm, about 3 hours or up to overnight. Wrap frozen dough ball individually in plastic and store in zipper-lock bag in freezer for up to 2 weeks. To thaw, unwrap ball, place in lightly oiled bowl, cover with plastic, and let sit in refrigerator for 12 to 24 hours before shaping.)

3 shape dough Combine 2 tablespoons oil and garlic in small bowl and microwave until fragrant, about 1 minute; set aside until ready to serve. Brush 8-inch round cake pan with 1 tablespoon oil. Press down on dough to deflate. Transfer dough to clean counter and pat into 6-inch square. Divide dough into 36 equal pieces and cover loosely with greased plastic wrap. Working with 1 piece of dough at a time (keep remaining pieces covered), form into rough ball by stretching dough around your thumb and pinching edges together so that top is smooth. Place ball seam side down on clean counter and, using your cupped hand, drag in small circles until dough feels taut and round. Repeat with remaining dough pieces.

4 second rise Arrange dough balls seam side down in prepared pan. Sprinkle with 2 tablespoons za'atar, cover loosely with greased plastic, and let sit until dough balls are puffy and have risen slightly (about ½ inch), 1 to 2 hours.

5 bake Adjust oven rack to middle position and heat oven to 400 degrees. Gently brush tops of dough balls with remaining 1 tablespoon oil. Bake until light golden brown, 20 to 25 minutes, rotating halfway through baking. Transfer pan to wire rack and let cool for 5 minutes. Transfer bread to large plate or serving platter, brush with garlic oil, sprinkle with remaining 1 tablespoon za'atar, and let cool for 5 minutes. Sprinkle with sea salt and serve.

ZA'ATAR

makes about ⅓ cup

- **2** tablespoons dried thyme
- **1** tablespoon dried oregano
- **1½** tablespoons sumac
- **1** tablespoon sesame seeds, toasted
- **¼** teaspoon table salt

Grind thyme and oregano using spice grinder or mortar and pestle until finely ground and powdery. Transfer to bowl and stir in sumac, sesame seeds, and salt. (Za'atar can be stored in airtight container at room temperature for up to 1 year.)

total time 26½ hours

25 min.	24 hours	40 min.	1 hour	20 min.	10 min.
make dough	first rise	shape dough	second rise	bake	cool

» **Take your time** To make over 3 or 4 days, let dough rise for up to 3 days in step 2.

total time 25 hours

25 min.	24 hours	10 min.	10 min.	5 min.
make dough	rise	shape dough	bake	cool

» **Take your time** To make over 3 or 4 days, let dough rise for up to 3 days in step 3.

GARLIC AND HERB BREADSTICKS

makes 18 breadsticks

- 1½ cups (8¼ ounces) bread flour
- 1 teaspoon sugar
- ¼ teaspoon instant or rapid-rise yeast
- ⅔ cup (5⅓ ounces) ice water
- 1½ teaspoons extra-virgin olive oil
- 1 teaspoon table salt, divided
- 2 teaspoons minced fresh thyme
- 2 teaspoons dried oregano
- 1 teaspoon granulated garlic
- ¼ teaspoon pepper
- 3 tablespoons unsalted butter, melted

why this recipe works   Dip in soup, dip in tomato sauce, or rush to grab one (or several) and eat it right off the sheet—no matter how you snack on these sticks, you'll learn that the homemade version well surpasses the overly doughy ones you can get delivered. A simple pizza dough that can be made in advance is easy to shape and provides consistent results. Baking the butter-coated dough on parchment paper keeps the butter from burning and simplifies the cleanup. For flavor, we sprinkle the dough with granulated garlic, fresh thyme, dried oregano, salt, and pepper before baking. Wait to make the thyme mixture until just before you're ready to sprinkle it; otherwise, the moisture from the fresh thyme can cause it to clump.

1   make dough   Pulse flour, sugar, and yeast in food processor until combined, about 5 pulses. With processor running, slowly add ice water and process until dough is just combined and no dry flour remains, about 10 seconds. Let dough rest for 10 minutes.

2   Add oil and ¾ teaspoon salt to dough and process until dough forms satiny, sticky ball that clears sides of bowl, 30 to 60 seconds. Transfer dough to lightly floured counter and knead by hand to form smooth, round ball, about 30 seconds.

3   rise   Place dough seam side down in lightly greased large bowl or container and cover tightly with plastic wrap. Refrigerate dough for at least 24 hours or up to 3 days. (To freeze dough, refrigerate it for 24 hours. Place on baking sheet or plate lined with parchment paper, cover loosely with plastic wrap, and freeze until firm, about 3 hours or up to overnight. Wrap frozen dough ball individually in plastic and store in zipper-lock bag in freezer for up to 2 weeks. To thaw, unwrap ball, place in lightly oiled bowl, cover with plastic, and let sit in refrigerator for 12 to 24 hours before shaping.)

4   shape dough   Adjust oven rack to middle position and heat oven to 450 degrees. Line rimmed baking sheet with parchment paper. Press down on dough to deflate. Transfer dough to lightly floured counter and divide in half. Cover dough loosely with greased plastic. Working with 1 piece of dough at a time (keep remaining piece covered), roll and stretch dough into 9 by 5-inch rectangle. Transfer dough to half of prepared sheet, with short ends parallel to long sides of sheet. Repeat with remaining dough piece and place on other half of sheet.

5   Stir thyme, oregano, granulated garlic, remaining ¼ teaspoon salt, and pepper together in bowl. Using pastry brush, brush top of dough pieces with half of melted butter and sprinkle with half of thyme mixture. Flip dough rectangles, brush with remaining melted butter, and sprinkle with remaining thyme mixture. Cut rectangles crosswise at 1-inch intervals to create nine 5-inch breadsticks from each piece of dough, but do not separate breadsticks.

6   bake   Bake until golden brown, 9 to 12 minutes. Let cool for 5 minutes. Pull breadsticks apart at seams. Serve.

PAN DE COCO

makes 12 buns

- **4** cups (20 ounces) all-purpose flour
- **2¼** teaspoons active dry yeast
- **1½** teaspoons table salt
- **1¼** cup (10 ounces) unsweetened canned coconut milk, room temperature
- **½** cup water
- **3** tablespoons sugar
- **2** tablespoons coconut oil, melted, divided, plus more for greasing pans
- **⅓** cup shredded coconut

why this recipe works   The Garifuna people of Honduras make a roll that covers all bases: Tender and plush, pan de coco are coconut milk rolls that are eaten in both savory and sweet settings, complementing anything from beans and stew to jam and dulce de leche. Pan de coco is traditionally made without eggs or dairy (making them naturally vegan), so the coconut milk plays a vital role in flavoring, tenderizing, and hydrating the dough. We add a touch of coconut oil and a sprinkling of shredded coconut to amplify the coconut flavor further. These rolls are sometimes flattened and griddled; other times they are made as pull-apart rolls, as in this recipe. We recommend using unrefined coconut oil here for maximum coconut flavor. Be sure to stir the coconut milk before measuring to ensure that the thick coconut cream layer and thinner coconut milk are thoroughly combined. We prefer topping the rolls with sweetened coconut, but you can use unsweetened coconut. If you're using the coconut topping, be sure to gauge doneness by the color of the rolls, not the color of the coconut.

1   make dough   Whisk flour, yeast, and salt together in bowl of stand mixer. Whisk coconut milk, water, sugar and 1 tablespoon oil in 4-cup liquid measuring cup until sugar has dissolved. Using dough hook on low speed, slowly add coconut milk mixture to flour mixture and mix until cohesive dough starts to form and no dry flour remains, about 2 minutes, scraping down bowl as needed. Increase speed to medium-low and knead until dough is smooth and elastic and clears sides of bowl (dough may stick to bottom of bowl), about 8 minutes. Transfer dough to lightly floured counter and knead by hand to form smooth, round ball, about 30 seconds.

2   first rise   Place dough seam side down in lightly greased large bowl or container, cover with plastic wrap, and let rise until doubled in volume, 1½ to 2 hours.

3   shape   Brush 13 by 9-inch baking pan with 1 teaspoon oil. Press down on dough to deflate. Transfer dough to clean counter, divide into 12 equal pieces, and cover loosely with plastic. Working with 1 piece of dough at a time (keep remaining pieces covered), form into rough ball by stretching dough around your thumb and pinching edges together so that top is smooth. Place ball seam side down on clean counter and, using your cupped hand, drag in small circles until dough feels taut and round. Repeat with remaining dough pieces. Arrange dough balls in prepared pan.

4   second rise   Cover with plastic and let rise until nearly doubled in size (sides of dough balls will be touching) and dough springs back minimally when poked gently with your finger, 45 minutes to 1 hour.

5   bake   Adjust oven rack to middle position and heat oven to 350 degrees. Gently brush rolls with remaining 1 tablespoon oil and sprinkle with shredded coconut, if using. Bake until rolls are golden brown, 25 to 30 minutes rotating pan halfway through baking. Let rolls cool in pan for 15 minutes, then transfer to wire rack. Serve warm or at room temperature.

total time 3¾ hours

35 min.	1½ hours	15 min.	45 min.	25 min.	15 min.
make dough	first rise	shape dough	second rise	bake	cool

LOP CHEUNG BAO

makes 10 buns

¾ cup whole milk, warm

3 tablespoons sugar

1 teaspoon instant or
  rapid-rise yeast

1 tablespoon vegetable oil

2 cups (10 ounces) bleached
  all-purpose flour

2 tablespoons cornstarch

1 teaspoon baking powder

⅛ teaspoon table salt

10 lop cheung

why this recipe works Lop cheung bao (sometimes written as lap cheong bao) is one of the best pigs in a blanket the world has to offer. A snow-white yeasted dough is twirled around a cured Chinese sausage (lop cheung), and the buns are steamed until the dough turns fluffy and firm. The snap of the rich sausage when you bite into the pillowy, slightly sweet bun is heavenly. This recipe was developed by Jacqueline Church, who leads food and culture tours in Boston's Chinatown. When purchasing lop cheung, look for good distribution of fat throughout the sausage and some alcohol in the ingredient list; avoid sausage containing liver here. This recipe is best made in a stacking bamboo steamer basket set inside a skillet. Using bleached all-purpose flour will create the bright-white color that is traditional and prized for these buns; you can also use unbleached all-purpose flour, though the bao will be less bright white.

1 make dough Whisk milk, sugar, and yeast in 2-cup liquid measuring cup until sugar has dissolved, then let sit until foamy, about 5 minutes. Whisk in oil. Pulse flour, cornstarch, baking powder, and salt in food processor until combined, about 3 pulses. With processor running, slowly add milk mixture and process until no dry flour remains, about 30 seconds. Transfer dough to lightly floured counter and knead by hand to form smooth, round ball, about 30 seconds.

2 first rise Transfer dough to lightly oiled large bowl, turning to coat dough ball in oil, arranging dough seam side down. Cover with plastic wrap and let rise until doubled in volume, about 1 hour.

3 While dough rises, place plate in bamboo steamer basket and arrange sausages in single layer on plate. Set steamer basket over simmering water in skillet and cook, covered, until sausages are plump and color is muted, 10 to 15 minutes. (Add boiling water to skillet as needed while steaming.) Set aside plate with sausages and let cool completely. Remove basket from simmering water and set aside.

4 shape dough Cut ten 6 by 4-inch rectangles of parchment paper; set aside. Press down on dough to deflate. Transfer dough to clean counter and portion into 10 equal pieces (about 2 ounces each); cover loosely with plastic. Working with 1 piece of dough at a time (keep remaining pieces covered), form each piece into rough ball by stretching dough around your thumb and pinching edges together so top is smooth. Place ball seam side down on clean counter and, using your cupped hand, drag in small circles until dough feels taut and round. Cover dough balls with plastic.

5 Working with 1 dough ball at a time (keep remaining pieces covered) and starting at center, gently and evenly roll and stretch dough into 10-inch-long rope. Wrap dough around 1 cooled sausage, starting 1 inch from 1 end of sausage (dough should wrap around sausage at least 3 times and sausage should be roughly centered on dough) and place in basket on 1 prepared parchment rectangle, tucking ends of dough underneath sausage. Cover with damp dish towel while forming remaining bao, spacing bao about 1 inch apart.

6 second rise Let bao sit until slightly puffy, about 20 minutes.

7 cook Remove damp dish towel and set covered steamer basket over cold water in skillet. Bring water to simmer over high heat and, once steam begins to escape from sides of basket, reduce heat to medium and steam until bao are puffy and firm, 10 to 15 minutes. (Add boiling water to skillet as needed while steaming.) Remove basket from simmering water and let bao cool for 5 minutes before serving.

total time 2½ hours

20 min.	1 hour	25 min.	20 min.	15 min.	5 min.
make dough	first rise	shape dough	second rise	cook	cool

CHAPTER THREE

sandwich slices

WHITE SANDWICH BREAD

Bagged loaves of sliced sandwich bread can line a whole aisle at the supermarket. If there are so many options and their purchase is so routine, making good sandwich bread—loaves with a tall rise, fluffy crumb, and a tender but present crust—must be a real challenge outside of the commercial kitchen, right? Wrong, of course. We think sandwich breads baked in a loaf pan are some of the most simple breads to make. They require straightforward kneading in the stand mixer and a common rolled shaping method.

White Sandwich Bread is a classic display of these techniques, and the white bread is a blank flavor slate for swirls, savory and sweet, a seeded coating, or a blanket of cheese. Not only is incorporating these flavor enhancements simple, it also makes sandwich combinations nearly endless (read: no sad desk lunch). When's the last time you found spicy zhoug-swirled sandwich bread at the store? The best part of these incorporations is that they don't require any changes to the core shaping method you'll use, so every loaf you turn out will come together with muscle memory.

WHITE SANDWICH BREAD

how-to

makes 1 loaf

2½ cups (13¾ ounces) bread flour

 2 teaspoons instant or
   rapid-rise yeast

1½ teaspoons table salt

 ¾ cup (6 ounces) whole milk,
   room temperature

 ⅓ cup (2⅔ ounces) water,
   room temperature

 2 tablespoons unsalted butter,
   melted

 2 tablespoons honey

The quintessential sandwich loaf—tall and domed, with a fine, snowy-white crumb and a light brown crust—is an American staple. Since it's a go-to, we wanted to develop a recipe that wasn't just better than bouncy plastic-wrapped bread, but the best—an impressive loaf that would be a worthy base for satisfying sandwiches. For a nice soft crumb we include a fair amount of fat; we use whole milk for a majority of the liquid and then enrich the dough further with 2 tablespoons of melted butter. These amounts are enough to tenderize the bread without making it too rich. A couple spoonfuls of honey gives the bread the faint sweetness we'd expect. But because our dough contains milk, butter, and honey, the crust is prone to browning before the inside is done. We tested oven temperatures of 350, 375, and 400 degrees and found that the lowest temperature provides a soft crust and avoids a doughy interior. The test kitchen's preferred loaf pan measures 8½ by 4½ inches; if you use a 9 by 5-inch loaf pan, increase the shaped rising time and start checking for doneness 10 minutes earlier than advised in the recipe.

1 make dough Whisk flour, yeast, and salt together in bowl of stand mixer. Whisk milk, water, melted butter, and honey in 4-cup liquid measuring cup until honey has dissolved. Using dough hook on low speed, slowly add milk mixture to flour mixture and mix until cohesive dough starts to form and no dry flour remains, about 2 minutes, scraping down bowl as needed. Increase speed to medium-low and knead until dough is smooth and elastic and clears sides of bowl, about 8 minutes. Transfer dough to lightly floured counter and knead by hand to form smooth, round ball, about 30 seconds.

2 first rise Place dough seam side down in lightly greased large bowl, cover tightly with plastic wrap, and let rise until doubled in volume, 1½ to 2 hours.

3 shape dough Grease 8½ by 4½-inch loaf pan. Press down on dough to deflate. Turn dough out onto lightly floured counter (side of dough that was against bowl should now be facing up). Press and stretch dough into 8 by 6-inch rectangle, with long side parallel to counter edge. Roll dough away from you into firm cylinder, keeping roll taut by tucking it under itself as you go. Pinch seam closed and place loaf seam side down in prepared pan, tucking ends as needed to match size of pan and pressing dough gently into corners.

4 second rise Cover loosely with greased plastic and let rise until loaf reaches 1 inch above lip of pan and dough springs back minimally when poked gently with your finger, 1 to 1½ hours.

5 bake Adjust oven rack to lower-middle position and heat oven to 350 degrees. Mist loaf with water and bake until deep golden brown and loaf registers at least 205 degrees, 35 to 40 minutes, rotating pan halfway through baking. Let loaf cool in pan for 15 minutes. Remove loaf from pan and let cool completely on wire rack, about 3 hours, before serving.

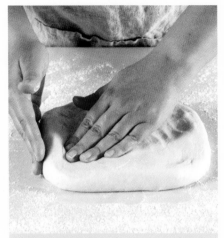
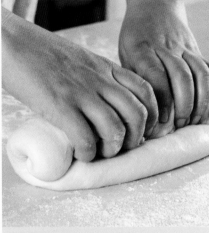

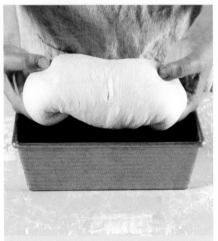
VARIATION

PARMESAN-BLACK PEPPER SANDWICH BREAD

Add ¾ teaspoon coarsely ground pepper to flour mixture in step 1. After misting loaf with water in step 5, sprinkle top evenly with ½ cup shredded Parmesan cheese, pressing gently to adhere.

total time 7 hours

30 min.	1½ hours	10 min.	1 hour	35 min.	3¼ hours
make dough	first rise	shape dough	second rise	bake	cool

CINNAMON RAISIN SWIRL BREAD

makes 1 loaf

Swirl a little sugar into your loaf—without doing much extra. You'll mix finely chopped raisins into our White Sandwich Bread dough (to taste their flavor without disrupting the delicate crumb), roll the dough into a larger rectangle, and then you'll slather on melted butter and cinnamon sugar, roll the dough, and proceed as normal. Your reward? A bread that's great for breakfast toast, holding peanut butter and jelly or bananas, or, if you like a little sweet and savory, sandwiching roast turkey. The test kitchen's preferred loaf pan measures 8½ by 4½ inches; if you use a 9 by 5-inch loaf pan, increase the shaped rising time and start checking for doneness 10 minutes earlier than advised in the recipe.

dough

- **1** recipe White Sandwich Bread, made through step 1, substituting 2 tablespoons sugar for honey and reducing kneading time to 6 minutes
- **⅓** cup raisins, chopped fine

filling

- **¼** cup (1¾ ounces) sugar
- **2** teaspoons ground cinnamon
- **1** tablespoon unsalted butter, melted

1   After kneading dough, reduce mixer speed to low, slowly add raisins and mix until mostly incorporated, about 2 minutes. Transfer dough to lightly floured counter and knead dough until smooth, round ball forms and raisins are fully incorporated, about 30 seconds.

2   first rise   Place dough seam side down in lightly greased large bowl or container, cover with plastic wrap, and let rise until doubled in size, 1½ to 2 hours.

3   make filling   Grease 8½ by 4½-inch loaf pan. Combine sugar and cinnamon in small bowl.

4   shape dough   Press down on dough to deflate. Transfer dough to lightly floured counter (side of dough that was against bowl should now be facing up). Press and stretch dough into 18 by 8-inch rectangle, with short side parallel to counter edge. Brush dough with melted butter and sprinkle evenly with sugar mixture. Roll dough away from you into firm cylinder, keeping roll taut by tucking it under itself as you go and pinch seam closed. Place loaf seam side down in prepared pan, tucking ends as needed to match size of pan and pressing dough gently into corners.

5   second rise   Cover dough loosely with greased plastic and let rise until loaf reaches 1 inch above lip of pan and dough springs back minimally when poked gently with your finger, 1 to 1½ hours.

6   bake   Adjust oven rack to lower-middle position and heat oven to 350 degrees. Mist loaf with water and bake until deep golden brown and loaf registers at least 205 degrees, 35 to 40 minutes, rotating pan halfway through baking. Let loaf cool in pan for 15 minutes. Remove loaf from pan and let cool completely on wire rack, about 3 hours, before serving.

Top dough with sugar mixture.

Roll dough into firm cylinder.

ZHOUG SWIRL BREAD

makes 1 loaf

2 cups coarsely chopped fresh cilantro leaves and stems

2 Thai chiles, stemmed

2 garlic cloves, peeled

½ teaspoon ground coriander

½ teaspoon ground cumin

½ teaspoon table salt

1 recipe White Sandwich Bread, made through step 2

2 tablespoons extra-virgin olive oil

A swirl doesn't have to be sweet. Spice up your sandwiches, literally, by incorporating a spicy swirl, here of the verdant Yemeni hot sauce zhoug. With this bread, ordinary fillings like deli lunchmeat or rotisserie chicken get an instant boost before condiments even make the sandwich. And the loaf takes no more work than making our beloved White Sandwich Bread and blitzing some herbs and spices in the food processor. The test kitchen's preferred loaf pan measures 8½ by 4½ inches; if you use a 9 by 5-inch loaf pan, increase the shaped rising time and start checking for doneness 10 minutes earlier than advised in the recipe.

1 Grease 8½ by 4½-inch loaf pan. Pulse cilantro, Thai chiles, garlic, coriander, cumin, and salt in food processor until coarsely chopped, 8 to 10 pulses.

2 shape dough Press down on dough to deflate. Transfer dough to lightly floured counter (side of dough that was against bowl should now be facing up). Press and stretch dough into 18 by 8-inch rectangle, with short side parallel to counter edge. Brush dough with oil and sprinkle evenly with zhoug, leaving ½ inch border on all sides. Roll dough away from you into firm cylinder, keeping roll taut by tucking it under itself as you go. Pinch seam closed and place loaf seam side down in prepared pan, tucking ends as needed to match size of pan and pressing dough gently into corners.

3 second rise Cover pan loosely with greased plastic and let loaf rise until it reaches 1 inch above lip of pan and dough springs back minimally when poked gently with your finger, 1 to 1½ hours.

4 bake Adjust oven rack to lower-middle position and heat oven to 350 degrees. Mist loaf with water and bake until deep golden brown and loaf registers at least 205 degrees, 35 to 40 minutes, rotating pan halfway through baking. Let loaf cool in pan for 15 minutes. Remove loaf from pan and let cool completely on wire rack, about 3 hours, before serving.

SANDWICH BREAD WITH EVERYTHING BAGEL CRUST

makes 1 loaf

3 tablespoons plus 1 teaspoon **Everything Bagel Seasoning** (recipe follows), divided

1 **recipe White Sandwich Bread, made through step 2**

A seeded outside is a nice contrast to the soft insides of white sandwich bread. Here, a thorough coating of seeds and flavorings that make up everything bagel seasoning (like poppy seeds, caraway seeds, and minced dried onion) not only give the loaf crunch but also cover it in really savory flavor. While the coating may be superficial, its strong flavors thoroughly jazz up any sandwich or piece of toast. Simply make our White Sandwich Bread dough, place it in a pan coated with the seasoning (homemade or store-bought is fine), sprinkle on some more, and it will bake into the golden exterior of your bread. The test kitchen's preferred loaf pan measures 8½ by 4½ inches; if you use a 9 by 5-inch loaf pan, increase the shaped rising time and start checking for doneness 10 minutes earlier than advised in the recipe.

1 Grease 8½ by 4½-inch loaf pan. Add 2 tablespoons everything bagel seasoning to pan and shake until bottom and sides of pan are evenly coated. Press down on dough to deflate. Transfer dough to lightly floured counter (side of dough that was against bowl should now be facing up).

2 shape dough Press and stretch dough into 8 by 6-inch rectangle, with long side parallel to counter edge. Roll dough away from you into firm cylinder, keeping roll taut by tucking it under itself as you go and pinch seam closed. Place loaf seam side down in prepared pan, tucking ends as needed to match size of pan and pressing dough gently into corners. Cover loosely with greased plastic and let rise until loaf reaches 1 inch above lip of pan and dough springs back minimally when poked gently with your finger, 1 to 1½ hours.

3 bake Adjust oven rack to lower-middle position and heat oven to 350 degrees. Mist loaf with water, then sprinkle with remaining 4 teaspoons everything bagel seasoning. Bake until deep golden brown and loaf registers at least 205 degrees, 35 to 40 minutes, rotating pan halfway through baking. Let loaf cool in pan for 15 minutes. Remove loaf from pan and let cool completely on wire rack, about 3 hours, before serving.

EVERYTHING BAGEL SEASONING

makes about ½ cup

Toast the seeds in a dry skillet over medium heat until fragrant (about 1 minute), and then remove the skillet from the heat so the seeds won't scorch.

Coat pan in seasoning.

Top loaf with seasoning.

2 **tablespoons sesame seeds, toasted**

2 **tablespoons poppy seeds**

1 **tablespoon caraway seeds, toasted**

1 **tablespoon kosher salt**

1 **tablespoon dried minced onion**

1 **tablespoon dried minced garlic**

Combine all ingredients in bowl. (Seasoning can be stored in airtight container for up to 3 months.)

total time 5 hours

20 min.	20 min.	20 min.	40 min.	3¼ hours
make dough	first rise	second rise	bake	cool

EASY SANDWICH BREAD

makes 1 loaf

2 cups (11 ounces) bread flour

6 tablespoons (2 ounces) whole-wheat flour

2¼ teaspoons instant or rapid-rise yeast

1¼ cups plus 2 tablespoons (11 ounces) warm water, divided

3 tablespoons unsalted butter, melted, divided

1 tablespoon honey

¾ teaspoon table salt

1 large egg, beaten with 1 tablespoon water and pinch table salt

why this recipe works   You can bake soft, well-risen, even-crumbed bread that's perfect for any sandwich without kneading or shaping—and it takes just 2 hours to make (with most of that time being hands-off). To encourage maximum gluten development in a short amount of time, we use higher-protein bread flour and make a wet, batter-like dough; increasing the amount of water enhances the gluten structure without requiring prolonged kneading. We also use slightly less fat and sugar and withhold salt until the second mix, which gives our bread more spring and lift. Using the mixer's paddle instead of the dough hook and increasing the speed to medium not only shortens the mixing time but also gives the loose dough enough structure to rise into a dome shape. The test kitchen's preferred loaf pan measures 8½ by 4½ inches; if you use a 9 by 5-inch loaf pan, increase the shaped rising time and start checking for doneness 10 minutes earlier than advised in the recipe. To prevent the loaf from deflating as it rises, do not let the batter come in contact with the plastic wrap.

1   make dough   Whisk bread flour, whole-wheat flour, and yeast together in bowl of stand mixer. Whisk 1¼ cups warm water, 2 tablespoons melted butter, and honey in 4-cup liquid measuring cup until honey has dissolved. Using paddle on low speed, slowly add water mixture to flour mixture and mix until batter comes together, about 1 minute. Increase speed to medium and mix for 4 minutes, scraping down bowl and paddle as needed.

2   first rise   Cover bowl tightly with plastic wrap and let batter rise until doubled in volume, about 20 minutes.

3   Adjust oven rack to lower-middle position and heat oven to 375 degrees. Grease 8½ by 4½-inch loaf pan. Dissolve salt in remaining 2 tablespoons warm water, then add to batter and mix on low speed until water mixture is mostly incorporated, about 40 seconds. Increase speed to medium and mix until thoroughly combined, about 1 minute.

4   second rise   Transfer batter to prepared pan and smooth top. Cover tightly with plastic and let rise until batter reaches ½ inch below lip of pan, 15 to 20 minutes. Uncover and continue to let rise until center of batter is level with lip of pan, 5 to 10 minutes.

5   bake   Gently brush loaf with egg wash and bake until deep golden brown and loaf registers at least 205 degrees, 40 to 45 minutes, rotating pan halfway through baking. Let loaf cool in pan for 15 minutes. Remove loaf from pan and transfer to wire rack. Brush top and sides with remaining melted butter. Let cool completely, about 3 hours, before serving.

ENGLISH MUFFIN BREAD

makes 2 loaves

---

2 tablespoons cornmeal

5 cups (27½ ounces) bread flour

1½ tablespoons instant or rapid-rise yeast

1 tablespoon sugar

2 teaspoons table salt

1 teaspoon baking soda

3 cups (24 ounces) warm whole milk

why this recipe works A good loaf of English muffin bread has the same chewy crumb and porous texture as individual English muffins—and it takes a fraction of the time to make. Our recipe makes two loaves so you can freeze one for later (or, if you're feeling generous, you can give one away to a friend). Bread flour gives the loaves their chewy yet light consistency, and because it absorbs more water than all-purpose flour, it can handle a high hydration so the dough bakes into loaves full of consistently sized holes. A dusting of cornmeal gives the crust that signature English muffin crunch. The test kitchen's preferred loaf pan measures 8½ by 4½ inches; if you use a 9 by 5-inch loaf pan, increase the shaped rising time and start checking for doneness 10 minutes earlier than advised in the recipe. English muffin bread is designed to be toasted after it is sliced.

1 make dough Grease two 8½ by 4½-inch loaf pans. Add cornmeal to prepared pans and shake until bottom and sides of pans are evenly coated; set aside. Combine flour, yeast, sugar, salt, and baking soda in large bowl. Stir in warm milk until combined, about 1 minute.

2 first rise Cover bowl with greased plastic wrap and let dough rise for 30 minutes, or until dough is bubbly and has doubled in volume.

3 second rise Stir dough and divide between prepared pans, pushing into corners with greased rubber spatula. (Pans should be about two-thirds full.) Cover pans with greased plastic and let dough rise until it reaches edges of pans, about 30 minutes.

4 bake Adjust oven rack to middle position and heat oven to 375 degrees. Bake until bread is well browned and registers at least 205 degrees, 30 to 35 minutes, switching and rotating pans halfway through baking. Remove loaves from pans and let cool completely on wire rack, about 1 hour. Slice, toast, and serve.

total time 2¾ hours

10 min.	30 min.	30 min.	30 min.	1 hour
make dough	first rise	second rise	bake	cool

total time 7½ hours

30 min.	1½ hours	10 min.	1 hour	35 min.	3¼ hours
make dough	first rise	shape dough	second rise	bake	cool

BUTTERMILK DILL BREAD

makes 1 loaf

- 2½ cups (13¾ ounces) bread flour
- 1 tablespoon sugar
- 2 teaspoons instant or rapid-rise yeast
- 1½ teaspoons table salt
- 1¼ cups (9 ounces) plus 1 tablespoon buttermilk, divided, room temperature
- ¼ cup minced fresh chives
- 3 tablespoons chopped fresh dill, divided
- 2 tablespoons unsalted butter, melted

why this recipe works   We can't wait to slice up this tangy and aromatic sandwich bread speckled with dill and chives. It's perfect for an end-of-summer BLT with tomatoes fresh from the garden, or as toast with scrambled eggs for breakfast. To showcase buttermilk's characteristic tang, we use it as the only liquid. Honey, which we use in our other sandwich breads, cancels out the buttermilk's flavor, so instead we include a bare minimum of neutral-flavored sugar to feed the yeast. After testing both fresh and dried herbs in different amounts, we preferred a generous ¼ cup of minced fresh chives to create a savory backdrop that still let a couple tablespoons of fresh dill shine through. Brushing the loaf with buttermilk before baking gives a bit more color and sheen to the top, and a sprinkle of chopped dill fronds makes for not only a fragrant bake in the oven, but a pretty one as well. The test kitchen's preferred loaf pan measures 8½ by 4½ inches; if you use a 9 by 5-inch loaf pan, increase the shaped rising time and start checking for doneness 10 minutes earlier than advised in the recipe.

1   make dough   Whisk flour, sugar, yeast, and salt together in bowl of stand mixer. Whisk 1¼ cups buttermilk, chives, 2 tablespoons dill, and melted butter together in 4-cup liquid measuring cup. Using dough hook on low speed, slowly add milk mixture to flour mixture and mix until cohesive dough starts to form and no dry flour remains, about 2 minutes, scraping down bowl as needed. Increase speed to medium-low and knead until dough is smooth and elastic and clears sides of bowl but still sticks to bottom, about 8 minutes. Transfer dough to lightly floured counter and knead by hand to form smooth, round ball, about 30 seconds.

2   first rise   Place dough seam side down in lightly greased large bowl or container, cover with plastic wrap, and let rise until doubled in volume, 1½ to 2 hours.

3   shape dough   Grease 8½ by 4½-inch loaf pan. Press down on dough to deflate. Turn dough out onto lightly floured counter (side of dough that was against bowl should now be facing up). Press and stretch dough into 8 by 6-inch rectangle, with long side parallel to counter edge. Roll dough away from you into firm cylinder, keeping roll taut by tucking it under itself as you go. Pinch seam closed and place loaf seam side down in prepared pan, tucking ends as needed to match size of pan and pressing dough gently into corners.

4   second rise   Cover loosely with greased plastic and let rise until loaf reaches 1 inch above lip of pan and dough springs back minimally when poked gently with your finger, 1 to 1½ hours.

5   bake   Adjust oven rack to lower-middle position and heat oven to 350 degrees. Gently brush loaf with remaining 1 tablespoon buttermilk, then sprinkle with remaining 1 tablespoon dill. Bake until golden brown and loaf registers at least 205 degrees, 35 to 40 minutes, rotating pan halfway through baking. Let loaf cool in pan for 15 minutes. Remove loaf from pan and let cool completely on wire rack, about 3 hours, before serving.

OATMEAL SANDWICH BREAD

makes 1 loaf

2 cups (11 ounces) bread flour

1½ teaspoons instant or rapid-rise yeast

1¼ teaspoons table salt

⅔ cup (2 ounces) old-fashioned rolled oats

½ cup (4 ounces) boiling water

2 tablespoons unsalted butter, cut into 4 pieces

⅔ cup (5⅓ ounces) whole milk, room temperature

2 tablespoons honey

why this recipe works   Sandwich bread shouldn't be heavy, and the addition of oats in this version makes it anything but—the bread is tender and fluffy and captures the sweetness and nuttiness from the oats without displaying their more robust texture. Incorporating the oats as meal made with boiling water and butter makes the loaf moist but not leaden and distributes the oatmeal throughout. Some honey complements the oat flavor. This bread works with just about any sandwich, from a simple PB&J to a turkey sandwich with all the fixings. The test kitchen's preferred loaf pan measures 8½ by 4½ inches; if you use a 9 by 5-inch loaf pan, increase the shaped rising time and start checking for doneness 10 minutes earlier than advised in the recipe. High-protein King Arthur Bread Flour works best with this recipe; other bread flours will suffice but the loaf will be squatter and more dense. For an accurate measurement of boiling water, bring a kettle of water to a boil and then measure out the desired amount.

1   make dough   Whisk together flour, yeast, and salt in bowl of stand mixer. Stir oats, boiling water, and butter together in medium bowl and let sit until water is absorbed and oats have cooled to room temperature, about 15 minutes. Add milk and honey and stir to combine. Using dough hook on low speed, slowly add oat mixture to flour mixture and mix until cohesive dough starts to form and no dry flour remains, about 2 minutes. Increase speed to medium-low and knead until dough clears sides of bowl (it will still stick to bottom), about 8 minutes, scraping down dough hook halfway through mixing. Transfer dough to lightly floured counter and knead to form smooth, round ball, about 30 seconds.

2   first rise   Place dough seam side down in lightly greased large bowl or container, cover with plastic wrap, and let rise until doubled in volume, 1 to 1½ hours.

3   shape dough   Grease 8½ by 4½-inch loaf pan. Press down on dough to deflate. Transfer dough to lightly floured counter (side of dough that was against bowl should now be facing up). Press and stretch dough into 8 by 6-inch rectangle, with long side parallel to counter edge. Roll dough away from you into firm cylinder, keeping roll taut by tucking it under itself as you go. Pinch seam closed and place loaf seam side down in prepared pan, tucking ends as needed to match size of pan and pressing dough gently into corners.

4   second rise   Cover loosely with greased plastic and let rise until loaf reaches 1 inch above lip of pan and dough springs back minimally when poked gently with your finger, about 1 hour. (Loaf may be refrigerated immediately after shaping for at least 8 hours and up to 16 hours; let loaf sit at room temperature for 1 hour before baking.)

5   bake   Adjust oven rack to lower-middle position and heat oven to 350 degrees. Mist loaf with water and bake until deep golden brown and loaf registers at least 205 degrees, 35 to 40 minutes, rotating pan halfway through baking. Let loaf cool in pan for 15 minutes. Remove loaf from pan and let cool completely on wire rack, about 3 hours, before serving.

total time 6¾ hours

45 min.	1 hour	5 min.	1 hour	35 min.	3¼ hours
make dough	first rise	shape dough	second rise	bake	cool

FURIKAKE JAPANESE MILK BREAD

makes 1 loaf

3   **tablespoons plus 2 cups bread flour (11 ounces), divided**

½   **cup (4 ounces) water, room temperature**

½   **cup (4 ounces) whole milk, room temperature**

1   **large egg, room temperature**

1½   **teaspoons instant or rapid-rise yeast**

6   **tablespoons furikake, divided**

2   **tablespoons sugar**

1½   **teaspoons table salt**

3   **tablespoons unsalted butter, cut into 3 pieces and softened**

1   **large egg, beaten with 1 table-spoon water and pinch salt**

1   **tablespoon toasted sesame oil**

FURIKAKE

makes about ½ cup

2   **sheets nori, torn into 1-inch pieces**

3   **tablespoons sesame seeds, toasted**

1½   **tablespoons bonito flakes**

1½   **teaspoons sugar**

1½   **teaspoons flake sea salt**

Process nori using spice grinder until coarsely ground and pieces are no larger than ½ inch, about 15 seconds. Add sesame seeds, bonito flakes, and sugar and pulse until coarsely ground and pieces of nori are no larger than ¼ inch, about 2 pulses. Transfer to small bowl and stir in salt. (Furikake can be stored in airtight container at room temperature for up to 3 weeks.)

why this recipe works   A plush bread with an incredibly fluffy texture, this is no ordinary white sandwich bread. The uniquely shaped dough for Japanese milk bread (also called Hokkaido milk bread) is rolled thin and formed into tight spirals, which allows the loaf to bake up into feathery strands. Shaping the dough into two spirals before arranging them in the pan builds an orderly structure, creating this bread's gossamer-thin layers. The tangzhong technique (see page 32) works well to make a moist but not sticky dough. While Japanese milk bread is wonderful as is, our rendition ups the flavor ante by adding furikake. This spice blend of nori, sesame seeds, bonito flakes, salt, and sugar is at once briny, earthy, nutty, and sweet. We add furikake to not only the dough but also the outer crust: Sprinkling the interior of the loaf pan as well as the top of the bread results in a beautiful crust that packs an umami punch and a pleasingly delicate crunch. A final brush of sesame oil on the warm baked loaf gives the bread a rich finish. To go all in on the nori flavor, we recommend serving slices of this bread with Nori Butter (page 95). The test kitchen's preferred loaf pan measures 8½ by 4½ inches; if you use a 9 by 5-inch loaf pan, increase the shaped rising time and start checking for doneness 10 minutes earlier than advised in the recipe.

1   make dough   Whisk 3 tablespoons flour and water in bowl until no lumps remain. Microwave, whisking every 20 seconds, until mixture thickens to stiff, smooth, pudding-like consistency that forms mound when dropped from end of whisk into bowl, 40 to 80 seconds.

2   Whisk milk, egg, and flour paste in bowl of stand mixer until smooth. Add yeast and remaining 2 cups flour. Using dough hook on low speed, mix until cohesive dough starts to form and no dry flour remains, about 2 minutes, scraping down bowl as needed. Cover bowl tightly with plastic wrap and let dough rest for 15 minutes.

3   Add 3 tablespoons furikake, sugar, and salt to dough and mix on low speed, about 5 minutes. With mixer running, add butter, 1 piece at a time, allowing each piece to incorporate before adding next, about 3 minutes total, scraping down bowl and dough hook as needed. Increase speed to medium and knead until dough is smooth and elastic and clears sides of bowl but sticks to bottom, 7 to 9 minutes. Transfer dough to lightly floured counter and knead by hand to form smooth, round ball, about 30 seconds.

4   first rise   Place dough seam side down in lightly greased large bowl or container, cover with plastic, and let rise until doubled in volume, 1 to 1½ hours.

5   shape dough   Grease 8½ by 4½-inch loaf pan. Add 2 tablespoons furikake to prepared pan and shake until bottom and sides of pan are evenly coated. Press down on dough to deflate. Turn out dough onto lightly floured counter (side of dough that was against bowl should now be facing up). Press and roll dough into 24 by 4-inch rectangle, with short side parallel to counter edge. Using pizza cutter or chef's knife, cut rectangle lengthwise into 2 equal strips. Roll 1 strip of dough into snug cylinder; pinch seam closed; and place seam side down in prepared pan, with spiral against long side of pan. Repeat with remaining strip of dough, placing it adjacent to other in pan.

6 second rise Cover loosely with greased plastic and let rise until loaf is level with lip of pan and dough springs back minimally when poked gently with your finger, 30 minutes to 1 hour.

7 bake Adjust oven rack to lowest position and heat oven to 375 degrees. Gently brush loaf with egg wash and sprinkle with remaining 1 tablespoon furikake. Bake until loaf is deep golden brown and registers at least 205 degrees, 30 to 35 minutes, rotating pan halfway through baking. Let loaf cool in pan on wire rack for 15 minutes. Remove loaf from pan and transfer to wire rack. Brush top and sides with oil. Let cool completely, about 3 hours, before serving.

total time 6½ hours

55 min.	1 hour	10 min.	30 min.	30 min.	3¼ hours
make dough	first rise	shape dough	second rise	bake	cool

total time 7 hours

30 min.	1½ hours	10 min.	1 hour	35 min.	3¼ hours
make dough	first rise	shape dough	second rise	bake	cool

WHOLE-WHEAT SANDWICH BREAD

makes 1 loaf

1½ cups (8¼ ounces) bread flour

1 cup (5½ ounces) whole-wheat flour

3 tablespoons toasted wheat germ

2 teaspoons instant or rapid-rise yeast

1½ teaspoons table salt

¾ cup (6 ounces) whole milk, room temperature

⅓ cup (2⅔ ounces) water, room temperature

3 tablespoons honey

2 tablespoons unsalted butter, melted

why this recipe works While the flavor profile of our whole-wheat bread is nuttier, wheatier, and a little sweeter, if we're honest, it isn't much different than our classic White Sandwich Bread (page 158). And that's a good thing: You can go white or whole-wheat whenever you're in the mood for one or the other. Since whole-wheat flour alone creates a dense loaf, we use a good amount of bread flour for structure, and we amplify the whole-wheat flavor with the addition of a little wheat germ. This multipurpose bread tastes great in nearly any sandwich or toast application. The test kitchen's preferred loaf pan measures 8½ by 4½ inches; if you use a 9 by 5-inch loaf pan, increase the shaped rising time and start checking for doneness 10 minutes earlier than advised in the recipe.

1 make dough Whisk bread flour, whole-wheat flour, wheat germ, yeast, and salt together in bowl of stand mixer. Whisk milk, water, honey, and melted butter in 4-cup liquid measuring cup until honey has dissolved. Using dough hook on low speed, slowly add milk mixture to flour mixture and mix until cohesive dough starts to form and no dry flour remains, about 2 minutes, scraping down bowl as needed. Increase speed to medium-low and knead until dough is smooth and elastic and clears sides of bowl, about 8 minutes. Transfer dough to lightly floured counter and knead by hand to form smooth, round ball, about 30 seconds.

2 first rise Place dough seam side down in lightly greased large bowl or container, cover tightly with plastic wrap, and let rise until doubled in volume, 1½ to 2 hours.

3 shape dough Grease 8½ by 4½-inch loaf pan. Press down on dough to deflate. Turn dough out onto lightly floured counter (side of dough that was against bowl should now be facing up). Press and stretch dough into 8 by 6-inch rectangle, with long side parallel to counter edge. Roll dough away from you into firm cylinder, keeping roll taut by tucking it under itself as you go. Pinch seam closed and place loaf seam side down in prepared pan, tucking ends as needed to match size of pan and pressing dough gently into corners.

4 second rise Cover loosely with greased plastic and let rise until loaf reaches 1 inch above lip of pan and dough springs back minimally when poked gently with your finger, 1 to 1½ hours.

5 bake Adjust oven rack to lower-middle position and heat oven to 350 degrees. Mist loaf with water and bake until deep golden brown and loaf registers at least 205 degrees, 35 to 40 minutes, rotating pan halfway through baking. Let loaf cool in pan for 15 minutes. Remove loaf from pan and let cool completely on wire rack, about 3 hours, before serving.

WHOLE-WHEAT OATMEAL LOAF

makes 1 loaf

1½ cups (8¼ ounces) bread flour

¾ cup (4⅛ ounces) whole-wheat flour

1½ teaspoons instant or rapid-rise yeast

1 teaspoon table salt

¾ cup (2¼ ounces) old-fashioned rolled oats, plus 4 teaspoons for sprinkling

⅔ cup (5⅓ ounces) boiling water, plus ½ cup (4 ounces) room temperature water

2 tablespoons unsalted butter, cut into 4 pieces

¼ cup molasses

why this recipe works Our delightfully homey Oatmeal Dinner Rolls (page 116) are a favorite recipe for us. We decided to take that dough and bake it in a loaf pan: With a soft crumb, a sweet wheat-and-oat flavor, and a pretty exterior, it's ideal for dressing up sandwiches (and getting in whole grains at lunch to boot). The sandwich bread is just as plush and delicious as the rolls—and available by the slice. For an accurate measurement of boiling water, bring a kettle of water to a boil and then measure out the desired amount. We strongly recommend measuring the flour by weight. Avoid blackstrap molasses here, as it's too bitter. The test kitchen's preferred loaf pan measures 8½ by 4½ inches; if you use a 9 by 5-inch loaf pan, increase the shaped rising time and start checking for doneness 10 minutes earlier than advised in the recipe.

1 make dough Whisk bread flour, whole-wheat flour, yeast, and salt together in bowl of stand mixer. Stir ¾ cup oats, boiling water, and butter together in medium bowl and let sit until water is absorbed and oats have cooled to room temperature, about 15 minutes. Add remaining water and molasses and stir to combine. Using dough hook on low speed, slowly add oat mixture to flour mixture and mix until cohesive dough starts to form and no dry flour remains, about 2 minutes. Increase speed to medium-low and mix until dough clears sides of bowl (it will still stick to bottom), about 8 minutes, scraping down dough hook halfway through mixing. Transfer dough to lightly floured counter and knead to form smooth, round ball, about 30 seconds.

2 first rise Place dough seam side down in lightly greased large bowl or container, cover tightly with plastic wrap, and let rise until doubled in volume, 1 to 1½ hours.

3 shape dough Grease 8½ by 4½-inch loaf pan. Press down on dough to deflate. Transfer dough to lightly floured counter (side of dough that was against bowl should now be facing up). Press and stretch dough into 8 by 6-inch rectangle, with long side parallel to counter edge. Roll dough away from you into firm cylinder, keeping roll taut by tucking it under itself as you go. Pinch seam closed and place loaf seam side down in prepared pan, tucking ends as needed to match size of pan and pressing dough gently into corners.

4 second rise Cover loosely with greased plastic and let rise until loaf reaches ½ inch above lip of pan and dough springs back minimally when poked gently with your finger, about 1 hour.

5 bake Adjust oven rack to lower-middle position and heat oven to 350 degrees. Mist loaf with water and sprinkle with reserved oats. Bake until deep golden brown and loaf registers at least 205 degrees, 35 to 40 minutes, rotating pan halfway through baking. Let loaf cool in pan for 15 minutes. Remove loaf from pan and let cool completely on wire rack, about 3 hours, before serving.

total time 6¾ hours

45 min.	1 hour	10 min.	1 hour	35 min.	3¼ hours
make dough	first rise	shape dough	second rise	bake	cool

QUINOA WHOLE-WHEAT BREAD

makes 1 loaf

1 cup (8 ounces) water, room temperature, divided

⅓ cup (1¾ ounces) plus 1 teaspoon prewashed white quinoa, divided

1⅔ cups (9⅛ ounces) bread flour

1 cup (5½ ounces) whole-wheat flour

2 tablespoons plus 1 teaspoon flaxseeds, divided

1 tablespoon plus 1 teaspoon poppy seeds, divided

1 tablespoon plus 1 teaspoon sesame seeds, divided

2 teaspoons instant or rapid-rise yeast

1½ teaspoons table salt

¾ cup (6 ounces) whole milk, room temperature

2 tablespoons honey

1 tablespoon vegetable oil

1 large egg lightly beaten with 1 tablespoon water and pinch table salt

why this recipe works   This hearty sandwich bread made with quinoa; whole-wheat flour; and flax, poppy, and sesame seeds will fuel your day with fiber, protein, and heart-healthy fats, whether it's at breakfast as toast, or tucked into your lunchbox with your favorite sandwich fixings. Using primarily bread flour allows us to pack a good amount of quinoa into the dough, and cooking the quinoa in the microwave before adding it to the dough prevents it from sucking up moisture from the loaf, giving us a pleasantly chewy yet tender bread. A quarter-cup of seeds stirred into the dough adds fun crunchy pops that keep this healthy loaf from being stodgy, and we sprinkle more seeds, plus a little extra quinoa, on top. We like the convenience of prewashed quinoa; rinsing removes the quinoa's bitter protective coating (called saponin). If you buy unwashed quinoa, rinse it and then spread it out on a clean dish towel to dry for 15 minutes. The test kitchen's preferred loaf pan measures 8½ by 4½ inches; if you use a 9 by 5-inch loaf pan, increase the shaped rising time and start checking for doneness 10 minutes earlier than advised in the recipe.

1 make dough   Microwave ¾ cup water and ⅓ cup quinoa in covered bowl at 50 percent power until water is almost completely absorbed, 8 to 12 minutes, stirring halfway through microwaving. Uncover quinoa and let sit until cooled slightly and water is completely absorbed, about 10 minutes.

2   Whisk bread flour, whole-wheat flour, 2 tablespoons flaxseeds, 1 tablespoon poppy seeds, 1 tablespoon sesame seeds, yeast, and salt together in bowl of stand mixer. Whisk milk, honey, oil, and remaining ¼ cup water in 4-cup liquid measuring cup until honey has dissolved, then whisk in cooked quinoa. Using dough hook on low speed, slowly add milk-quinoa mixture to flour mixture and mix until cohesive dough starts to form and no dry flour remains, about 2 minutes, scraping down bowl as needed. Increase speed to medium-low and knead until dough is elastic but still sticky, about 8 minutes. Transfer dough to lightly floured counter and knead by hand to form smooth, round ball, about 30 seconds.

3 first rise   Place dough seam side down in lightly greased large bowl or container, cover bowl with plastic wrap, and let rise until doubled in volume, 1½ to 2 hours.

4 shape dough   Grease 8½ by 4½-inch loaf pan. Press down on dough to deflate. Transfer dough to lightly floured counter (side of dough that was against bowl should now be facing up) and press into 8 by 6-inch rectangle, with long side parallel to counter edge. Roll dough away from you into firm cylinder, keeping roll taut by tucking it under itself as you go. Pinch seam closed then place loaf seam side down in prepared pan, tucking ends as needed to match size of pan and pressing dough gently into corners.

5 second rise Cover dough loosely with greased plastic and let rise until loaf reaches 1 inch above lip of pan at lowest point and dough springs back minimally when poked gently with your finger, 1 to 1½ hours.

6 bake Adjust oven rack to lower-middle position and heat oven to 350 degrees. Combine remaining 1 teaspoon quinoa, 1 teaspoon flax-seeds, 1 teaspoon poppy seeds, and 1 teaspoon sesame seeds in bowl. Brush loaf gently with egg wash and sprinkle with quinoa mixture. Bake until golden brown and loaf registers at least 205 degrees, 45 to 50 minutes, rotating pan halfway through baking. Let loaf cool in pan for 15 minutes. Remove loaf from pan and let cool completely on wire rack, about 3 hours, before serving.

total time 7½ hours

50 min.	1½ hours	5 min.	1 hour	45 min.	3¼ hours
make dough	first rise	shape dough	second rise	bake	cool

CHAPTER FOUR

no-knead
dutch oven breads

NO-KNEAD RUSTIC LOAF

Great loaves of artisan-style rustic bread display some distinct characteristics—they're beautifully browned, with a thick-yet-crisp crust that breaks to a chewy, open interior. The word "artisan" implies you need professional skills—and plenty of time—to turn out loaves in this style, but that isn't true. Enter: the no-knead method of bread baking. We've updated and perfected this beloved technique to create our quintessential rustic loaf that requires just a mix and some hand-folds and is done on a convenient timetable. You can discover our steps for developing this superlative new version in the book's introduction (see page 21), and learn all about why the technique works.

While the boule, a generously sized perky round loaf, is a timeless shape for this kind of bread, we've made our hydrated, airy core dough ultra-adaptable: Coax your dough into an elongated bâtard perfect for slicing. With a dead-simple shaping technique, make thin and crispy appetizer flatbreads with just the right amount of chewy interior for soaking up olive oil. Make crusty rolls for dinner or sandwich-size ones for a bakery-style lunch. Even bake a rustic sandwich bread in a loaf pan—who says sandwich slices have to be soft and tight-crumbed? Introduce flavor through mix-ins like dried fruit, seeds, even chocolate, and alternative flours. Your new go-to loaf will also be the most impressive in your repertoire.

NO-KNEAD RUSTIC LOAF

how-to   how-to

makes 1 loaf

2¾ cups (15⅛ ounces) bread flour

1½ teaspoons table salt

¼ teaspoon instant or rapid-rise yeast

¾ cup plus 2 tablespoons (7 ounces) water, room temperature

½ cup (4 ounces) mild lager, room temperature

1 tablespoon distilled white vinegar

Not only is it possible to make a bakery-quality rustic loaf for your home table, it's now easier than ever with our new and improved no-knead rustic bread. Instead of kneading our exemplary loaf, we make a very wet dough and rely on a rest and some structure-building folds to slowly develop a strong gluten network—one that can support a dramatic open crumb initiated by baking the bread in the humid environment of a preheated Dutch oven. While handling wet doughs can be a real challenge, a long built-in rest allows the dry ingredients to absorb a lot of the moisture. And our fear-free folding method is extra forgiving. We use a mild American lager, such as Budweiser; strongly flavored beers will make this bread taste bitter. While we prefer the flavor that beer adds, you can substitute an equal amount of water. You will need a bowl that is at least 9 inches wide and 4 inches deep to cover the dough in step 6.

1 make dough   Whisk flour, salt, and yeast together in large bowl. Using rubber spatula, fold water, beer, and vinegar into flour mixture, scraping up dry flour from bottom of bowl and pressing dough until cohesive and shaggy and all flour is incorporated.

2 first rise   Cover bowl tightly with plastic wrap and let sit at room temperature for at least 8 hours or up to 18 hours.

3 fold and rest   Using greased bowl scraper or your wet fingertips, fold dough over itself by lifting and folding edge of dough toward middle and pressing to seal. Turn bowl 90 degrees and fold dough again; repeat turning bowl and folding dough 6 more times (for a total of 8 folds). Flip dough seam side down in bowl, cover with plastic, and let rest for 15 minutes.

4 shape dough   Lay 18 by 12-inch sheet of parchment paper on counter and spray lightly with vegetable oil spray. Transfer dough seam side up onto lightly floured counter and pat into rough 9-inch circle using your lightly floured hands. Using bowl scraper or your floured fingertips, lift and fold edge of dough toward center, pressing to seal. Repeat 5 more times (for a total of 6 folds), evenly spacing folds around circumference of dough. Press down on dough to seal, then use bench scraper to gently flip dough seam side down.

total time 13¾ hours

25 min.	8 hours	20 min.	15 min.	1 hour	40 min.	3 hours
make dough	first rise	fold + rest	shape dough	second rise	bake	cool

» **Take your time** To make over 24 hours, let dough sit for up to 18 hours in step 2.

Press to create shaggy dough.

Fold dough toward middle.

Turn bowl, fold again; repeat.

Pat dough into 9-inch circle.

Fold edge toward center.

Repeat folds 5 more times.

Cup dough and pull toward you.

5   Using both hands, cup side of dough farthest away from you and pull dough toward you, keeping pinky fingers and side of palm in contact with counter and applying slight pressure to dough as it drags to create tension. (If dough slides across surface of counter without rolling, remove excess flour. If dough sticks to counter or hands, lightly sprinkle counter or hands with flour.) Rotate dough ball 90 degrees, reposition dough ball at top of counter, and repeat pulling dough until taut round ball forms, at least 4 more times. Using your floured hands or bench scraper, transfer dough seam side down to center of prepared parchment.

6   second rise   Cover dough with inverted large bowl. Let rise until dough has doubled in size and springs back minimally when poked gently with your finger, 1 to 2 hours.

7   Thirty minutes before baking, adjust oven rack to middle position, place Dutch oven with lid on rack, and heat oven to 475 degrees. Using sharp knife or single-edge razor blade, make one 6-inch-long, ½-inch-deep slash with swift, fluid motion along top of loaf. Carefully remove hot pot from oven and, using parchment as sling, gently transfer dough to hot pot. Working quickly and reinforcing score in top of loaf if needed, cover pot and return to oven.

8   bake   Reduce oven temperature to 425 degrees and bake loaf in covered pot for 30 minutes. Remove lid and continue to bake until loaf is deep golden brown and registers at least 205 degrees, 10 to 15 minutes. Using parchment sling, carefully remove loaf from hot pot and transfer to wire rack; discard parchment. Let cool completely, about 3 hours, before slicing.

NO-KNEAD
RUSTIC BÂTARD

how-to

makes 1 loaf

1 recipe No-Knead Rustic Loaf, made through step 3

We created this book to accommodate rustic artisan bread in a common round Dutch oven, and you can make every recipe in this chapter in one to create a boule. A boule is a classic, but if you have an oval-shaped Dutch oven, you can make a simple modification to the shape for variety. A torpedo-shaped bâtard doesn't take much more manipulating and creates an even loaf from end to end, particularly appropriate for slicing for sandwiches or lunch toasts. The long slash it gets opens to create more of a crispy ear (the raised bit of crust along a loaf's slash) than with a boule. Some might even find a bâtard simpler to shape than a boule—there's no rolling it around the counter to create a taut exterior. You need an oval Dutch oven that holds 8 quarts or more for this recipe. You can also use a Challenger Pan (see page 11) if you happen to own one.

1 shape dough   After letting dough rest in step 3, lightly spray 18 by 12-inch sheet of parchment with vegetable oil spray. Transfer dough seam side up onto lightly floured counter and pat into rough 7-inch square. Fold top corners of dough diagonally into center of square and press gently to seal. Stretch and fold upper third of dough toward center and press seam gently to seal. Stretch and fold dough in half toward you to form rough 8 by 4-inch loaf and pinch seam closed. Roll loaf seam side down. Gently slide your hands underneath each end of loaf and transfer seam side down to prepared parchment. Reshape loaf as needed, tucking edges under to form taut torpedo shape.

2 second rise   Cover loosely with plastic wrap and let rise until dough has doubled in size and springs back minimally when poked gently with your finger, 1 to 2 hours.

3   Thirty minutes before baking, adjust oven rack to middle position, place oval Dutch oven with lid on rack, and heat oven to 475 degrees. Using sharp knife or single-edge razor blade, make one 6-inch-long, ½-inch-deep slash with swift, fluid motion along top of loaf. Carefully remove hot pot from oven and, using parchment as sling, gently transfer dough to hot pot.

4 bake   Working quickly and reinforcing score in top of loaf if needed, cover pot and return to oven. Reduce oven temperature to 425 degrees and bake loaf in covered pot for 30 minutes. Remove lid and continue to bake until loaf is deep golden brown and registers at least 205 degrees, 10 to 15 minutes. Using parchment sling, carefully remove loaf from hot pot and transfer to wire rack; discard parchment. Let cool completely, about 3 hours, before slicing.

Pat dough into 7-inch square.

Fold top corners into center.

Fold corner toward center.

Fold dough in half toward you.

Pinch seam closed.

Transfer dough to parchment.

Tuck edges under to form torpedo shape.

(ALMOST) NO-KNEAD RUSTIC FLATBREADS

makes 2 loaves

---

1 recipe No-Knead Rustic Loaf, made through step 2

1 teaspoon extra-virgin olive oil

Flake sea salt

Drizzled with olive oil; sprinkled with flaky salt, maybe some fresh rosemary; served with briny olives and an aperitif, crispy-chewy flatbreads are a refined and elegant first course. If you know how to make our no-knead bread dough, producing these flatbreads from it is a breeze—they might be the easiest rustic bread in this book to make and shape. Skip all the folding, divide the dough in half, and simply knead each piece a few times. Stretch the dough into rounds and transfer them to a preheated baking stone to turn deeply golden during baking. These flatbreads have the typical shape for ripping, dipping, and sharing, but they're crustier and chewier than most, thin and crispy but not cracker-like, and sturdy enough to absorb fruity olive oil without getting soft. They display all the best qualities of our No-Knead Rustic Loaf in squatter, sharable form.

1 Thirty minutes before baking, adjust oven rack to middle position, set baking stone on rack, and heat oven to 475 degrees.

2 rest Transfer dough to well-oiled counter and divide in half; cover loosely with greased plastic wrap. Using your oiled hands, knead each piece of dough 8 to 10 times. Cover with plastic and let rest for 30 minutes.

3 shape dough Working with 1 piece of dough at a time, press and stretch dough into even 10-inch round on well-oiled counter (keep remaining piece covered). Carefully transfer dough to 18 by 12-inch sheet of parchment paper, reshaping as needed. Drizzle dough with ½ teaspoon extra-virgin olive oil and, using pizza peel or rimless baking sheet, carefully slide parchment with dough onto stone.

4 bake Bake for 12 to 16 minutes, until dark, spotty brown. Transfer to cutting board and let cool for 5 minutes before sprinkling with flake sea salt to taste and slicing. Repeat with remaining dough and oil.

NO-KNEAD RUSTIC ROLLS

makes 6 rolls

1 recipe No-Knead Rustic Loaf, made through step 3

Miniaturizing a boule has its benefits: Chewy, crusty rolls make elite sandwiches or a rustic side to a warming main course. You can simply divide the same dough you've mastered to make the rustic bread archetype, our No-Knead Rustic Loaf, into smaller rounds that also bake brilliantly in your Dutch oven. Each roll is made like a little boule. These make generously sized rolls that can accommodate a delicious sandwich filling. For smaller rolls, shape into eight balls. Use a bowl that measures at least 10 inches wide to cover the rolls in step 3. You will need a Dutch oven that holds 5½ quarts or more for this recipe.

1 Lay 18 by 12-inch sheet of parchment paper on counter and, using pencil, draw 9-inch circle in center of parchment. Flip parchment ink side down and spray lightly with vegetable oil spray.

2 shape dough Transfer dough seam side up onto lightly floured counter and pat into rough 6 by 9-inch rectangle with short side parallel to counter edge. Cut dough into 6 equal pieces and cover loosely with plastic wrap. Working with 1 piece of dough at a time, pat dough into disk. Working around circumference of dough, fold edges of dough toward center until ball forms. Place ball seam side down on counter and, using your cupped hand, drag in small circles until dough feels taut and round. (Tackiness of dough against counter and circular motion should work dough into smooth, even ball, but if dough sticks to your hands, lightly dust top of dough with flour.)

3 second rise Arrange dough balls evenly within circle on prepared parchment (5≈rolls around perimeter and 1 roll in center) and cover with inverted large bowl. Let rise until dough has doubled in size and springs back minimally when poked gently with your finger, 1 to 2 hours.

4 Thirty minutes before baking, adjust oven rack to middle position, place Dutch oven with lid on rack, and heat oven to 475 degrees. Using sharp knife or single-edge razor blade, make one 1½-inch-long, ½-inch-deep slash with swift, fluid motion along top of each roll. Carefully remove hot pot from oven and, using parchment as sling, gently transfer dough to hot pot. Working quickly and reinforcing scores in top of rolls if needed, cover pot and return to oven.

5 bake Reduce oven temperature to 425 degrees and bake rolls in covered pot for 30 minutes. Remove lid and continue to bake until rolls are deep golden brown and register at least 205 degrees, 10 to 15 minutes. Using parchment sling, carefully remove rolls from hot pot and transfer to wire rack; discard parchment. Let cool completely, about 1 hour, before serving.

Arrange dough balls within circle on parchment.

Cover with inverted bowl.

Make slash in top of each roll.

Transfer dough to pot.

NO-KNEAD RUSTIC
SANDWICH LOAF

makes 1 loaf

**1 recipe No-Knead Rustic Loaf,
made through step 3**

We have a whole chapter of sandwich breads baked in a loaf pan (see page 154). Some are swirled with a filling, some are made a bit heartier with whole grains, and some have a substantial coating of seeds, but their main elements are constant: a plush, easy-to-slice crumb and a delicate crust. But who says a square slice of sandwich bread can't have the stronger chew and crackling crust of a free-form rustic bread? Form this dough into a loaf, place in the pan, bake the loaf in the pan right in the preheated Dutch oven (yes, really!) and you have the best of both worlds. Slices of this bread will fit in your lunch bag but also hold up to the most slathered and stacked of sandwich fillings. A toasted slice can support as much avocado as you can eat, the largest heirloom tomato slices, or a luxuriously liberal spreading of butter. You will need a Dutch oven that holds 5½ quarts or more for this recipe.

1 shape dough After letting dough rest in step 3, grease 8½ by 4½-inch loaf pan. Transfer dough seam side up onto lightly floured counter and, using your lightly floured hands, pat into rough 8 by 6-inch rectangle, with long side parallel to counter edge. Roll dough away from you into firm cylinder, keeping roll taut by tucking it under itself as you go. Pinch seam closed and place loaf seam side down in prepared pan, pressing dough gently into corners.

2 second rise Cover loosely with greased plastic and let rise until loaf reaches 1 inch above lip of pan and dough springs back minimally when poked gently with your knuckle, 1 to 1½ hours.

3 Thirty minutes before baking, adjust oven rack to middle position, place Dutch oven with lid on rack, and heat oven to 475 degrees. Using sharp knife or single-edge razor blade, make one 3-inch-long, ½-inch-deep slash with swift, fluid motion along top of loaf. Carefully remove hot pot from oven and gently transfer pan with dough to hot pot. Working quickly, cover pot and return to oven.

4 bake Reduce oven temperature to 425 degrees and bake loaf in covered pot for≈30 minutes. Remove lid and continue to bake until loaf is deep golden brown and registers at least 205 degrees, 10 to 15 minutes. Carefully remove loaf and pan from hot pot and transfer to wire rack to cool for 15 minutes. Remove loaf from pan and let cool completely on wire rack, about 3 hours, before slicing.

Pat dough into rectangle.

Roll dough into firm cylinder.

Pinch seam closed.

Place dough in pan.

Place loaf pan in Dutch oven.

WHOLE-WHEAT RUSTIC LOAF

makes 1 loaf

- **2** cups (11 ounces) bread flour
- **1** cup (5½ ounces) whole-wheat flour
- **1½** teaspoons table salt
- **¼** teaspoon instant or rapid-rise yeast
- **1** cup (8 ounces) water, room temperature
- **½** cup (4 ounces) mild-flavored lager, room temperature
- **1** tablespoon distilled white vinegar

why this recipe works Add the nutty, complex taste of whole-wheat flour to a rustic loaf, and you have a texture and flavor marvel. But the structure-interrupting properties of whole-wheat flour can be even more challenging to overcome with rustic breads than with rolls and sandwich loaves—a strong gluten network is absolutely essential to the chewy, open crumb expected of these loaves. We replace a third of the flour in our original No-Knead Rustic Loaf (page 186) with whole-wheat flour and subtly increase the hydration to produce a light and appropriately moist loaf with a dark, chewy crust. Yes, a marvel. We prefer King Arthur brand bread flour in this recipe; the dough will be slightly stickier if you use a lower-protein bread flour. While we prefer the flavor that beer adds, you can substitute an equal amount of water. You will need a bowl that is at least 9 inches wide and 4 inches deep to cover the dough in step 6.

1 make dough Whisk bread flour, whole-wheat flour, salt, and yeast together in large bowl. Using rubber spatula, fold water, beer, and vinegar into flour mixture, scraping up dry flour from bottom of bowl and pressing dough until cohesive and shaggy and all flour is incorporated.

2 first rise Cover bowl tightly with plastic wrap and let sit at room temperature for at least 8 hours or up to 18 hours.

3 fold and rest Using greased bowl scraper or your wet fingertips, fold dough over itself by lifting and folding edge of dough toward middle and pressing to seal. Turn bowl 90 degrees and fold dough again; repeat turning bowl and folding dough 6 more times (for a total of 8 folds). Flip dough seam side down in bowl, cover with plastic, and let rest for 15 minutes.

4 shape dough Lay 18 by 12-inch sheet of parchment paper on counter and spray lightly with vegetable oil spray. Transfer dough seam side up onto lightly floured counter and pat into rough 9-inch circle using your lightly floured hands. Using bowl scraper or your floured fingertips, lift and fold edge of dough toward center, pressing to seal. Repeat 5 more times (for a total of 6 folds), evenly spacing folds around circumference of dough. Press down on dough to seal, then use bench scraper to gently flip dough seam side down.

5 Using both hands, cup side of dough furthest away from you and pull dough toward you, keeping pinky fingers and side of palm in contact with counter and applying slight pressure to dough as it drags to create tension. (If dough slides across surface of counter without rolling, remove excess flour. If dough sticks to counter or your hands, lightly sprinkle counter or hands with flour.) Rotate dough ball 90 degrees, reposition dough ball at top of counter, and repeat pulling dough until taut round ball forms, at least 4 more times. Using your floured hands or bench scraper, transfer dough seam side down to center of prepared parchment.

6 **second rise** Cover dough with inverted large bowl. Let rise until dough has doubled in size and dough springs back minimally when poked gently with your finger, 1 to 2 hours.

7 Thirty minutes before baking, adjust oven rack to middle position, place Dutch oven with lid on rack and heat oven to 475 degrees. Using sharp knife or single-edge razor blade, make one 6-inch-long, ½-inch-deep slash with swift, fluid motion along top of loaf. Carefully remove hot pot from oven and, using parchment as sling, gently transfer dough to hot pot. Working quickly and reinforcing score in top of loaf if needed, cover pot, and return to oven.

8 **bake** Reduce oven temperature to 425 degrees and bake loaf in covered pot for 30 minutes. Remove lid and continue to bake until loaf is deep golden brown and registers at least 205 degrees, 10 to 15 minutes. Using parchment sling, carefully remove loaf from hot pot and transfer to wire rack; discard parchment. Let cool completely, about 3 hours, before slicing.

total time 13¾ hours

25 min.	8 hours	20 min.	15 min.	1 hour	40 min.	3 hours
make dough	first rise	fold + rest	shape dough	second rise	bake	cool

» **Take your time** To make over 24 hours, let dough sit for up to 18 hours in step 2.

CRANBERRY WALNUT BREAD

makes 1 loaf

2 cups (11 ounces) bread flour

1 cup (5½ ounces) whole-wheat flour

½ cup dried cranberries

½ cup walnuts, toasted and chopped

1½ teaspoons table salt

¼ teaspoon instant or rapid-rise yeast

1½ cups plus 2 tablespoons (13 ounces) water, room temperature

1 tablespoon distilled white vinegar

why this recipe works   Tart dried cranberries and rich walnuts stud this hearty, chewy loaf that would be great toasted and slathered with butter for breakfast, or equally delicious as a vehicle for a stellar post-Thanksgiving turkey sandwich. To get the best distribution of cranberries and walnuts, we add them at the mixing stage, toasting the walnuts first to bring out their nuttiness. Using bread flour and whole-wheat flour creates the chewy yet hearty texture we look for, and incorporating a bit more water than in our regular whole-wheat loaf keeps the crumb moist and tender even when adding a generous amount of thirsty dried fruit. We prefer King Arthur brand bread flour in this recipe; the dough will be slightly stickier if you use a lower-protein bread flour. You will need a bowl that is at least 9 inches wide and 4 inches deep to cover the dough in step 6.

1   make dough   Whisk bread flour, whole-wheat flour, cranberries, walnuts, salt, and yeast together in large bowl. Using rubber spatula, fold water and vinegar into flour mixture, scraping up dry flour from bottom of bowl and pressing dough until cohesive and shaggy and all flour is incorporated.

2   first rise   Cover bowl tightly with plastic wrap and let sit at room temperature for at least 8 hours or up to 18 hours.

3   fold and rest   Using greased bowl scraper or your m fingertips, fold dough over itself by lifting and folding edge of dough toward middle and pressing to seal. Turn bowl 90 degrees and fold dough again; repeat turning bowl and folding dough 6 more times (for a total of 8 folds). Flip dough seam side down in bowl, cover with plastic, and let rest for 15 minutes.

4   shape dough   Lay 18 by 12-inch sheet of parchment paper on counter and spray lightly with vegetable oil spray. Transfer dough seam side up onto lightly floured counter and pat into rough 9-inch circle using your lightly floured hands. Using bowl scraper or your floured fingertips, lift and fold edge of dough toward center, pressing to seal. Repeat 5 more times (for a total of 6 folds), evenly spacing folds around circumference of dough. Press down on dough to seal, then use bench scraper to gently flip dough seam side down.

5   Using both hands, cup side of dough furthest away from you and pull dough toward you, keeping pinky fingers and side of palm in contact with counter and applying slight pressure to dough as it drags to create tension. (If dough slides across surface of counter without rolling, remove excess flour. If dough sticks to counter or your hands, lightly sprinkle counter or hands with flour.) Rotate dough ball 90 degrees, reposition dough ball at top of counter, and repeat pulling dough until taut round ball forms, at least 4 more times.

6   second rise   Using your floured hands or bench scraper, transfer dough seam side down to center of prepared parchment and cover with inverted large bowl. Let rise until dough has doubled in size and dough springs back minimally when poked gently with your finger, 1 to 2 hours.

7 Thirty minutes before baking, adjust oven rack to middle position, place Dutch oven with lid on rack, and heat oven to 475 degrees. Using sharp knife or single-edge razor blade, make one 6-inch-long, ½-inch-deep slash with swift, fluid motion along top of loaf. Carefully remove hot pot from oven and, using parchment as sling, gently transfer dough to hot pot. Working quickly and reinforcing score in top of loaf if needed, cover pot, and return to oven.

8 bake Reduce oven temperature to 425 degrees and bake loaf in covered pot for 30 minutes. Remove lid and continue to bake until loaf is deep golden brown and registers at least 205 degrees, 10 to 15 minutes. Using parchment sling, carefully remove loaf from hot pot and transfer to wire rack; discard parchment. Let cool completely, about 3 hours, before slicing.

total time 13¾ hours

25 min.	8 hours	25 min.	15 min.	1 hour	40 min.	3 hours
make dough	first rise	fold + rest	shape dough	second rise	bake	cool

» **Take your time** To make over 24 hours, let dough sit for up to 18 hours in step 2.

SEEDED OAT BREAD

makes 1 loaf

- **3** tablespoons raw pepitas
- **3** tablespoons raw sunflower seeds
- **4** teaspoons sesame seeds
- **4** teaspoons poppy seeds
- **2** teaspoons caraway seeds
- **⅔** cup (2 ounces) old-fashioned rolled oats
- **½** cup (4 ounces) boiling water plus ¾ cup (6 ounces) room temperature water
- **½** cup (4 ounces) mild lager, room temperature
- **1** tablespoon distilled white vinegar
- **2** cups (11 ounces) bread flour
- **⅔** cup (3⅔ ounces) whole-wheat flour
- **1½** teaspoons table salt
- **¼** teaspoon instant or rapid-rise yeast

why this recipe works   We're absolutely wild about this loaf. It's superlatively hearty—you can really sink your teeth into it—yet still maintains the moist texture and springy crumb of a proper rustic loaf. We pack in three starring players: oats, seeds, and whole-wheat flour. So many water-hungry components can lead to an overly dense loaf. To avoid this, we hydrate old-fashioned rolled oats with boiling water and up the overall hydration of the loaf. For the best distribution of a variety of seeds, we incorporate them during mixing, and then cover the loaf with more seeds for nutty crunch. We prefer King Arthur brand bread flour in this recipe; the dough will be slightly stickier if you use a lower-protein bread flour. While we prefer the flavor that beer adds, you can substitute an equal amount of water. You will need a bowl that is at least 9 inches wide and 4 inches deep to cover dough in step 7. For an accurate measurement of boiling water, bring a kettle of water to a boil and then measure out the desired amount.

1   make dough   Adjust oven rack to middle position and heat oven to 325 degrees. Combine pepitas, sunflower seeds, sesame seeds, poppy seeds, and caraway seeds in bowl. Measure out 6 tablespoons seed mixture, spreading into even layer on rimmed baking sheet, and roast until seeds are lightly golden and fragrant, about 10 minutes. Transfer to wire rack and set aside to cool for 15 minutes. Reserve remaining untoasted seed mixture.

2   Meanwhile, combine oats and boiling water in medium bowl; let sit until water is absorbed and oats have cooled to room temperature, about 15 minutes. Stir in room-temperature water, beer, and vinegar. Whisk bread flour, whole-wheat flour, salt, yeast, and cooled toasted seed mixture together in large bowl. Using rubber spatula, fold oat and water mixture into flour mixture, scraping up dry flour from bottom of bowl and pressing dough until cohesive and shaggy and all flour is incorporated.

3   first rise   Cover bowl tightly with plastic wrap and let sit at room temperature for at least 8 hours or up to 18 hours.

4   fold and rest   Using greased bowl scraper or your wet fingertips, fold dough over itself by lifting and folding edge of dough toward middle and pressing to seal. Turn bowl 90 degrees and fold dough again; repeat turning bowl and folding dough 6 more times (for a total of 8 folds). Flip dough seam side down in bowl, cover with plastic, and let rest for 15 minutes.

5 shape dough   Lay 18 by 12-inch sheet of parchment paper on counter and spray lightly with vegetable oil spray. Transfer dough seam side up onto lightly floured counter and pat into rough 9-inch circle using your lightly floured hands. Using bowl scraper or your floured fingertips, lift and fold edge of dough toward center, pressing to seal. Repeat 5 more times (for a total of 6 folds), evenly spacing folds around circumference of dough. Press down on dough to seal, then use bench scraper to gently flip dough seam side down.

6   Using both hands, cup side of dough furthest away from you and pull dough toward you, keeping pinky fingers and side of palm in contact with counter and applying slight pressure to dough as it drags to create tension. (If dough slides across surface of counter without rolling, remove excess flour. If dough sticks to counter or your hands, lightly sprinkle counter or hands with flour.) Rotate dough ball 90 degrees, reposition dough ball at top of counter, and repeat pulling dough until taut round ball forms, at least 4 more times. Using your floured hands or bench scraper, transfer dough seam side down to center of prepared parchment, then spray or gently brush top of loaf with water. Sprinkle reserved untoasted seed mixture over top and use your hands to gently press seeds onto sides of loaf.

7 second rise   Cover dough with inverted large bowl and let rise until dough has doubled in size and dough springs back minimally when poked gently with your finger, 1 to 2 hours.

8   Thirty minutes before baking, adjust oven rack to middle position, place Dutch oven with lid on rack, and heat oven to 475 degrees. Using sharp knife or single-edge razor blade, make one 6-inch-long, ½-inch-deep slash with swift, fluid motion along top of loaf. Carefully remove hot pot from oven and, using parchment as sling, gently transfer dough to hot pot. Working quickly and reinforcing score in top of loaf if needed, cover pot and return to oven.

9 bake   Reduce oven temperature to 425 degrees and bake loaf in covered pot for 30 minutes. Remove lid and continue to bake until loaf is deep golden brown and registers at least 205 degrees, 10 to 15 minutes. Using parchment sling, carefully remove loaf from hot pot and transfer to wire rack; discard parchment. Let cool completely, about 3 hours, before slicing.

total time 14¼ hours

55 min.	8 hours	20 min.	20 min.	1 hour	40 min.	3 hours
make dough	first rise	fold + rest	shape dough	second rise	bake	cool

»   **Take your time**   To make over 24 hours, let dough sit for up to 18 hours in step 3.

seeded oat bread (page 200)

sprouted wheat berry bread (page 204)

SPROUTED WHEAT BERRY BREAD

makes 1 loaf

¼ cup (1¾ ounces) wheat berries, rinsed

2 cups (16 ounces) water, room temperature, divided

2 cups (11 ounces) bread flour

1 cup (5½ ounces) sprouted wheat flour

1½ teaspoons table salt

¼ teaspoon instant or rapid-rise yeast

½ cup (4 ounces) mild lager, room temperature

1 tablespoon distilled white vinegar

1 tablespoon honey

why this recipe works Sprouted grains have nutritional benefits beyond common whole-grain flour, plus a wholesome flavor and texture, that have boosted their popularity. When grains begin to sprout, or germinate, their digestibility increases dramatically. In our quest for the ideal sprouted grain to use in our bread we tried quinoa, millet, lentils, buckwheat, and wheat berries. We chose wheat berries for their exceptionally nutty flavor and pleasant chew. We also employ sprouted wheat flour: Apart from adding nutrition, sprouted grain flours have a longer shelf life and initiate higher enzymatic activity, breaking down more starches in the dough into fermentable sugars for the yeast to feed on. What this means for your loaf is increased volume and a more open and soft crumb. A touch of honey balances the earthy flavors of the whole grains. If you cannot find sprouted wheat flour, traditional whole-wheat flour will work. We prefer King Arthur brand bread flour in this recipe; the dough will be slightly stickier if you use a lower-protein bread flour. While we prefer the flavor that beer adds, you can substitute an equal amount of water. You will need a bowl that is at least 9 inches wide and 4 inches deep to cover the dough in step 7.

1 Combine wheat berries and 1 cup water in medium bowl, cover tightly with plastic wrap, and let sit at room temperature until wheat berries are softened, at least 8 hours or up to 16 hours. Drain wheat berries in fine-mesh strainer, return to bowl and cover with plastic. Puncture plastic with a paring knife 8 to 10 times. Let grains sit at room temperature, rinsing and draining grains every 8 hours, until grains begin to sprout, 24 to 36 hours.

2 make dough Whisk bread flour, sprouted wheat flour, salt, and yeast together in large bowl. Whisk remaining 1 cup water, beer, vinegar, and honey in 2-cup liquid measuring cup until honey is dissolved. Using rubber spatula, fold sprouted wheat berries and water mixture into flour mixture, scraping up dry flour from bottom of bowl andpressing dough until cohesive and shaggy and all flour is incorporated.

3 first rise Cover bowl tightly with plastic and let sit at room temperature for at least 8 hours or up to 18 hours.

4 fold and rest Using greased bowl scraper or your wet fingertips, fold dough over itself by lifting and folding edge of dough toward middle and pressing to seal. Turn bowl 90 degrees and fold dough again; repeat turning bowl and folding dough 6 more times (for a total of 8 folds). Flip dough seam side down in bowl, cover with plastic, and let rest for 15 minutes.

Drain softened wheat berries.

Puncture plastic 8 to 10 times.

Rinse and drain every 8 hours.

Finish once beginning to sprout.

5   shape dough   Lay 18 by 12-inch sheet of parchment paper on counter and spray lightly with vegetable oil spray. Transfer dough seam side up onto lightly floured counter and pat into rough 9-inch circle using your lightly floured hands. Using bowl scraper or your floured fingertips, lift and fold edge of dough toward center, pressing to seal. Repeat 5 more times (for a total of 6 folds), evenly spacing folds around circumference of dough. Press down on dough to seal, then use bench scraper to gently flip dough seam side down.

6   Using both hands, cup side of dough furthest away from you and pull dough toward you, keeping pinky fingers and side of palm in contact with counter and applying slight pressure to dough as it drags to create tension. (If dough slides across surface of counter without rolling, remove excess flour. If dough sticks to counter or your hands, lightly sprinkle counter or hands with flour.) Rotate dough ball 90 degrees, reposition dough ball at top of counter, and repeat pulling dough until taut round ball forms, at least 4 more times. Using your floured hands or bench scraper, transfer dough seam side down to center of prepared parchment.

7   second rise   Cover dough with inverted large bowl. Let rise until dough has doubled in size and dough springs back minimally when poked gently with your finger, 1 to 2 hours.

8   Thirty minutes before baking, adjust oven rack to middle position, place Dutch oven with lid on rack and heat oven to 475 degrees. Using sharp knife or single-edge razor blade, make one 6-inch-long, ½-inch-deep slash with swift, fluid motion along top of loaf. Carefully remove hot pot from oven and, using parchment as sling, gently transfer dough to hot pot. Working quickly and reinforcing score in top of loaf if needed, cover pot and return to oven.

9   bake   Reduce oven temperature to 425 degrees and bake loaf in covered pot for 30 minutes. Remove lid and continue to bake until loaf is deep golden brown and registers at least 205 degrees, 10 to 15 minutes. Using parchment sling, remove loaf from pot and transfer to wire rack; discard parchment. Let cool completely, about 3 hours, before serving.

total time 13¾ hours, plus 24 hours sprouting

5 min.	8 hours	20 min.	15 min.	1 hour	40 min.	3 hours
make dough	first rise	fold + rest	shape dough	second rise	bake	cool

» **Take your time** To make over 48 hours, let dough sit for up to 18 hours in step 3.

SPELT BREAD

makes 1 loaf

- **2 cups (11 ounces) bread flour**
- **1 cup (5½ ounces) spelt flour**
- **1½ teaspoons table salt**
- **¼ teaspoon instant or rapid-rise yeast**
- **1 cup (8 ounces) water, room temperature**
- **½ cup (4 ounces) mild lager, room temperature**
- **1 tablespoon distilled white vinegar**

why this recipe works   There are a lot of reasons to like spelt flour, the ancient grain that's seen a surge in popularity in the West in the last 10 years. It's full of fiber, protein, and vitamins, and, because of its high water solubility, its nutrients are quickly absorbed by the body. But as recipe developers, we're most delighted by the grain's rich, sweet, nutty flavor. We use it to make a rustic bread that puts these flavors on display. Combining the spelt flour with bread flour, as we usually do with whole-grain flours, gives us a sturdy loaf with wheaty flavor and the appropriate chew. While we prefer the flavor that beer adds, you can substitute an equal amount of water. You will need a bowl that is at least 9 inches wide and 4 inches deep to cover the dough in step 6.

1   make dough   Whisk bread flour, spelt flour, salt, and yeast together in large bowl. Using rubber spatula, fold water, beer, and vinegar into flour mixture, scraping up dry flour from bottom of bowl and pressing dough until cohesive and shaggy and all flour is incorporated.

2   first rise   Cover bowl tightly with plastic wrap and let sit at room temperature for at least 8 hours or up to 18 hours.

3   fold and rest   Using greased bowl scraper or your wet fingertips, fold dough over itself by lifting and folding edge of dough toward middle and pressing to seal. Turn bowl 90 degrees and fold dough again; repeat turning bowl and folding dough 6 more times (for a total of 8 folds). Flip dough seam side down in bowl, cover with plastic, and let rest for 15 minutes.

4   shape dough   Lay 18 by 12-inch sheet of parchment paper on counter and spray lightly with vegetable oil spray. Transfer dough seam side up onto lightly floured counter and pat into rough 9-inch circle using your lightly floured hands. Using bowl scraper or your floured fingertips, lift and fold edge of dough toward center, pressing to seal. Repeat 5 more times (for a total of 6 folds), evenly spacing folds around circumference of dough. Press down on dough to seal, then use bench scraper to gently flip dough seam side down.

5   Using both hands, cup side of dough furthest away from you and pull dough toward you, keeping pinky fingers and side of palm in contact with counter and applying slight pressure to dough as it drags to create tension. (If dough slides across surface of counter without rolling, remove excess flour. If dough sticks to counter or your hands, lightly sprinkle counter or hands with flour.) Rotate dough ball 90 degrees, reposition dough ball at top of counter, and repeat pulling dough until taut round ball forms, at least 4 more times. Using your floured hands or bench scraper, transfer dough seam side down to center of prepared parchment.

6   second rise   Cover dough with inverted large bowl. Let rise until dough has doubled in size and dough springs back minimally when poked gently with your finger, 1 to 2 hours.

7 Thirty minutes before baking, adjust oven rack to middle position, place Dutch oven with lid on rack, and heat oven to 475 degrees. Using sharp knife or single-edge razor blade, make one 6-inch-long, ½-inch-deep slash with swift, fluid motion along top of loaf. Carefully remove hot pot from oven and, using parchment as sling, gently transfer dough to hot pot. Working quickly and reinforcing score in top of loaf if needed, cover pot and return to oven.

8 bake Reduce oven temperature to 425 degrees and bake loaf in covered pot for 30 minutes. Remove lid and continue to bake until loaf is deep golden brown and registers at least 205 degrees, 10 to 15 minutes. Using parchment sling, carefully remove loaf from hot pot and transfer to wire rack; discard parchment. Let cool completely, about 3 hours, before slicing.

total time 13¾ hours

25 min.	8 hours	20 min.	15 min.	1 hour	40 min.	3 hours
make dough	first rise	fold + rest	shape dough	second rise	bake	cool

» **Take your time** To make over 24 hours, let dough sit for up to 18 hours in step 2.

SPICY OLIVE SPELT BREAD

makes 1 loaf

how-to

2 cups (11 ounces) bread flour

1 cup (5½ ounces) spelt flour

1½ teaspoons table salt

¼ teaspoon instant or rapid-rise yeast

1 cup (8 ounces) water, room temperature

½ cup (4 ounces) mild lager, room temperature

1 tablespoon distilled white vinegar

¾ cup pitted olives, rinsed, patted dry, and chopped

2 tablespoons minced fresh oregano

1 tablespoon minced, stemmed oil-packed Calabrian chiles

why this recipe works Olives bring enlivening briny bites to hearty breads (see page 206); we wanted to kick them up further by adding some heat to an olive loaf. After trying a few different chiles, we landed on vibrantly hot Calabrian chiles (jarred, as any fresh chile was too harsh). As for the olives, patting them dry before chopping and folding them in prevents their moisture from altering the hydration, which would make the dough sticky and unworkable. We enjoy the contrast between these pockets of flavor and the deep, nutty taste of spelt flour. You'll love cutting generous slices of this bread for cheese and charcuterie boards and Italian sandwiches, as well as serving with soups and stews. We prefer King Arthur brand bread flour in this recipe; the dough will be slightly stickier if you use a lower-protein bread flour. While we prefer the flavor that beer adds, you can substitute an equal amount of water. If you can't find Calabrian chiles, you can use 1½ teaspoons red pepper flakes. Avoid oil-cured olives in this recipe as their flavor will be too intense. You will need a bowl that is at least 9 inches wide and 4 inches deep to cover dough in step 6.

1 make dough Whisk bread flour, spelt flour, salt, and yeast together in large bowl. Using rubber spatula, fold water, beer, and vinegar into flour mixture, scraping up dry flour from bottom of bowl and pressing dough until cohesive and shaggy and all flour is incorporated.

2 first rise Cover bowl tightly with plastic wrap and let sit at room temperature for at least 8 hours or up to 18 hours.

3 fold and rest Mix olives, oregano, and chiles together in small bowl. Sprinkle half of olive mixture evenly over dough. Using greased bowl scraper or your wet fingertips, fold dough over itself by lifting and folding edge of dough toward middle and pressing to seal. Turn bowl 90 degrees and fold dough again; repeat turning bowl and folding dough 2 more times. Sprinkle remaining olive mixture over dough and repeat folding dough 4 more times (for a total of 8 folds). Flip dough seam side down in bowl, cover with plastic, and let rest for 15 minutes.

total time 13¾ hours

25 min.	8 hours	25 min.	15 min.	1 hour	40 min.	3 hours
make dough	first rise	fold + rest	shape dough	second rise	bake	cool

» **Take your time** To make over 24 hours, let dough sit for up to 18 hours in step 2.

4 shape dough Lay 18 by 12-inch sheet of parchment paper on counter and spray lightly with vegetable oil spray. Transfer dough seam side up onto lightly floured counter and pat into rough 9-inch circle using your lightly floured hands. Using bowl scraper or your floured fingertips, lift and fold edge of dough toward center, pressing to seal. Repeat 5 more times (for a total of 6 folds), evenly spacing folds around circumference of dough. Press down on dough to seal then use bench scraper to gently flip dough seam side down.

5 Using both hands, cup side of dough furthest away from you and pull dough toward you, keeping pinky fingers and side of palm in contact with counter and applying slight pressure to dough as it drags to create tension. (If dough slides across surface of counter without rolling, remove excess flour. If dough sticks to counter or your hands, lightly sprinkle counter or hands with flour.) Rotate dough ball 90 degrees, reposition dough ball at top of counter, and repeat pulling dough until taut round ball forms, at least 4 more times. Using your floured hands or bench scraper, transfer dough seam side down to center of prepared parchment.

6 second rise Cover dough with inverted large bowl and let rise until dough has doubled in size and dough springs back minimally when poked gently with your finger, 1 to 2 hours.

7 Thirty minutes before baking, adjust oven rack to middle position, place Dutch oven with lid on rack and heat oven to 475 degrees. Using sharp knife or single-edge razor blade, make one 6-inch-long, ½-inch-deep slash with swift, fluid motion along top of loaf. Carefully remove hot pot from oven and, using parchment as sling, gently transfer dough to hot pot. Working quickly and reinforcing score in top of loaf if needed, cover pot and return to oven.

8 bake Reduce oven temperature to 425 degrees and bake loaf in covered pot for 30 minutes. Remove lid and continue to bake until loaf is deep golden brown and registers at least 205 degrees, 10 to 15 minutes. Using parchment sling, carefully remove loaf from hot pot and transfer to wire rack; discard parchment. Let cool completely, about 3 hours, before slicing.

Sprinkle olive mixture over dough.

Fold dough over itself toward middle, pressing to seal.

spicy olive spelt bread (page 208)

anadama bread (page 212)

ANADAMA BREAD

makes 1 loaf

- **½ cup (2½ ounces) plus 2 table-spoons cornmeal, divided**
- **½ cup (4 ounces) boiling water plus 1 cup (8 ounces) water, room temperature**
- **¼ cup molasses**
- **1 tablespoon distilled white vinegar**
- **2½ cups (13¾ ounces) bread flour**
- **¼ cup (¾ ounce) nonfat dry milk powder**
- **1½ teaspoons table salt**
- **¼ teaspoon instant or rapid-rise yeast**

why this recipe works Anadama bread is a New England classic with two defining ingredients, molasses and cornmeal, that have a centuries-old association with the region. We love the flavor and texture of the bread so we thought it was a great candidate for the no-knead treatment. We presoak the cornmeal with boiling water to hydrate it so the bread's interior is moist, soft, and pillowy. Anadama recipes typically include a dairy component to enrich the dough and enhance its softness. Because the dough rises at room temperature for a while, we opted for dry milk powder, which also produces a lighter, more open crumb than other options. A dialed-back amount of molasses adds flavor without weighing down the dough or turning the loaf too dark in the oven. Anadama makes the perfect accompaniment to hearty winter stew, and it's great toasted and spread with butter or even sliced for an everyday sandwich bread. You will need a bowl that is at least 9 inches wide and 4 inches deep to cover dough in step 8. Yellow steel-ground cornmeal works best here; don't use stone-ground whole-grain or white cornmeal in this recipe.

1 make dough Combine ½ cup cornmeal and boiling water in medium bowl; let sit until water is absorbed and cornmeal has cooled to room temperature, about 15 minutes. Add room-temperature water, molasses, and vinegar to cooled cornmeal mixture, whisking until molasses is dissolved.

2 Whisk flour, milk powder, salt, and yeast together in large bowl. Using rubber spatula, fold cornmeal mixture into flour mixture, scraping up dry flour from bottom of bowl and pressing dough until cohesive and shaggy and all flour is incorporated.

3 first rise Cover bowl tightly with plastic wrap and let sit at room temperature for at least 8 hours or up to 18 hours.

4 fold and rest Using greased bowl scraper or your wet fingertips, fold dough over itself by lifting and folding edge of dough toward middle and pressing to seal. Turn bowl 90 degrees and fold dough again; repeat turning bowl and folding dough 6 more times (for a total of 8 folds). Flip dough seam side down in bowl, cover with plastic, and let rest for 15 minutes.

5 shape dough Lay 18 by 12-inch sheet of parchment paper on counter and spray lightly with vegetable oil spray. Transfer dough seam side up to lightly floured counter and pat into rough 9-inch circle using your lightly floured hands. Using bowl scraper or your floured fingertips, lift and fold edge of dough toward center, pressing to seal. Repeat 5 more times (for a total of 6 folds), evenly spacing folds around circumference of dough. Press down on dough to seal then use bench scraper to gently flip dough seam side down.

6 Using both hands, cup side of dough furthest away from you and pull dough toward you, keeping pinky fingers and side of palm in contact with counter and applying slight pressure to dough as it drags to create tension. (If dough slides across surface of counter without rolling, remove excess flour. If dough sticks to counter or your hands, lightly sprinkle counter or hands with flour.) Rotate dough ball 90 degrees, reposition dough ball at top of counter, and repeat pulling dough until taut round ball forms, at least 4 more times.

7 Using your floured hands or bench scraper, transfer dough seam side down to center of prepared parchment then spray or gently brush top of loaf with water. Sprinkle remaining 2 tablespoons cornmeal over top and use your hands to gently press cornmeal onto sides of loaf.

8 second rise Cover dough with inverted large bowl and let rise until dough has doubled in size and dough springs back minimally when poked gently with your finger, 1 to 2 hours.

9 Thirty minutes before baking, adjust oven rack to middle position, place Dutch oven with lid on rack, and heat oven to 475 degrees. Using sharp knife or single-edge razor blade, make one 6-inch-long, ½-inch-deep slash with swift, fluid motion along top of loaf. Carefully remove hot pot from oven and, using parchment as sling, gently transfer dough to hot pot. Working quickly and reinforcing score in top of loaf if needed, cover pot and return to oven.

10 bake Reduce oven temperature to 425 degrees and bake loaf in covered pot for 30 minutes. Remove lid and continue to bake until loaf is deep golden brown and registers at least 205 degrees, 10 to 15 minutes. Using parchment sling, carefully remove loaf from hot pot and transfer to wire rack; discard parchment. Let cool completely, about 3 hours, before slicing.

total time 14¾ hours

45 min.	8 hours	20 min.	20 min.	1 hour	40 min.	3 hours
make dough	first rise	fold + rest	shape dough	second rise	bake	cool

» **Take your time** To make over 24 hours, let dough sit for up to 18 hours in step 3.

RYE BREAD

makes 1 loaf

- **2 cups (11 ounces) bread flour**
- **1 cup (5½ ounces) medium rye flour**
- **1½ teaspoons table salt**
- **¼ teaspoon instant or rapid-rise yeast**
- **1¼ cups plus 2 tablespoons (11 ounces) water, room temperature**
- **1 tablespoon distilled white vinegar**

why this recipe works   To maintain a moist, sliceable texture, rye breads barely incorporate rye flour (you might mistake its flavor for that of the caraway seeds that are sometimes in the dough). We wanted the nuttiness of a really rye-forward loaf, not with the closed crumb of a deli bread but with the chewy, open, rustic texture of our other Dutch-oven breads. To pack in more rye flour without making the loaf dry or crumbly, we add more water than most recipes call for. For the fermented tang of these breads, beer tasted out of place with the rye flour. We incorporated a splash of vinegar instead with great result. We prefer King Arthur brand bread flour in this recipe; the dough will be slightly stickier if you use a lower-protein bread flour. You will need a bowl that is at least 9 inches wide and 4 inches deep to cover dough in step 6.

1 make dough   Whisk bread flour, rye flour, salt, and yeast together in large bowl. Using rubber spatula, fold water and vinegar into flour mixture, scraping up dry flour from bottom of bowl and pressing dough until cohesive and shaggy and all flour is incorporated.

2 first rise   Cover bowl tightly with plastic wrap and let sit at room temperature for at least 8 hours or up to 18 hours.

3 fold and rest   Using greased bowl scraper or your wet fingertips, fold dough over itself by lifting and folding edge of dough toward middle and pressing to seal. Turn bowl 90 degrees and fold dough again; repeat turning bowl and folding dough 6 more times (for a total of 8 folds). Flip dough seam side down in bowl, cover with plastic, and let rest for 15 minutes.

4 shape dough   Lay 18 by 12-inch sheet of parchment paper on counter and spray lightly with vegetable oil spray. Transfer dough seam side up to lightly floured counter and pat into rough 9-inch circle using your lightly floured hands. Using bowl scraper or your floured fingertips, lift and fold edge of dough toward center, pressing to seal. Repeat 5 more times (for a total of 6 folds), evenly spacing folds around circumference of dough. Press down on dough to seal then use bench scraper to gently flip dough seam side down.

5   Using both hands, cup side of dough furthest away from you and pull dough toward you, keeping pinky fingers and side of palm in contact with counter and applying slight pressure to dough as it drags to create tension. (If dough slides across surface of counter without rolling, remove excess flour. If dough sticks to counter or your hands, lightly sprinkle counter or hands with flour.) Rotate dough ball 90 degrees, reposition dough ball at top of counter, and repeat pulling dough until taut round ball forms, at least 4 more times. Using your floured hands or bench scraper, transfer dough seam side down to center of prepared parchment.

6 **second rise** Cover dough with inverted large bowl. Let rise until dough has doubled in size and dough springs back minimally when poked gently with your finger, 1 to 2 hours.

7 Thirty minutes before baking, adjust oven rack to middle position, place Dutch oven with lid on rack, and heat oven to 475 degrees. Using sharp knife or single-edge razor blade, make one 6-inch-long, ½-inch-deep slash with swift, fluid motion along top of loaf. Carefully remove hot pot from oven and, using parchment as sling, gently transfer dough to hot pot. Working quickly and reinforcing score in top of loaf if needed, cover pot and return to oven.

8 **bake** Reduce oven temperature to 425 degrees and bake loaf in covered pot for 30 minutes. Remove lid and continue to bake until loaf is deep golden brown and registers at least 205 degrees, 10 to 15 minutes. Using parchment sling, carefully remove loaf from hot pot and transfer to wire rack; discard parchment. Let cool completely, about 3 hours, before slicing.

total time 13¾ hours

25 min.	8 hours	20 min.	15 min.	1 hour	40 min.	3 hours
make dough	first rise	fold + rest	shape dough	second rise	bake	cool

» **Take your time** To make over 24 hours, let dough sit for up to 18 hours in step 2.

COCOA CHERRY RYE BREAD

makes 1 loaf

---

2 cups (11 ounces) bread flour

1 cup (5½ ounces) medium rye flour

⅓ cup (1 ounce) Dutch-processed cocoa powder

2 tablespoons packed brown sugar

1½ teaspoons table salt

¼ teaspoon instant or rapid-rise yeast

1½ cups plus 2 tablespoons (13 ounces) water, room temperature

1 tablespoon distilled white vinegar

¾ cup dried cherries, divided

why this recipe works   Chocolate and rye are a pair that's become popular in baked goods from cookies to coffee cake for good reason: The bitter notes of chocolate pair well with the earthy, nutty rye flour for a flavor that's quite sophisticated. To create a chocolate-rye bread studded with dried fruit, we add cocoa powder (and a little extra water) to our Rye Bread (see page 214). We found that Dutch-processed cocoa powder created a taller, more open-crumbed loaf than one made with more acidic natural cocoa. To balance the dark, earthy backdrop, we add a couple tablespoons of brown sugar and a handful of tart dried cherries. Slather a slice with butter and sprinkle with flaky salt for a unique indulgence. We prefer King Arthur brand bread flour in this recipe; the dough will be slightly stickier if you use a lower-protein bread flour. You will need a bowl that is at least 9 inches wide and 4 inches deep to cover dough in step 6.

1   make dough   Whisk bread flour, rye flour, cocoa powder, brown sugar, salt, and yeast together in large bowl. Using rubber spatula, fold water and vinegar into flour mixture, scraping up dry flour from bottom of bowl and pressing dough until cohesive and shaggy and all flour is incorporated.

2   first rise   Cover bowl tightly with plastic wrap and let sit at room temperature for at least 8 hours or up to 18 hours.

3   fold and rest   Sprinkle half of dried cherries over dough. Using greased bowl scraper or your wet fingertips, fold dough over itself by lifting and folding edge of dough toward middle and pressing to seal. Turn bowl 90 degrees and fold dough again; repeat turning bowl and folding dough 2 more times. Sprinkle remaining dried cherries over dough, and fold dough 4 more times (for a total of 8 folds). Flip dough seam side down in bowl, cover with plastic, and let rest for 15 minutes.

4   shape dough   Lay 18 by 12-inch sheet of parchment paper on counter and spray lightly with vegetable oil spray. Transfer dough seam side up to lightly floured counter and pat into rough 9-inch circle using your lightly floured hands. Using bowl scraper or your floured fingertips, lift and fold edge of dough toward center, pressing to seal. Repeat 5 more times (for a total of 6 folds), evenly spacing folds around circumference of dough. Press down on dough to seal then use bench scraper to gently flip dough seam side down.

5   Using both hands, cup side of dough furthest away from you and pull dough toward you, keeping pinky fingers and side of palm in contact with counter and applying slight pressure to dough as it drags to create tension. (If dough slides across surface of counter without rolling, remove excess flour. If dough sticks to counter or your hands, lightly sprinkle counter or hands with flour.) Rotate dough ball 90 degrees, reposition dough ball at top of counter, and repeat pulling dough until taut round ball forms, at least 4 more times. Using your floured hands or bench scraper, transfer dough seam side down to center of prepared parchment.

6 **second rise** Cover dough with inverted large bowl. Let rise until dough has doubled in size and dough springs back minimally when poked gently with your finger, 1 to 2 hours.

7 Thirty minutes before baking, adjust oven rack to middle position, place Dutch oven with lid on rack, and heat oven to 475 degrees. Using sharp knife or single-edge razor blade, make one 6-inch-long, ½-inch-deep slash with swift, fluid motion along top of loaf. Carefully remove hot pot from oven and, using parchment as sling, gently transfer dough to hot pot. Working quickly and reinforcing score in top of loaf if needed, cover pot and return to oven.

8 **bake** Reduce oven temperature to 425 degrees and bake loaf in covered pot for 30 minutes. Remove lid and continue to bake until loaf registers at least 205 degrees, 10 to 15 minutes. Using parchment sling, carefully remove loaf from hot pot and transfer to wire rack; discard parchment. Let cool completely, about 3 hours, before slicing.

total time 13¾ hours

make dough	first rise	fold + rest	shape dough	second rise	bake	cool
25 min.	8 hours	20 min.	15 min.	1 hour	40 min.	3 hours

» **Take your time** To make over 24 hours, let dough sit for up to 18 hours in step 2.

SESAME DURUM BREAD

makes 1 loaf

2 cups (10 ounces) durum flour (see page 12)

1 cup (5½ ounces) bread flour

1½ teaspoons table salt

¼ teaspoon instant or rapid-rise yeast

1½ cups (12 ounces) water, room temperature

1 tablespoon distilled white vinegar

¼ cup sesame seeds, divided

why this recipe works   Loaves made with durum flour are common in Italy where the same flour is also used for pasta and pizza doughs. They have a delightfully light, open, tender crumb with a deep golden color. We tested multiple ratios of durum flour to bread flour and landed on a generous 65 percent durum flour. This amount lets us increase the hydration for the trademark wide-open crumb and custard-y texture, without having to deal with a sticky, unworkable dough. A coating of sesame seeds complements the sweet, nutty nature of the durum flour and gives additional texture to the exterior— we particularly love the nutty flavor of the browned seeds on the bottom of the loaf. Use durum flour in this recipe, which is more finely ground than semolina flour. Avoid Caputo Semola Rimacinata (found commonly in grocery stores). We prefer King Arthur brand bread flour in this recipe; the dough will be slightly stickier if you use a lower-protein bread flour. You will need a bowl that is at least 9 inches wide and 4 inches deep to cover the dough in step 6.

1 make dough   Whisk durum flour, bread flour, salt, and yeast together in large bowl. Using rubber spatula, fold water and vinegar into flour mixture, scraping up dry flour from bottom of bowl and pressing dough until cohesive and shaggy and all flour is incorporated.

2 first rise   Cover bowl tightly with plastic wrap and let sit at room temperature for at least 8 hours or up to 18 hours.

3 fold and rest   Using greased bowl scraper or your wet fingertips, fold dough over itself by lifting and folding edge of dough toward middle and pressing to seal. Turn bowl 90 degrees and fold dough again; repeat turning bowl and folding dough 6 more times (for a total of 8 folds). Flip dough seam side down in bowl, cover with plastic, and let rest for 15 minutes.

4 shape dough   Lay 18 by 12-inch sheet of parchment paper on counter and spray lightly with vegetable oil spray. Sprinkle one-third of sesame seeds in center of parchment and spread into rough 9-inch round; set aside. Transfer dough seam side up to lightly floured counter and pat into rough 9-inch circle using your lightly floured hands. Using bowl scraper or your floured fingertips, lift and fold edge of dough toward center, pressing to seal. Repeat 5 more times (for a total of 6 folds), evenly spacing folds around circumference of dough. Press down on dough to seal, then use bench scraper to gently flip dough seam side down.

5   Using both hands, cup side of dough furthest away from you and pull dough toward you, keeping pinky fingers and side of palm in contact with counter and applying slight pressure to dough as it drags to create tension. (If dough slides across surface of counter without rolling, remove excess flour. If dough sticks to counter or your hands, lightly sprinkle counter or hands with flour.) Rotate dough ball 90 degrees, reposition dough ball at top of counter, and repeat pulling dough until taut round ball forms, at least 4 more times. Using your floured hands or bench scraper, transfer dough seam side down to center of prepared parchment then spray or gently brush top of loaf with water. Sprinkle remaining ⅔ sesame seeds over top and use your hands to gently press seeds onto sides of loaf.

6   second rise   Cover dough with inverted large bowl and let rise until dough has doubled in size and dough springs back minimally when poked gently with your finger, 1 to 2 hours.

7   Thirty minutes before baking, adjust oven rack to middle position, place Dutch oven with lid on rack, and heat oven to 475 degrees. Using sharp knife or single-edge razor blade, make one 6-inch-long, ½-inch-deep slash with swift, fluid motion along top of loaf. Carefully remove hot pot from oven and, using parchment as sling, gently transfer dough to hot pot. Working quickly and reinforcing score in top of loaf if needed, cover pot and return to oven.

8   bake   Reduce oven temperature to 425 degrees and bake loaf in covered pot for 30 minutes. Remove lid and continue to bake until loaf is deep golden brown and registers at least 205 degrees, 10 to 15 minutes. Using parchment sling, carefully remove loaf from hot pot and transfer to wire rack; discard parchment. Let cool completely, about 3 hours, before slicing.

total time 13¾ hours

25 min.	8 hours	20 min.	20 min.	1 hour	40 min.	3 hours
make dough	first rise	fold + rest	shape dough	second rise	bake	cool

» **Take your time** To make over 24 hours, let dough sit for up to 18 hours in step 2.

sesame durum bread (page 218)

orange-chocolate durum bread (page 222)

ORANGE-CHOCOLATE DURUM BREAD

makes 1 loaf

---

2 **cups (10 ounces) durum flour (see page 12)**

1 **cup (5½ ounces) bread flour**

1½ **teaspoons table salt**

¼ **teaspoon instant or rapid-rise yeast**

1 **cup (8 ounces) water, room temperature**

1 **tablespoon grated orange zest plus ½ cup (4 ounces) orange juice**

1 **tablespoon distilled white vinegar**

4 **ounces bittersweet chocolate, chopped no larger than ¼ inch**

why this recipe works   Enjoyed as a sweet treat alongside coffee or sliced thick and used for French toast, this bread with generous pockets of chocolate throughout a moist, orange-scented durum loaf is sure to make your rotation. Simply adding orange zest at the beginning of mixing impedes proofing, while folding the zest into the dough doesn't distribute its flavor very well. Our fix is to use orange juice as well as zest; we add the juice with the other wet ingredients for bread with an open crumb and sweet orange flavor throughout. The orange juice also amplifies the loaf's golden color. Use durum flour in this recipe, which is more finely ground than semolina flour. Avoid Caputo Semola Rimacinata (found commonly in grocery stores). We prefer King Arthur brand bread flour in this recipe; the dough will be slightly stickier if you use a lower-protein bread flour. It's important to chop the chocolate fine with pieces no larger than ¼ inch. Alternatively, you can use mini chocolate chips. You will need a bowl that is at least 9 inches wide and 4 inches deep to cover the dough in step 6.

1 make dough   Whisk durum flour, bread flour, salt, and yeast together in large bowl. Using rubber spatula, fold water, orange juice, and vinegar into flour mixture, scraping up dry flour from bottom of bowl and pressing dough until cohesive and shaggy≈and all flour is incorporated.

2 first rise   Cover bowl tightly with plastic wrap and let sit at room temperature for at least 8 hours or up to 18 hours.

3 fold and rest   Mix chocolate and orange zest together in bowl, breaking up large clumps of zest with your fingers. Sprinkle half of chocolate mixture evenly over dough. Using greased bowl scraper or your wet fingertips, fold dough over itself by lifting and folding edge of dough toward middle and pressing to seal. Turn bowl 90 degrees and fold dough again; repeat turning bowl and folding dough 2 more times. Sprinkle remaining chocolate mixture over dough and repeat folding dough 4 more times (for a total of 8 folds). Flip dough seam side down in bowl, cover with plastic, and let rest for 15 minutes.

4   Lay 18 by 12-inch sheet of parchment paper on counter and spray lightly with vegetable oil spray. Transfer dough seam side up to lightly floured counter and pat into rough 9-inch circle using your lightly floured hands. Using bowl scraper or your floured fingertips, lift and fold edge of dough toward center, pressing to seal. Repeat 5 more times (for a total of 6 folds), evenly spacing folds around circumference of dough. Press down on dough to seal, then use bench scraper to gently flip dough seam side down.

5 shape dough   Using both hands, cup side of dough furthest away from you and pull dough toward you, keeping pinky fingers and side of palm in contact with counter and applying slight pressure to dough as it drags to create tension. (If dough slides across surface of counter without rolling, remove excess flour. If dough sticks to counter or your hands, lightly sprinkle counter or hands with flour.) Rotate dough ball 90 degrees, reposition dough ball at top of counter, and repeat pulling dough until taut round ball forms, at least 4 more times. Using your floured hands or bench scraper, transfer dough seam side down to center of prepared parchment.

6 second rise   Cover dough with inverted large bowl. Let rise until dough has doubled in size and dough springs back minimally when poked gently with your finger, 1 to 2 hours.

7   Thirty minutes before baking, adjust oven rack to middle position, place Dutch oven with lid on rack, and heat oven to 475 degrees. Using sharp knife or single-edge razor blade, make one 6-inch-long, ½-inch-deep slash with swift, fluid motion along top of loaf. Carefully remove hot pot from oven and, using parchment as sling, gently transfer dough to hot pot. Working quickly and reinforcing score in top of loaf if needed, cover pot and return to oven.

8 bake   Reduce oven temperature to 425 degrees and bake loaf in covered pot for 30 minutes. Remove lid and continue to bake until loaf is deep golden brown and registers at least 205 degrees, 10 to 15 minutes. Using parchment sling, carefully remove loaf from hot pot and transfer to wire rack; discard parchment. Let cool completely, about 3 hours, before slicing.

total time 13¾ hours

25 min.	8 hours	20 min.	15 min.	1 hour	40 min.	3 hours
make dough	first rise	fold + rest	shape dough	second rise	bake	cool

» **Take your time** To make over 24 hours, let dough sit for up to 18 hours in step 2.

CHAPTER FIVE

pizza and flatbreads

THIN-CRUST PIZZA

Pizza varies from region to region, whether you're in Italy or in the U.S. It's a common favorite food, and it is communal food. It's also a meal, good for lunch or dinner or even breakfast—whether that means a "breakfast pizza," or a refrigerated slice of last night's leftovers. But at its most basic, pizza is *bread* with stuff on it. So even though there's a topping, making pizza is similar to making other breads.

Thin-crust pizza is maybe the most iconic pizza and it transcends regions (although you might have more opinions on the thin pie if you live in the New York City Tri-State area). We've developed the ultimate recipe for a dough for thin-crust pizza: It comes together with little effort and has tons of flavor (crust should have a flavor of its own separate from the topping), plus chew from a flexible long fermentation time (up to three days) and generous hydration. Those characteristics also make the dough easy to roll beyond the expected circular pie. Smoothly form the dough into a rectangle, fit it into a baking sheet, and make pizza for breakfast (an especially fun one—Shakshuka Breakfast Pizza). Stuff rounds of the dough with ample filling to mimic a Florida favorite that slices like cake. Wrap the dough around hearty vegetables and cured meat, and you get a new dish entirely: a satisfying, party-ready stromboli.

THIN-CRUST PIZZA

serves 4 to 6

how-to

dough

- **3** cups (16½ ounces) bread flour
- **2** teaspoons sugar
- **½** teaspoon instant or rapid-rise yeast
- **1⅓** cups (10⅔ ounces) ice water
- **1** tablespoon vegetable oil
- **1½** teaspoons table salt

sauce and toppings

- **1** (28-ounce) can whole peeled tomatoes, drained with juice reserved
- **1** tablespoon extra-virgin olive oil
- **2** garlic cloves, minced
- **1** teaspoon red wine vinegar
- **1** teaspoon dried oregano
- **½** teaspoon table salt
- **¼** teaspoon pepper
- **1** ounce Parmesan cheese, grated fine (½ cup), divided
- **8** ounces whole-milk mozzarella cheese, shredded (2 cups), divided

Classic New York–style pizza is something special: It has a thin, crisp, and spotty charred exterior and is tender yet chewy within. But with home ovens that reach only 500 degrees (far lower than a pizzeria oven) and recipes for dough that is impossible to stretch thin, the savviest cooks struggle to produce parlor-quality thin-crust pies at home. For the perfect crust in a home oven, we make the dough fairly wet so it's easy to stretch and becomes chewy after baking. This also makes it possible to knead the dough in the food processor; the blade's rapid action turns the dough elastic in just about a minute (after a brief rest). We chill the dough in the refrigerator for a day or so to develop great flavor. The final step is getting browning and crunch. Most recipes call for placing pizza on the bottom oven rack, close to the heating element. That placement browns the bottom but dries out the crust. Situating the baking steel or stone on the highest rack mimics the shallow chamber of a commercial pizza oven where heat rises, radiates off the top of the oven, and browns the pizza before the interior dries out. And heating the broiler for 10 minutes before each bake superheats the oven to get it a little closer to the temperature of a professional one. Shape the second dough ball while the first pizza bakes, but don't top the pizza until right before you bake it. If you add more toppings, keep them light or they may weigh down the thin crust.

1 make dough Pulse flour, sugar, and yeast in food processor until combined, about 5 pulses. With processor running, slowly add ice water and process until dough is just combined and no dry flour remains, about 10 seconds. Let dough rest for 10 minutes.

2 Add oil and salt to dough and process until dough forms satiny, sticky ball that clears sides of bowl, 30 to 60 seconds. Transfer dough to lightly oiled counter and knead by hand to form smooth, round ball, about 30 seconds.

3 rise Place dough seam side down in lightly greased large bowl or container, cover with plastic wrap, and refrigerate for at least 24 hours or up to 3 days. (To freeze dough, refrigerate it for 24 hours. Place on baking sheet or plate lined with parchment paper, cover loosely with plastic wrap, and freeze until firm, about 3 hours or up to overnight. Wrap frozen dough ball individually in plastic and store in zipper-lock bag in freezer for up to 2 weeks. To thaw, unwrap ball, place in lightly oiled bowl, cover with plastic, and let sit in refrigerator for 12 to 24 hours before shaping.)

4 make sauce and toppings Process drained tomatoes, oil, garlic, vinegar, oregano, salt, and pepper in clean, dry workbowl until smooth, about 30 seconds. Transfer mixture to 2-cup liquid measuring cup and add reserved tomato juice until sauce measures 2 cups. Reserve 1 cup sauce. Set aside remaining sauce for another use (it can be refrigerated for up to 1 week or frozen for up to 1 month).

5 shape dough Press down on dough to deflate. Transfer dough to clean counter, divide in half, and cover loosely with greased plastic. Pat 1 piece of dough (keep remaining piece covered) into 4-inch round. Working around circumference of dough, fold edges toward center until ball forms. Flip ball seam side down and, using your cupped hands, drag in small circles on counter until dough feels taut and round and all seams are secured on underside. (If dough sticks to your hands, lightly dust top of dough with flour.) Repeat with remaining piece of dough.

6 rest Space dough balls 3 inches apart, cover loosely with greased plastic, and let rest for 1 hour. One hour before baking, adjust oven rack 4 to 5 inches from broiler element, set baking steel or stone on rack, and heat oven to 500 degrees.

7 Heat broiler for 10 minutes. Coat 1 dough ball generously with flour and place on well-floured counter. Using your fingertips, gently flatten into 8-inch round, leaving 1 inch of outer edge slightly thicker than center. Using your hands, gently stretch dough into 12-inch round, working along edge and giving disk quarter turns.

8 Transfer dough to well-floured pizza peel and stretch into 13-inch round. Using back of spoon or ladle, spread ½ cup tomato sauce in even layer over surface of dough, leaving ¼-inch border around edge. Sprinkle ¼ cup Parmesan evenly over sauce, followed by 1 cup mozzarella.

9 bake Slide pizza carefully onto baking steel or stone and set oven to 500 degrees. Bake until crust is well browned and cheese is bubbly and partially browned, 8 to 10 minutes, rotating pizza halfway through baking. Transfer pizza to wire rack and let cool for 5 minutes before slicing and serving. Heat broiler for 10 minutes. Repeat with remaining dough, sauce, and toppings, setting oven to 500 degrees when pizza is placed on steel or stone.

total time 26¼ hours

20 min.	24 hours	15 min.	1 hour	40 min.
make dough	rise	shape dough	rest	bake

» **Take your time** To make over 3 or 4 days, let dough rise for up to 3 days in step 3.

SHAKSHUKA BREAKFAST PIZZA

serves 4 to 6

½ recipe Thin-Crust Pizza, made through step 3

3 tablespoons extra-virgin olive oil, divided, plus extra for drizzling

1 small onion, chopped fine

1 yellow bell pepper, stemmed, seeded, and chopped fine

1¼ cups jarred piquillo peppers, rinsed, patted dry, and chopped

2 garlic cloves, minced

1 teaspoon tomato paste

½ teaspoon ground cumin

½ teaspoon smoked paprika

½ teaspoon table salt

⅛ teaspoon pepper

Pinch cayenne pepper

2 tablespoons plus ¼ cup coarsely chopped fresh cilantro, divided

2 tablespoons water

6 large eggs

3 ounces feta cheese, crumbled (¾ cup)

¼ cup pitted kalamata olives, sliced

To reimagine the presentation of shakshuka, the classic dish of eggs simmered in a sauce of tomatoes, peppers, and spices, we put the breakfast on top of a pizza featuring our thin-crust dough. Our goal is a crispy crust, but also eggs with still-jammy yolks (or soft-cooked if you'd prefer). We easily coax our well-hydrated dough into a rectangle and, for a thick sauce that doesn't make the crust soggy, we use a little tomato paste for flavor instead of liquid-y fresh or canned tomatoes. Making wells in the sauce with the back of a spoon provides the eggs the perfect holding place for the bake. To achieve the perfect crust without overcooking the eggs, we cook the pizza like most—hot and fast—and use the lowest oven rack to shield the delicate eggs. A garnish of feta cheese, olives, and plenty of cilantro gives the rich sauce and eggs briny pops of flavor and welcome grassy freshness. Jarred roasted red peppers can be substituted for the piquillo peppers.

1 rest   After refrigerating dough in step 3, let dough rest at room temperature for 1 hour.

2   Meanwhile, adjust oven rack to lowest position, place pizza stone on rack, and heat oven to 500 degrees. Heat 1 tablespoon oil in 12-inch nonstick skillet over medium-high heat until shimmering. Add onion, bell pepper, and piquillo peppers and cook until softened and beginning to brown, 8 to 10 minutes. Add garlic, tomato paste, cumin, paprika, salt, pepper, and cayenne and cook, stirring frequently, until tomato paste begins to darken, about 2 minutes. Transfer pepper mixture to bowl and stir in 2 tablespoons cilantro. Transfer 1 cup sauce to blender, add water, and process until smooth, about 60 seconds, scraping down sides of blender jar as needed. Return puree to bowl with remaining sauce, stirring to combine; set aside. (Sauce can be refrigerated for up to 24 hours.)

3 shape dough   Lightly spray rimmed baking sheet with vegetable oil spray. Brush bottom of pan with remaining 2 tablespoons oil. Transfer dough to floured counter and roll and press into rough 14 by 10-inch rectangle of even thickness. Transfer rectangle to prepared sheet, reshaping as needed. (If dough resists stretching, let it rest for 10 to 20 minutes before trying to stretch again.)

4   Spread reserved sauce into thin layer over surface of dough, leaving ½-inch border around edges. Create 2 rows of 3 evenly spaced small wells in sauce, each about 4 inches in diameter (6 wells total). Crack 1 egg into each well.

5 bake   Place baking sheet on stone and bake pizza until crust is light golden around edges and egg whites are set, 8 to 10 minutes, rotating sheet halfway through baking. Transfer pizza to wire rack, sprinkle with feta, and let sit for 5 minutes. Sprinkle with olives and remaining ¼ cup cilantro and drizzle with oil, then slice and serve.

Spread sauce on dough.

Make wells in sauce.

Crack eggs into wells.

STUFFED PIZZA

serves 8

pizza

- **4 ounces hot Italian sausage, casings removed**
- **4 ounces thinly sliced pepperoni, quartered**
- **4 ounces thinly sliced Black Forest deli ham, cut into ½-inch pieces**
- **4 ounces salami, cut into ¼-inch cubes**
- **¾ teaspoon dried oregano, divided**
- **1 recipe Thin-Crust Pizza, made through step 5**
- **1 pound whole-milk mozzarella cheese, shredded (4 cups)**
- **2 tablespoons unsalted butter, cut into 2 pieces**
- **1 garlic clove, minced**

sauce

- **1 (14.5-ounce) can whole peeled tomatoes, drained**
- **1½ teaspoons extra-virgin olive oil**
- **1 small garlic clove, minced**
- **½ teaspoon red wine vinegar**
- **½ teaspoon table salt**
- **½ teaspoon dried oregano**

We wanted to re-create the impressive stuffed pizza served at Michelangelo Pizzeria and Italian Restaurant in Sarasota, Florida, using our thin-crust pizza dough as the base. We stuff two rounds of dough with a mixture of mozzarella, hot Italian sausage, ham, pepperoni, and salami. Pressing on the pizza compacts the ingredients, ensuring that the filling holds together when sliced. Finishing the baked pizza with garlic butter and dried oregano gives it a beautiful sheen and a distinctly "pizza" aroma. Finally, we allow the pizza to cool so that it holds its shape when sliced. Buy a 4-ounce chunk of salami rather than sliced salami from the deli.

1 make pizza Adjust oven rack to lowest position and heat oven to 425 degrees. Cook sausage in 8-inch nonstick skillet over medium heat, breaking up meat with wooden spoon, until no longer pink, 5 to 7 minutes. Transfer to medium bowl and let cool completely, about 20 minutes. Add pepperoni, ham, salami, and ½ teaspoon oregano to bowl with sausage and toss to combine.

2 After forming dough balls in step 5, turn 1 ball onto well-floured 16 by 12-inch sheet parchment paper. Using your hands, flatten into 8-inch disk. Using rolling pin, roll dough into 12-inch circle, dusting with flour as needed. Sprinkle 1 cup mozzarella evenly over dough, leaving ½-inch border. Sprinkle one-third of sausage mixture (about 1 heaping cup) over cheese. Repeat layering until cheese and meat mixture are used up (top layer should be cheese).

3 Roll remaining dough ball into 12-inch circle on well-floured counter, dusting with flour as needed. Brush edges of dough on parchment with water. Loosely roll dough on counter around rolling pin and gently unroll it directly over dough on parchment and filling. Press dough edges together firmly to seal. Using pizza cutter, trim and discard dough just beyond sealed edge of pizza, about ¼ inch from filling. Using paring knife, cut 1-inch hole in top center of pizza. Lifting parchment, transfer pizza to rimmed baking sheet. Using your hands, press down on top of pizza to compress filling into even layer.

4 bake Bake pizza until deep golden brown, 20 to 25 minutes. Slide pizza from sheet onto wire rack. Microwave butter and garlic in small bowl until butter is melted and mixture is fragrant, about 1 minute. Brush top of hot pizza with garlic butter, then sprinkle with remaining ¼ teaspoon oregano. Let pizza cool on rack for at least 45 minutes.

5 make sauce Meanwhile, process all sauce ingredients in food processor until smooth, about 30 seconds. Transfer to serving dish. (Sauce can be refrigerated for up to 3 days or frozen for up to 1 month.)

6 To serve, adjust oven rack to lowest position and heat oven to 425 degrees. Slice pizza into 8 wedges and place on parchment paper–lined rimmed baking sheet. Bake pizza slices until hot throughout, about 10 minutes. Microwave sauce until hot, about 2 minutes, stirring occasionally. Serve pizza with sauce.

Brush edges of dough with water.

Unroll dough from rolling pin on top.

Press edges firmly to seal.

BROCCOLI RABE AND SALAMI STROMBOLI

serves 4

½ recipe Thin-Crust Pizza, made through step 3

1 teaspoon extra-virgin olive oil

2 garlic cloves, minced

¼ teaspoon red pepper flakes

6 ounces broccoli rabe, trimmed and cut into ¼-inch pieces

2 tablespoons water

4 ounces thinly sliced aged provolone cheese

2 ounces thinly sliced Genoa salami

4 ounces mozzarella cheese, shredded (1 cup)

1 large egg, beaten with 1 tablespoon water and pinch table salt

1 teaspoon sesame seeds

Here, we take our thin-crust pizza dough and roll it around a filling rather than putting it under toppings, then bake it up for a nice restyling of pizza with the same great flavor and texture. We like the substantial, satisfying filling of broccoli rabe in this stromboli; Genoa salami and two kinds of cheese offset its earthiness with richness and a pleasing cheese pull. You may substitute broccoli florets for the broccoli rabe.

1 After refrigerating dough in step 3, let dough rest at room temperature for 1 hour. Adjust oven rack to middle position and heat oven to 375 degrees. Line rimmed baking sheet with aluminum foil and grease foil. Heat oil in 12-inch nonstick skillet over medium heat until shimmering. Add garlic and pepper flakes and cook until fragrant, about 30 seconds. Add broccoli rabe and water, cover, and cook until just tender, about 1 minute. Uncover and cook until liquid has evaporated, about 1 minute. Transfer broccoli rabe to dish towel; gather corners of towel and squeeze out excess moisture.

2 shape dough Roll dough into 12 by 10-inch rectangle on floured counter with long side parallel to counter edge. Shingle provolone evenly over dough, leaving ½-inch border along top and sides. Layer salami over provolone. Sprinkle mozzarella and broccoli rabe evenly over salami.

3 Brush borders with egg wash (reserve remaining egg wash for brushing top of stromboli). Fold bottom third of stromboli in toward middle. Fold top third of stromboli down to cover first fold, creating log. Pinch seam firmly to seal. Transfer stromboli to prepared sheet, seam side down. Pinch ends firmly to seal and tuck underneath.

4 bake Brush top of stromboli with remaining egg wash. Using sharp knife, make 5 evenly spaced ½-inch-deep slashes, 2 inches long, on top of stromboli. Sprinkle with sesame seeds. Bake until crust is golden and center registers 200 degrees, 30 to 35 minutes, rotating sheet halfway through baking. Transfer stromboli to wire rack and let cool for 10 minutes before cutting into 2-inch-thick slices. Serve.

Add toppings to dough.

Fold over bottom third of dough.

Fold over top third of dough.

Pinch seam to seal.

Transfer stromboli to sheet.

Pinch ends firmly to seal and tuck underneath.

ONE-HOUR PIZZA

serves 4 to 6

dough

- 1⅓ cups (7⅓ ounces) bread flour
- ½ cup (3 ounces) semolina flour
- 2 teaspoons instant or rapid-rise yeast
- 2 teaspoons sugar
- ½ cup plus 2 tablespoons (5 ounces) warm water
- ¼ cup (2 ounces) mild lager
- 2 teaspoons distilled white vinegar
- 1½ teaspoons extra-virgin olive oil
- 1 teaspoon table salt
- Vegetable oil spray

sauce

- 1 (28-ounce) can whole peeled tomatoes, drained
- 1 tablespoon extra-virgin olive oil
- 3 anchovy fillets, rinsed and patted dry (optional)
- 1 teaspoon table salt
- 1 teaspoon dried oregano
- ½ teaspoon sugar
- ¼ teaspoon pepper
- ⅛ teaspoon red pepper flakes
- 1 ounce Parmesan cheese, grated fine (½ cup), divided
- 6 ounces whole-milk mozzarella, shredded (1½ cups), divided

why this recipe works   Most of our pizzas feature doughs that can be made ahead so homemade pizza on a weeknight is possible. But a recipe that takes an hour? From start to table? Yes, and we also perfected pizza à la minute with a crust that's crisp, tender, and light for an unplanned pizza night. First, we use a high percentage of yeast and warm water in the dough to make sure, instead of prolonged proofing, it takes only 30 minutes. To take full advantage of the minimal proofing time, we had to rethink the way we prepare the dough. Instead of the usual process of proofing the dough and then rolling it out, we reverse the order of operations so the dough proofs in its ready round shape. We also use a combination of semolina and all-purpose flours, which makes the dough more extensible than with all-purpose alone. Extra sauce can be refrigerated for up to a week or frozen for up to a month.

1 make dough   Adjust oven rack 4 to 5 inches from broiler element, set baking steel or stone on rack, and heat oven to 500 degrees.

2   While oven heats, process bread flour, semolina flour, yeast, and sugar in food processor until combined, about 2 seconds. With processor running, slowly add warm water, lager, vinegar, and oil and process until dough is just combined and no dry flour remains, about 10 seconds. Let dough rest for 10 minutes. Add salt to dough and process until dough forms satiny, sticky ball that clears sides of bowl, 30 to 60 seconds. Transfer dough to lightly floured counter and knead by hand to form smooth, round ball, about 30 seconds. Divide dough into 2 equal pieces and shape each into smooth ball.

3 shape dough   Spray 11-inch circle in center of large sheet of parchment paper with oil spray. Place 1 ball of dough in center of parchment. Spray top of dough with oil spray. Using rolling pin, roll dough into 10-inch circle. Cover with second sheet of parchment. Using rolling pin and your hands, continue to roll and press dough into 11½-inch circle. Set aside and repeat rolling with second ball of dough.

4 rise   Let dough sit at room temperature until slightly puffy, about 30 minutes.

5 make sauce   Process all sauce ingredients in food processor until smooth, about 30 seconds. Transfer to medium bowl.

6   When dough has rested for 20 minutes, heat broiler for 10 minutes. Remove top piece of parchment from 1 disk of dough and dust top of dough lightly with all-purpose flour. Using your hands or pastry brush, spread flour evenly over dough, brushing off any excess. Liberally dust pizza peel with all-purpose flour. Flip dough onto peel, parchment side up. Carefully remove parchment and discard.

7 Using back of spoon or ladle, spread ½ cup sauce in thin layer over surface of dough, leaving ¾-inch border around edge. Sprinkle ¼ cup Parmesan evenly over sauce, followed by ¾ cup mozzarella.

8 bake Slide pizza carefully onto steel or stone and set oven to 500 degrees. Bake until crust is well browned and cheese is bubbly and beginning to brown, 8 to 12 minutes, rotating pizza halfway through baking. Transfer pizza to wire rack and let cool for 5 minutes before slicing and serving. Repeat steps 6 and 7 to top and bake second pizza.

total time 1 hour

15 min.	5 min.	30 min.	10 min.	5 min.
make dough	shape dough	rise	bake	cool

PEPPERONI SHEET-PAN PIZZA

serves 4 to 6

dough

- 3 cups (15 ounces) all-purpose flour
- 2 teaspoons instant or rapid-rise yeast
- 2 teaspoons sugar
- 1⅓ cups (10⅔ ounces) water, room temperature
- 1 teaspoon table salt
- ¼ cup extra-virgin olive oil

sauce

- 1¼ cups canned crushed tomatoes
- 2 tablespoons extra-virgin olive oil
- 2 garlic cloves, minced
- 3 anchovy fillets, minced
- 1½ teaspoons dried oregano
- 1 teaspoon sugar
- ½ teaspoon red pepper flakes
- ½ teaspoon table salt

- 1 ounce Parmesan cheese, grated (½ cup), plus extra for sprinkling
- 12 ounces whole-milk block mozzarella cheese, shredded (3 cups)
- 4 ounces thinly sliced pepperoni

  Red pepper flakes, for sprinkling

why this recipe works We wanted a stunning, easy-to-make sheet-pan pizza with an airy, focaccia-like crust and ultracrispy edges. The best part about sheet-pan pizza is that it requires minimal shaping, which gives us flexibility with the dough. We simply transfer a highly hydrated dough straight to a well-oiled rimmed baking sheet, eliminating the need for extended handling or rolling. Greasing the pan with both olive oil and vegetable oil spray ensures that the dough never sticks during the process. After topping the pie with a potent stir-together tomato sauce, generous amounts of Parmesan and mozzarella (all the way to the sides for crispy lacy edges), and sliced pepperoni, we bake it at 500 degrees on a baking stone that has been preheated for a full hour on the bottom oven rack (closest to the heating element). The hot oven and constant direct heat of the stone results in strong oven spring to create the right crumb. We prefer to buy link pepperoni and slice it thin rather than using presliced pepperoni. Avoid preshredded cheese; it contains added starch, which gives the melted cheese a drier, chewier texture.

1 make dough Whisk flour, yeast, and sugar together in bowl of stand mixer. Using dough hook on low speed, slowly add water to flour mixture and mix until cohesive dough starts to form and no dry flour remains, 2 to 4 minutes, scraping down bowl as needed. Cover bowl and let rest for 10 minutes.

2 Add salt and mix on medium speed until dough forms satiny, sticky ball that clears sides of bowl, 6 to 8 minutes. Lightly spray rimmed baking sheet with vegetable oil spray. Rub bottom and sides of pan with olive oil. Using dough scraper or your greased hands, transfer dough to oiled sheet and turn to coat. With your greased hands, stretch dough into rough 12 by 8-inch rectangle of even thickness.

3 first rise Cover pan with plastic wrap and let rise until puffed and nearly doubled in volume, about 1 hour.

4 make sauce Meanwhile, adjust oven rack to lowest position, place baking stone on rack, and heat oven to 500 degrees. Combine all sauce ingredients in bowl. (Sauce can be refrigerated for up to 24 hours.)

5 shape dough Using your greased hands, gently stretch dough to corners of sheet, pressing lightly with your fingertips to deflate dough and carefully lifting corners and edges of dough to pull toward edges of sheet. (It's OK if dough shrinks back slightly from corners of sheet at this point.)

6 second rise Cover loosely with plastic and let rest until slightly puffed, about 20 minutes.

7 Using your greased hands, press dough all the way to edges and corners of sheet. Using your fingertips, pinch edges of dough against sides of sheet to form small lip. Using bottom of ½-cup dry measuring cup or large spoon, spread sauce into thin layer over surface of dough, leaving ½-inch border. Sprinkle Parmesan evenly over sauce. Sprinkle mozzarella over entire surface of dough, making sure some cheese sits on edges of dough against sheet. Top pizza with pepperoni.

8   bake   Place baking sheet on stone and bake pizza until cheese is bubbly and well browned, about 15 minutes, rotating sheet halfway through baking. Run knife around edge of sheet to loosen pizza and transfer pizza to wire rack. Let cool for 5 minutes. Slice and serve, sprinkled with extra Parmesan and pepper flakes as desired.

total time 2½ hours

45 min.	1 hour	5 min.	20 min.	15 min.	5 min.
make dough	**first rise**	**shape dough**	**second rise**	**bake**	**cool**

CAPRESE SHEET-PAN PIZZA

You can use homemade pesto (recipe follows) or store-bought. Balsamic glaze is a reduced, concentrated version of balsamic vinegar that's used as a condiment; you can find it alongside the vinegars at the supermarket.

While dough is rising in step 3, toss 10 ounces cherry tomatoes, sliced ¼ inch thick; ½ teaspoon table salt; ½ teaspoon sugar; and 1 minced garlic clove together in bowl. Transfer to colander set over bowl and drain. Omit sauce in step 4 and spread 1¼ cups pesto over surface of dough in step 7 instead. Omit Parmesan and pepperoni. Substitute 10 ounces fresh mozzarella, sliced into ¼-inch-thick rounds for shredded whole-milk mozzarella. Sprinkle pizza with drained tomatoes, ½ teaspoon pepper, and ¼ teaspoon table salt. Before serving, top baked pizza with ½ cup shaved Parmesan, ⅓ cup torn fresh basil leaves, and 2 tablespoons balsamic glaze (optional).

SHEET-PAN PIZZA WITH 'NDUJA, RICOTTA, AND CHERRY PEPPERS

While dough is rising in step 3, pulse ½ cup room temperature 'nduja with ½ cup whole-milk ricotta cheese in food processor until smooth, about 15 pulses; set aside at room temperature. Substitute additional ¼ cup room temperature 'nduja for olive oil and anchovies in sauce in step 4, using fork to mash 'nduja into sauce until uniform. Substitute Pecorino Romano for Parmesan. Omit pepperoni. Before serving, drop rough 2-teaspoon-size dollops of 'nduja-ricotta mixture evenly over baked pizza and smear lightly with back of spoon. Garnish with ⅓ cup shredded fresh basil and ⅓ cup thinly sliced jarred hot cherry peppers.

PESTO

makes 1½ cups

You can refrigerate this pesto for up to 3 days or freeze it for up to 3 months. To prevent browning, press plastic wrap flush to the surface, or top the pesto with a thin layer of olive oil. Bring to room temperature before using.

- **6** garlic cloves, unpeeled
- **½** cup pine nuts
- **4** cups fresh basil leaves
- **¼** cup fresh parsley leaves
- **1** cup extra-virgin olive oil
- **1** ounce Parmesan cheese, grated fine (½ cup)

1   Toast garlic in 8-inch skillet over medium heat, shaking skillet occasionally, until softened and spotty brown, about 8 minutes. When garlic is cool enough to handle, remove and discard skins and chop coarsely.

2   Toast pine nuts in now-empty skillet over medium heat, stirring often, until golden and fragrant, 4 to 5 minutes.

3   Place basil and parsley in 1-gallon zipper-lock bag. Pound bag with flat side of meat pounder or with rolling pin until all leaves are bruised.

4   Process garlic, pine nuts, and herbs in food processor until finely chopped, about 1 minute, scraping down sides of bowl as needed. With processor running, slowly add oil until incorporated. Transfer pesto to bowl, stir in Parmesan, and season with salt and pepper to taste.

total time 3¼ hours

1 hour	2 hours	15 min.	5 min.
make dough	rise	bake	cool

DETROIT-STYLE PIZZA

serves 4 to 6

dough

1 tablespoon extra-virgin olive oil

2¼ cups (11¼ ounces) all-purpose flour

1½ teaspoons instant or rapid-rise yeast

1½ teaspoons sugar

1 cup (8 ounces) water, room temperature

¾ teaspoon table salt

sauce

1 cup canned crushed tomatoes

1 tablespoon extra-virgin olive oil

1 tablespoon chopped fresh basil

1 garlic clove, minced

1 teaspoon dried oregano

1 teaspoon dried basil

½ teaspoon sugar

½ teaspoon pepper

¼ teaspoon table salt

10 ounces Monterey Jack cheese, shredded (2½ cups)

why this recipe works   Our challenge in creating a recipe for topsy-turvy Detroit pizza—a crispy pan pizza from the Motor City—was figuring out how to mimic the tender crumb, the buttery melty brick cheese (which can be found only in Michigan), and the vibrant tomato sauce that covers the cheese in stripes. The stand mixer does most of the kneading for us; a hydrated dough that requires a 15-minute rest and a 2-hour rise produces the tender, almost fluffy crust. We top the pizza with handfuls of Monterey Jack cheese, which we think is the only acceptable substitute for the brick cheese typically used on Detroit pizzas. It has enough fat to fry the pizza's essential crisp edges as it bakes. A combination of dried herbs, sugar, and canned crushed tomatoes gives our sauce authentic flavor and texture. To add more toppings, such as pepperoni or sausage, press them into the dough before adding the cheese.

1 make dough   Spray 13 by 9-inch nonstick baking pan with vegetable oil spray, then brush bottom and sides of pan with olive oil. Whisk flour, yeast, and sugar together in bowl of stand mixer. Using dough hook on low speed, slowly add room temperature water to flour mixture and mix until cohesive dough forms and no dry flour remains, about 2 minutes, scraping down bowl as needed. Cover and let rest for 10 minutes.

2   Add salt and knead on medium speed until dough forms satiny, sticky ball that clears sides of bowl, 6 to 8 minutes. Transfer dough to lightly floured counter and knead by hand to form smooth, round ball, about 30 seconds. Transfer dough to prepared pan, cover with plastic, and let rest for 15 minutes. Using your well-oiled hands, press dough into corners of pan. (If dough resists stretching, let it rest for another 10 minutes before trying again to stretch.)

3 rise   Cover with plastic and let dough rise at room temperature until nearly tripled in volume and large bubbles form, 2 to 3 hours.

4 make sauce   Adjust oven rack to lowest position and heat oven to 500 degrees. Combine all sauce ingredients in bowl. (Sauce can be refrigerated for up to 24 hours.)

5   Sprinkle Monterey Jack evenly over dough to edges of pan. Spoon three 1-inch-wide strips of sauce, using ⅓ cup sauce for each, over cheese evenly down length of pan.

6 bake   Bake until cheese is bubbly and browned, about 15 minutes. Let pizza cool in pan on wire rack for 5 minutes. Run knife around edge of pan to loosen pizza. Using spatula, slide pizza onto cutting board. Cut into pieces and serve.

THIN-CRUST WHOLE-WHEAT PIZZA WITH GARLIC OIL, THREE CHEESES, AND BASIL

serves 4 to 6

dough

- 1½ cups (8¼ ounces) whole-wheat flour
- 1 cup (5½ ounces) bread flour
- 2 teaspoons honey
- ¾ teaspoon instant or rapid-rise yeast
- 1¼ cups (10 ounces) ice water
- 2 tablespoons extra-virgin olive oil
- 1¾ teaspoons table salt

garlic oil

- ¼ cup extra-virgin olive oil
- 2 garlic cloves, minced
- 2 anchovy fillets, rinsed, patted dry, and minced (optional)
- ½ teaspoon pepper
- ½ teaspoon dried oregano
- ⅛ teaspoon red pepper flakes
- ⅛ teaspoon table salt

- 1 cup fresh basil leaves, divided
- 1 ounce Pecorino Romano cheese, grated (½ cup), divided
- 8 ounces whole-milk mozzarella cheese, shredded (2 cups), divided
- 6 ounces (¾ cup) whole-milk ricotta cheese, divided

why this recipe works For a whole-wheat pizza that's as crisp and chewy as the standard and offers a good, but not overwhelming, wheat flavor, we use a combination of 60 percent whole-wheat flour and 40 percent bread flour. To ensure that this combination produces a great crust, we use proportionately more water than for our other thin-crust dough (page 228), which results in better gluten development and chew. To compensate for the added moisture, we employ the broiler to speed the baking process and guarantee a crisp crust and tender interior. Traditional toppings clash with the whole-wheat flavor, so we opt for an oil-based sauce to enliven three complementary cheeses, plus some aromatic fresh basil. We prefer King Arthur brand bread flour for this recipe.

1 make dough Process whole-wheat flour, bread flour, honey, and yeast in food processor until combined, about 2 seconds. With processor running, add water and process until dough is just combined and no dry flour remains, about 10 seconds. Let dough rest for 10 minutes.

2 Add oil and salt to dough and process until it forms satiny, sticky ball that clears sides of workbowl, 45 to 60 seconds. Transfer dough to lightly oiled counter and knead by hand to form smooth, round ball, about 30 seconds.

3 rise Place dough seam side down in lightly greased large bowl or container, cover with plastic wrap, and refrigerate for at least 18 hours or up to 2 days.

4 make garlic oil Heat oil in 8-inch skillet over medium-low heat until shimmering. Add garlic; anchovies, if using; pepper; oregano; pepper flakes; and salt. Cook, stirring constantly, until fragrant, about 30 seconds. Transfer to bowl and let cool completely before using.

5 shape dough One hour before baking pizza, adjust oven rack 4 to 5 inches from broiler element, set baking steel or stone on rack, and heat oven to 500 degrees. Divide dough in half. Shape each half into smooth, tight ball. Place balls on lightly oiled baking sheet, spacing them at least 3 inches apart.

6 rest Cover dough loosely with greased plastic and let stand for 1 hour.

7 Heat broiler for 10 minutes. Meanwhile, coat 1 ball of dough generously with flour and place on well-floured counter. Using your fingertips, gently flatten into 8-inch disk, leaving 1 inch of outer edge slightly thicker than center. Lift edge of dough and, using back of your hands and knuckles, gently stretch disk into 12-inch round, working along edges and giving disk quarter turns as you stretch. Transfer dough to well-floured peel and stretch into 13-inch round. Using back of spoon, spread half of garlic oil over surface of dough, leaving ¼-inch border. Layer ½ cup basil leaves over pizza. Sprinkle with ¼ cup Pecorino, followed by 1 cup mozzarella.

8 bake Slide pizza carefully onto steel or stone and return oven to 500 degrees. Bake until crust is well browned and cheese is bubbly and partially browned, 8 to 10 minutes, rotating pizza halfway through baking. Remove pizza and place on wire rack. Dollop half of ricotta over surface of pizza. Let pizza rest for 5 minutes, slice, and serve.

9 Heat broiler for 10 minutes. Repeat process of stretching, topping, and baking with remaining dough and toppings, returning oven to 500 degrees when pizza is placed on steel or stone.

total time 20¼ hours

20 min.	18 hours	15 min.	1 hour	40 min.
make dough	**rise**	**shape dough**	**rest**	**bake**

» **Take your time** To make over 3 days, let dough rise for up to 2 days in step 3.

PIZZA AL TAGLIO WITH POTATOES AND SOPPRESSATA

serves 4 to 6

dough

- 2⅔ cups (14⅔ ounces) bread flour
- 1 teaspoon instant or rapid-rise yeast
- 1½ cups (12 ounces) water, room temperature
- 2 tablespoons extra-virgin olive oil
- 1¼ teaspoons table salt
- Vegetable oil spray

sauce

- 1 (14.5-ounce) can whole peeled tomatoes, drained
- 1 tablespoon extra-virgin olive oil
- 2 anchovy fillets, rinsed
- 1 teaspoon dried oregano
- ½ teaspoon table salt
- ¼ teaspoon red pepper flakes

topping

- 3 tablespoons extra-virgin olive oil, divided
- 6 ounces thinly sliced soppressata
- 10 ounces thinly sliced provolone cheese
- 1 pound small Yukon Gold potatoes, peeled and sliced thin
- ½ teaspoon pepper
- 2 teaspoons chopped fresh parsley

why this recipe works   The singular Roman invention known as pizza al taglio is baked in rectangular pans and cut into slabs as big or as small as the buyer desires. Roman pizzerias display their many varieties behind glass in deli-style cases, where it is sold by the length and cut with scissors (al taglio means "by the cut"). This pizza has a unique crust: It is full of irregularly sized holes, tender and chewy in equal measure, with an audibly crisp yet delicate bottom and a complex, yeasty flavor. It's also one of the easiest pizzas you'll ever make. Because the dough is so wet, we fold it by hand to develop gluten, then place in a baking pan and let it proof overnight in the refrigerator to develop flavor and relax for easy stretching to its final dimensions. We then coat the top of the dough with olive oil and turn it out onto a baking sheet, stretching it to the edges of the sheet and allowing it to proof for an hour until bubbly and risen. Finally, we top the pizza: Savory tomato sauce, soppressata, and cheese combine for a salty-savory punch, and sliced Yukon Gold potatoes become lightly crisped, browned, and curled at the edges. We prefer King Arthur brand bread flour in this recipe. Use small potatoes measuring 1 to 2 inches in diameter and slice them just before topping the pizza; otherwise, they won't lie flat.

1   make dough   Whisk flour and yeast together in medium bowl. Add room temperature water and oil and stir with wooden spoon until shaggy mass forms and no dry flour remains. Cover bowl with plastic wrap and let rest for 10 minutes. Sprinkle salt over dough and mix until fully incorporated. Cover bowl with plastic and let dough rest for 20 minutes.

2   fold and rest   Using your wet fingertips, fold dough over itself by gently lifting and folding edge of dough toward middle. Turn bowl 90 degrees; fold again. Turn bowl and fold dough 4 more times (total of 6 turns). Cover bowl with plastic and let dough rest for 20 minutes. Repeat folding technique, turning bowl each time, until dough tightens slightly, 3 to 6 turns total. Cover bowl with plastic and let dough rest for 10 minutes.

3   Spray bottom of 13 by 9-inch baking pan liberally with oil spray. Transfer dough to prepared pan and spray top of dough lightly with oil spray. Gently press dough into 10 by 7-inch oval of even thickness.

4   first rise   Cover pan tightly with plastic and refrigerate for at least 16 hours or up to 24 hours.

5 make sauce While dough rests, process all ingredients in blender until smooth, 20 to 30 seconds. Transfer sauce to bowl, cover, and refrigerate until needed. (Sauce can be refrigerated in airtight container for up to 2 days).

6 shape dough Brush top of dough with 2 tablespoons oil. Spray rimmed baking sheet (including rim) with oil spray. Invert prepared sheet on top of pan and flip, allowing dough to fall onto sheet (you may need to lift pan and nudge dough at 1 end to release). Using your fingertips, gently dimple dough into even thickness and stretch toward edges of sheet to form 15 by 11-inch oval.

7 second rise Spray top of dough lightly with oil spray, cover loosely with plastic, and let rest until slightly puffy, 1 to 1¼ hours.

8 Thirty minutes before baking, adjust oven rack to lowest position and heat oven to 450 degrees. Just before baking, use your fingertips to gently dimple dough into even thickness, pressing into corners of sheet. Using back of spoon or ladle, spread ½ cup sauce in even layer over surface of dough. (Remaining sauce can be frozen for up to 2 months.) Lay soppressata in even layer over sauce, followed by provolone. Toss potatoes with pepper and remaining 1 tablespoon oil. Starting in 1 corner, shingle potatoes to form even row across bottom of pizza, overlapping each slice by about one-quarter. Continue to layer potatoes in rows, overlapping each row by about one-quarter.

9 bake Transfer sheet to oven and bake until bottom of crust is evenly browned, and potatoes are browned around edges, 20 to 25 minutes, rotating sheet halfway through baking. Transfer sheet to wire rack and let pizza cool for 5 minutes. Run knife around rim of sheet to loosen pizza. Transfer pizza to cutting board and cut into 8 rectangles. Sprinkle with parsley and serve.

total time 19 hours

50 min.	35 min.	16 hours	5 min.	1 hour	20 min.	5 min.
make dough	fold + rest	first rise	shape dough	second rise	bake	cool

» **Take your time** To make over 27 hours, refrigerate dough for up to 24 hours in step 4.

pizza al taglio with potatoes and soppressata (page 246)

focaccia di recco (page 250)

FOCACCIA DI RECCO

serves 4 to 6

- 1⅔ cups (9 ounces) bread flour
- ¾ teaspoon table salt
- ½ cup plus 2 tablespoons (5 ounces) water
- ¼ cup plus 2 teaspoons extra-virgin olive oil, divided
- 12 ounces (1¼ cups) stracchino cheese
- ⅛ teaspoon flake sea salt, crumbled

why this recipe works: Barely known outside of Liguria, pizza-like focaccia di recco consists of two paper-thin, chewy-crisp sheets of dough sandwiching molten cheese and lashed with peppery olive oil and crunchy salt. To roll the flatbreads so thin, the dough needs to be extra extensible. High-protein bread flour, moderately high hydration, and a few tablespoons of olive oil make for an elastic but sturdy dough that we can stretch paper-thin without tearing. Briefly baking the focaccia on a baking stone preheated in a 525-degree oven yields a flatbread with a deeply tanned yet still chewy bottom and a crisp, lightly charred top. Stracchino (also known as Crescenza) is a young, mild, spreadable cow's milk cheese; look for it at specialty cheese shops and Italian markets or online. If it's unavailable, substitute Robiola or a mixture of 8 ounces cream cheese and 4 ounces (1 cup) shredded fontina (use a young Italian cheese) processed in a food processor until combined. Using high-protein King Arthur brand bread flour makes the dough easier to stretch, but other bread flours will work. If your oven does not go to 525 degrees, set it to the highest possible temperature and extend the baking time slightly. Minimize the time between assembling and baking the focaccia to prevent it from sticking to the pan. Serve as a snack with cocktails or as an appetizer.

1 make dough In food processor fitted with metal blade, process flour and table salt until combined, about 2 seconds. Combine water and 2 tablespoons oil in liquid measuring cup. With processor running, slowly add water mixture; process until dough forms satiny, sticky ball that clears sides of work bowl, 30 to 60 seconds. Remove dough from bowl and knead briefly on lightly floured counter until smooth, about 2 minutes. Divide dough in half. Working with 1 half at a time, cup dough between palms of your hands and work in circular motions on counter to form smooth, taut ball.

2 rest Wrap each piece with plastic wrap and let rest for 45 minutes to 1 hour.

3 When dough has been resting for 20 minutes, adjust oven rack to lower-middle position, set baking stone on rack, and heat oven to 525 degrees. Invert rimmed baking sheet on counter. Place second rimmed baking sheet, right side up, on top and arrange so that short sides sit parallel to edge of counter (bottom baking sheet will act as platform). Coat bottom and sides of top baking sheet with 1 tablespoon oil.

4 shape dough Roll 1 dough ball into 8 by 12-inch rectangle on lightly floured counter. Brush with pastry brush to remove excess flour. Lift dough, drape over your knuckles, and gently stretch into 16 by 12-inch rectangle. Center dough over prepared pan and lower onto pan. Gently stretch dough, rotating pan as needed, until it hangs 2 inches over all sides. Working with 1 side at a time, gently lift dough, let it contract slightly and then relax into pan so just 1 inch remains draped over rim and dough lines bottom of pan.

Stretch dough into rectangle.

Stretch to hang over pan 2 inches.

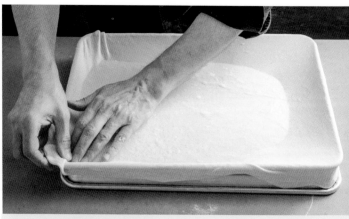
Lift dough and let relax into pan to 1-inch overhang.

Dollop cheese on dough.

Place dough on top of cheese.

Cut away overhanging dough with rolling pin.

5   Dollop generous tablespoons of stracchino evenly over surface of dough, leaving 1-inch border from edge of pan. Repeat rolling and stretching second dough ball into 16 by 12-inch rectangle. Place dough directly on top of dollops of cheese. Gently stretch dough (making sure not to disturb cheese) until it hangs 1 inch over all sides of pan. Press firmly around rim of pan to seal edges. Run rolling pin along outside edge of pan rim to cut away overhanging dough. Using kitchen shears, cut 2-inch slit just to side of each dollop of cheese. Using your fingertips, roll dough edges down into pan to create border. Press to seal. Drizzle with 1 tablespoon oil and sprinkle with sea salt.

6   bake   Place baking sheet on stone and bake until focaccia is crisp and well browned, 8 to 9 minutes, rotating pan halfway through baking. Slide thin spatula under focaccia to loosen on all sides and transfer to wire rack. Let cool for 1 minute, then transfer bread to cutting board. Drizzle with remaining 2 teaspoons oil, slice into 12 squares, and serve immediately.

total time 1½ hours

15 min.	45 min.	20 min.	10 min.
make dough	rest	shape dough	bake

MANA'EESH ZA'ATAR

Flatbreads might be the most ancient processed food, originating in the Fertile Crescent and spreading outward. They remain a key food in Middle Eastern and surrounding cuisines today, often served alongside full meals or as a vehicle for dips or pools of fragrant extra-virgin olive oil. They are morning, noon, or night breads: Find them with cheese, eggs, and salads at breakfast, rolled up for lunch on the go or a snack, or as a warm addition to the dinner table.

Mana'eesh are delicious Lebanese flatbreads in all of their iterations; it can be hard to pick a single flavor to take home. Luckily, if you learn how to make a common version topped with olive oil and za'atar, it's easy to swap out toppings. Perhaps something a little fresher, with burst tomatoes, or something a little richer, with cheese. The dough can be rolled thicker or thinner depending on the application. Our Labneh Mana'eesh Za'atar are sandwich wraps and so we simply roll the disks of dough thinner than for the individual breads, bake for less time, and cover the rounds when they come out of the oven, essentially steaming them so they're pliable.

MANA'EESH ZA'ATAR

serves 4 to 6

dough

- 2½ cups (12½ ounces) all-purpose flour
- 1½ teaspoons instant or rapid-rise yeast
- 1 teaspoon table salt
- ¾ cup plus 2 tablespoons (7 ounces) cold water
- 2 tablespoons extra-virgin olive oil

topping

- 3 tablespoons za'atar
- 3 tablespoons extra-virgin olive oil
- ½ teaspoon table salt

  Semolina flour

In Lebanon, mana'eesh are beloved street and bakery food and a common addition to the daily at-home table. Bakers prepare these flavorful breads using superhot ovens. In Lebanese, the word "man'oushe" (the singular form of mana'eesh) means "engraved" and refers to the indentations in the bread made by tapping the dough with your fingertips before baking. This keeps the dough from puffing too much in the oven and also creates pockets for the spice-and-oil mixture to pool. For this version, a food processor speedily mixes the simple dough. Placing a baking steel or stone on the middle rack of your oven and heating it at 500 degrees for a solid hour goes a long way toward mimicking bakery ovens. The high heat encourages slight bubbles with delicate char to form on top of the bread while the bottom turns an even golden brown. See page 147 for our recipe for za'atar, or use a store-bought blend. We found that semolina flour works best for transferring the flatbreads to the baking steel or stone. All-purpose flour can be substituted, but make sure the peel is generously coated.

1 make dough Process flour, yeast, and salt in food processor until combined, about 2 seconds. Combine cold water and oil in liquid measuring cup. With processor running, slowly add water mixture and process until dough forms sticky ball that clears sides of bowl, 30 to 60 seconds. Transfer dough to clean counter and knead by hand to form smooth, round ball, about 30 seconds.

2a rise Place dough seam side down in lightly greased large bowl or container, cover bowl with plastic wrap, and let rise until almost doubled in volume, 2 to 2½ hours.

2b for an overnight rise Refrigerate dough for 24 hours.

3 make topping Meanwhile, combine za'atar, oil, and salt in bowl; set aside. One hour before baking, adjust oven rack to middle position, set baking steel or stone on rack, and heat oven to 500 degrees.

4 shape dough Divide dough into 3 equal pieces on clean counter. Shape each piece of dough into ball; cover loosely with plastic and let rest for 15 minutes.

5 Coat 1 dough ball lightly with flour and, using your fingertips, flatten into 6- to 7-inch disk on lightly floured counter. Using rolling pin, roll into 9- to 10-inch circle. Dust baking peel with semolina flour. Slide dough round onto peel. Spread one-third of topping (about 1½ tablespoons) over surface of dough with back of spoon, stopping ½ inch from edge. Firmly tap dough all over with your fingertips, about 6 times.

6 bake Slide dough onto baking steel or stone and bake bread until lightly bubbled and brown on top, about 5 minutes. Using baking peel, transfer man'oushe to wire rack. Repeat with remaining dough and topping. Serve.

Flatten dough into disks.

Roll disks into circles.

Slide dough onto baking peel.

Spread topping on dough.

Tap dough with your fingertips.

Slide dough onto baking stone.

VARIATIONS

CHEESE MANA'EESH

Omit topping. Combine 1½ cups shredded whole-milk block mozzarella cheese and ½ cup crumbled feta in small bowl. After tapping dough in step 5, sprinkle one-third cheese mixture evenly over each dough round, followed by ¾ teaspoon nigella seeds, stopping ½ inch from edge. Proceed with step 6.

TOMATO MANA'EESH

Omit topping. Toss 12 ounces quartered cherry tomatoes and ½ tablespoon table salt in colander set over bowl. Let drain for 15 minutes. Discard liquid. Combine drained tomatoes, 1 thinly sliced shallot, 2 tablespoons extra-virgin olive oil, 2 teaspoons minced fresh thyme, and ¼ teaspoon table salt in bowl. After tapping dough in step 5, distribute one-third of tomato mixture over each dough round, stopping ½ inch from edge. Proceed with recipe.

total time 2¾ hours

10 min.	2 hours	20 min.	15 min.
make dough	**rise**	**shape dough**	**bake**

» **Take your time** To bake the next day, refrigerate dough for 24 hours in step 2.

LABNEH MANA'EESH ZA'ATAR

serves 4

2 **Persian cucumbers, cut into ¼-inch-wide lengths**

1 **tomato, cored and chopped**

½ **teaspoon table salt**

¼ **cup pitted kalamata olives, chopped coarse**

3 **tablespoons shredded fresh mint**

1 **tablespoon extra-virgin olive oil**

1 **tablespoon lemon juice**

¼ **teaspoon pepper**

1 **recipe Mana'eesh Za'atar, made through step 3**

½ **cup labneh, divided**

Not only are mana'eesh versatile due to their delicious topping options, they also can be eaten any time of day. Sure you could serve the flatbreads with your fried eggs, but we encourage you to try a popular Lebanese breakfast item, labneh mana'eesh. By adding schmears of labneh (a creamy yogurt cheese) and a refreshing cucumber-tomato salad to our Za'atar Mana'eesh and rolling them up, the flatbreads become portable wraps. We divide the dough into quarters instead of thirds so they roll out thinner for the proper size wrap. The original flatbreads are a little too stiff to roll up; lowering the bake time and tenting the flatbreads with foil allows them to soften enough to surround the fillings without cracking. The labneh adds a bright and welcome tang while also acting as a glue for the filling.

1   Combine cucumbers, tomato, and salt in colander set over bowl; let drain for 15 minutes and discard liquid. Toss drained cucumber-tomato mixture, olives, mint, oil, lemon juice, and pepper together in bowl; set salad aside.

2   **shape dough**   Divide dough into 4 equal pieces on clean counter. Shape each piece of dough into ball; cover loosely with plastic and let rest for 15 minutes.

3   Coat 1 dough ball lightly with flour and, using your fingertips, flatten into 6- to 7-inch disk on lightly floured counter. Using rolling pin, roll into 9- to 10-inch circle. Dust baking peel with semolina flour. Slide dough round onto peel. Spread one-quarter of za'atar topping (about 1 tablespoon) over surface of dough with back of spoon, stopping ½ inch from edge. Firmly tap dough all over with your fingertips, about 6 times.

4   **bake**   Slide dough onto hot baking steel or stone and bake bread until lightly bubbled and baked through (there won't be much browning), about 4 minutes. Transfer man'oushe to plate and tent with foil. Repeat with remaining dough and za'atar topping.

5   Working with 1 man'oushe at a time, spread 2 tablespoons labneh evenly over ⅓ of flatbread, then top with one-quarter cucumber-tomato salad, making sure the cucumbers are aligned. Roll flatbread tightly around filling then wrap tightly in aluminum foil. Cut each wrap in half crosswise before serving.

LAHMAJUN

serves 4

dough

3¼ cups (16¼ ounces) all-purpose flour

⅛ teaspoon instant or rapid-rise yeast

1¼ cups (10 ounces) ice water

1 tablespoon vegetable oil

1½ teaspoons table salt

Vegetable oil spray

topping

1 red bell pepper, stemmed, seeded, and cut into 1-inch pieces

¼ small onion

¼ cup fresh parsley leaves and tender stems

2 tablespoons mild biber salçası

1 tablespoon tomato paste

1 garlic clove, peeled

1 teaspoon ground allspice

1 teaspoon paprika

½ teaspoon ground cumin

½ teaspoon table salt

⅛ teaspoon pepper

⅛ teaspoon cayenne pepper

6 ounces ground lamb, broken into small pieces

why this recipe works   Thin and crispy lahmajun are meat-and-vegetable-topped Armenian flatbreads that are eaten whole, cut or folded in half, or wrapped around a salad to make a sandwich. The dough starts with an all-purpose flour with a higher protein content to develop plenty of gluten for both crispness and tenderness (but not so much that the flatbreads turn tough). Using very little yeast and letting the dough ferment slowly in the refrigerator maximizes flavor and minimizes the formation of gas bubbles that would make the dough difficult to roll. The lengthy rest also allows the gluten to relax so that the dough can be stretched thin. The topping for lahmajun is more like a meaty veneer than a sauce—moist but not wet and concentrated in flavor so that each bite tastes vibrant despite the thin layer. It's heady from garlic, spices, and biber salçası, a thick, cardinal-red Turkish pepper paste made from either sweet or a combination of sweet and hot peppers. Using plastic wrap to spread the topping over the dough rounds gives you the dexterity of using your fingers for a thin layer but avoids a mess. Use a mild variety of biber salçası; if it's unavailable, increase the tomato paste in the topping to 2 tablespoons and increase the paprika to 4 teaspoons. You can substitute 85 percent lean ground beef for the lamb, if desired. We prefer King Arthur brand all-purpose flour in this recipe. We like to serve the lahmajun with lemon wedges.

1   make dough   Process flour and yeast in food processor until combined, about 2 seconds. With processor running, slowly add ice water and process until dough is just combined and no dry flour remains, about 10 seconds. Let dough rest for 10 minutes.

2   Add oil and salt and process until dough forms shaggy ball, 30 to 60 seconds. Transfer dough to lightly oiled counter and knead by hand to form smooth, round ball, about 30 seconds (texture will remain slightly rough). Divide dough into 4 equal pieces. Working with 1 piece of dough at a time, form into rough ball by stretching dough around your thumbs and pinching edges together so that top is smooth. Place ball seam side down on clean counter and, using your cupped hands, drag in small circles until dough feels taut and round; transfer, seam side down, to rimmed baking sheet coated with oil spray. Spray tops of balls lightly with oil spray.

3   rise   Cover baking sheet tightly with plastic wrap and refrigerate dough for at least 16 hours or up to 2 days.

total time 17 hours

25 min.	16 hours	10 min.	25 min.
make dough	rise	shape dough	bake

» **Take your time**   To make over 3 days, refrigerate dough for up to 2 days in step 3.

4 make topping In now-empty processor, process bell pepper, onion, parsley, biber salçası, tomato paste, garlic, allspice, paprika, cumin, salt, pepper, and cayenne until smooth, scraping down sides of bowl as needed, about 15 seconds. Add lamb and pulse to combine, 8 to 10 pulses. Transfer to container, cover, and refrigerate until needed (topping can be refrigerated for up to 24 hours).

5 One hour before baking, remove dough from refrigerator and let stand at room temperature until slightly puffy and no longer cool to touch. Meanwhile, adjust oven rack to upper-middle position (rack should be 4 to 5 inches from broiler element), set baking steel or stone on rack, and heat oven to 500 degrees.

6 shape dough Place 1 dough ball on unfloured counter and dust top lightly with flour. Using heel of your hand, press dough ball into 5-inch disk. Using rolling pin, gently roll into 12-inch circle of even thickness. (Use tackiness of dough on counter to aid with rolling; if dough becomes misshapen, periodically peel round from counter, reposition, and continue to roll.) Dust top of round lightly but evenly with flour and, starting at 1 edge, peel dough off counter and flip, floured side down, onto floured baking peel (dough will spring back to about 11 inches in diameter). Place one-quarter of topping (about ½ cup) in center of dough. Cover dough with 12 by 12-inch sheet of plastic and, using your fingertips and knuckles, gently spread filling evenly across dough, leaving ⅛-inch border. Starting at 1 edge, peel away plastic, leaving topping in place (reserve plastic for topping remaining lahmajun).

7 bake Carefully slide lahmajun onto baking steel or stone and bake until bottom crust is browned, edges are lightly browned, and topping is steaming, 4 to 6 minutes. While lahmajun bakes, begin rolling next dough ball. Transfer baked lahmajun to wire rack. Repeat rolling, topping, and baking remaining 3 dough balls.

Roll dough into 12-inch circle, repositioning as needed.

Spread filing across dough with plastic wrap.

Peel away plastic.

lahmajun (page 258)

alu parathas (page 262)

ALU PARATHAS

serves 4

---

potato stuffing

- **1** pound russet potatoes, peeled and cut into 1-inch pieces
- **2** tablespoons minced fresh cilantro
- **1** tablespoon grated fresh ginger
- **1** Thai chile, stemmed and minced
- **1½** teaspoons amchoor
- **1** teaspoon ground cumin
- **¾** teaspoon table salt
- **¼** teaspoon nigella seeds
- **¼** teaspoon ajwain

dough

- **1⅔** cups (8⅓ ounces) all-purpose flour
- **½** teaspoon table salt
- **½** teaspoon sugar
- **2** tablespoons vegetable oil
- **½** cup plus **1** tablespoon (4½ ounces) cold water
- **¼** cup ghee, melted

why this recipe works   These potato-stuffed flatbreads hail from Punjab and are a staple across the northern part of the Indian subcontinent and in big cities such as Mumbai and Delhi. Alu parathas are made by wrapping disks of dough around a boldly spiced potato stuffing, rolling the stuffed balls into slim rounds, and browning the rounds (brushed with ghee) until crisp brown patches develop. The steamy, pliable breads are typically enjoyed as the center of a meal. We start by making a compact, flavorful potato stuffing of mashed russets, aromatics, and a bold mix of spices and seeds: amchoor, cumin, nigella seeds, and ajwain. Next, we mix a quick dough in the food processor, letting it rest for 30 minutes so the gluten relaxes. After stuffing the potato balls into disks of dough, we roll the packages thin and griddle them in a cast-iron skillet using plenty of nutty ghee. Flipping the breads only four times ensures they stay pliable while still developing lots of crisp brown spots. Ghee, nigella seeds (known in India as kalonji), ajwain, and amchoor can all be purchased at a South Asian market or online. Ajwain has an oregano-like flavor and is often added to fried food to aid digestion; if you can't find it, it's OK to leave it out. If preferred, you can substitute ¼ teaspoon cayenne pepper for the Thai chile in the stuffing. Serve the parathas as an entrée with raita, prepared mango pickle, or Tamatya-Kandyachi Koshimbir (recipe follows) for breakfast, lunch, or dinner.

1   make potato stuffing   Place potatoes in large saucepan, add cold water to cover by 1 inch, and bring to boil over high heat. Reduce heat to maintain simmer and cook until potatoes are very tender, about 16 minutes. Drain well and process through ricer or mash with potato masher until completely smooth. Set aside and let partially cool, about 20 minutes.

2   Stir cilantro, ginger, Thai chile, amchoor, cumin, salt, kalonji, and ajwain into potatoes. Season with salt to taste. Cover and set aside. (Potato stuffing can be refrigerated for up to 24 hours; let come to room temperature before using.)

3   make dough   Process flour, salt, and sugar in food processor until combined, about 2 seconds. Add oil and pulse until incorporated, about 5 pulses. With processor running, slowly add cold water and process until dough is combined and no dry flour remains, about 30 seconds. Transfer dough to clean counter and knead by hand to form smooth, round ball, about 30 seconds.

4   rest   Place dough seam side down in lightly greased large bowl or container, cover with plastic, and let rest for 30 minutes.

5 shape dough Divide potato stuffing into 8 equal portions and roll into balls (they will be about 1½ inches wide); cover with plastic. Divide dough into 8 equal pieces, about 1¾ ounces each, and cover loosely with plastic. Working with 1 piece of dough at a time (keep remaining pieces covered), form into rough ball by stretching dough around your thumb and pinching edges together so that top is smooth. Place ball seam side down on clean counter and, using your cupped hand, drag in small circles until dough feels taut and round. Let dough balls rest, covered, for 15 minutes. While dough balls rest, line rimmed baking sheet with parchment paper.

6 Roll 1 dough ball into 4-inch disk on lightly floured counter. Place 1 stuffing ball in center of dough disk. Gather edges of dough around stuffing to enclose completely; pinch to seal. Place seam side down on lightly floured counter, gently flatten, and lightly and gently roll to even ⅛-inch-thick round (about 8 inches wide). Transfer to prepared sheet and cover loosely with plastic. Repeat with remaining dough balls, stacking parathas between layers of parchment.

7 cook Heat 10-inch cast-iron skillet over medium heat for 5 minutes, then reduce heat to low. Brush any remaining flour from both sides of 1 paratha, then gently place in hot skillet, being careful not to stretch paratha. Cook until large bubbles begin to form on surface, underside of paratha is light blond, and paratha moves freely in skillet, 30 to 60 seconds. (Paratha may puff.) Using metal spatula, flip paratha; brush with ghee. Cook until underside is spotty brown and moves freely in skillet, 20 to 60 seconds, pressing any puffed edges firmly onto skillet with spatula to ensure even contact. Flip paratha back onto first side. Repeat brushing with ghee, pressing, cooking, and flipping once more until paratha is even more spotty brown on both sides and no longer looks raw, about 30 seconds per side. Transfer cooked paratha to second rimmed baking sheet, let cool slightly, then cover loosely with dish towel.

8 Repeat with remaining parathas, wiping out skillet with paper towels between each paratha and briefly removing skillet from heat if it begins to smoke or if paratha browns too quickly. Serve hot. (Parathas can be stacked between layers of parchment paper, placed in zipper-lock bag, and refrigerated for up to 2 days; to refresh, heat 10-inch cast-iron skillet over medium heat for 5 minutes, then reduce heat to low. Cook paratha until warmed through, flipping 3 times, 10 to 15 seconds per side.)

TAMATYA-KANDYACHI KOSHIMBIR

serves 4

If you are not fond of raw onion, substitute ¼ cup chopped peanuts.

- **4 large, firm tomatoes, cored and cut into ¼-inch dice**
- **½ teaspoon table salt**
- **1 Thai green chile, sliced**
  Pinch sugar
- **1 large onion, chopped fine**
- **¼ teaspoon ground cumin**
- **2 tablespoons grated fresh coconut (optional)**
- **2 tablespoons finely chopped fresh cilantro (optional)**

Stir tomatoes, salt, Thai chile, and sugar together in bowl. Let sit for 5 minutes to allow flavors to meld. Stir in onion and cumin. Serve, garnishing with coconut and cilantro, if using.

total time 2¾ hours

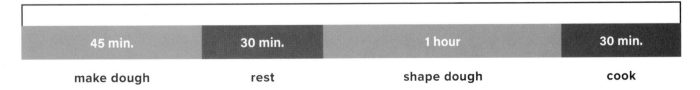

make dough	rest	shape dough	cook
45 min.	30 min.	1 hour	30 min.

ADJARULI KHACHAPURI

serves 6

dough

1¾ cups (8¾ ounces) all-purpose flour

1½ teaspoons sugar

1 teaspoon instant or rapid-rise yeast

¾ teaspoon table salt

½ cup plus 2 tablespoons (5 ounces) ice water

1 tablespoon extra-virgin olive oil

topping

6 ounces whole-milk mozzarella cheese, shredded (1½ cups)

6 ounces feta cheese, crumbled (1½ cups)

1 large egg yolk

1 tablespoon unsalted butter

why this recipe works   This cheese-filled bread is so beloved in the country of Georgia that it's the national dish. Different versions of khachapuri are shaped and filled in different ways; the adjaruli version is distinguished by its distinctive wide, flat boat shape. When the bread is still hot from the oven, the molten cheese is usually topped with an egg and butter and stirred together tableside. Diners tear off chunks of the crust to swipe into the center. This dough uses all-purpose flour, which provides enough structure to contain the oozy cheese and gives the bread a lightly chewy texture. A blend of mozzarella and feta cheeses approximates the briny, salty tang and desirable stringy texture found in the Georgian cheeses traditionally used, such as sulguni and imeruli. Stirring in an egg yolk and a pat of butter right before serving makes the filling smooth, stretchy, and ultrarich. Use block mozzarella here.

1   make dough   Process flour, sugar, yeast, and salt in food processor until combined, about 2 seconds. With processor running, slowly add ice water and oil and process until dough forms sticky ball that clears sides of bowl, 30 to 60 seconds. Transfer dough to clean counter and knead by hand to form smooth, round ball, about 30 seconds.

2a   first rise   Place dough seam side down in lightly greased large bowl or container, cover bowl with plastic wrap, and let rise until almost doubled in volume, 2 to 2½ hours.

2b   for an overnight rise   Refrigerate dough for 24 hours. Let dough sit at room temperature, about 2 hours.

3   shape dough   Turn dough onto lightly floured 16 by 12-inch sheet of parchment paper and coat lightly with flour. Flatten into 8-inch disk using your hands. Using rolling pin, roll dough into 12-inch circle, dusting dough lightly with flour as needed. Roll bottom edge of dough 2½ inches in toward center. Rotate parchment 180 degrees and roll bottom edge of dough (directly opposite first rolled side) 2½ inches toward center. (Opposing edges of rolled sides should be 7 inches apart.) Roll ends of rolled sides toward centerline and pinch firmly together to form football shape about 12 inches long and about 7 inches across at its widest point. Transfer parchment with dough to rimmed baking sheet.

4   second rise   Cover loosely with plastic and let rise until puffy, 30 minutes to 1 hour. Adjust oven rack to middle position and heat oven to 450 degrees.

5   make topping   Combine mozzarella and feta in bowl. Fill dough with cheese mixture, lightly compacting and mounding in center (cheese will be piled higher than edge of dough).

6   bake   Bake until crust is well browned and cheese is bubbly and beginning to brown in spots, 15 to 17 minutes. Transfer sheet to wire rack. Add egg yolk and butter to cheese filling and stir with fork until fully incorporated and cheese is smooth and stretchy. Lift parchment off sheet and slide bread onto serving dish. Serve immediately.

Roll bottom edge of dough toward center.

Roll second edge of dough toward center.

Roll ends of rolled sides toward center line.

Pinch ends to form football shape.

total time 3¼ hours

10 min.	2 hours	10 min.	30 min.	20 min.
make dough	first rise	shape dough	second rise	bake

» **Take your time** To bake the next day, refrigerate dough for 24 hours in step 2.

adjaruli khachapuri (page 264)

mushroom musakhan (page 268)

MUSHROOM MUSAKHAN

serves 4 to 6

dough

1½ cups (8¼ ounces) whole-wheat flour

1 cup (5½ ounces) bread flour

¾ teaspoon instant or rapid-rise yeast

1¼ cups (10 ounces) ice water

2 teaspoons honey

2 tablespoons extra-virgin olive oil

1¾ teaspoons table salt

topping

½ cup extra-virgin olive oil, divided

2 tablespoons minced fresh oregano or 2 teaspoons dried

4 garlic cloves, minced

1½ tablespoons ground sumac

¼ teaspoon ground allspice

⅛ teaspoon ground cardamom

2 pounds onions, halved and sliced ¼ inch thick

2 teaspoons packed light brown sugar

1½ teaspoons table salt, divided

¼ cup pine nuts

2 pounds portobello mushroom caps, gills removed, caps halved and sliced ½ inch thick, divided

2 tablespoons minced fresh chives, divided

why this recipe works   Musakhan is a popular Palestinian dish featuring flatbread that's usually topped with roasted chicken, caramelized onions, pine nuts, and tart ground sumac. This version focuses on just the bread part and includes the traditional caramelized onions, pine nuts, and sumac, but showcases mushrooms rather than chicken. Sautéed portobello mushrooms, with their robust flavor and meaty texture, make a satisfying savory topping. The traditional base for musakhan is taboon bread, a thick, crisp flatbread that is traditionally cooked in a clay oven called a taboon. To ensure crisp edges on these flatbreads with a standard oven, we cook them on a preheated baking steel or stone in the hottest oven we can achieve. If you don't have a baking stone, use a preheated overturned rimmed baking sheet. Serve with plain yogurt for dolloping on top, if you like.

1   make dough   Pulse whole-wheat flour, bread flour, and yeast in food processor until combined, about 5 pulses. With processor running, slowly add ice water and honey and process until dough is just combined and no dry flour remains, about 10 seconds. Let dough rest for 10 minutes.

2   Add oil and salt to dough and process until dough forms satiny, sticky ball that clears sides of bowl, 30 to 60 seconds. Transfer dough to lightly oiled counter and knead by hand to form smooth, round ball, about 30 seconds.

3   rise   Place dough seam side down in lightly greased large bowl or container, cover with plastic wrap, and refrigerate for at least 18 hours or up to 2 days.

4   make topping   Combine 1 tablespoon oil, oregano, garlic, sumac, allspice, and cardamom in bowl. Heat 2 tablespoons oil in 12-inch nonstick skillet over high heat until shimmering. Add onions, sugar, and ½ teaspoon salt and stir to coat. Cook, stirring occasionally, until onions begin to soften and release some moisture, about 5 minutes. Reduce heat to medium and continue to cook, stirring often, until onions are well caramelized, 35 to 40 minutes. (If onions are sizzling or scorching, reduce heat. If onions are not browning after 15 to 20 minutes, increase heat.) Push onions to sides of skillet. Add oregano-garlic mixture to center and cook, mashing mixture into skillet, until fragrant, about 30 seconds. Stir oregano-garlic mixture into onions. Transfer onion mixture to food processor and pulse to jam-like consistency, about 5 pulses. Transfer to bowl, stir in pine nuts, and season with salt and pepper to taste; let cool completely before using.

5 Wipe skillet clean with paper towels. Heat 2 tablespoons oil in now-empty skillet over medium-high heat until shimmering. Add half of mushrooms and ½ teaspoon salt and cook, stirring occasionally, until evenly browned, 8 to 10 minutes; transfer to separate bowl. Repeat with 2 tablespoons oil, remaining mushrooms, and remaining ½ teaspoon salt; transfer to bowl and let cool completely before using.

6 shape dough One hour before baking, adjust oven rack 4 to 5 inches from broiler element, set baking stone on rack, and heat oven to 500 degrees. Press down on dough to deflate. Transfer dough to clean counter, divide in half, and cover loosely with greased plastic. Pat 1 piece of dough (keep remaining piece covered) into 4-inch round. Working around circumference of dough, fold edges toward center until ball forms.

7 Flip ball seam side down and, using your cupped hands, drag in small circles on counter until dough feels taut and round and all seams are secured on underside. (If dough sticks to your hands, lightly dust top of dough with flour.) Repeat with remaining piece of dough. Space dough balls 3 inches apart.

8 rest Cover dough loosely with greased plastic and let rest for 1 hour.

9 Heat broiler for 10 minutes. Meanwhile, generously coat 1 dough ball with flour and place on well-floured counter. Press and roll into 12 by 8-inch oval. Transfer oval to well-floured baking peel and stretch into 15 by 8-inch oval. (If dough resists stretching, let it relax for 10 to 20 minutes before trying to stretch it again.) Using fork, poke entire surface of oval 10 to 15 times. Spread half of onion mixture evenly on dough, edge to edge, and arrange half of mushrooms on top.

10 bake Slide flatbread carefully onto baking stone and return oven to 500 degrees. Bake until bottom crust is evenly browned and edges are crisp, about 10 minutes, rotating flatbread halfway through baking. Transfer flatbread to wire rack and let cool for 5 minutes. Drizzle with 1½ teaspoons oil and sprinkle with 1 tablespoon chives. Slice and serve. Heat broiler for 10 minutes. Repeat with remaining dough and toppings, returning oven to 500 degrees when flatbread is placed on stone.

total time 20¼ hours

20 min.	18 hours	15 min.	1 hour	30 min.	5 min.
make dough	rise	shape dough	rest	bake	cool

» **Take your time** To make over 3 days, refrigerate dough for up to 2 days in step 3.

COQUES WITH SPINACH, RAISINS, AND PINE NUTS

serves 6 to 8

dough

- **3 cups (16½ ounces) bread flour**
- **2 teaspoons sugar**
- **½ teaspoon instant or rapid-rise yeast**
- **1½ cups (10⅔ ounces) ice water**
- **3 tablespoons extra-virgin olive oil**
- **1½ teaspoons table salt**

topping

- **9 tablespoons extra-virgin olive oil, divided, plus extra for drizzling**
- **½ cup golden raisins, chopped**
- **1 large shallot, minced**
- **2 anchovy fillets, rinsed, patted dry, and minced**
- **½ teaspoon red pepper flakes**
- **3 garlic cloves, minced**
- **2 pounds frozen spinach, thawed and squeezed dry**
- **1 tablespoon grated lemon zest plus 1 tablespoon juice**
- **1¼ teaspoons table salt**
- **¼ cup pine nuts**
- **Flake sea salt**

why this recipe works Thin and crunchy and topped with a myriad of savory (or sweet) toppings, these Catalan flatbreads are ubiquitous in Spanish tapas bars. Although coques are sometimes referred to as the Spanish version of pizza, we don't think that captures the dish. The flatbreads have an almost-fried crispiness; to achieve that we use more olive oil than is typical in a pizza dough, and we brush each coca with more olive oil before baking. Parbaking the dough before topping it further promotes an evenly crispy, sturdy base—all the better to support a classic combination of spinach, raisins, and pine nuts. Thawed frozen spinach saves time and effort of prepping and cooking fresh greens, and a healthy dose of garlic, red pepper flakes, lemon, and just a touch of anchovies make the topping taste bright, complex, and savory. With a final drizzle of olive oil and a sprinkle of flaky salt, your coca is ready to accompany a glass of wine for a light dinner or be part of an appetizer spread. If you cannot fit two coques on a single baking sheet, bake them in two batches. We prefer King Arthur brand bread flour in this recipe.

1 make dough Pulse flour, sugar, and yeast in food processor until combined, about 5 pulses. With processor running, slowly add ice water and process until dough is just combined and no dry flour remains, about 10 seconds. Let dough rest for 10 minutes.

2 Add oil and salt to dough and process until dough forms satiny, sticky ball that clears sides of bowl, 30 to 60 seconds. Transfer dough to lightly floured counter and knead by hand to form smooth, round ball, about 30 seconds.

3 rise Place dough seam side down in lightly greased large bowl or container, cover tightly with plastic wrap, and refrigerate dough for at least 24 hours or up to 3 days.

4 shape dough Press down on dough to deflate. Transfer dough to clean counter, divide into quarters, and cover loosely with greased plastic. Working with 1 piece of dough at a time (keep remaining pieces covered), form into rough ball by stretching dough around your thumb and pinching edges together so that top is smooth. Place ball seam side down on counter and, using your cupped hands, drag in small circles until dough feels taut and round. Space dough balls 3 inches apart.

5 rest Cover dough loosely with greased plastic, and let rest for 1 hour.

6 make topping Combine ¼ cup oil, raisins, shallot, anchovies, and pepper flakes in Dutch oven. Cook over medium heat, stirring frequently, until shallots are softened, 3 to 5 minutes. Stir in garlic and cook until fragrant, about 30 seconds. Off heat, stir in spinach, lemon zest and juice, and salt; let cool while rolling out dough.

7 Adjust oven racks to upper-middle and lower-middle positions and heat oven to 500 degrees. Coat 2 rimmed baking sheets with 2 tablespoons oil each. Transfer 1 dough ball to well-floured counter. Press and roll into 14 by 5-inch oval. Arrange oval on prepared sheet, with long edge fitted snugly against 1 long side of sheet, reshaping as needed. (If dough resists stretching, let rest for 10 to 20 minutes before trying to stretch again.) Repeat with remaining dough balls, arranging 2 ovals on each sheet, spaced ½ inch apart. Using fork, poke surface of dough 10 to 15 times.

8 bake Brush dough ovals with remaining 1 tablespoon oil and bake until puffed, 6 to 8 minutes, switching and rotating sheets halfway through baking. Scatter spinach topping evenly over flat-breads, then sprinkle with pine nuts. Bake until topping is heated through and edges of flatbreads are deep golden brown and crisp, 10 to 12 minutes, switching and rotating sheets halfway through baking. Let flatbreads cool on sheets for 10 minutes, then transfer to cutting board. Drizzle with extra oil and sprinkle with sea salt. Slice and serve.

total time 26 hours

25 min.	24 hours	5 min.	1 hour	18 min.	10 min.
make dough	rise	shape dough	rest	bake	cool

» **Take your time** To make over 2 to 4 days, refrigerate dough for up to 3 days in step 3.

total time 40 minutes

20 min.	20 min.
make batter	**cook**

SOCCA WITH SAUTÉED ONIONS AND ROSEMARY

serves 6 to 8

batter

- 1½ cups (12 ounces) water
- 1⅓ cups (6 ounces) chickpea flour
- ¼ cup extra-virgin olive oil, divided
- 1 teaspoon table salt
- ¼ teaspoon ground cumin

topping

- 2 tablespoons extra-virgin olive oil, plus extra for drizzling
- 2 cups thinly sliced onions
- ½ teaspoon table salt
- 1 teaspoon chopped fresh rosemary
- Coarse sea salt

why this recipe works These thin, crisp, nutty-tasting chickpea pancakes will transport you right to the French Riviera, where they are a popular snacking choice as street food or alongside a glass of chilled rosé at an outdoor café. Traditionally, the socca batter is baked in a large cast-iron skillet in a very hot wood-burning oven. Then the large pancake with a blistered top and smoky flavor is cut into wedges for serving. To make socca at home, we cook supereasy smaller versions entirely on the stovetop, using a preheated nonstick skillet and flipping them to get a great crust on both sides. These smaller socca are easier to flip than one large pancake, and the direct heat of the stovetop ensures a crispy exterior on both sides, giving the socca a higher ratio of crunchy crust to tender interior. A topping of golden caramelized onions, enhanced with rosemary, complements the savory flatbreads.

1 make batter Adjust oven rack to middle position and heat oven to 200 degrees. Set wire rack in rimmed baking sheet and place in oven. Whisk water, flour, 4 teaspoons oil, salt, and cumin in bowl until no lumps remain. Let batter rest while preparing topping, at least 10 minutes.

2 make topping Heat oil in 10-inch nonstick skillet over medium-high heat until just smoking. Add onions and table salt and cook until onions start to brown around edges but still have some texture, 7 to 10 minutes. Add rosemary and cook until fragrant, about 1 minute. Transfer onion mixture to bowl; set aside. Wipe skillet clean with paper towels.

3 cook Heat 2 teaspoons oil in now-empty skillet over medium-high heat until just smoking. Lift skillet off heat and pour ½ cup batter into far side of skillet; swirl gently in clockwise direction until batter evenly covers bottom of skillet. Return skillet to heat and cook socca, without moving it, until well browned and crisp around bottom edge, 3 to 4 minutes (you can peek at underside of socca by loosening it from side of skillet with rubber spatula). Flip socca with rubber spatula and cook until second side is just cooked, about 1 minute. Transfer socca, browned side up, to prepared wire rack in oven.

4 Repeat 3 more times, using 2 teaspoons oil and ½ cup batter per batch. Transfer socca to cutting board and cut each into wedges. Serve, topped with sautéed onions, drizzled with extra oil, and sprinkled with sea salt.

KESRA RAKHSIS

serves 6 to 8

2 tablespoons sesame seeds

2¾–3 cups (16½ to 18 ounces) fine semolina flour

1¼ teaspoons table salt

1 teaspoon active dry yeast

1 teaspoon sugar

1 teaspoon nigella seeds

1 teaspoon chia seeds (optional)

1 cup (8 ounces) warm water

½ cup extra-virgin olive oil

why this recipe works   Kesra rakhsis (also often called "rek-sas") is an Algerian flatbread that comes together relatively quickly and makes a great snack, side, or vessel for dips. Our recipe is adapted from Wafa Bahloul, chef and co-owner of Kayma, a restaurant serving Algerian food in the La Cocina Municipal Marketplace in San Francisco. The base of the bread is semolina flour, which is made with whole-grain durum wheat. This flour gives the bread the signature chew and deep flavor that Bahloul enhances with sugar, salt, deeply toasted sesame seeds, chia seeds, nigella seeds, and a hefty dose of olive oil (preferably Algerian olive oil). When she lived in Algeria, Bahloul cooked this bread in a tagine (a sort of clay skillet without a handle) on the stovetop. We call for using a preheated cast-iron skillet on the stovetop to mimic the crisp edges created by the original cooking method. You can substitute black sesame seeds for the nigella seeds, if desired. We had the best results with a very fine semolina flour such as Caputo Durum Wheat Semolina. The dough's texture should be similar to that of Play-Doh. If your dough is too soft in step 2, add extra flour. Serve the bread warm with butter and/or olives or alongside dips or soup.

1   make dough   Toast sesame seeds in 8-inch skillet over medium heat until deep golden brown and fragrant, 4 to 6 minutes. Transfer sesame seeds to large bowl. Add 2¾ cups flour, salt, yeast, sugar, nigella seeds, and chia seeds, if using. Stir in warm tap water and oil until fully combined. (Dough should be soft and tacky but still workable. If dough is too wet, stir in additional flour, 1 tablespoon at a time, up to ¼ cup, until dough can hold its shape.) Turn out dough onto clean counter and knead by hand until dough feels less sticky and springs back when pressed lightly with your fingertip (continue kneading if it doesn't), 3 to 5 minutes.

2   Divide dough into 2 equal pieces (about 14 ounces each). Shape each piece into ball. Working with 1 dough ball at a time, place seam side down on clean counter and drag in small circles until dough feels taut and round.

3   rise   Cover dough balls loosely with plastic wrap and let rest for 1 hour.

4   shape dough   Roll 1 dough ball into 8-inch round. Repeat with remaining dough ball.

5   cook   Heat 12-inch cast-iron skillet over medium-low heat for 10 minutes. Prick dough round all over with fork. Loosely roll dough around rolling pin and gently and carefully unroll it into skillet. Cook until underside is deep golden brown, about 5 minutes, rotating flatbread as needed for even browning. Flip flatbread and continue to cook until second side is deep golden brown, about 4 minutes. Transfer to large plate. Repeat pricking and cooking remaining dough round (you needn't preheat skillet again). Tear or cut into wedges and serve warm.

total time 2 hours

25 min.	1 hour	5 min.	25 min.
make dough	rise	shape dough	cook

PAN-GRILLED FLATBREADS

serves 4

2½ cups (13¾ ounces) bread flour

¼ cup (1⅓ ounces) whole-wheat flour

2¼ teaspoons instant or rapid-rise yeast

1½ teaspoons table salt

1 cup (8 ounces) water, room temperature

¼ cup (2 ounces) plain whole-milk yogurt, room temperature

2 tablespoons extra-virgin olive oil, divided

2 teaspoons sugar

1½ tablespoons unsalted butter, melted

Coarse sea salt

why this recipe works   Inspired by the soft pillowy texture and versatility of Indian naan, we set out to make flavorful, rustic-looking, tender-chewy all-purpose flatbreads that could go with just about anything. These are easy enough to cook while dinner is bubbling or to make to serve with prepared salads and spreads. To give the simple flatbreads a wheat flavor without compromising the texture, we add a small amount of whole-wheat flour—just ¼ cup—to bread flour. Taking a cue from naan, we enrich the dough with yogurt and oil, which tenderize it. A little sugar and salt improve the flavor of the bread. For the cooking vessel, we turn to a cast-iron skillet and its great heat retention to help create spotty brown flecks. To avoid a tough crust on these plush flatbreads, we first mist the dough with water before cooking to moisten the flour that coats it. Then we cover the pan during the bread's brief cooking time, trapping steam and moisture. Brushing the finished breads with melted butter and sprinkling them with sea salt adds a final layer of flavor. We prefer a cast-iron skillet here, but any 12-inch nonstick skillet will work fine. For efficiency, stretch the next ball of dough while each flatbread is cooking.

1 make dough   Whisk bread flour, whole-wheat flour, yeast, and table salt together in bowl of stand mixer. Whisk water, yogurt, 1 tablespoon oil, and sugar in 4-cup liquid measuring cup until sugar has dissolved. Using dough hook on low speed, slowly add water mixture to flour mixture and mix until cohesive dough starts to form and no dry flour remains, about 2 minutes, scraping down bowl as needed. Increase speed to medium-low and knead until dough is smooth and elastic and clears sides of bowl but sticks to bottom, about 8 minutes. Transfer dough to lightly floured counter and knead by hand to form smooth, round ball, about 30 seconds.

2 rise   Place dough seam side down in lightly greased large bowl or container, cover with plastic wrap, and let rise until doubled in volume, 1½ to 2 hours.

3 shape dough   Adjust oven rack to middle position and heat oven to 200 degrees. Transfer dough to clean counter, divide into quarters, and cover loosely with greased plastic. Working with 1 piece of dough at a time (keep remaining pieces covered), form into rough ball by stretching dough around your thumb and pinching edges together so that top is smooth. Place ball seam side down on clean counter and, using your cupped hand, drag in small circles until dough feels taut and round. Let balls rest, covered, for 10 minutes.

4 Grease 12-inch cast-iron skillet with remaining 1 tablespoon oil and heat over medium heat for 5 minutes. Meanwhile, press and roll 1 dough ball into 9-inch round of even thickness, sprinkling dough and counter with flour as needed to prevent sticking. Using fork, poke entire surface of round 20 to 25 times.

5 cook Using paper towels, carefully wipe out skillet, leaving thin film of oil on bottom and sides. Mist top of dough with water. Place dough moistened side down in skillet, then mist top of dough with water. Cover and cook until flatbread is lightly puffed and bottom is spotty brown, 2 to 4 minutes. Flip flatbread, cover, and continue to cook until spotty brown on second side, 2 to 4 minutes. (If large air pockets form, gently poke with fork to deflate.)

6 Brush 1 side of flatbread with about 1 teaspoon melted butter and sprinkle with sea salt. Serve immediately or transfer to ovensafe plate, cover loosely with aluminum foil, and keep warm in oven. Repeat with remaining dough balls, melted butter, and sea salt. Serve.

total time 2¾ hours

25 min.	1½ hours	20 min.	25 min.
make dough	rise	shape dough	cook

PITA BREAD

serves 8

2⅔ cups (14⅔ ounces) bread flour

2¼ teaspoons instant or rapid-rise yeast

1⅓ cups (10½ ounces) ice water

¼ cup extra-virgin olive oil

4 teaspoons honey

1¼ teaspoons table salt

Vegetable oil spray

why this recipe works The tender chew and complex flavor of fresh-baked pitas are revelatory—they make it hard to go back to bagged versions. Our recipe creates tender, chewy pitas with perfect pockets, every time. We start with high-protein bread flour, which creates the structure to support the expansion necessary for pocket formation and good chew. A high hydration level and a generous amount of oil helps keep the pitas tender, and honey adds a touch of sweetness. After quickly making the dough in the stand mixer, we shape it into balls and let them proof overnight in the refrigerator to develop complex flavor. We then roll the dough balls into thin, even rounds before baking them on a hot baking steel or stone placed on the lowest oven rack, ensuring that the breads puff up quickly and fully. We prefer King Arthur brand bread flour for this recipe. If using another bread flour, reduce the amount of water in the dough by 2 tablespoons (1 ounce).

1 make dough Whisk flour and yeast together in bowl of stand mixer. Add ice water, oil, and honey on top of flour mixture. Fit stand mixer with dough hook and mix on low speed until all flour is moistened, 1 to 2 minutes. Let dough rest for 10 minutes.

2 Add salt to dough and mix on medium speed until dough forms satiny, sticky ball that clears sides of bowl, 6 to 8 minutes. Transfer dough to lightly oiled counter and knead until smooth, about 1 minute.

3 Divide dough into 8 equal pieces. Working with 1 piece of dough at a time (keep remaining pieces covered), form into rough ball by stretching dough around your thumb and pinching edges together so that top is smooth. Place ball seam side down on clean counter and, using your cupped hand, drag in small circles until dough feels taut and round. Transfer, seam side down, to rimmed baking sheet coated with oil spray.

4 rise Spray tops of balls lightly with oil spray, then cover tightly with plastic wrap and refrigerate for at least 16 hours or up to 24 hours.

5 shape dough One hour before baking, adjust oven rack to lowest position, set baking steel or stone on rack, and heat oven to 425 degrees. Remove dough from refrigerator. Coat 1 dough ball generously on both sides with flour and place on well-floured counter, seam side down. Use heel of your hand to press dough ball into 5-inch circle. Using rolling pin, gently roll into 7-inch circle, adding flour as necessary to prevent sticking. Roll slowly and gently to prevent any creasing. Repeat with second dough ball. Brush both sides of each dough round with pastry brush to remove any excess flour. Transfer dough rounds to unfloured baking peel, making sure side that was facing up when you began rolling is face up again.

6 bake Slide both dough rounds carefully onto steel or stone and bake until evenly inflated and lightly browned on undersides, 1 to 3 minutes. Using peel, slide pitas off stone and, using your hands or spatula, gently invert. (If pitas do not puff after 3 minutes, flip immediately to prevent overcooking.) Return pitas to stone and bake until lightly browned in center of second side, 1 minute. Transfer pitas to wire rack to cool, covering loosely with clean dish towel. Repeat shaping and baking with remaining 6 pitas in 3 batches. Let pitas cool for 10 minutes before serving. (The pitas are best eaten within 24 hours of baking. Reheat leftover pitas by wrapping them in aluminum foil, placing them in a cold oven, setting the temperature to 300 degrees, and baking for 15 to 20 minutes.)

total time 17¾ hours

40 min.	16 hours	35 min.	20 min.	10 min.
make dough	**rise**	**shape dough**	**bake**	**cool**

» **Take your time** To make over 26 hours, refrigerate dough for up to 24 hours in step 4.

WHOLE-WHEAT PITA BREAD

serves 8

1⅓ cups (7⅓ ounces) whole-wheat flour

1⅓ cups (7⅓ ounces) bread flour

2¼ teaspoons instant or rapid-rise yeast

1 cup plus 2 tablespoons (9 ounces) ice water

¼ cup extra-virgin olive oil

4 teaspoons honey

1¼ teaspoons table salt

Vegetable oil spray

why this recipe works   Adding significant whole-wheat flavor to pita breads is surprisingly simple. We use a 50/50 combination of bread flour and whole-wheat flour for the perfect amount of nuttiness without compromising the pita's pocket. The oil in the recipe ensures the pitas are still moist. We prefer King Arthur brand bread flour in this recipe. The pitas are best eaten within 24 hours of baking. Reheat leftover pitas by wrapping them in aluminum foil, placing them in a cold oven, setting the temperature to 300 degrees, and baking for 15 to 20 minutes.

1   make dough   Sift whole-wheat flour through fine-mesh strainer into bowl of stand mixer; discard bran remaining in strainer. Whisk bread flour and yeast into whole-wheat flour. Add ice water, oil, and honey on top of flour mixture. Fit stand mixer with dough hook and mix on low speed until all flour is moistened, 1 to 2 minutes. Let dough rest for 10 minutes.

2   Add salt to dough and mix on medium speed until dough forms satiny, sticky ball that clears sides of bowl, 6 to 8 minutes. Transfer dough to lightly oiled counter and knead until smooth, about 1 minute.

3   Divide dough into 8 equal pieces. Working with 1 piece of dough at a time (cover remaining pieces), form into rough ball by stretching dough around your thumbs and pinching edges together so that top is smooth. Place ball seam side down on clean counter and, using your cupped hand, drag in small circles until dough feels taut and round.

4   rise   Spray tops of balls lightly with oil spray, then cover tightly with plastic wrap and refrigerate for at least 16 hours or up to 24 hours.

5   shape dough   One hour before baking, adjust oven rack to lowest position, set baking stone on rack, and heat oven to 425 degrees. Remove dough from refrigerator. Coat 1 dough ball generously on both sides with flour and place on well-floured counter, seam side down. Use heel of your hand to press dough ball into 5-inch circle. Using rolling pin, gently roll into 7-inch circle, adding flour as necessary to prevent sticking. Roll slowly and gently to prevent any creasing. Repeat with second dough ball. Brush both sides of each dough round with pastry brush to remove any excess flour. Transfer dough rounds to unfloured peel, making sure side that was facing up when you began rolling is face up again.

6   bake   Slide both dough rounds carefully onto steel or stone and bake until evenly inflated and lightly browned on undersides, 1 to 3 minutes. Using peel, slide pitas off stone and, using your hands or spatula, gently invert. (If pitas do not puff after 3 minutes, flip immediately to prevent overcooking.) Return pitas to steel or stone and bake until lightly browned in center of second side, 1 minute. Transfer pitas to wire rack to cool, covering loosely with clean dish towel. Repeat shaping and baking with remaining 6 pitas in 3 batches. Let pitas cool for 10 minutes before serving.

total time 17¾ hours

40 min.	16 hours	35 min.	20 min.	10 min.
make dough	rise	shape dough	bake	cool

» **Take your time** To make over 26 hours, refrigerate dough for up to 24 hours in step 4.

total time 1¾ hours

25 min.	30 min.	15 min.	25 min.
make dough	rest	shape dough	cook

PIADINE

serves 4

2 cups (10 ounces)
all-purpose flour

¾ teaspoon baking powder

½ teaspoon table salt

3 tablespoons vegetable oil

¾ cup (6 ounces) water

why this recipe works   Once a poor man's bread in the Emilia-Romagna region of Italy, piadine are now found both as street food and at the table in most restaurants in the region. The rustic, tender-chewy rounds, tailor-made for filling with cured meat, cheese, and/or vegetables, can be made without yeast, lengthy rising times, or even your oven. For an appropriately open crumb, we add baking powder to the dough. Ample amounts of fat and water dilute the gluten strands, keeping the dough soft and pliable without making it too rich. Rolling the dough into 9-inch rounds creates substantial breads that fit in a cast-iron pan, which we preheat thoroughly so the flatbread browns quickly without drying out. A nonstick skillet can be used in place of cast iron; increase the heat to medium-high and preheat the empty skillet with ½ teaspoon of oil until shimmering; wipe out the oil before proceeding with the recipe.

1   make dough   Process flour, baking powder, and salt in food processor until combined, about 2 seconds. Add oil and process until no visible bits of fat remain, about 10 seconds. With processor running, slowly add water and process until most of dough forms soft, slightly tacky ball that clears sides of workbowl, 30 to 60 seconds (there may be small bits of loose dough).

2   Transfer dough to counter and gently knead until smooth, about 15 seconds. Divide dough into 4 equal pieces and shape each into ball. Working with 1 piece of dough at a time (keep remaining pieces covered), form into rough ball by stretching dough around your thumb and pinching edges together so that top is smooth. Place ball seam side down on clean counter and, using your cupped hand, drag in small circles until dough feels taut and round.

3   rest   Cover dough balls loosely with plastic wrap. Let rest for 30 minutes.

4   shape dough   Pat 1 dough ball into 5-inch disk on lightly floured counter (keep remaining dough balls covered). Roll disk into 9-inch circle, flouring counter as needed to prevent sticking. Repeat with remaining dough balls.

5   cook   Heat 12-inch cast-iron skillet over medium heat until drop of water dripped onto surface sizzles immediately, about 3 minutes. Prick 1 dough round all over with fork, then carefully place in skillet. Cook until underside is spotty brown, 1 to 2 minutes, using fork to pop any large bubbles that form. Flip round and cook until second side is spotty brown, 1 to 2 minutes (flatbread should still be pliable). Transfer piadina to plate, gently fold in half, and cover with clean dish towel to keep warm. Repeat with remaining dough rounds, stacking piadine and re-covering with towel as they finish. Serve warm. (Piadine can be stored in zipper-lock bag for up to 2 days. Reheat in cast-iron skillet over medium-high heat for 20 to 30 seconds per side, until warmed through.)

CHAPATIS

serves 4

¾ **cup (4⅛ ounces)
whole-wheat flour**

¾ **cup (3¾ ounces)
all-purpose flour**

1 **teaspoon table salt**

½ **cup (4 ounces) warm water**

3 **tablespoons plus 2 teaspoons
vegetable oil, divided**

why this recipe works   Chapatis are wheaty, unleavened Indian flatbreads often used as utensils for scooping up a number of sumptuous dishes. They're traditionally made from a finely ground hard wheat flour known as atta. We found that a combination of whole-wheat and all-purpose flours yields a more tender and elastic chapati than one made with only (comparatively coarse) American whole-wheat flour. To simulate the results achieved by cooking chapatis on the griddle known as a tava, we turn to a well-seasoned cast-iron skillet. This recipe can easily be doubled.

1   make dough   Whisk flours and salt together in bowl. Stir in water and 3 table-spoons oil until cohesive dough forms. Transfer dough to lightly floured counter and knead by hand to form smooth ball, 1 minute.

2   Divide dough into 4 pieces and cover with plastic wrap. Working with 1 piece of dough at a time (keep remaining pieces covered), form into rough ball by stretching dough around your thumb and pinching edges together so that top is smooth. Place ball seam side down on clean counter and, using your cupped hand, drag in small circles until dough feels taut and round. Repeat with remaining dough pieces. Place on plate seam side down.

3   rest   Cover dough with plastic wrap and let sit for 30 minutes. (Dough can be refrigerated for up to 3 days.)

4   shape dough   Line rimmed baking sheet with parchment paper. Roll 1 dough ball into 9-inch circle on lightly floured counter (keep remaining pieces covered). Transfer to prepared sheet and top with additional sheet of parchment. Repeat with remaining dough balls.

5   cook   Heat 12-inch cast-iron or nonstick skillet over medium heat for 3 minutes. Add ½ teaspoon oil to skillet, then use paper towels to carefully wipe out skillet, leaving thin film of oil on bottom; skillet should be just smoking. (If using 12-inch nonstick skillet, heat ½ teaspoon oil over medium heat in skillet until shimmering, then wipe out skillet.) Place 1 dough round in hot skillet and cook until dough is bubbly and bottom is browned in spots, about 2 minutes. Flip dough and cook until puffed and second side is spotty brown, 1 to 2 minutes. Transfer to clean plate and cover with dish towel to keep warm. Repeat with remaining dough rounds and oil. Serve. (Cooked chapatis can be refrigerated for up to 3 days or frozen for up to 3 months. To freeze, layer wraps between parchment and store in zipper-lock bag. To serve, stack wraps on plate, cover with damp dish towel, and microwave until warm, 60 to 90 seconds.)

total time 1¼ hours

15 min.	30 min.	5 min.	25 min.
make dough	rest	shape dough	cook

» **Take your time** To make over 2 to 4 days, refrigerate dough for up to 3 days in step 3.

CHAPTER SIX

enriched breads

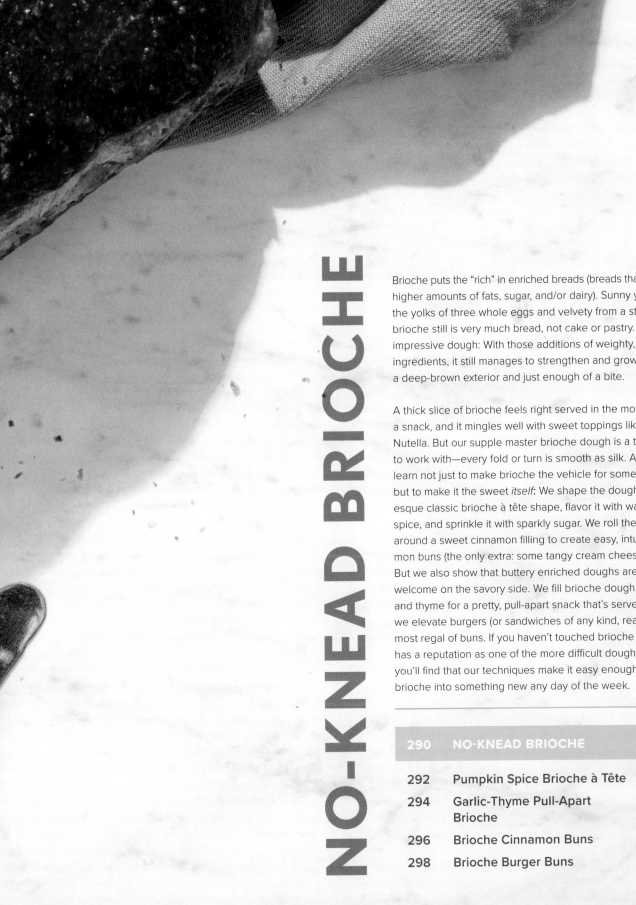

NO-KNEAD BRIOCHE

Brioche puts the "rich" in enriched breads (breads that incorporate higher amounts of fats, sugar, and/or dairy). Sunny yellow from the yolks of three whole eggs and velvety from a stick of butter, brioche still is very much bread, not cake or pastry. And it's one impressive dough: With those additions of weighty, tenderizing ingredients, it still manages to strengthen and grow, to develop a deep-brown exterior and just enough of a bite.

A thick slice of brioche feels right served in the morning or as a snack, and it mingles well with sweet toppings like jam or Nutella. But our supple master brioche dough is a true dream to work with—every fold or turn is smooth as silk. And so you'll learn not just to make brioche the vehicle for something sweet but to make it the sweet *itself*: We shape the dough into a statu-esque classic brioche à tête shape, flavor it with warm pumpkin spice, and sprinkle it with sparkly sugar. We roll the dough around a sweet cinnamon filling to create easy, intuitive cinna-mon buns (the only extra: some tangy cream cheese frosting). But we also show that buttery enriched doughs are more than welcome on the savory side. We fill brioche dough with garlic and thyme for a pretty, pull-apart snack that's served warm, and we elevate burgers (or sandwiches of any kind, really) with the most regal of buns. If you haven't touched brioche because it has a reputation as one of the more difficult doughs to execute, you'll find that our techniques make it easy enough to shape brioche into something new any day of the week.

NO-KNEAD BRIOCHE

makes 1 loaf

how-to

- 1⅔ cups (9⅛ ounces) bread flour
- 1¼ teaspoons instant or rapid-rise yeast
- ¾ teaspoon table salt
- 3 large eggs, room temperature
- 8 tablespoons unsalted butter, melted and slightly cooled
- ¼ cup (2 ounces) water, room temperature
- 3 tablespoons sugar
- 1 large egg, beaten with 1 tablespoon water and pinch table salt

The most impressive recipes take the most work, right? That was certainly the case with the brioche of the past, where the gradual kneading process traditionally took upwards of 20 minutes, during which time the dough could break from an abundance of incorporated butter. We've made brioche not only a simple process but a foolproof one by melting the butter and employing our favored folding method (see page 25) rather than kneading. Combine those techniques with a prolonged refrigerator fermentation (where the dough doesn't run the risk of overproofing and collapsing) for flavor and workability and a unique shaping method that strengthens the dough, and the bread reliably bakes as fine and tall as any classic brioche. The test kitchen's preferred loaf pan measures 8½ by 4½ inches; if you use a 9 by 5-inch loaf pan, increase the shaped rising time by 20 to 30 minutes and start checking for doneness 10 minutes earlier than advised in the recipe.

1 make dough Whisk flour, yeast, and salt together in large bowl. Whisk eggs, melted butter, water, and sugar in second bowl until sugar has dissolved. Using rubber spatula, fold egg mixture into flour mixture, scraping up dry flour from bottom of bowl until cohesive dough starts to form and no dry flour remains. Cover bowl tightly with plastic wrap and let dough rest for 10 minutes.

2 fold and rest Using greased bowl scraper or your wet fingertips, fold dough over itself by lifting and folding edge of dough toward middle and pressing to seal. Turn bowl 90 degrees and fold dough again; repeat turning bowl and folding dough 2 more times (total of 4 folds). Cover tightly with plastic and let rest for 30 minutes. Repeat folding and resting every 30 minutes, 3 more times. After fourth set of folds, cover bowl tightly with plastic.

3 first rise Refrigerate dough for at least 16 hours or up to 48 hours.

4 shape dough Transfer dough to well-floured counter, divide in half, and cover loosely with greased plastic. Using your well-floured hands, press 1 piece of dough into rough 4-inch circle (keep remaining piece covered). Using your floured fingertips and working around circumference of dough, lift and fold edge of dough toward center, pressing to seal, until ball forms (for a total of 6 folds). Repeat with remaining piece of dough.

5 Flip each dough ball seam side down and, using your cupped hands, drag in small circles on counter until dough feels taut and round. (If dough sticks to your hands, lightly dust top of dough with flour.) Cover dough rounds loosely with greased plastic and let rest for 5 minutes. Grease 8½ by 4½-inch loaf pan. Flip each dough ball seam side up, press into 4-inch disk, and repeat folding and rounding steps. Place rounds seam side down, side by side, into prepared pan, pressing dough gently into corners.

6 second rise Cover pan loosely with greased plastic and let rise until loaf reaches ½ inch below lip of pan and dough springs back minimally when poked gently with your finger, 1½ to 2 hours.

7 bake Adjust oven rack to middle position and heat oven to 350 degrees. Gently brush loaf with egg wash and bake until deep golden brown and loaf registers at least 190 degrees, 35 to 40 minutes, rotating pan halfway through baking. Let loaf cool in pan for 15 minutes. Remove loaf from pan and let cool completely on wire rack, about 3 hours, before serving.

Press dough half into 4-inch circle.

Fold edges of dough toward center.

Drag ball in circles until taut and round.

Repeat and transfer balls to pan.

total time 23¾ hours

35 min.	1½ hours	16 hours	15 min.	1½ hours	35 min.	3¼ hours
make dough	fold + rest	first rise	shape dough	second rise	bake	cool

» **Take your time** To make over 2 or 3 days, refrigerate dough for up to 48 hours in step 3.

PUMPKIN SPICE BRIOCHE À TÊTE

makes 1 loaf

1 recipe No-Knead Brioche, made through step 3, adding 2 teaspoons pumpkin pie spice to butter and stirring occasionally when melting

2 teaspoons turbinado sugar

Traditional brioche comes in a few typical shapes including rolls and this brioche à tête (or brioche parisienne)—a round bread baked in a fluted mold with a head, or smaller dough ball, crowning it. But since our brioche uses a nontraditional technique, we give it nontraditional flavor: Pumpkin spice (bloomed in the melted butter) in the dough gives the buttery bread a beautiful warmth, and a prebake sprinkling of turbinado sugar adds sweetness, crunch, and some show-stopping sparkle to an already-impressive bread. If you can shape the dough in two balls, you can make this brioche à tête with ease.

1 shape dough Transfer dough to well-floured counter. Remove golf ball–size piece of dough to create large and small ball. Pat large piece of dough into 8-inch disk and small piece of dough into 3-inch disk. Starting with large piece of dough, work around circumference; fold edges of dough toward center until ball forms. Flip dough over and, without applying pressure, move your hands in small circular motions to form dough into smooth, taut round. (Tackiness of dough against counter and circular motion should work dough into smooth, even ball, but if dough sticks to your hands, lightly dust top of dough with flour.) Repeat with remaining small piece of dough. Cover dough rounds loosely with plastic and let rest for 5 minutes.

2 Grease 8- to 8½-inch fluted brioche pan. Place larger round, seam side down, into prepared pan; press gently into corners and dimple center of dough using your fingers. Place smaller round, seam side down, in center of larger round, pushing down so that only top half of smaller round is showing.

3 second rise Cover dough loosely with plastic and let rise at room temperature until almost doubled in size (dough should rise to about ½ inch below top edge of pan), 1½ to 2 hours.

4 bake Adjust oven rack to middle position and preheat oven to 325 degrees. Brush loaf gently with egg wash. Sprinkle with turbinado sugar and bake until golden brown and internal temperature registers 190 degrees, 50 minutes to 1 hour, rotating pan halfway through baking and tenting with foil if bread begins to brown too quickly. Transfer pan to wire rack and let cool for 5 minutes. Remove loaf from pan, return to wire rack, and let cool completely before slicing and serving, about 3 hours.

Dimple large dough round.

Add small dough round to dimple.

GARLIC-THYME PULL-APART BRIOCHE

makes 1 loaf

6 tablespoons unsalted butter, divided

2 teaspoons minced fresh thyme

¾ teaspoon garlic powder

¾ teaspoon water

¼ teaspoon table salt

2 teaspoons garlic, minced to paste

1 recipe No-Knead Brioche, made through step 3

Any enriched dough is delightful when layered: Think of pastries like croissants; breads like butter fan rolls (see page 126); and even milk bread (see page 174), made of feathery spirals. Pulling off a layer is a satisfying treat made even more satisfying when there is a flavor sandwiched between layers, like the garlic-butter-thyme paste in this accordion-like loaf of brioche. By spreading the paste over squares of dough, folding them, and placing them in a row in the loaf pan, you create slices that merge together like soft, extra-buttery pieces of garlic bread. Serve the loaf warm and let diners dive in. You must use an 8½ by 4½-inch loaf pan for this recipe.

1   Combine 3 tablespoons butter, thyme, garlic powder, water, and salt in small bowl; set aside. Place remaining 3 tablespoons butter in small bowl and microwave, covered, until melted, about 30 seconds. Stir in garlic and continue to microwave, covered, until mixture is bubbling around edges, about 1 minute, stirring halfway through microwaving. Transfer melted butter mixture to bowl with butter-thyme mixture and whisk until homogeneous loose paste forms. (If mixture melts, set aside and let solidify before using.)

2   shape dough   Grease 8½ by 4½-inch loaf pan. Transfer dough to well-floured counter. Press and roll dough into 16 by 12-inch rectangle, with short side parallel to counter's edge. Spread garlic paste evenly over dough. Using pizza cutter or chef's knife, cut dough lengthwise into thirds, then cut each strip into quarters crosswise (you should have 12 roughly 4-inch squares). Working with 1 dough square at a time, fold in half with garlic paste on inside, then place in prepared pan folded edge down. Repeat with remaining dough squares.

3   second rise   Cover loosely with greased plastic wrap and let rise until dough is puffy and has risen slightly, about 1 hour.

4   bake   Adjust oven rack to middle position and heat oven to 350 degrees. Remove plastic and bake until golden brown and loaf registers at least 190 degrees, 40 to 45 minutes, rotating pan halfway through baking and covering with foil if bread begins to brown too quickly. Let loaf cool in pan for 5 minutes. Remove loaf from pan and let cool for 10 minutes on wire rack. Serve warm.

Cut dough lengthwise into thirds.

Cut each strip into quarters.

Fold dough squares in half and add to pan.

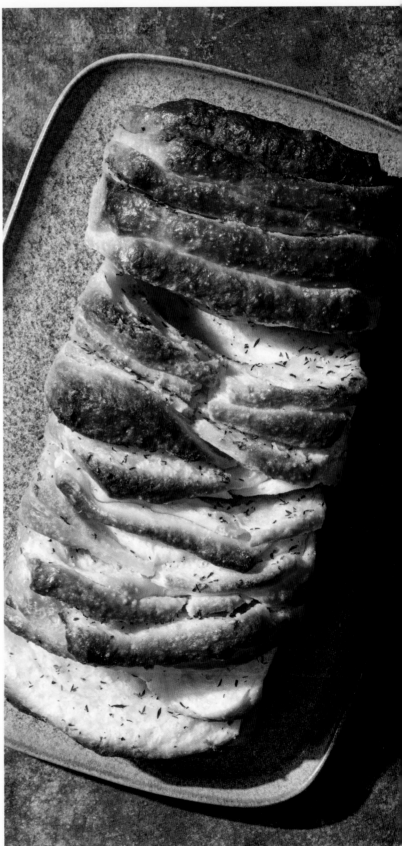

BRIOCHE CINNAMON BUNS

makes 8 buns

filling

- ½ cup packed (3½ ounces) brown sugar
- 2 teaspoons ground cinnamon
  Pinch table salt
- 3 tablespoons unsalted butter, softened

- 1 recipe No-Knead Brioche, made through step 3

icing

- 1 cup (4 ounces) confectioners' sugar
- 3 ounces cream cheese, softened
- 2 tablespoons milk
- ½ teaspoon vanilla extract
- ⅛ teaspoon table salt

Maybe it's because many of us grew up with the supermarket cans of cinnamon buns that were hot and ready fast, or it's because they sport such a hypnotizing cinnamon spiral, but breakfast cinnamon buns can seem out of the average baker's reach. When you make cinnamon buns out of something familiar—our great brioche dough—you'll never pop a can again. Roll out the supple dough, fill it with sweet goodness, shape it into a cylinder, cut buns, and achieve some of the softest, richest cinnamon buns without difficult new techniques. And, as with our master brioche recipe, although the recipe isn't made as swiftly as canned buns, you can make the buns when it's convenient for you. Let the dough sit in the fridge for a whole two days if you like and then shape the buns when the weekend, and the craving for a sweet, warm breakfast, comes around.

1   make filling   Grease 9-inch round cake pan, line with parchment paper, and grease parchment. Combine sugar, cinnamon, and salt in bowl; set aside.

2   shape dough   Transfer dough to well-floured counter. Press and roll dough into 12 by 9-inch rectangle, with long side parallel to counter edge. Spread butter over dough, leaving ½-inch border on far edge. Sprinkle dough evenly with cinnamon-sugar mixture, then press filling firmly into dough. Roll dough away from you into firm cylinder, keeping roll taut by tucking it under itself as you go. Pinch seam closed, then roll log seam side down. Using serrated knife, cut cylinder into 8 pieces. Gently re-form ends that were pinched during cutting then arrange buns in prepared pan (1 bun in center and others around perimeter of pan) seam sides facing in.

3   second rise   Cover loosely with greased plastic wrap and let rise until doubled in size, about 1 hour.

4   bake   Adjust oven rack to middle position and heat oven to 350 degrees. Bake buns until golden brown, 30 to 35 minutes, rotating pan halfway through baking. Loosen buns from sides of pan with paring knife and let cool for 5 minutes. Invert large plate over cake pan. Using pot holders, flip plate and pan upside down; remove pan and parchment. Reinvert buns onto wire rack, set wire rack inside parchment-lined rimmed baking sheet, and let cool for 5 minutes.

5   make icing   While buns cool, whisk all ingredients in bowl until smooth. Spread icing evenly over tops of buns to cover. Serve.

Roll dough into firm cylinder.

Pinch seam closed.

Cut into 8 pieces.

BRIOCHE BURGER BUNS

makes 5 buns

1 recipe No-Knead Brioche, made through step 3

2 teaspoons sesame seeds (optional)

There are plain white burger buns, sesame-seeded potato burger buns (a delicious standard; see page 138), and then there are brioche buns—the richest, most luxurious burger buns you can make for soaking up the savory juices from your fancy pub burgers and wildest burger creations. Once you've made the brioche dough, the recipe is as easy as shaping into burger-size rolls, much like you learned in chapter 2 of this book.

1 shape dough Line rimmed baking sheet with parchment paper. Transfer dough to well-floured counter, divide into 5 equal pieces, and cover loosely with greased plastic. Working with 1 piece of dough at a time, pat dough into disk using your well-floured hands (keep remaining pieces covered). Using your floured fingertips and working around circumference of dough, lift and fold edge of dough toward center until ball forms (total of 6 folds). Flip dough over and, using your cupped hands, drag in small circles on counter until dough feels taut and round. (If dough sticks to your hands, lightly dust top of dough with flour.)

2 second rise Arrange buns on prepared sheet, cover loosely with plastic, and let rise at room temperature until almost doubled in size, 1 to 1½ hours.

3 bake Adjust oven rack to middle position and heat oven to 350 degrees. Gently brush rolls with egg wash and sprinkle with sesame seeds, if using. Bake until golden brown and rolls register at least 190 degrees, 15 to 20 minutes, rotating sheet halfway through baking. Transfer sheet to wire rack and let cool for 5 minutes. Transfer buns to wire rack and let cool completely.

QUICKER CINNAMON BUNS

makes 8 buns

filling

- ¾ cup packed (5¼ ounces) light brown sugar
- ¼ cup (1¾ ounces) granulated sugar
- 1 tablespoon ground cinnamon
- ⅛ teaspoon table salt
- 2 tablespoons unsalted butter, melted
- 1 teaspoon vanilla extract

dough

- 1¼ cups (10 ounces) whole milk, room temperature, divided
- 2 tablespoons granulated sugar, divided
- 4 teaspoons instant or rapid-rise yeast
- 2¾ cups (13¾ ounces) all-purpose flour
- 2½ teaspoons baking powder
- ¾ teaspoon table salt
- 6 tablespoons unsalted butter, melted, divided

glaze

- 1 cup (4 ounces) confectioners' sugar, sifted
- 3 ounces cream cheese, softened
- 2 tablespoons unsalted butter, melted
- 2 tablespoons whole milk
- ½ teaspoon vanilla extract
- ⅛ teaspoon table salt

why this recipe works We love our rich, plush, decadent Brioche Cinnamon Buns (page 296), but their 17-plus-hour proof makes them best for times when you want to space out your baking. These tender, yeasty cinnamon buns can be made the morning you want to eat. For a quick rise, we supplement the yeast (which we proof in warm milk for extra speed) with baking powder. A mere 2 minutes of hand-kneading and a single 30-minute rise are enough to give us the flavor and texture of the best buns. A 375-degree oven temperature is perfect: It gives the yeast time to rise and develop more flavor before the tops of the buns set, and then eventually they brown and caramelize. Brown sugar and butter in the filling and a touch of vanilla in our tangy cream cheese glaze make these buns ultrarich and indulgent.

1 make filling Combine brown sugar, granulated sugar, cinnamon, and salt in bowl. Stir in melted butter and vanilla until mixture resembles wet sand; set aside.

2 make dough Grease dark 9-inch round cake pan, line with parchment paper, and grease parchment. Pour ¼ cup milk in small bowl and microwave until 110 degrees, 15 to 20 seconds. Stir in 1 teaspoon sugar and yeast and let sit until mixture is bubbly, about 5 minutes.

3 Whisk flour, baking powder, salt, and remaining 5 teaspoons sugar together in large bowl. Stir in 2 tablespoons melted butter, yeast mixture, and remaining 1 cup milk until dough forms (dough will be sticky). Transfer dough to well-floured counter and knead until smooth ball forms, about 2 minutes.

4 shape dough Roll dough into 12 by 9-inch rectangle, with long side parallel to counter edge. Brush dough all over with 2 tablespoons melted butter, leaving ½-inch border on far edge. Sprinkle dough evenly with filling, then press filling firmly into dough. Using bench scraper or metal spatula, loosen dough from counter. Roll dough away from you into firm cylinder and pinch seam to seal. Roll log seam side down and, using serrated knife, cut into 8 equal pieces. Gently re-form ends that were pinched during cutting, then arrange buns cut side down in prepared pan (1 bun in center and others around perimeter of pan), seam sides facing in. Brush tops of buns with remaining 2 tablespoons melted butter.

5 rise Cover buns loosely with greased plastic wrap and let rise for 30 minutes.

6 bake Adjust oven rack to lowest position and heat oven to 375 degrees. Bake buns until edges are well browned, 29 to 32 minutes, rotating pan halfway through baking. Loosen buns from sides of pan with paring knife and let cool for 5 minutes. Invert large plate over cake pan. Using pot holders, flip plate and pan upside down; remove pan and parchment. Reinvert buns onto wire rack, set wire rack inside parchment-lined rimmed baking sheet, and let cool for 5 minutes.

7 make glaze Whisk all ingredients in bowl until smooth. Pour glaze evenly over tops of buns, spreading with spatula to cover. Serve.

total time 2 hours

30 min.	10 min.	30 min.	30 min.	15 min.
make dough	shape dough	rise	bake	cool

STICKY BUNS

makes 12 buns

dough

- **3 cups (16½ ounces) bread flour, divided**
- **⅔ cup (5⅓ ounces) water, room temperature**
- **⅔ cup (5⅓ ounces) milk, room temperature**
- **1 large egg plus 1 large yolk, room temperature**
- **2 teaspoons instant or rapid-rise yeast**
- **3 tablespoons granulated sugar**
- **1½ teaspoons table salt**
- **6 tablespoons unsalted butter, cut into 6 pieces and softened**

topping

- **6 tablespoons unsalted butter, melted**
- **½ cup packed (3½ ounces) dark brown sugar**
- **¼ cup (1¾ ounces) granulated sugar**
- **¼ cup dark or light corn syrup**
- **¼ teaspoon table salt**
- **2 tablespoons water**
- **1 cup pecans, toasted and chopped (optional)**

filling

- **¾ cup packed (5¼ ounces) dark brown sugar**
- **1 teaspoon ground cinnamon**

why this recipe works Many recipes for sticky buns call for a firm, dry dough that's easy to manipulate into the required spiral and sturdy enough to support a generous amount of topping. But firm, dry sticky buns aren't very appealing. To make a softer, more tender, and moist sticky bun, we added tangzhong (see page 32). The cooked flour-and-water paste traps water, so the dough isn't sticky or difficult to work with when spiraling into buns, and the increased hydration converts to steam during baking, which makes the bread fluffy and light. The added water also keeps the crumb moist and tender. To ensure that the soft bread won't collapse under the weight of the topping, we strengthen the crumb by adding a resting period and withholding the sugar and salt until the gluten is firmly established. And since not much is better than a warm, squidgy sticky bun, we build in an optional overnight rise so you can wake up and bake these treats. The slight tackiness of the dough aids in flattening and stretching it in step 6, so resist the urge to use a lot of bench flour. Rolling the dough cylinder tightly in step 6 will result in misshapen rolls; keep the cylinder a bit slack. Bake these buns in a metal, not glass or ceramic, baking pan.

1 make dough Whisk ¼ cup flour and water in small bowl until no lumps remain. Microwave, whisking every 20 seconds, until mixture thickens to stiff, smooth, pudding-like consistency that forms mound when dropped from end of whisk into bowl, 40 to 80 seconds. In bowl of stand mixer, whisk flour paste and milk until smooth. Add egg and yolk and whisk until incorporated. Add remaining 2¾ cups flour and yeast. Fit stand mixer with dough hook and mix on low speed until all flour is moistened, 1 to 2 minutes. Let rest for 15 minutes.

2 Add sugar and salt to dough and mix on medium-low speed for 5 minutes. Stop mixer and add butter. Continue to mix on medium-low speed for 5 minutes longer, scraping down dough hook and sides of bowl halfway through (dough will stick to bottom of bowl). Transfer dough to lightly floured counter. Knead briefly to form ball.

3 first rise Place dough seam side down in lightly greased bowl or container and lightly coat surface of dough with oil spray. Cover with plastic wrap and let rise until just doubled in volume, 40 minutes to 1 hour.

4 make topping While dough rises, grease 13 by 9-inch metal baking pan. Whisk melted butter, brown sugar, granulated sugar, corn syrup, and salt in medium bowl until smooth. Add water and whisk until incorporated. Pour mixture into prepared pan and tilt pan to cover bottom. Sprinkle evenly with pecans, if using.

5 make filling Stir sugar and cinnamon in small bowl until thoroughly combined; set aside.

6 shape Press down on dough to deflate. Transfer dough to lightly floured counter. Pat and stretch dough into 18 by 15-inch rectangle with long side parallel to counter edge. Sprinkle dough evenly with filling, leaving 1-inch border on far edge, then press filling firmly into dough. Roll dough away from you into cylinder, taking care not to roll too tightly. Pinch seam to seal and roll log seam side down. Using serrated knife, cut into 12 equal pieces. Gently re-form ends that were pinched during cutting then arrange buns cut side down in prepared pan, seam sides facing in. Cover pan loosely with plastic.

7a second rise Let buns rise until puffy and touching one another, 40 minutes to 1 hour.

7b for an overnight rise Refrigerate buns for up to 14 hours. Remove from refrigerator and let buns sit at room temperature until puffy and touching one another, 1 to 1½ hours.

8 bake Adjust oven racks to lower-middle and lowest positions. Place rimmed baking sheet on lower rack to catch any drips and heat oven to 375 degrees. Bake buns on upper rack until golden brown, 20 to 25 minutes. Rotate pan; cover loosely with aluminum foil; and bake until center of dough registers at least 200 degrees, 10 to 15 minutes longer. Let buns cool in pan on wire rack for 5 minutes. Place rimmed baking sheet over buns and carefully invert. Remove pan and let buns cool for 5 minutes. Using spoon, scoop any glaze on sheet onto buns. Let cool for at least 10 minutes longer before serving.

total time 3¼ hours

1 hour	40 min.	10 min.	40 min.	30 min.	20 min.
make dough	first rise	shape dough	second rise	bake	cool

» **Take your time** To bake the next day, refrigerate dough for up to 14 hours in step 7.

sticky buns (page 302)

sausage and chive pull-apart rolls (page 306)

SAUSAGE AND CHIVE PULL-APART ROLLS

makes 12 buns

dough

- **3** cups (16½ ounces) bread flour, divided
- **⅔** cup (5⅓ ounces) water, room temperature
- **⅔** cup (5⅓ ounces) whole milk, room temperature
- **1** large egg plus 1 large yolk, room temperature
- **2** teaspoons instant or rapid-rise yeast
- **3** tablespoons granulated sugar
- **1½** teaspoons table salt
- **6** tablespoons unsalted butter, cut into 6 pieces and softened

  Vegetable oil spray

filling

- **1½** pounds bulk pork sausage
- **1½** teaspoons pepper
- **1** teaspoon ground fennel
- **1** teaspoon ground sage
- **8** ounces sharp cheddar cheese, shredded (2 cups)
- **¼** cup minced fresh chives

why this recipe works   These comforting rolls are just as much at home on the breakfast table alongside eggs as they are accompanying a cozy bowl of tomato or vegetable soup at lunch or dinner. Instead of rolling up the enriched dough with cinnamon sugar like with many breakfast buns, we layer in a deeply flavorful filling of sautéed pork sausage, fennel seeds, and sage, topping that with cheddar cheese. A handful of fresh chives finishes the baked rolls. Like with our Sticky Buns (page 302), we use the tangzhong method (see page 32) for workable dough and moist, fluffy results. The slight tackiness of the dough aids in flattening and stretching it in step 5, so resist the urge to≈use a lot of flour on the counter. Rolling the dough cylinder too tightly will result in misshapen rolls; keep the cylinder a bit slack. Bake these buns in a metal, not glass or ceramic, baking pan.

1   make dough   Whisk ¼ cup flour and water in small bowl until no lumps remain. Microwave, whisking every 20 seconds, until mixture thickens to stiff, smooth, pudding-like consistency that forms mound when dropped from end of whisk into bowl, 40 to 80 seconds. In bowl of stand mixer, whisk flour paste and milk until smooth. Add egg and yolk and whisk until incorporated. Add yeast and remaining 2¾ cups flour. Fit mixer with dough hook and mix on low speed until all flour is moistened, 1 to 2 minutes. Let rest for 15 minutes.

2   Add sugar and salt and mix on medium-low speed for 5 minutes. Stop mixer and add butter. Continue to mix on medium-low speed for 5 minutes longer, scraping down dough hook and side of bowl halfway through (dough will stick to bottom of bowl). Transfer dough to lightly floured counter. Knead briefly to form ball.

3   first rise   Place dough seam side down in lightly greased bowl or container and lightly coat surface of dough with vegetable oil spray. Cover with plastic wrap and let rise until just doubled in volume, 40 minutes to 1 hour.

4   make filling   While dough rises, grease 13 by 9-inch metal baking pan; set aside. Cook sausage in 12-inch nonstick skillet over medium heat until no longer pink, about 8 minutes, breaking up meat with wooden spoon into pieces no larger than ¼ inch. Stir in pepper, fennel, and sage and cook until fragrant, about 30 seconds. Using slotted spoon, transfer sausage to bowl and let cool completely, about 20 minutes.

5 shape dough Press down on dough to deflate. Transferdough to lightly floured counter. Pat and stretch dough into 18 by 15-inch rectangle with long side parallel to counter edge. Sprinkle dough evenly with cooled sausage, leaving 1-inch border on far edge. Smooth filling into even layer, then sprinkle cheese evenly over top. Press filling firmly into dough. Roll dough away from you into cylinder, taking care not to roll too tightly. Pinch seam to seal and roll log seam side down. Using serrated knife, cut into 12 equal pieces. Gently re-form ends that were pinched during cutting then arrange buns cut side down in prepared pan, seam sides facing in. Cover pan loosely with plastic.

6a second rise Let buns rise until puffy and touching one another, 40 minutes to 1 hour.

6b for an overnight rise Refrigerate buns for up to 14 hours. Remove from refrigerator and let buns sit at room temperature until puffy and touching one another, 1 to 1½ hours.

7 bake Adjust oven rack to middle position and heat oven to 375 degrees. Bake buns until golden brown, 20 to 25 minutes. Rotate pan; cover loosely with aluminum foil; and bake until center of dough registers at least 200 degrees, 10 to 15 minutes longer. Let buns cool in pan on wire rack for 5 minutes. Place rimmed baking sheet over buns and carefully invert. Remove pan and let buns cool for 5 minutes. Place serving platter over buns and carefully reinvert. Let cool for at least 10 minutes longer before sprinkling with chives. Serve.

total time 3¼ hours

1 hour	40 min.	10 min.	40 min.	30 min.	20 min.
make dough	first rise	shape dough	second rise	bake	cool

» **Take your time** To bake the next day, refrigerate dough for up to 14 hours in step 6.

CHALLAH

makes 1 loaf

how-to

flour paste

- ½ cup (4 ounces) water
- 3 tablespoons bread flour

dough

- 1 large egg plus 2 large yolks, room temperature
- ¼ cup (2 ounces) water, room temperature
- 2 tablespoons vegetable oil
- 2¾ cups (15⅛ ounces) bread flour
- 1¼ teaspoons instant or rapid-rise yeast
- ¼ cup (1¾ ounces) sugar
- 1 teaspoon table salt
- 1 large egg, beaten with 1 tablespoon water and pinch table salt
- 1 tablespoon sesame seeds or poppy seeds (optional)

why this recipe works   With its beautiful braids, high rise, and even, burnished exterior, challah looks like it should take expert hands. To make workable challah for all, with dough that is moist but malleable, we combine a short rest during kneading with a long fermentation; this builds a sturdy but stretchy gluten network that makes the dough easy to handle. We also employ tangzhong (see page 32) for moisture without stickiness to aid all that shaping. Ample amounts of oil and eggs make the baked bread plush. Brushing an egg wash over the braided dough encourages rich browning as the loaf bakes. This dough will be firmer and drier than most bread doughs, which makes it easy to braid. Some friction is necessary for rolling and braiding the ropes, so resist the urge to dust your counter with flour. If your counter is too narrow to stretch the ropes, slightly bend the pieces at the 12 o'clock and 6 o'clock positions. Sometimes the top of the braid can use some tightening and adjusting once you've braided down the length of the strips. To do this, un-braid and then re-braid the top in the reverse direction of the rest of the dough. You do not need to brush the larger loaf with egg wash if you're proofing the loaf overnight in step 6; just brush the entire loaf before baking.

1   make flour paste   Whisk water and flour in small bowl until smooth Microwave, whisking every 20 seconds, until mixture thickens to stiff, smooth, pudding-like consistency that forms mound when dropped from end of whisk into bowl, 40 to 80 seconds.

2   make dough   Whisk flour paste, egg and yolks, water, and oil in bowl of stand mixer until smooth. Add flour and yeast. Fit mixer with dough hook and mix on low speed until all flour is moistened, 3 to 4 minutes. Let rest for 20 minutes.

3   Add sugar and salt and mix on medium speed for 9 minutes, until smooth and elastic (dough will be quite firm and dry). Transfer dough to clean counter and knead by hand to form smooth, round ball, about 30 seconds.

4   first rise   Place dough seam side down in lightly greased large bowl or container, cover with plastic wrap, and let dough rise until doubled in volume, about 1½ hours.

5   shape dough   Line rimmed baking sheet with parchment paper and set inside second rimmed baking sheet. Press down on dough to deflate. Transfer dough to counter and press into 6-inch square. Divide dough into 2 pieces, one roughly half the size of the other. Divide each piece into thirds and cover loosely with greased plastic. Working with 1 piece of dough at a time (keep remaining pieces covered), stretch and roll dough pieces into 16-inch ropes (3 ropes will be much thicker)

6   Arrange 3 thicker ropes side by side, perpendicular to counter edge, and pinch far ends together. Braid ropes into 10-inch length and pinch remaining ends together. Transfer loaf to prepared sheet and brush top with egg wash. Repeat braiding remaining ropes into second 10-inch length and place on top of larger loaf.

Divide 2 dough pieces into thirds.

Roll pieces into 16-inch ropes.

Pinch far ends of thicker ropes.

Braid thicker ropes and pinch.

Brush top with egg wash.

Braid thinner ropes and pinch.

Place second braid on top of loaf.

Brush risen loaf with egg wash.

7a second rise Loosely cover loaf with plastic and let rise until loaf is puffy and increases in size by a third, 45 minutes to 1 hour.

7b for an overnight rise Refrigerate challah for at least 8 hours or up to 16 hours. Let challah sit at room temperature for 1 hour before baking.

8 bake Adjust oven rack to middle position and heat oven to 350 degrees. Brush loaf with remaining egg wash and sprinkle with poppy or sesame seeds, if using. Bake until loaf is deep golden brown and registers at least 195 degrees, 35 to 40 minutes. Let cool on sheets for 20 minutes. Transfer loaf to wire rack and let cool completely before serving, about 2 hours.

total time 6½ hours

1 hour	1½ hours	20 min.	45 min.	35 min.	2¼ hours
make dough	first rise	shape dough	second rise	bake	cool

» **Take your time** To bake the next day, refrigerate loaf for at least 8 hours or up to 16 hours in step 7.

challah (page 308)

prosciutto and fig pinwheel bread (page 312)

PROSCIUTTO AND FIG PINWHEEL BREAD

how-to

makes 1 loaf

2 cups (10 ounces)
all-purpose flour

2 tablespoons minced fresh thyme

2 teaspoons minced fresh sage

2 teaspoons ground fennel

1½ teaspoons instant or
rapid-rise yeast

½ teaspoon table salt

½ cup (4 ounces) whole milk,
room temperature

¼ cup (1¾ ounces) sugar

2 large egg yolks,
room temperature

8 tablespoons unsalted butter, cut
into 8 pieces and softened

6 ounces thinly sliced prosciutto

¼ cup fig jam

1 large egg, beaten with
1 tablespoon water and
pinch table salt

why this recipe works   This showstopper is a stunning centerpiece for holidays—or any other special occasion. We roll out layers of dough into rounds, add a savory and sweet filling, and then stack the rounds, cutting them partially into strips and twisting to end up with a jaw-dropping sunburst-shaped bread. Making this showpiece is not nearly as difficult as you might think. We start by making an egg-enriched dough, packing in plenty of thyme, sage, and fennel for savory flavor that complements the filling, a match made in heaven of prosciutto and fig jam. Brushing on egg wash before baking gives this masterpiece a beautiful sheen.

1   make dough   Whisk flour, thyme, sage, fennel, yeast, and salt together in bowl of stand mixer. Whisk milk, sugar, and egg yolks in 4-cup liquid measuring cup until sugar has dissolved. Using dough hook on low speed, slowly add milk mixture to flour mixture and mix until cohesive dough starts to form and no dry flour remains, about 2 minutes, scraping down bowl as needed.

2   Increase speed to medium-low and, with mixer running, add butter 1 piece at a time, allowing each piece to incorporate before adding next, about 3 minutes total, scraping down bowl and dough hook as needed. Continue to knead until dough is smooth and elastic and clears sides of bowl, 10 to 12 minutes. Transfer dough to lightly floured counter and knead by hand to form smooth, round ball, about 30 seconds.

3   rest and rise   Place dough seam side down in lightly greased large bowl or container, cover with plastic wrap, and let rise at room temperature until increased in volume by about half, 1½ to 2 hours. Place in refrigerator until dough is firm, at least 1 hour or up to 24 hours. (If dough is chilled longer than 1 hour, let rest at room temperature for 15 minutes before rolling out.)

4   shape   Press down on dough to deflate. Transfer to clean counter, cut into 4 pieces, then knead each piece by hand to form smooth round ball; cover with plastic. Transfer 1 dough ball to center of double layer of parchment paper on counter and press and roll dough into 12-inch circle on parchment (keep remaining dough balls covered). Shingle half of prosciutto evenly over dough. Using parchment as sling, transfer dough and parchment to cutting board.

5   Transfer second dough ball to lightly floured counter and press and roll into 12-inch circle. Carefully top prosciutto-topped dough round with second dough round. Microwave fig jam until loosened, about 30 seconds, then evenly brush over top dough round.

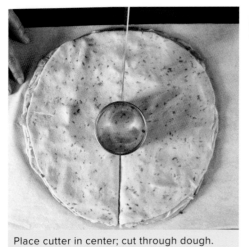
Place cutter in center; cut through dough.

Make 16 cuts around cutter.

Twist strips 2½ turns and pinch.

6 Transfer third dough ball to lightly floured counter and press and roll into 12-inch circle. Carefully top fig-topped dough round with third dough round. Shingle remaining prosciutto over top. Transfer final dough ball to lightly floured counter and press and roll into 12-inch circle, then lay dough round on top of stack.

7 Place 3-inch wide cookie cutter or overturned bowl in center of dough (do not press into dough). Using sharp knife positioned at 12 o'clock, cut through all 4 layers of dough and filling, starting from edge of cookie cutter and finishing at edge of dough round (be sure to cut firmly through prosciutto layers). Repeat cut on opposite side of cookie cutter, at 6 o'clock. Continue to repeat cuts around dough round to make 16 evenly spaced cuts around cookie cutter. Remove cookie cutter.

8 Grasping ends of 2 adjacent strips and twisting in opposite directions, twist strips twice, then twist another half turn and pinch ends together to seal. Repeat with remaining strips. Using parchment as sling, carefully lift star and place on rimmed baking sheet (use caution as some cuts may have sliced through top parchment layer).

9 second rise Cover bread loosely with greased plastic and let rise until puffy, 40 to 60 minutes.

10 bake Adjust oven rack to middle position and heat oven to 350 degrees. Brush pinwheel with egg wash and bake until golden brown, 30 to 40 minutes (if edges brown faster than center, shield edges with aluminum foil). Transfer sheet to wire rack and let cool for 15 minutes. Serve warm or at room temperature.

total time 5 hours

40 min.	2½ hours	30 min.	40 min.	30 min.	15 min.
make dough	rest + rise	shape dough	second rise	bake	cool

» **Take your time** To bake the next day, let dough rise for up to 24 hours in step 3.

CHOCOLATE BABKA

makes 1 loaf

how-to

dough

2¼ cups (12⅓ ounces) bread flour

1½ teaspoons instant or
    rapid-rise yeast

½ cup (4 ounces) whole milk,
   room temperature

2 large eggs, room temperature

1 tablespoon grated orange zest
   (optional)

1 teaspoon vanilla extract

¼ cup (1¾ ounces)
   granulated sugar

½ teaspoon table salt

6 tablespoons unsalted butter,
   cut into 6 pieces and softened

filling

8 ounces bittersweet chocolate,
   chopped fine

8 tablespoons unsalted butter

½ cup (2 ounces) confectioners'
   sugar, sifted

½ cup (1½ ounces) unsweetened
   cocoa powder, sifted

½ teaspoon table salt

syrup

½ cup (3½ ounces)
   granulated sugar

¼ cup (2 ounces) water

why this recipe works   We think if you're going to make chocolate babka—the rolling, the filling, the braiding—the loaf should be able to hold the deepest, darkest spirals of decadent chocolate. We start with a yeasted dough that we flavor with some aromatic orange zest and vanilla extract. Then we make a luscious chocolate filling by microwaving melted butter and chocolate together and stirring in confectioners' sugar, cocoa, and salt until the filling is smooth. To ensure layers of chocolate throughout the loaf, we use a technique called the Russian braiding: We split the log in half lengthwise, lay the halves next to each other cut sides up, and twist them together five times total. We bake the loaf uncovered for 30 minutes and then cover it with foil to finish baking to ensure browning without burning for this sweet loaf. For an extra-special finish, we make a sugar syrup and brush it over the warm babka. The test kitchen's preferred loaf pan measures 8½ by 4½ inches; if you use a 9 by 5-inch loaf pan, start checking for doneness 15 minutes earlier than advised in the recipe. If the chocolate filling becomes too stiff to spread in step 5, use a rubber spatula to work it back to a softer texture.

1   make dough   Whisk flour and yeast together in bowl of stand mixer. Whisk milk; eggs; orange zest, if using; and vanilla in 2-cup liquid measuring cup until combined. Using dough hook on low speed, slowly add milk mixture to flour mixture and mix until cohesive dough starts to form and no dry flour remains, about 2 minutes, scraping down bowl as needed. Let rest for 15 minutes.

2   Add sugar and salt and knead on medium-low speed until incorporated, about 30 seconds. Increase speed to medium and, with mixer running, add butter 1 piece at a time, allowing each piece to incorporate before adding next, about 3 minutes total, scraping down bowl and dough hook as needed. Continue to knead on medium-high speed until dough begins to pull away from sides of bowl, 7 to 10 minutes longer.

3   rest and rise   Transfer dough to greased large bowl or container, cover with plastic, and let rise at room temperature until slightly puffy, about 1 hour. Refrigerate until firm, at least 2 hours or up to 24 hours.

4   make filling   Just before removing dough from refrigerator, place chocolate in medium bowl. Melt butter in small saucepan over medium heat. Immediately pour melted butter over chocolate and stir to combine. Microwave at 50 percent power, stirring often, until chocolate is fully melted and smooth, about 30 seconds. Stir in sugar, cocoa, and salt until combined; set aside.

5 shape dough Adjust oven rack to middle position and≈heat oven to 325 degrees. Grease 8½ by 4½-inch loaf pan. Press down on dough to deflate. Transfer dough to lightly floured counter and press and roll into 18 by 12-inch rectangle, with short side parallel to counter edge. Using offset spatula, spread chocolate mixture evenly over dough, leaving ½-inch border on far edge. Roll dough away from you into even 12-inch cylinder, keeping roll taut by tucking it under itself as you go. Pinch seam to seal and reshape as needed. Arrange dough log so that short side is parallel to counter edge, then use greased bench scraper or sharp knife to cut in half lengthwise. Turn dough halves cut side up and arrange side by side. Pinch top ends together. Forming tight twist, cross left log over right log. Continue twisting, 5 times total, keeping cut sides facing up as much as possible. Pinch bottom ends together and carefully transfer to prepared pan cut sides up, reshaping as needed to fit into pan.

6 bake Set wire rack in rimmed baking sheet and center loaf pan on wire rack. Bake for 30 minutes. Rotate pan, cover loosely with aluminum foil, and bake until bread registers at least 200 degrees, 50 minutes to 1 hour.

7 make syrup Meanwhile, combine sugar and water in small saucepan and heat over medium heat until sugar dissolves. Set aside off heat.

8 Remove babka from oven. Leaving babka in loaf pan, brush syrup evenly over entire surface of hot babka (use all of it). Let cool in loaf pan on wire rack for 1 hour. Carefully remove babka from pan and let cool completely on wire rack, about 2 hours. Slice 1 inch thick and serve.

total time 8¼ hours

50 min.	3 hours	10 min.	1¼ hours	3 hours
make dough	rest + rise	shape dough	bake	cool

» **Take your time** To bake the next day, refrigerate dough for up to 24 hours in step 3.

chocolate babka (page 314)

pizza babka (page 318)

PIZZA BABKA

makes 1 loaf

dough

- 2¼ cups (12⅓ ounces) bread flour
- 1½ teaspoons instant or rapid-rise yeast
- ½ cup (4 ounces) whole milk, room temperature
- 2 large eggs, room temperature
- 1 tablespoon sugar
- ½ teaspoon table salt
- 6 tablespoons unsalted butter, cut into 6 pieces and softened

filling

- 3 tablespoons extra-virgin olive oil
- 2 garlic cloves, minced
- ½ teaspoon dried oregano
- ¼ teaspoon red pepper flakes
- ½ cup tomato paste
- 1 teaspoon red wine vinegar
- ½ cup chopped fresh basil
- 6 ounces provolone piccante, shredded (1½ cups)
- 1½ ounces Pecorino Romano cheese, grated (¾ cup), divided
- 1 large egg, beaten with 1 tablespoon water and pinch salt

why this recipe works Babka is usually sweet (see page 314), but filling this enriched dough with savory ingredients instead makes for something truly special. The flavor inspiration for this impressive babka comes from Sicilian scaccia, a baked good featuring thin layers of unenriched dough, tomato sauce, and caciocavallo cheese in a swirled and multilayered loaf. We love the extra richness a babka dough brings to the braid. To pack the filling with pizza flavor, we combine tomato paste, garlic, oil, wine vinegar, oregano, and red pepper flakes. A blend of provolone piccante (aka sharp provolone) and Pecorino Romano creates superbly cheesy layers. If, when testing the bread for doneness, the thermometer comes out with a temperature below 190, try in a different spot. (Hitting a pocket of cheese may give a false reading.) The test kitchen's preferred loaf pan measures 8½ by 4½ inches; if you use a 9 by 5-inch loaf pan, increase the shaped rising time by 20 to 30 minutes and start checking for doneness 15 minutes earlier than advised in the recipe.

1 make dough Whisk flour and yeast together in bowl of stand mixer. Whisk milk and eggs in 2-cup liquid measuring cup until combined. Using dough hook on medium-low speed, slowly add milk mixture to flour mixture and mix until cohesive dough forms and no dry flour remains, about 2 minutes, scraping down bowl as needed. Let rest for 15 minutes.

2 Add sugar and salt and knead on medium-low speed until incorporated, about 30 seconds. Increase speed to medium and, with mixer running, add butter, 1 piece at a time, allowing each piece to incorporate before adding next, about 3 minutes total, scraping down bowl and dough hook as needed. Continue to knead on medium-high speed until dough begins to pull away from sides of bowl, 7 to 10 minutes longer.

3 rest and rise Transfer dough to greased large bowl or container, cover with plastic, and let rise at room temperature until slightly puffy, about 1 hour. Refrigerate until firm, at least 2 hours or up to 24 hours.

4 make filling Combine oil, garlic, oregano, and pepper flakes in bowl and microwave until fragrant, 45 to 60 seconds, stirring halfway through microwaving; let cool completely. Stir in tomato paste and vinegar and season with salt and pepper to taste.

5 shape dough Grease 8½ by 4½-inch loaf pan. Press down on dough to deflate. Transfer dough to lightly floured counter and press and roll dough into 18 by 7-inch rectangle, with short side parallel to counter edge. Spread filling evenly over dough, leaving ½-inch border on far edge, then sprinkle basil, provolone, and ¼ cup Pecorino over filling. Roll dough away from you into even 7-inch cylinder, keeping roll taut by tucking it under itself as you go. Pinch seam and ends to seal and reshape as needed. Wrap in plastic, transfer to rimmed baking sheet, and refrigerate until firm but still supple, about 30 minutes.

6 Transfer chilled dough log to lightly floured counter with short side facing you. Using bench scraper or sharp knife, cut log in half lengthwise. Turn dough halves cut side up and arrange side by side. Gently stretch each half into 14-inch length, then pinch top ends together. Forming tight twist, cross left log over right log. Continue twisting until you reach bottom of log, keeping cut sides facing up as much as possible. Pinch bottom ends together and carefully transfer to prepared pan cut sides up, reshaping as needed to fit into pan.

7 second rise Cover loaf loosely with greased plastic and let rise until almost doubled in size, 1 to 1½ hours (top of loaf should rise about 1 inch over lip of pan).

8 bake Adjust oven rack to middle position and heat oven to 350 degrees. Gently brush loaf with egg wash, sprinkle with remaining ½ cup Pecorino, and bake until loaf is deep golden brown and registers at least 200 degrees, 40 to 55 minutes, rotating pan halfway through baking. Let loaf cool in pan on wire rack for 1 hour. Remove loaf from pan and let cool completely on wire rack, about 2 hours, before serving.

total time 8¾ hours

50 min.	3 hours	10 min.	1 hour	45 min.	3 hours
make dough	rest + rise	shape dough	second rise	bake	cool

» **Take your time** To bake the next day, refrigerate dough for up to 24 hours in step 3.

CAST IRON CINNAMON SWIRL BREAD

makes 1 loaf

3¼ cups (16¼ ounces)
 all-purpose flour

2 teaspoons table salt

2 teaspoons ground cinnamon,
 divided

1 cup (8 ounces) warm whole milk

8 tablespoons unsalted butter,
 melted, divided

¼ cup (1¾ ounces)
 granulated sugar

2 tablespoons warm water

2¼ teaspoons instant or
 rapid-rise yeast

½ cup packed (3½ ounces)
 light brown sugar

1 large egg, beaten with
 1 tablespoon water and
 pinch table salt

why this recipe works Take cinnamon buns and make them an elegant braided, babka-like loaf, and you have this cinnamon swirl bread that's quite simple despite the sophisticated presentation. Adding some cinnamon directly to the dough, rather than just to the filling, ensures fragrance in every bite. To wind the braided dough into a spiral that doesn't budge, we start with a Russian braid (see page 314), which tightly seals the pieces of dough together while providing plenty of escape routes for the excess air that would otherwise compress the dough and create tunnels in the loaf or oozing. The dough proofs in the skillet; as it rises, it nuzzles up against the sides of the skillet, gaining great height and creating an impressive dome shape—like a giant cinnamon bun.

1 make dough Whisk flour, salt, and 1 teaspoon cinnamon together in bowl of stand mixer. Whisk milk, 6 tablespoons melted butter, granulated sugar, warm water, and yeast in 2-cup liquid measuring cup until yeast has dissolved. Using dough hook on low speed, slowly add milk mixture to flour mixture and mix until cohesive dough starts to form and no dry flour remains, about 2 minutes, scraping down bowl as needed. Increase speed to medium and knead until dough is smooth and elastic and clears sides of bowl, about 10 minutes. Transfer dough to lightly floured counter and knead by hand to form smooth, round ball, about 30 seconds.

2 first rise Place dough seam side down in lightly greased large bowl or container, cover bowl with greased plastic wrap, and let rise until doubled in volume, about 1 hour.

3 shape dough Mix brown sugar and remaining 1 teaspoon cinnamon in bowl until thoroughly combined. Press down on dough to deflate. Transfer dough to lightly floured counter and press and roll into 16 by 12-inch rectangle with long side parallel to counter edge. Brush remaining 2 tablespoons melted butter over dough, leaving ½-inch border around edges. Sprinkle cinnamon-sugar mixture over butter, leaving ¾-inch border on far edge, then press filling firmly to adhere. Roll dough away from you into even 16-inch cylinder, keeping roll taut by tucking it under itself as you go. Pinch seam and ends to seal and reshape as needed. (If dough log is very soft, carefully transfer to parchment-lined rimmed baking sheet and refrigerate until chilled, about 30 minutes.)

4 Grease 10-inch cast-iron skillet. Arrange dough log so that short side is parallel to counter edge, then use bench scraper or sharp knife to cut in half lengthwise. Turn dough halves cut side up and arrange side by side. Pinch top ends together. Forming tight twist, cross left log over right log. Continue twisting until you reach bottom of log, keeping cut sides facing up as much as possible. Pinch bottom ends together. Starting at 1 end, wind log into coil and tuck end underneath coil. Transfer loaf to prepared skillet.

5 second rise Cover skillet with greased plastic, and let dough rise until doubled in size, 45 minutes to 1 hour.

6 bake Adjust oven rack to lower-middle position and heat oven to 325 degrees. Brush loaf with egg wash, transfer skillet to oven, and bake until loaf is deep golden brown and filling is melted, 45 to 55 minutes, rotating skillet halfway through baking. Using potholders, transfer skillet to wire rack and let loaf cool for 10 minutes. Being careful of hot skillet handle, remove loaf from skillet, return to rack, and let cool completely, about 2 hours, before serving.

total time 5½ hours

35 min.	1 hour	15 min.	45 min.	45 min.	2¼ hours
make dough	first rise	shape dough	second rise	bake	cool

total time 4¾ hours

35 min.	1½ hours	10 min.	1 hour	50 min.	40 min.
make dough	first rise	shape dough	second rise	bake	cool

SPICY CHEESE BREAD

makes 1 loaf

bread

3¼ cups (16¼ ounces) all-purpose flour

¼ cup (1¾ ounces) sugar

1 tablespoon instant or rapid-rise yeast

1½ teaspoons red pepper flakes

1¼ teaspoons table salt

½ cup (4 ounces) water, room temperature

2 large eggs plus 1 large yolk, room temperature

4 tablespoons unsalted butter, melted

6 ounces Monterey Jack cheese, cut into ½-inch cubes (1½ cups), room temperature

6 ounces provolone cheese, cut into ½-inch cubes (1½ cups), room temperature

topping

1 large egg, beaten with 1 tablespoon water and pinch table salt

1 teaspoon red pepper flakes

1 tablespoon unsalted butter, melted

why this recipe works This softly chewy, cheesy snack bread speckled with red pepper flakes is legendary in its homeland of Wisconsin. Our homage to this bakery favorite features an eggy dough, which bakes up soft with a thin, deeply golden crust. To incorporate enough cheese to make the bread worthy of its name—without ending up with a heavy, greasy, oozing loaf—we roll out the dough after its first rise, top it with cubes of cheese, roll the dough into a log to seal in the cheese, and spiral the whole thing into a cake pan for its second rise. An equal mix of provolone and Monterey Jack provides a great flavor-to-meltability ratio. The cake pan helps contain the cheese and also helps the bread keep its shape as it bakes up into a beautiful domed loaf. If, when testing the bread for doneness, the thermometer comes out with a temperature below 190, try in a different spot. (Hitting a pocket of cheese may give a false reading.) Take the cheese out of the refrigerator when you start the recipe to ensure that it comes to room temperature by the time you need it. Otherwise, the cold cheese will prevent the dough from rising properly.

1 make bread Whisk flour, sugar, yeast, pepper flakes, and salt together in bowl of stand mixer. Whisk water, eggs and yolk, and melted butter in 2-cup liquid measuring cup until combined. Using dough hook on low speed, slowly add water mixture to flour mixture and mix until cohesive dough starts to form and no dry flour remains. Increase speed to medium and knead until dough clears bottom and sides of bowl, about 6 minutes. Transfer dough to clean counter and knead by hand to form smooth, round ball, about 30 seconds.

2 first rise Place dough seam side down in greased large bowl or container, cover with plastic wrap, and let rise until doubled in volume, 1½ to 2 hours.

3 shape dough Grease 9-inch round cake pan. Press down on dough to deflate. Transfer dough to clean counter and press and roll into 18 by 12-inch rectangle with long side parallel to counter edge. Sprinkle Monterey Jack and provolone evenly over dough, leaving 1-inch border. Roll dough away from you into cylinder, keeping roll taut by tucking it under itself as you go. Pinch seam and ends to seal, then roll log so seam side is down. Roll log back and forth on counter, applying gentle, even pressure, until log reaches 30 inches in length. If any tears occur, pinch to seal. Starting at 1 end, wind log seam side down into tight coil; tuck end underneath coil.

4 second rise Place loaf in prepared pan and cover loosely with plastic. Let dough rise until doubled in size, 1 to 1½ hours.

5 make topping Adjust oven rack to lower-middle position and heat oven to 350 degrees. Brush top of loaf with egg wash, then sprinkle with pepper flakes.

6 bake Place pan on rimmed baking sheet and bake until loaf is golden brown, about 25 minutes. Rotate pan, cover loosely with aluminum foil, and continue to bake until loaf registers at least 190 degrees, 25 to 30 minutes. Transfer pan to wire rack and brush bread with melted butter. Let cool for 10 minutes. Run knife around edge of pan to loosen bread then slide onto wire rack, using spatula as needed for support. Let cool for 30 minutes before slicing. Serve warm.

BOLOS LÊVEDOS

makes 8 cakes

flour paste

⅔ cup (5⅓ ounces) water

¼ cup (1¼ ounces) all-purpose flour

dough

6 tablespoons (3 ounces) whole milk, room temperature

4 tablespoons unsalted butter, cut into 4 pieces and softened

2 large eggs, room temperature

3 cups (15 ounces) all-purpose flour, divided

1 teaspoon instant or rapid-rise yeast

½ cup (3½ ounces) sugar

1 teaspoon table salt

1 teaspoon vegetable oil

why this recipe works   Though they look a lot like English muffins, these Portuguese "cakes" ("bolos" means "cakes" and "lêvedos" means "leavened"), originally from the Azores, are denser and richer, with a fair amount of sweetness and a rich crumb thanks to whole milk, eggs, and butter. Inspired by a visit to Central Bakery, a Portuguese bakery in Tiverton, Rhode Island, that turns out dozens of bolos lêvedos a day, we set out to create a smaller-scale recipe for the home kitchen. First, to ensure that the dough is hydrated enough to create a tender finished product, we follow the tangzhong method (see page 32). To further ensure full hydration and tender bolos, we include an autolyse or resting step (see page 2) to fully hydrate the flour and get a head start on gluten development. After a traditional two-stage rise, we brown our bolos in a skillet and finish cooking them in the oven, which yields slightly sweet, moist cakes fit for breakfast, lunch, and dinner. Split the bolos with a knife. Serve them with butter or use them as sandwich bread or burger buns.

1   make flour paste   Whisk water and flour in small bowl until smooth. Microwave, whisking every 20 seconds, until mixture thickens to stiff, smooth, pudding-like consistency that forms mound when dropped from end of whisk into bowl, 40 to 80 seconds.

2   make dough   Whisk flour paste and milk in bowl of stand mixer until smooth. Whisk in butter until fully incorporated, then whisk in eggs. Add flour and yeast. Fit stand mixer with dough hook and mix on low speed until all flour is moistened, 1 to 2 minutes. Let rest for 15 minutes.

3   Add sugar and salt to dough and mix on low speed until incorporated, about 1 minute. Increase speed to medium and mix until dough is elastic and pulls away from sides of bowl but still sticks to bottom (dough will be sticky), about 8 minutes.

4   first rise   Place dough in greased large bowl, cover with plastic wrap, and let rise until doubled in volume, about 1½ hours.

5   shape dough   Line rimmed baking sheet with parchment paper. Press down on dough to deflate. Transfer dough to clean counter, divide into 8 equal pieces, and cover loosely with plastic. Working with 1 piece of dough at a time (keep remaining pieces covered), form into rough ball by stretching dough around your thumb and pinching edges together so that top is smooth. Place ball seam side down on clean counter and, using your cupped hand, drag in small circles until dough feels taut and round.

6   Sprinkle ¼ cup flour on counter. Working with 1 dough ball at a time, turn dough ball in flour and press with your hand to flatten into 3½- to 4-inch disk. Transfer dough disks to prepared sheet. Lay second sheet of parchment over dough disks, then place second rimmed baking sheet on top to keep disks flat during second rise. Let rise for 30 minutes.

7 cook Adjust oven rack to middle position and heat oven to 350 degrees. Heat oil in 12-inch nonstick skillet over medium-low heat until shimmering. Using paper towels, carefully wipe out oil from skillet. Transfer 4 dough disks to skillet and cook until deeply browned on both sides, 2 to 4 minutes per side. Return toasted disks to sheet. Repeat with remaining 4 dough disks. Bake until cakes register at least 190 degrees in center, 11 to 14 minutes. Transfer cakes to wire rack and let cool for 30 minutes. Serve.

VARIATION

BOLOS LÊVEDOS WITH LEMON AND CINNAMON

Add 1½ teaspoons grated lemon zest and ¼ teaspoon ground cinnamon with remaining flour and yeast in step 2.

total time 3¾ hours

30 min.	1½ hours	20 min.	30 min.	25 min.	30 min.
make dough	first rise	shape dough	second rise	cook	cool

GLAZED DOUGHNUTS

makes 12 doughnuts

dough

- 4½ cups (22½ ounces) all-purpose flour
- ½ cup (3½ ounces) granulated sugar
- 1 teaspoon instant or rapid-rise yeast
- 1½ cups (12 ounces) milk, room temperature
- 1 large egg, room temperature
- 1½ teaspoons table salt
- 8 tablespoons unsalted butter, cut into ½-inch pieces and softened
- 2 quarts vegetable oil for frying

glaze

- 3¼ cups (13 ounces) confectioners' sugar
- ½ cup (4 ounces) hot water
- Pinch table salt

why this recipe works   Our yeasted doughnuts are moist but light with a tender chew and restrained sweetness, thanks to a careful balance of fat, sugar, and moisture in the dough. We chill the dough overnight so that it's faster to make the doughnuts in the morning—if that's when you want to eat them. The dough also develops more complex flavor and is easier to handle when cold. Shutting the cut doughnuts in the oven with a loaf pan of boiling water—a makeshift baker's proof box—encourages them to rise quickly and doesn't influence the flavor of these fried treats. We then briefly fry them on both sides in moderately hot oil until they turn golden brown. To give them donut shop appeal, we dip the doughnuts in a thin glaze, which sets into a sheer, matte shell. You'll need two large baking sheets and two wire racks for this recipe. You'll also need 3-inch and 1-inch round cutters. Use a Dutch oven that holds 6 quarts or more for frying the doughnuts. You can omit the plain glaze and frost the doughnuts with one of our variations on page 328— chocolate, coffee, matcha, or raspberry. Or, simply roll the just-fried doughnuts in sugar.

1   make dough   Whisk flour, sugar, and yeast together in bowl of stand mixer. Whisk milk and egg in 2-cup liquid measuring cup until combined. Using dough hook on low speed, slowly add milk mixture to flour mixture and mix until cohesive dough starts to form and no dry flour remains, about 2 minutes, scraping down bowl as needed. Let rest for 20 minutes.

2   Add salt and knead on medium-low speed until dough is smooth and elastic and clears sides of bowl, 5 to 7 minutes. With mixer running, add butter, 1 piece at a time, allowing each piece to incorporate before adding next, about 3 minutes total, scraping down bowl and dough hook as needed. Continue to knead until dough is smooth and elastic and clears sides of bowl, 7 to 13 minutes longer, scraping down bowl halfway through mixing.

3   first rise   Transfer dough to greased large bowl, flip dough, and form into ball. Cover with plastic and let rest for 1 hour. Transfer to refrigerator and rest for at least 8 hours or up to 48 hours.

4 shape dough Adjust oven racks to lowest and middle positions. Place loaf pan on lower rack. Line rimmed baking sheet with parchment paper and grease parchment. Press down on dough to deflate. Transfer dough to lightly floured counter and press into 8-inch square of even thickness. Roll dough into 10 by 13-inch rectangle, about ½ inch thick. Using 3-inch round cutter dipped in flour, cut 12 rounds. Using 1-inch cutter dipped in flour, cut hole out of center of each round. Transfer doughnuts and holes to prepared sheet. (If desired, use 1-inch cutter to cut small rounds from remaining dough. Transfer to sheet with doughnuts.) Bring kettle or small saucepan of water to boil.

5 second rise Pour 1 cup boiling water into loaf pan. Place sheet on upper rack, uncovered. Close oven and allow doughnuts to rise until dough increases in height by 50 percent and springs back very slowly when pressed with your knuckle, 45 minutes to 1 hour.

6 make glaze Whisk sugar, water, and salt together in medium bowl until smooth.

7 fry About 20 minutes before end of rising time, add oil to large Dutch oven until it measures about 1½ inches deep and heat over medium-low heat to 360 degrees. Set wire rack in second rimmed baking sheet and line with triple layer of paper towels. Using both your hands, gently place 4 risen doughnuts in oil. Cook until golden brown on undersides, 1 to 1½ minutes, adjusting burner as necessary to maintain oil temperature between 350 and 365 degrees. Using spider skimmer, flip doughnuts and cook until second sides are browned, 1 to 1½ minutes. Transfer doughnuts to prepared rack. Return oil to 360 degrees and repeat with remaining doughnuts. For doughnut holes, transfer all to oil and stir gently and constantly until golden brown, about 2 minutes. Transfer to prepared rack to cool. Let doughnuts sit until cool enough to handle, at least 5 minutes.

8 cool Set clean wire rack in now-empty sheet. Working with 1 doughnut at a time, dip both sides of doughnut in glaze, allowing excess to drip back into bowl. Place on unlined rack. Repeat with doughnut holes. Let doughnuts and holes stand until glaze has become slightly matte and dry to touch, 15 to 30 minutes, before serving.

total time 11½ hours

1 hour	9 hours	10 min.	45 min.	15 min.	30 min.
make dough	first rise	shape dough	second rise	fry	cool

» **Take your time** To make the doughnuts over 2 or 3 days, refrigerate dough for up to 48 hours in step 3.

CHOCOLATE FROSTING

makes 1½ cups

4 ounces bittersweet chocolate, chopped fine

½ cup water

2 cups (8 ounces) confectioners' sugar

2 tablespoons unsweetened cocoa powder

Pinch table salt

1 While doughnuts cool, microwave chocolate and water in medium bowl at 50 percent power until chocolate is melted, about 30 seconds. Whisk in sugar, cocoa, and salt until smooth and fluid. Let cool slightly.

2 Set clean wire rack in now-empty sheet. Dip top half of 1 cooled doughnut into frosting until evenly coated, allowing excess to drip back into bowl. Invert doughnut and place on wire rack. Repeat with remaining doughnuts. Let doughnuts stand until frosting is dry to touch, 15 to 30 minutes, before serving.

MATCHA FROSTING

makes ¾ cup

2 cups (8 ounces) confectioners' sugar

2 teaspoons matcha powder

Pinch table salt

3 tablespoons hot water

1 While doughnuts cool, whisk sugar, matcha powder, and salt together in medium bowl. Add hot water and whisk until smooth.

2 Set clean wire rack in now-empty sheet. Dip top half of 1 cooled doughnut into frosting until evenly coated, allowing excess to drip back into bowl. Invert doughnut and place on wire rack. Repeat with remaining doughnuts. Let doughnuts stand until frosting is slightly matte and dry to touch, 15 to 30 minutes, before serving.

COFFEE FROSTING

makes ¾ cup

2 cups (8 ounces) confectioners' sugar

1 tablespoon instant espresso powder

Pinch table salt

¼ cup (2 ounces) hot water

1 While doughnuts cool, whisk together sugar, espresso powder, and salt in medium bowl. Whisk in hot water until smooth.

2 Set clean wire rack in now-empty sheet. Dip top half of 1 cooled doughnut into frosting until evenly coated, allowing excess to drip back into bowl. Invert doughnut and place on wire rack. Repeat with remaining doughnuts. Let doughnuts stand until glaze is slightly matte and dry to touch, 15 to 30 minutes, before serving.

RASPBERRY FROSTING

makes 1 cup

8 ounces (1⅔ cups) frozen raspberries, thawed

2 cups (8 ounces) confectioners' sugar

Pinch table salt

Rainbow sprinkles (optional)

1 While doughnuts cool, process raspberries in blender until smooth. Strain puree through fine-mesh strainer into bowl or measuring cup. Measure out 6 tablespoons puree for frosting (reserve remaining puree for another use). In medium bowl, whisk sugar, salt, and puree until smooth.

2 Set clean wire rack in now-empty sheet. Dip top half of 1 cooled doughnut into frosting until evenly coated, allowing excess to drip back into bowl. Invert doughnut and place on wire rack. Top doughnut with sprinkles, if using. Repeat with remaining doughnuts. Let doughnuts stand until glaze is slightly matte and dry to touch, 15 to 30 minutes, before serving.

HAM AND CHEESE WOOL ROLL

makes 1 loaf

2¼ cups (12⅓ ounces) bread flour

1½ teaspoons instant or rapid-rise yeast

½ cup (4 ounces) whole milk, room temperature

2 large eggs, room temperature

1 tablespoon sugar

½ teaspoon table salt

6 tablespoons unsalted butter, cut into 6 pieces and softened

4 teaspoons Dijon mustard

4 ounces thinly sliced ham (about 8 slices), torn into rough 3-inch pieces

3 ounces Gruyère cheese, shredded (1½ cups)

why this recipe works   As its name suggests, this loaf resembles a neatly wound roll of wool, and it's just as soft and plush as one too. Half of each portion of dough is topped with a sweet or savory filling and the other half is sliced into thin strips. The dough is rolled into a log starting with the filled side so it ends up adorned with the strips that give the loaf a slinky-like appearance. Once baked, the strips turn the wreath into a pull-apart loaf. It sounds intricate, but you should find the shaping surprisingly simple. While the options for fillings are endless, ranging from custard to chocolate to cheese, we landed on a ham and Gruyère combination with a schmear of Dijon mustard. This rich, sharp, cheesy bread is perfect for a picnic, football party, or fun after-school snack—everyone can pull off a piece of their liking. The slight tackiness of the dough aids in rolling and shaping, so resist the urge to flour the counter.

1 make dough   Whisk flour and yeast together in bowl of stand mixer. Whisk milk and eggs in 2-cup liquid measuring cup until combined. Using dough hook on low speed, slowly add milk mixture to flour mixture and mix until cohesive dough starts to form and no dry flour remains, about 2 minutes, scraping down sides of bowl with rubber spatula as needed (dough will look fairly dry). Cover bowl and let rest for 15 minutes.

2   Add sugar and salt and knead on medium speed until incorporated, about 30 seconds. With mixer running, add butter 1 piece at a time, allowing each piece to incorporate before adding next, about 3 minutes total, scraping down dough hook and sides of bowl as needed. Continue to knead on medium speed until dough begins to pull away from sides of bowl, 7 to 10 minutes. Transfer dough to clean counter and knead by hand to form smooth, round ball, about 30 seconds.

3 first rise   Place dough seam side down in lightly greased large bowl or container, cover tightly with plastic wrap, and let rise until slightly puffy, about 1 hour. Refrigerate until firm, at least 2 hours or up to 24 hours.

4 shape dough   Grease 9-inch cake pan. Press down on dough to deflate. Transfer dough to clean counter so that side of dough touching bowl is now touching counter. Pat into 7- by 8-inch rectangle, using bench scraper to help square off corners. Divide dough into 4 equal pieces and cover loosely with plastic.

5   Roll 1 piece of dough into 12 by 6-inch rectangle with short side parallel to counter edge (keep remaining pieces covered). Starting from left side of rectangle, measure ¼ inch in from edge and, using bench scraper or pizza wheel, cut 5-inch-long by ¼-inch-wide strip lengthwise from top edge of dough. Measure ¼ inch from cut mark and repeat cutting dough lengthwise. Repeat measuring and cutting across width of dough until you reach the right edge. (You should have about 20 strips.)

Cut bottom of dough into strips.

Spread dough with mustard.

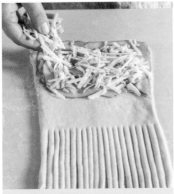
Top with cheese and ham.

Roll up dough.

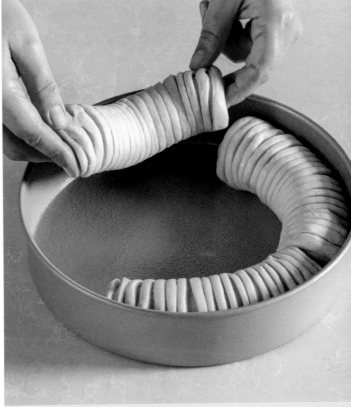
Place dough portions in pan.

6 Evenly spread 1 teaspoon mustard over uncut portion of dough, leaving 2 inch border between beginning of cuts and mustard in center of dough. Arrange one-quarter of ham evenly over mustard, then sprinkle with one-quarter of cheese. Roll dough away from you into firm cylinder, keeping roll taut by tucking it under itself as you go. Roll log seam side down, curl ends of dough away from you, and transfer to prepared pan, making sure seam is down and facing corner of pan. Repeat with remaining dough, mustard, ham, and cheese.

7 second rise Cover pan with plastic and let dough rise until puffy, about 1 hour.

8 bake Adjust oven rack to middle position and heat oven to 350 degrees. Bake until loaf is deep golden brown and registers at least 190 degrees, 35 to 45 minutes, rotating pan halfway through baking. Let loaf cool in pan on wire rack for 15 minutes. Remove loaf from pan and let cool on rack for 30 minutes. Slice and serve warm.

total time 6¾ hours

50 min.	3 hours	25 min.	1 hour	35 min.	45 min.
make dough	first rise	shape dough	second rise	bake	cool

» **Take your time** To bake the next day, refrigerate dough for up to 24 hours in step 3.

ham and cheese wool roll (page 330)

conchas (page 334)

CONCHAS

makes 12 conchas

dough

- 3⅔ cups (20⅛ ounces) bread flour
- 1 tablespoon instant or rapid-rise yeast
- 1¼ cups (10 ounces) water, room temperature
- 2 large eggs, room temperature
- ¼ cup (1¾ ounces) sugar
- 2 teaspoons table salt
- 13 tablespoons unsalted butter, cut into 13 pieces and softened

vanilla crust

- 1 cup (4 ounces) confectioners' sugar
- ¾ cup (4⅛ ounces) bread flour, plus extra for rolling
- 10 tablespoons (4 ounces) vegetable shortening
- 2 teaspoons vanilla extract
- ⅛ teaspoon table salt

VARIATION

CHOCOLATE CONCHAS

Reduce bread flour in Vanilla Crust to ⅔ cup (3⅔ ounces) and add 3 tablespoons unsweetened cocoa powder.

why this recipe works   Mexico's best-known pan dulce (sweet bread), conchas are a lightly sweet, enriched bread topped with a cookie-like crust that's scored to look like a shell (concha means "seashell" in Spanish). An ideal concha is buttery, light, and tender—perfect for a dunk in hot chocolate or coffee—yet sturdy enough to support the crispy crust. Conchas derive from brioche, brought to Mexico through the migration of French and other European bakers by the 1800s, so we start with a brioche method to create the base. Then we add the flavorful, sweet topping (vanilla and chocolate are the most common versions), made from equal parts confectioners' sugar, flour, and vegetable shortening, by pressing it into a thin round to cover each bun. The higher melting point of the shortening helps the iconic seashell scoring hold during baking. A butter knife makes quick work of the design, without the need for a traditional concha cutter. When the coating sets, it gives the soft bun crunch and then melts in your mouth. Conchas are best eaten the day they are made.

1   make dough rolls   Whisk flour and yeast together in bowl of stand mixer. Whisk water and eggs in 4-cup liquid measuring cup until combined. Using dough hook on low speed, add water mixture to flour mixture and mix until cohesive dough starts to form and no dry flour remains, about 2 minutes, scraping down bowl as needed. Let rest for 15 minutes.

2   Add sugar and salt to dough and knead on medium-low speed until incorporated, about 30 seconds. Increase speed to medium and, with mixer running, add butter 1 piece at a time, allowing each piece to incorporate before adding next, 4 to 6 minutes total, scraping down bowl and dough hook as needed. Continue to knead until dough is elastic and pulls away cleanly from sides of bowl, about 10 minutes longer.

3   first rise   Transfer dough to greased large bowl or container, cover with greased plastic, and let dough rise at room temperature until doubled in volume, about 1 hour.

4   make vanilla crust   While dough rises, in clean, dry mixer bowl, combine confectioners' sugar, flour, vegetable shortening, vanilla, and salt. Fit mixer with paddle attachment and mix on low speed, scraping down bowl as needed, until mixture is homogeneous and has texture of Play-Doh, about 2 minutes. Transfer mixture to counter and divide into 12 equal pieces. Roll into balls, place on large plate, and cover with plastic; refrigerate for 30 minutes. Draw or trace 4-inch circle in center of 1 side of zipper-lock bag. Cut open seams along both sides of bag, leaving bottom seam intact so bag opens completely; set aside.

Toss ball of crust in flour.

Press crust into circle.

Place crust on top of concha.

Score pattern.

5 shape dough Line 2 rimmed baking sheets with parchment paper. Transfer concha dough to clean counter and divide into 12 equal pieces. Cover loosely with greased plastic. Form 1 piece of dough into rough ball by bringing edges of dough together and pinching edges to seal so that top is smooth. Place ball seam side down on clean counter and, using your cupped hand, drag in small circles until dough feels taut and round. Repeat with remaining dough pieces, scraping counter clean with bench scraper as needed (keep remaining pieces covered). Evenly space 6 dough balls on each prepared sheet. Poke any air bubbles in dough balls with tip of paring knife.

6 second rise Cover rolls loosely with greased plastic and let rise at room temperature until doubled in size, 1 to 1½ hours.

7 While rolls rise, place reserved cut bag marked side down on counter. Place ⅓ cup flour in small bowl; working with 1 ball of crust at a time, gently toss in flour to generously coat, then open bag and place ball in center of circle. Fold other side of bag over ball and, using glass pie plate or baking dish, gently press crust to 4-inch diameter, using circle drawn on bag as guide. Carefully peel bag away from crust to remove, then place crust on top of 1 ball of concha dough, pressing gently to mold crust to dough. Repeat with remaining balls of crust and remaining concha dough balls, wiping bag clean as needed. (Don't wait until after dough rises to top dough balls with crust.)

8 Using butter knife and pressing gently, score crust of each roll with series of concentric curved lines emanating from single point to create seashell pattern, being careful not to cut through topping completely.

9 bake Adjust oven racks to upper-middle and lower-middle positions and heat oven to 350 degrees. Bake until buns are golden brown and register at least 205 degrees, 20 to 25 minutes, switching and rotating sheets halfway through baking. Transfer sheets to wire racks and let cool for 15 minutes Serve.

total time 3¾ hours

55 min.	1 hour	15 min.	1 hour	20 min.	15 min.
make dough	first rise	shape dough	second rise	bake	cool

BOLO BAO

makes 20 buns

flour paste

- ½ cup (4 ounces) water
- 2 tablespoons all-purpose flour

dough

- ½ cup (4 ounces) cold whole milk
- 1 large egg, room temperature
- 2⅔ cups (13⅓ ounces) all-purpose flour
- ⅓ cup plus 4 teaspoons (3 ounces) sugar
- 3½ teaspoons nonfat dry milk powder
- 2¼ teaspoons instant or rapid-rise yeast
- 1 teaspoon table salt
- 4 tablespoons unsalted butter, cut into 4 pieces and softened

topping

- ⅔ cup plus 2 teaspoons (3½ ounces) all-purpose flour
- ¼ teaspoon baking powder
- ¼ teaspoon table salt
- 6 tablespoons unsalted butter, softened
- ⅔ cup (2⅔ ounces) confectioners' sugar
- 2 large eggs, lightly beaten
- 2 teaspoons vanilla extract

why this recipe works   A favorite in many Chinese bakeries is a slightly sweet baked bun called bolo bao (pineapple bun). Its moist, fluffy interior is the result of adding tangzhong (see page 32) to an already enriched bread dough. Most bakery-style versions come with a custardy, crackly topping with a crosshatched pattern that resembles the outside of a pineapple (hence the name). Our version is inspired by the bolo bao offered at Tim Ho Wan, a Michelin-starred dim sum restaurant in Hong Kong. The crust is smoother, lighter, and shatteringly crisp, a delightful contrast to the soft bun.

1   make flour paste   Whisk water and flour in medium bowl until smooth. Microwave, whisking every 20 seconds, until mixture thickens to stiff, smooth, pudding-like consistency that forms mound when dropped from end of whisk into bowl, 40 to 80 seconds.

2   make dough   Whisk flour paste and milk together in 4-cup liquid measuring cup. Whisk in egg. Whisk flour, sugar, milk powder, yeast, and salt together in bowl of stand mixer. Using dough hook on low speed, slowly add milk mixture and mix until cohesive dough starts to form and no dry flour remains, about 2 minutes, scraping down bowl as needed. Increase speed to medium-high and knead until dough is smooth and elastic and clears sides of bowl, 10 to 12 minutes.

3   Fit mixer with paddle. With mixer running on medium speed, add butter, 1 piece at a time, and beat for 30 seconds after each addition. Once all butter has been added, mix until butter is fully incorporated and dough is no longer shiny, 1 to 2 minutes. Transfer dough to lightly floured counter and knead by hand to form smooth, round ball.

4   first rise   Transfer dough seam side down to lightly greased large bowl or container, cover with plastic, and let dough rise until doubled in volume, 1 to 1½ hours.

5   make topping   Meanwhile, whisk flour, baking powder, and salt together in small bowl. Using clean, dry mixer bowl and paddle, beat butter and confectioners' sugar on medium-high speed until light, pale, and fluffy, about 3 minutes. With mixer running, gradually add eggs, then vanilla and mix until smooth, about 2 minutes, scraping down bowl as needed. Add flour mixture and mix on low speed until combined, about 30 seconds. Scrape down bowl, then use rubber spatula to ensure all flour is incorporated. Transfer mixture to 1-quart heavy-duty zipper-lock bag and snip off 1 corner, making hole no larger than ¼ inch (alternatively, transfer to pastry bag fitted with ¼-inch piping tip); set aside until ready to use (do not refrigerate).

6 shape dough   Line 2 rimmed baking sheets with parchment paper. Press down on dough to deflate. Transfer dough to clean counter, divide into 20 equal pieces, and cover loosely with plastic. Working with 1 piece of dough at a time (keep remaining pieces covered), form into rough ball by stretching dough around your thumb and pinching edges together so that top is smooth. Place ball seam side down on clean counter and, using your cupped hand, drag in small circles until dough feels taut and round. Space 10 balls evenly on each prepared sheet. Lightly spray tops of buns with vegetable oil spray.

7 second rise   Cover dough with plastic and let rise until doubled in size and dough springs back minimally when poked gently with your finger, about 1 hour.

8 bake   Adjust oven rack to middle position and heat oven to 375 degrees. Pipe about 2 tablespoons topping in tight spiral on top of each bun (topping should form circle roughly 2 inches in diameter and ¼ inch thick). Bake, 1 sheet at a time, until topping is golden brown, 14 to 16 minutes, rotating sheet halfway through baking. Transfer buns to wire rack and let cool for at least 10 minutes. Serve.

total time 3½ hours

45 min.	1 hour	15 min.	1 hour	20 min.	10 min.
make dough	first rise	shape dough	second rise	bake	cool

total time 21½ hours

35 min.	1½ hours	16 hours	20 min.	2 hours	20 min.	5 min.
make dough	fold + rest	first rise	shape dough	second rise	bake	cool

ORANGE BLOSSOM AND ANISE BUNS

makes 12 buns

3¼ cups (17¾ ounces) bread flour

2¼ teaspoons instant or rapid-rise yeast

1½ teaspoons table salt

1½ teaspoons anise seeds

6 large eggs, room temperature

16 tablespoons unsalted butter, melted and cooled slightly

½ cup water, room temperature

⅓ cup (2⅓ ounces) granulated sugar

5 teaspoons orange blossom water

1 large egg, beaten with 1 tablespoon water and pinch table salt

1 tablespoon sesame seeds

1 tablespoon turbinado or sparkling sugar

why this recipe works   Inspired by krachel, a Moroccan sweet bread flavored with two common aromas in Moroccan desserts, orange and anise, these fragrant rolls are equally at home on the breakfast table as they are eaten alongside tea. And in Morocco the krachel often break the Ramadan fast. Since we've made buns from our No-Knead Brioche (page 290) dough, it was a logical one to use for the base of our adaptation. We sprinkled the top with sesame seeds as is traditional in Morocco as well as turbinado sugar for crunch, sparkle, and sweetness. While we prefer anise seeds in this recipe, you can use fennel seeds. The dough will be quite sticky; if it is too sticky to handle after dividing into 12 pieces in step 3, refrigerate the dough for 15 minutes.

1 make dough   Whisk flour, yeast, salt, and anise seeds together in large bowl. Whisk eggs, melted butter, water, granulated sugar, and orange blossom water in 4-cup liquid measuring cup until sugar has dissolved. Using rubber spatula, gently fold egg mixture into flour mixture, scraping up dry flour from bottom of bowl, until cohesive dough starts to form and no dry flour remains. Let rest for 10 minutes.

2 fold and rest   Using greased bowl scraper or your wet fingertips, fold dough over itself by gently lifting and folding edge of dough toward middle. Turn bowl 45 degrees; fold again. Turn bowl and fold dough 6 more times (total of 8 folds). Cover with plastic wrap and let rise for 30 minutes. Repeat folding and rising every 30 minutes, 3 more times.

3 first rise   Cover bowl tightly with plastic and refrigerate for 16 hours.

4 shape dough   Line rimmed baking sheet with parchment paper. Press down on dough to deflate. Transfer dough to well-floured counter and divide into 12 equal pieces. Working with 1 piece of dough at a time, pat dough into disk. Working around circumference of dough, fold edges of dough toward center until ball forms. Place ball seam side down on counter and, using your cupped hand, drag in small circles until dough feels taut and round. (Tackiness of dough against counter and circular motion should work dough into smooth, even ball, but if dough sticks to your hands, lightly dust top of dough with flour.) Arrange buns seam side down on prepared sheet.

5 second rise   Cover dough loosely with plastic and let rise at room temperature until almost doubled in size and dough springs back minimally when poked gently with your finger, about 2 hours.

6 bake   Adjust oven rack to middle position and heat oven to 350 degrees. Gently brush rolls with egg wash and sprinkle with sesame seeds and turbinado sugar. Bake until rolls are golden brown and register at least 190 degrees, about 20 minutes, rotating sheet halfway through baking. Let rolls cool on sheet on wire rack for 5 minutes. Serve warm or at room temperature.

USE IT UP

If baking bread becomes part of your regular routine, you'll likely want ways to use it beyond simply digging in. Some of these recipes are great for using bread right away. Others work well when bread is a little past its prime. While you can freeze many breads, you might want bread that's a bit past its prime just to make some of these tasty treats and satisfying meal options.

BREAKFAST IDEAS

ENRICHED BREAD FRENCH TOAST

serves 4

After weaving and braiding and stacking your way to a beautiful loaf, you'll want more ways than one to use the long loaf challah. Or maybe your brioche brunch plans fell through. French toast is a great way to use these breads. Fun additions, like an almond crust or a little booze, make it even better. To prevent the butter from clumping during mixing, heat the milk in a microwave or small saucepan until it is warm to the touch (about 80 degrees) before adding the butter. All the slices of bread can be cooked together on an electric griddle, but the process may take an extra 2 to 3 minutes per side. Set the griddle temperature to 350 degrees and use the entire amount of unmelted butter (2 tablespoons) to grease the griddle. Serve with warm maple syrup.

8 slices Challah (page 308) or No-Knead Brioche (page 290)

1½ cups whole milk, warmed slightly

3 large egg yolks

3 tablespoons packed light brown sugar

2 tablespoons unsalted butter, melted, plus 2 tablespoons unsalted butter

1 tablespoon vanilla extract

½ teaspoon ground cinnamon

¼ teaspoon table salt

1 Adjust oven rack to middle position and heat oven to 300 degrees. Place bread on wire rack set in rimmed baking sheet. Bake until bread is almost dry throughout (center should remain slightly moist), about 16 minutes, flipping bread halfway through baking. Remove bread from rack and let cool for 5 minutes. Reduce oven temperature to 200 degrees and return sheet with wire rack to oven.

2 Whisk milk, egg yolks, sugar, melted butter, vanilla, cinnamon, and salt together in large bowl. Transfer mixture to 13 by 9-inch baking dish. Add bread to dish and soak until slices are saturated with milk mixture but not falling apart, 20 seconds per side. Using firm slotted spatula, transfer bread to second baking sheet, allowing excess milk mixture to drip back into dish.

3 Melt ½ tablespoon butter in 12-inch skillet over medium-low heat. Using slotted spatula, transfer 2 slices soaked bread to skillet and cook until golden brown, 3 to 4 minutes. Flip and continue to cook until second side is golden brown, 3 to 4 minutes longer. (If toast is browning too quickly, reduce temperature slightly.) Transfer French toast to prepared wire rack in oven to keep warm. Wipe skillet clean with paper towels. Repeat in 3 batches with remaining 1½ tablespoons butter and remaining 6 slices soaked bread. Serve warm.

VARIATIONS

ALMOND-CRUSTED FRENCH TOAST

Process ½ cup slivered almonds and 1 tablespoon packed light brown sugar in food processor until coarsely ground, 12 to 15 pulses (you should have about ½ cup). Add 1 tablespoon triple sec and 1 teaspoon grated orange zest to milk mixture in step 2. Sprinkle 1 tablespoon almond mixture over 1 side of each slice soaked bread. Cook as directed, starting with almond mixture side down.

EXTRA-CRISP FRENCH TOAST

Pulse 1 slice hearty bread, torn into 1-inch pieces; 1 tablespoon packed light brown sugar; and ¼ teaspoon ground cinnamon in food processor until finely ground, 8 to 12 pulses (you should have about ½ cup). Sprinkle 1 tablespoon bread-crumb mixture over 1 side of each slice soaked bread. Cook as directed, starting with crumb mixture side down.

EVERYDAY FRENCH TOAST

serves 4

If you need a way to use your many slices of sandwich bread, French toast works for that too. This one caters to a more delicate bread. You could make this French toast sweeter by using Cinnamon Raisin Swirl Bread (page 160), which goes great with maple syrup, or give things a nutty flavor with Whole-Wheat Sandwich Bread (page 177). Be sure to use vegetable oil spray here to prevent the toast from sticking. Top with maple syrup or confectioners' sugar, if desired.

  3 **large eggs**

  1 **tablespoon vanilla extract**

  2 **teaspoons packed brown sugar**

  ½ **teaspoon ground cinnamon**

  ¼ **teaspoon table salt**

  2 **tablespoons unsalted butter, melted**

  1 **cup milk**

  8 **slices White Sandwich Bread (page 158)**

1 Adjust 1 oven rack to lowest position and second rack 5 to 6 inches from broiler element. Heat oven to 425 degrees. Generously spray bottom and sides of 18 by 13-inch rimmed baking sheet with vegetable oil spray. Whisk eggs, vanilla, sugar, cinnamon, and salt in large bowl until sugar is dissolved and no streaks of egg remain. Whisking constantly, drizzle in melted butter. Whisk in milk.

2 Pour egg mixture into prepared sheet. Arrange bread in single layer in egg mixture, leaving small gaps between slices. Working quickly, use your fingers to flip slices in same order you placed them in sheet. Let sit until slices absorb remaining custard, about 1 minute.

3 Bake on lower rack until bottoms of slices are golden brown, 10 to 15 minutes. Transfer sheet to upper rack and heat broiler. (Leave sheet in oven while broiler heats.) Broil until tops of slices are golden brown, watching carefully and rotating sheet if necessary to prevent burning, 1 to 4 minutes. Using thin metal spatula, carefully flip each slice. Serve.

BISCUITS AND GRAVY

serves 8

Maybe you like to keep things simple and don't want to smother your just-baked biscuits, but don't mind us if we do. Here we create a unique spin using our Cast Iron Orange-Herb Biscuits: The fluffy buttermilk biscuits provide an awakening tang, and they're sturdy enough to absorb some gravy without completely turning to mush. The subtle orange-herb flavor really complements the porky flavor of a white gravy that's just rich enough.

¼	cup all-purpose flour
1½	teaspoons pepper
1	teaspoon ground fennel
1	teaspoon ground sage
1½	pounds bulk pork sausage
3	cups whole milk
1	recipe Cast Iron Orange-Herb Biscuits (page 50), cooled and split in half

Whisk flour, pepper, fennel, and sage together in small bowl. Cook sausage in 12-inch nonstick skillet over medium heat, breaking up meat with wooden spoon, until sausage is no longer pink, about 8 minutes. Sprinkle flour mixture over sausage and cook, stirring constantly, until flour is absorbed, about 1 minute. Slowly stir in milk and simmer until gravy thickens, about 5 minutes. Season with salt to taste. Serve over split biscuits.

HAM AND GRUYÈRE BREAKFAST SANDWICHES

serves 4

Everyone knows the best breakfast sandwiches are served on a toasted English muffin. If you've made a batch, there's no reason to stick to filling all of your nooks and crannies with butter and jam. And there's no reason to get your sandwich from a drive-through window. (Oh, and we still butter the muffins.)

4	English Muffins (page 141), split
3	tablespoons unsalted butter, softened
¼	cup mayonnaise
2	teaspoons Dijon mustard
4	large eggs
1	tablespoon vegetable oil
4	thin slices deli Black Forest ham (4 ounces)
4	ounces Gruyère cheese, shredded (1 cup)
1½	ounces (1½ cups) baby arugula
4	thin tomato slices

1 Adjust oven rack 5 inches from broiler element and heat broiler. Spread insides of muffins evenly with butter and arrange split side up on rimmed baking sheet. Combine mayonnaise and mustard in bowl; set aside. Crack 2 eggs into small bowl and season with salt and pepper. Repeat with remaining 2 eggs and second small bowl.

2 Broil muffins until golden brown, 2 to 4 minutes, rotating sheet halfway through broiling. Flip muffins and broil until just crisp on second side, 1 to 2 minutes; set aside.

3 Heat oil in 12-inch nonstick skillet over medium-high heat until shimmering. Working quickly, pour 1 bowl of eggs in 1 side of pan and second bowl of eggs in other side. Cover and cook for 1 minute. Working quickly, top each egg with 1 slice of ham and ¼ cup Gruyère. Cover pan, remove from heat, and let stand until Gruyère is melted and egg whites are cooked through, about 2 minutes.

4 Spread mayonnaise mixture on muffin bottoms and place 1 topped egg on each. Divide arugula evenly among sandwiches, then top with tomato slices and muffin tops. Serve.

SKILLET STRATA WITH CHEDDAR AND THYME

serves 4

A strata—like a savory, eggy breakfast bread pudding—can be a long affair of soaking, weighting, and baking. Baking bread takes long enough. Use leftovers in this quick version turned out in a skillet. This recipe works with any savory bread in chapter 3 except for English Muffin Bread or Quinoa Whole-Wheat Bread. Do not trim the crusts from the bread or the strata will be dense and eggy. Using a 10-inch skillet is crucial for the right thickness and texture of this dish.

 6 large eggs

1½ cups whole milk

 1 teaspoon minced fresh thyme or ¼ teaspoon dried

 ¼ teaspoon pepper

 4 ounces sharp cheddar cheese, shredded (1 cup)

 4 tablespoons unsalted butter

 1 onion, chopped fine

 ½ teaspoon table salt

 5 slices White Sandwich Bread (page 158), cut into 1-inch squares

1 Adjust oven rack to middle position and heat oven to 425 degrees. Whisk eggs, milk, thyme, and pepper together in bowl, then stir in cheddar.

2 Melt butter in 10-inch ovensafe nonstick skillet over medium-high heat. Add onion and salt and cook until onion is softened and lightly browned, about 6 minutes. Stir in bread until evenly coated and cook, stirring occasionally, until bread is lightly toasted, about 3 minutes.

3 Off heat, fold in egg mixture until slightly thickened and well combined with bread. Gently press on top of strata to help it soak up egg mixture. Transfer skillet to oven and cook until center of strata is puffed and edges have browned and pulled away slightly from sides of pan, about 12 minutes. Serve.

SAUTÉED GRAPE AND ALMOND BUTTER TOAST

serves 1

This is PB&J all grown up—earthy almond butter, not-so-sweet sautéed grape topping, and, of course, homemade rustic whole-grain bread. It's a treat you can make for yourself that's worth the time—really just 3 minutes beyond the normal PB&J to warm and soften the grapes. And it will fill and satisfy you beyond the classic sandwich too. This recipe also works with Sprouted Wheat Berry Bread (page 204), Spelt Bread (page 206), and Anadama Bread (page 212).

 ½ teaspoon extra-virgin olive oil

 3 ounces seedless red or green grapes, halved (¾ cup)

 ½ teaspoon honey

 ½ teaspoon minced fresh thyme or ⅛ teaspoon dried

   Pinch table salt

 ¼ teaspoon grated lemon zest plus ½ teaspoon juice

 2 tablespoons natural almond butter

 1 slice Whole-Wheat Rustic Loaf (page 196), about ½ inch thick, toasted

Heat oil in 8- or 10-inch nonstick skillet over medium-high heat until shimmering. Add grapes, honey, thyme, and salt and cook, stirring occasionally, until grapes begin to soften and juices thicken, 3 to 5 minutes. Off heat, stir in lemon zest and juice. Spread almond butter evenly over toasted bread, top with grape mixture, and serve.

CORN RICOTTA TOAST WITH PICKLED CORN AND CHERRY TOMATOES

serves 4

The toast should be golden brown and crunchy near the crust but still have spring in the center: Think bruschetta rather than crostini. We love this on any savory rustic bread in chapter 4.

1 cup water

⅔ cup distilled white vinegar

⅓ cup sugar

1 tablespoon kosher salt

2 cups (about 4 ears) corn kernels

1 large shallot, sliced thin

2 red Thai chiles, stemmed and seeded

4 (¾-inch-thick) slices No-Knead Rustic Loaf (page 186), toasted

6 ounces (¾ cup) ricotta cheese

5 ounces cherry tomatoes, halved

10 fresh basil leaves, torn into large pieces

1 Bring water, vinegar, sugar, and salt to boil in medium saucepan over high heat. Remove from heat and add corn, shallot, and chiles. Let steep for at least 45 minutes. (Pickled corn mixture can be refrigerated in airtight container for up to 1 week.)

2 Drain pickled corn mixture; discard chiles and pickling liquid. Divide ricotta among toasts and spread to edges. Divide pickled corn mixture and cherry tomatoes among toasts and top with basil. Season with flake sea salt and pepper to taste. Serve.

BROWN SUGAR TOAST

serves 1

Need a midday pick-me-up that's fast and satisfying and salty-sweet? This is the one. A blanket of banana slices is a great complement.

1 tablespoon salted butter, softened

1 tablespoon packed dark brown sugar

1 (1-inch-thick) slice White Sandwich Bread (page 158)

1 Mix butter and brown sugar together. Evenly spread half of mixture on 1 side of bread and place bread butter side down in small nonstick skillet. Spread remaining butter mixture on top of bread.

2 Cook in nonstick skillet over medium heat until browned and crisp on both sides, 3 to 4 minutes per side, watching carefully and adjusting heat to prevent burning. Transfer to wire rack to crisp and cool slightly before serving.

PITA AND SIMPLE HUMMUS

serves 8

Pita loves all kinds of dips but hummus is without a doubt a must-have accompaniment. Here's our easiest version with a spicy variation.

¼ cup water

2 tablespoons lemon juice

¼ cup tahini, stirred well

2 tablespoons extra-virgin olive oil

1 (15-ounce) can chickpeas, rinsed

1 garlic clove, minced

½ teaspoon table salt

¼ teaspoon ground cumin

   Pinch cayenne

1 recipe pita bread (see page 278 or 280)

1   Combine water and lemon juice in bowl; set aside. Whisk tahini and oil together in second bowl.

2   Process chickpeas, garlic, salt, cumin, and cayenne in food processor until coarsely ground, about 15 seconds, scraping down bowl as needed. With processor running, slowly add water mixture until incorporated and process until smooth, about 1 minute. With processor still running, slowly add tahini mixture until incorporated and process until creamy, about 15 seconds, scraping down bowl as needed.

3   Transfer hummus to serving bowl, cover with plastic wrap, and let sit until flavors meld, at least 30 minutes. (Hummus can be refrigerated for up to 5 days.) Serve with pita bread.

PITA AND SPICY ROASTED RED PEPPER HUMMUS

Increase cayenne to ⅛ teaspoon and add ¼ teaspoon smoked paprika to food processor with chickpeas. After incorporating tahini mixture in step 2, add ¼ cup jarred roasted red peppers, rinsed, patted dry, and chopped, and pulse until coarsely ground, 5 to 7 pulses.

HAM AND SWISS FOOTBALL SANDWICHES

serves 6

A roll can often be a slider-size sandwich bun. The appetizer fills sweet Hawaiian rolls with ham and cheese, brushes them with a savory butter sauce, and bakes them until slightly crisp on the outside, soft inside, and oozing melted cheese.

12 Hawaiian Sweet Rolls (page 120)

6 tablespoons yellow mustard, divided

8 ounces deli Black Forest ham (12 thin slices)

8 ounces deli Swiss cheese (12 thin slices)

4 tablespoons unsalted butter

2 tablespoons finely chopped onion

1 tablespoon poppy seeds

2 tablespoons Worcestershire sauce

1 teaspoon garlic powder

1   Adjust oven rack to middle position and heat oven to 350 degrees. Slice rolls in half horizontally. Spread 4 table-spoons mustard on cut sides of roll tops and bottoms. Arrange roll bottoms, cut side up and side by side, in 13 by 9-inch baking dish. Fold ham slices in thirds, then once in half; place 1 slice on each roll bottom. Fold Swiss like ham, then place over ham. Season with pepper and cap with roll tops.

2   Combine butter, onion, and poppy seeds in bowl. Microwave until butter is melted and onion is softened, about 1 minute. Whisk Worcestershire, garlic powder, and remaining 2 tablespoons mustard into butter mixture until combined. Generously brush tops and edges of sandwiches with all of butter mixture. Spoon any remaining solids over sandwiches.

3   Cover dish with aluminum foil and let sit for 10 minutes to allow sandwiches to absorb sauce. Bake for 20 minutes. Uncover and continue to bake until cheese is melted around edges and tops are slightly firm, 7 to 9 minutes. Let cool for 10 minutes. Serve.

to make ahead   Sandwiches can be brushed with sauce, covered, and refrigerated up to 1 day in advance. Bring to room temperature before cooking.

GROWN-UP GRILLED CHEESE WITH ROBIOLA AND CHIPOTLE

serves 4

The best bread for a grilled cheese is, in our opinion, simply one of our sandwich breads (pages 154–181). To make grilled cheese melty but also flavorful for adults, we process the cheese and other flavorings in the food processor until a smooth paste forms; then we spread it on buttered bread and grill. Look for a Robiola aged for about one year (avoid Robiola aged for longer; it won't melt well). To quickly bring the Robiola to room temperature, microwave the pieces until warm, about 30 seconds. The first two sandwiches can be held in a 200-degree oven on a wire rack set in a baking sheet. Following are some other favorite, intriguing combos.

7	ounces Robiola cheese, rind removed, cut into 24 equal pieces, room temperature
2	ounces Brie cheese, rind removed
2	tablespoons dry white wine or vermouth
¼	teaspoon minced canned chipotle chile in adobo sauce
3	tablespoons unsalted butter, softened
1	teaspoon Dijon mustard
8	slices Whole-Wheat Sandwich Bread (page 177)

1 Process Robiola, Brie, and wine in food processor until smooth paste forms, 20 to 30 seconds. Add chipotle and pulse to combine, 3 to 5 pulses. Combine butter and mustard in small bowl.

2 Working on parchment paper–lined counter, spread mustard butter evenly over 1 side of slices of bread. Flip 4 slices of bread over and spread cheese mixture evenly over slices. Top with remaining 4 slices of bread, buttered sides up.

3 Preheat 12-inch nonstick skillet over medium heat for 2 minutes. (Droplets of water should just sizzle when flicked onto pan.) Place 2 sandwiches in skillet; reduce heat to medium-low; and cook until both sides are crispy and golden brown, 6 to 9 minutes per side, moving sandwiches to ensure even browning. Remove sandwiches from skillet and let stand for 2 minutes before serving. Repeat with remaining 2 sandwiches. Serve.

GRILLED CHEESE WITH ASIAGO AND DATES

Substitute Asiago for Robiola, 4 teaspoons finely chopped dates for chipotle, and Whole-Wheat Oatmeal Loaf (page 178) for Whole-Wheat Sandwich Bread.

GRILLED CHEESE WITH CHEDDAR AND SHALLOT

Substitute aged cheddar for Robiola, 4 teaspoons minced shallot for chipotle, and Buttermilk Dill Bread (page 171) for Whole-Wheat Sandwich Bread.

GRILLED CHEESE WITH COMTÉ AND CORNICHON

Substitute Comté for Robiola, 4 teaspoons minced cornichon for chipotle, and Sandwich Bread with Everything Bagel Crust (page 164) for Whole-Wheat Sandwich Bread.

GRILLED CHEESE WITH GRUYÈRE AND CHIVES

Substitute Gruyère for Robiola, 4 teaspoons minced fresh chives for chipotle, and White Sandwich Bread (page 158) for Whole-Wheat Sandwich Bread.

SAVOY CABBAGE SOUP WITH HAM, RYE BREAD, AND FONTINA

serves 4

High in the Italian Alps, Valle d'Aosta is known for a regional wintertime dish, seupa alla valpellinentze, a decadent combination of rich beef broth, pancetta, cabbage, rye bread, and nutty fontina cheese. We love how present the cobblestone topping of our rye bread is in this recipe. You will need a 13 by 9-inch broiler-safe baking dish for this recipe.

12 ounces Rye Bread (page 214), cut into 1½-inch pieces

2 tablespoons extra-virgin olive oil

1 tablespoon unsalted butter

4 ounces pancetta, chopped fine

1 onion, halved and sliced thin

½ teaspoon table salt

3 garlic cloves, minced

1 head savoy cabbage (1½ pounds), cored and cut into 1-inch pieces

4 cups beef broth

2 bay leaves

4 ounces fontina cheese, shredded (1 cup)

1 tablespoon chopped fresh parsley

1 Adjust oven rack to middle position and heat oven to 250 degrees. Spread bread in even layer on rimmed baking sheet and bake, stirring occasionally, until dried and crisp throughout, about 45 minutes; let croutons cool completely.

2 Heat oil and butter in Dutch oven over medium-low heat until butter is melted. Add pancetta and cook until browned and fat is rendered, about 8 minutes. Stir in onion and salt and cook over medium heat until softened and lightly browned, 5 to 7 minutes. Stir in garlic and cook until fragrant, about 30 seconds. Stir in cabbage, broth, and bay leaves and bring to boil. Reduce heat to low, cover, and simmer until cabbage is tender, about 45 minutes.

3 Adjust oven rack 6 inches from broiler element and heat broiler. Discard bay leaves. Spread half of cabbage mixture evenly in bottom of 13 by 9-inch broiler-safe baking dish, then top with half of croutons. Repeat with remaining cabbage mixture and croutons. Gently press down on croutons until saturated. Sprinkle fontina over top and broil until melted and spotty brown, about 4 minutes. Sprinkle with parsley and serve.

SIMPLE TOMATO-BREAD SOUP

serves 4

This tomato soup is so savory, you'd never know it was born from thrift. Making the Tuscan-inspired soup with sandwich bread (rather than rustic bread) ensures consistency from batch to batch.

¼ cup extra-virgin olive oil, plus extra for drizzling

3 garlic cloves, sliced thin

¼ teaspoon red pepper flakes

1 (28-ounce) can crushed tomatoes

4 ounces White Sandwich Bread (page 158), cut into ½-inch cubes (3 cups)

2 cups chicken broth

1 sprig fresh basil plus 2 tablespoons chopped

½ teaspoon table salt

¼ teaspoon pepper

Grated Parmesan cheese

1 Combine oil, garlic, and pepper flakes in large saucepan and cook over medium heat until garlic is lightly browned, about 4 minutes.

2 Stir in tomatoes, bread, broth, basil sprig, salt, and pepper and bring to boil over high heat. Reduce heat to medium, cover, and simmer vigorously until bread has softened completely and soup has thickened slightly, about 15 minutes, stirring occasionally.

3 Off heat, discard basil sprig. Whisk soup until bread has fully broken down and soup has thickened further, about 1 minute. Sprinkle with Parmesan and chopped basil, drizzle with extra oil, and serve.

ACQUACOTTA

serves 8 to 10

This vegetable soup is a hearty one-bowl meal. If escarole is unavailable, you can substitute 8 ounces of kale. If your cheese has a rind, add it to the pot with the broth in step 3. Serve this soup the traditional way, with a poached or soft-cooked egg spooned on top of the toast before the broth is added.

soup

- 1 large onion, chopped coarse
- 2 celery ribs, chopped coarse
- 4 garlic cloves, peeled
- 1 (28-ounce) can whole peeled tomatoes
- ½ cup extra-virgin olive oil
- ¾ teaspoon table salt
- ⅛ teaspoon red pepper flakes
- 8 cups chicken broth
- 1 fennel bulb, 2 tablespoons fronds minced, stalks discarded, bulb halved, cored, and cut into ½-inch pieces
- 2 (15-ounce) cans cannellini beans, drained with liquid reserved, rinsed
- 1 small head escarole (10 ounces), trimmed and cut into ½-inch pieces (8 cups)
- 2 large egg yolks
- ½ cup chopped fresh parsley
- 1 tablespoon minced fresh oregano

  Grated Pecorino Romano cheese

  Lemon wedges

toast

- 10 (½-inch-thick) slices No-Knead Rustic Loaf (page 186)
- ¼ cup extra-virgin olive oil

1 for the soup   Pulse onion, celery, and garlic in food processor until very finely chopped, 15 to 20 pulses, scraping down sides of bowl as needed. Transfer onion mixture to Dutch oven. Add tomatoes and their juice to now-empty processor and pulse until tomatoes are finely chopped, 10 to 12 pulses; set aside.

2   Stir oil, salt, and pepper flakes into onion mixture. Cook over medium-high heat, stirring occasionally, until light brown fond begins to form on bottom of pot, 12 to 15 minutes. Stir in tomatoes, increase heat to high, and cook, stirring frequently, until mixture is very thick and rubber spatula leaves distinct trail when dragged across bottom of pot, 9 to 12 minutes.

3   Add broth and fennel bulb to pot and bring to simmer. Reduce heat to medium-low and simmer until fennel begins to soften, 5 to 7 minutes. Stir in beans and escarole and cook until fennel is fully tender, about 10 minutes.

4   Whisk egg yolks and reserved bean liquid together in bowl, then stir into soup. Stir in parsley, oregano, and fennel fronds. Season with salt and pepper to taste.

5 for the toast   Adjust oven rack about 5 inches from broiler element and heat broiler. Place bread on aluminum foil–lined rimmed baking sheet, drizzle with oil, and season with salt and pepper. Broil until bread is deep golden brown.

6   Place 1 slice bread in bottom of each bowl. Ladle soup over toasted bread. Serve, passing Pecorino and lemon wedges separately.

FATTOUSH

serves 4

This Levantine salad combines fresh, flavorful produce with crisp pita and bright herbs. It's a great way to use up and reimagine pita. We fend off soggy bread by making the pita moisture-repellent, brushing its craggy sides with plenty of olive oil before baking. The oil soaks into the bread and prevents the pita chips from absorbing the salad's moisture while still allowing them to take on some of its flavor. The success of this recipe depends on ripe, in-season tomatoes. You can use white or whole-wheat pita.

- 2 (8-inch) pita breads (page 278 and 280)
- 3 tablespoons plus ¼ cup extra-virgin olive oil, divided
- 3 tablespoons lemon juice
- ¼ teaspoon garlic, minced to paste
- ¼ teaspoon table salt
- 1 pound tomatoes, cored and cut into ¾-inch pieces
- 1 English cucumber, peeled and sliced ⅛ inch thick
- 1 cup arugula, chopped coarse
- ½ cup chopped fresh cilantro
- ½ cup chopped fresh mint
- 4 scallions, sliced thin

1   Adjust oven rack to middle position and heat oven to 375 degrees. Using kitchen shears, cut around perimeter of each pita and separate into 2 thin rounds. Cut each round in half. Place pita bread, smooth side down, on wire rack set in rimmed baking sheet. Brush 3 tablespoons oil over surface of pita. (Pita does not need to be uniformly coated. Oil will absorb and spread as it bakes.) Season with salt and pepper. Bake until pita is crisp and pale golden brown, 10 to 14 minutes.

2   While pita toasts, whisk lemon juice, garlic, and salt together in small bowl. Let stand for 10 minutes.

3   Place tomatoes, cucumber, arugula, cilantro, mint, and scallions in large bowl. Break pita into ½-inch pieces and place in bowl with vegetables. Add lemon-garlic mixture and remaining ¼ cup oil and toss to coat. Season with salt and pepper to taste. Serve immediately.

CORNBREAD AND TOMATO SALAD

serves 4

Bread is great with salad but bread in salad is a nice and surprising treatment for our Jalapeño-Cheddar Cornbread (page 60). This spin on panzanella gets a double dose of corn flavor from toasty cubes of the cornbread and sweet corn kernels. All that corn flavor combined with juicy tomatoes and complementary jalapeño-lime dressing makes a summer salad sensation.

- 1 recipe Jalapeño-Cheddar Cornbread (page 60), cut into ¾-inch pieces (about 4 cups)
- 6 tablespoons extra-virgin olive oil, divided
- 2 tablespoons mayonnaise
- 2 tablespoons minced jalapeño chile
- 2 tablespoons lime juice
- 1¼ teaspoons table salt
- ½ teaspoon pepper
- 1½ pounds mixed tomatoes, cored and cut into ¾-inch pieces
- 1 small red onion, sliced thin
- 2 ears corn, kernels cut from cobs
- ¼ cup fresh basil leaves, torn

1   Adjust oven rack to middle position and heat oven to 400 degrees. Toss cornbread with 2 tablespoons oil on rimmed baking sheet. Spread cornbread on sheet and bake until dry to touch and edges turn golden brown, about 15 minutes, stirring halfway through baking. Let cool for 10 minutes.

2   Whisk mayonnaise, jalapeño, lime juice, salt, pepper, and remaining ¼ cup oil together in large bowl. Add tomatoes, onion, and cornbread and toss gently to coat. Season with salt and pepper to taste. Transfer salad to serving platter and top with corn and basil. Serve.

WHITE BEAN AND MUSHROOM GRATIN

serves 4 to 6

This vegetarian entrée gratin features creamy white beans, meaty cremini mushrooms, tender carrots, and a crisp, toasty starring layer of homemade No-Knead Rustic Loaf (page 186). Other rustic loaves like Whole-Wheat Rustic Loaf (page 196), Spelt Bread (page 206), or Rye Bread (page 214) also work here. Cannellini or navy beans can be used in place of great Northern beans, if desired.

- ½ cup extra-virgin olive oil, divided
- 10 ounces cremini mushrooms, trimmed and sliced ½ inch thick
- ¾ teaspoon table salt
- ½ teaspoon pepper, divided
- 4–5 slices No-Knead Rustic Loaf (page 186), cut into ½-inch cubes (5 cups)
- ¼ cup minced fresh parsley, divided
- 1 cup water
- 1 tablespoon all-purpose flour
- 1 small onion, chopped fine
- 5 garlic cloves, minced
- 1 tablespoon tomato paste
- 1½ teaspoons minced fresh thyme
- ⅓ cup dry sherry
- 2 (15-ounce) cans great Northern beans
- 3 carrots, peeled, halved lengthwise, and cut into ¾-inch pieces

1 Adjust oven rack to middle position and heat oven to 300 degrees. Heat ¼ cup oil in 12-inch ovensafe skillet over medium-high heat until shimmering. Add mushrooms, salt, and ¼ teaspoon pepper and cook, stirring occasionally, until mushrooms are well browned, 8 to 12 minutes.

2 While mushrooms cook, toss bread, 3 tablespoons parsley, remaining ¼ cup oil, and remaining ¼ teaspoon pepper together in bowl. Set aside. Stir water and flour in second bowl until no lumps of flour remain. Set aside.

3 Reduce heat to medium, add onion to skillet, and continue to cook, stirring frequently, until onion is translucent, 4 to 6 minutes. Reduce heat to medium-low; add garlic, tomato paste, and thyme; and cook, stirring constantly, until bottom of skillet is dark brown, 2 to 3 minutes. Add sherry and cook, scraping up any browned bits.

4 Add beans and their liquid, carrots, and flour mixture. Bring to boil over high heat. Off heat, arrange bread mixture over surface in even layer. Transfer skillet to oven and bake for 40 minutes. (Liquid should have consistency of thin gravy.)

5 Leave skillet in oven and turn on broiler. Broil until crumbs are golden brown, 4 to 7 minutes. Remove gratin from oven and let stand for 20 minutes. Sprinkle with remaining 1 tablespoon parsley and serve.

PORK SCHNITZEL

serves 4

Need a way to use up a lot of sandwich bread at dinner without, well, feeling like you're eating a lot of bread? Making bread crumbs is great for working your way through a loaf. Pork schnitzel is a delectable option for using crumbs—rich, salty, and coated in a crispy browned puffed coating. Use a Dutch oven that holds 6 quarts or more.

- 7 slices White Sandwich Bread (page 158), crusts removed, cut into ¾-inch cubes
- ½ cup all-purpose flour
- 2 large eggs, plus 1 hard-cooked large egg, yolk and white separated and passed through fine-mesh strainer (optional)
- 1 tablespoon vegetable oil
- 1 (1¼-pound) pork tenderloin, trimmed
- 2 cups vegetable oil for frying
- 2 tablespoons chopped fresh parsley
- 2 tablespoons capers, rinsed
- Lemon wedges

1 Place bread on large plate. Microwave for 4 minutes, stirring well halfway through microwaving. Microwave at 50 percent power until bread is dry and few pieces start to lightly brown, 3 to 5 minutes, stirring every minute. Process bread in food processor to very fine crumbs, about 45 seconds. Transfer bread crumbs (you should have about 1¼ cups) to shallow dish. Spread flour in second shallow dish. Beat 2 eggs with 1 tablespoon oil in third shallow dish.

2 Set wire rack in rimmed baking sheet and line plate with triple layer of paper towels. Cut tenderloin on angle into 4 equal pieces. Working with 1 piece at a time, place pork cut side down between 2 sheets of parchment paper or plastic wrap and pound with meat pounder to even ⅛- to ¼-inch thickness. Pat cutlets dry with paper towels and season with salt and pepper. Working with 1 cutlet at a time, dredge cutlets thoroughly in flour, shaking off excess; dip in egg mixture, letting excess drip off to ensure very thin coating; and coat evenly with bread crumbs, pressing on crumbs to adhere. Transfer breaded cutlets to prepared rack in single layer; let coating dry for 5 minutes.

3 Heat 2 cups oil in large Dutch oven over medium-high heat to 375 degrees. Lay 2 cutlets in pot, without overlapping them, and cook, shaking pot gently and continuously, until cutlets are wrinkled and light golden brown on both sides, 1 to 2 minutes per side. Transfer cutlets to paper towel–lined plate and flip cutlets several times to blot excess oil. Return oil to 375 degrees and repeat with remaining cutlets. Serve cutlets sprinkled with parsley; capers; and hard-cooked egg, if using, passing lemon wedges separately.

RICH DESSERTS

BERRY PUDDING

serves 6

Rich, eggy challah makes a sliceable dessert flavored deeply with sweet berry juices. "Staling" it (even if it's day-old) in the oven makes it even sturdier.

8	(¼-inch-thick) slices Challah (page 308), crusts removed
12	ounces strawberries, hulled and chopped (2 cups)
8	ounces blackberries, halved (1½ cups)
8	ounces (1½ cups) blueberries
5	ounces (1 cup) raspberries
½	cup (3½ ounces) granulated sugar
1	teaspoon unflavored gelatin
2	tablespoons cold water
½	cup (5½ ounces) apricot preserves
1	cup heavy cream, chilled
1	tablespoon confectioners' sugar

1 Adjust oven rack to middle position and heat oven to 350 degrees. Line 8½ by 4½-inch loaf pan with plastic wrap, pushing plastic into corners and up sides of pan and allowing excess to overhang long sides. Make cardboard cutout just large enough to fit inside pan.

2 Place challah on wire rack set in rimmed baking sheet. Bake until dry, about 10 minutes, flipping challah and rotating sheet halfway through baking. Let challah cool completely.

3 Combine strawberries, blackberries, blueberries, and raspberries in bowl. Transfer half of mixture to medium saucepan, add granulated sugar, and bring to simmer over medium-low heat, stirring occasionally. Reduce heat to low and continue to cook until berries release their juices and raspberries begin to break down, about 5 minutes. Off heat, stir in remaining berries. After 2 minutes, strain berries through fine-mesh strainer set over medium bowl for 10 minutes, gently stirring once halfway through straining. Reserve juice. (You should have ¾ to 1 cup.)

4 Sprinkle gelatin over water in bowl and let sit until gelatin softens, about 5 minutes. Microwave until mixture is bubbling around edges and gelatin dissolves, about 30 seconds. Whisk preserves and gelatin mixture together in large bowl. Fold in strained berries.

5 Trim 4 slices of challah to fit snugly side by side in bottom of loaf pan (you may have extra challah). Dip slices in reserved berry juice until saturated, about 30 seconds per side, then place in bottom of pan. Spoon berry mixture over challah. Trim remaining 4 slices of challah to fit snugly side by side on top of berries (you may have extra challah). Dip slices in reserved berry juice until saturated, about 30 seconds per side, then place on top of berries. Cover pan loosely with plastic and place in 13 by 9-inch baking dish. Place cardboard cutout on top of pudding. Top with 3 soup cans to weigh down pudding. Refrigerate pudding for at least 8 hours or up to 24 hours.

6 Using stand mixer fitted with whisk attachment, whip cream and confectioners' sugar on medium-low speed until foamy, about 1 minute. Increase speed to high and whip until soft peaks form, 1 to 3 minutes. Transfer to serving bowl. Remove cans, cardboard, and plastic from top of pudding. Loosen pudding by pulling up on edges of plastic. Place inverted platter over top of loaf pan and flip platter and pan upside down to unmold pudding. Discard plastic. Slice pudding with serrated knife and serve with whipped cream.

APPLE-BLACKBERRY BROWN BETTY

serves 6 to 8

An apple Betty is like an apple crisp, but instead of a crumbly butter/sugar/flour topping, it has slightly sweetened bread crumbs both above and below the apples. Brioche is buttery and delicious with the warm fruit. We like the flavor of nutmeg here, but substitute ½ teaspoon of ground cinnamon if you prefer it. This dessert is best served freshly baked and warm, but you can cover any leftovers tightly with foil and refrigerate them for up to two days; warm before serving.

7 slices No-Knead Brioche (page 290), cut into 1-inch pieces

½ cup packed (3½ ounces) plus ⅓ cup packed (2⅓ ounces) light brown sugar, divided

¾ teaspoon table salt, divided

6 tablespoons unsalted butter, melted

1½ pounds Golden Delicious apple, peeled, cored, and cut into ½-inch pieces

1 pound Granny Smith apples, peeled, cored, and cut into ½-inch pieces

2 tablespoons water

1 teaspoon vanilla extract

¼ teaspoon ground nutmeg

3¾ ounces (¾ cup) blackberries, berries larger than ¾ inch cut in half crosswise

Vanilla ice cream or sweetened whipped cream

1 Adjust oven racks to upper-middle and lower-middle positions and heat oven to 375 degrees. Pulse bread in food processor until coarsely ground, about 15 pulses. Add ½ cup sugar and ½ teaspoon salt and pulse to combine, about 5 pulses. Drizzle with melted butter and pulse until evenly distributed, about 5 pulses. Scatter 2½ cups bread-crumb mixture in 8-inch square baking dish. Press gently to create even layer.

2 Combine apples, water, vanilla, nutmeg, remaining ⅓ cup sugar, and remaining ¼ teaspoon salt in bowl. Pile apple mixture atop bread crumb mixture in dish and spread and press into even layer. Sprinkle blackberries over apples (dish will be very full). Distribute remaining bread-crumb mixture evenly over blackberries and press lightly to form uniform layer. Cover tightly with aluminum foil. (Uncooked Betty can be refrigerated for up to 2 days.) Place on rimmed baking sheet and bake on lower rack until apples are soft, 1 hour to 1 hour 10 minutes.

3 Remove foil and transfer dish to upper rack. Bake until crumbs on top are crisp and well browned, about 15 minutes. Transfer to wire rack and let cool for at least 20 minutes. Serve with ice cream.

Cornbread and Tomato Salad (page 349)

Pita and Spicy Roasted Red Pepper Hummus (page 345)

Acquacotta (page 348)

Berry Pudding (page 351)

 RAPID-FIRE BREAD IDEAS

Toasted Seeded Oat Bread (page 200) + lemon vinaigrette + mashed avocado + red pepper flakes = **AVOCADO TOAST**

Toasted No-Knead Rustic Loaf (page 186) + dark bar chocolate + drizzle of olive oil + flake sea salt = **CHOCOLATE OLIVE OIL TOAST**

Cocoa Cherry Rye Bread (page 216) + mascarpone + vanilla extract = **CHOCOLATE AND VANILLA TOAST**

Toasted Spelt Bread (page 206) + garlic + tomatoes + basil + salt = **TOMATO TOAST**

White Sandwich Bread (page 158) processed to crumbs + pasta + fried egg = **SIMPLE PASTA DISH**

Egg fried in cut-out hole of Buttermilk Dill Bread (page 171) = **EGG IN A HOLE**

Flourless Nut and Seed Loaf (page 70) + cream cheese + smoked salmon + chives = **GLUTEN-FREE SALMON TOASTS**

Pretzel Buns (page 136) + deli pastrami or roast beef + spicy mustard = **DELI SANDWICH SLIDERS**

Split Glazed Doughnuts (page 326) + burger + American cheese + bacon = **DONUT SHOP BURGERS**

Toasted Orange-Chocolate Durum Bread (page 222) + drizzle of olive oil + flake sea salt = **ORANGE-CHOCOLATE OLIVE OIL TOAST**

Brioche Burger Buns (page 298) or Orange Blossom and Anise Buns (page 339) + scoop of gelato = **SICILIAN-STYLE ICE CREAM SANDWICH**

Olive oil + salt + pepper + toasted cubed bread of your choice = **CROUTONS**

NUTRITIONAL INFORMATION FOR OUR RECIPES

To calculate the nutritional values of our recipes per serving, we used *The Food Processor SQL by ESHA research*. When using this program, we entered all the ingredients, using weights wherever possible. We also used our preferred brands in these analyses. Any ingredient listed as "optional" was excluded from the analyses. If there is a range in the serving size, we used the highest number of servings to calculate nutritional values. We did not include additional salt for food that's seasoned to taste.

	CALORIES	TOTAL FAT (G)	SAT FAT (G)	CHOL (MG)	SODIUM (MG)	TOTAL CARB (G)	DIETARY FIBER (G)	TOTAL SUGARS (G)	PROTEIN (G)
CHAPTER 1: QUICK BREADS									
Easiest-Ever Drop Biscuits	320	18	11	55	440	35	1	3	6
Cinnamon Sugar Biscuits	380	23	15	70	470	38	0	13	5
Ginger Biscuits	380	17	11	55	470	48	0	16	6
Miso-Scallion Biscuits	330	18	11	55	520	35	0	4	6
Sun-Dried Tomato, Garlic, and Za'atar Biscuits	330	21	13	60	500	30	1	2	6
Cheese-Stuffed Biscuits	430	27	17	80	620	34	0	3	11
Pig in a Biscuit	190	12	6	40	340	13	0	1	6
Potato Biscuits with Bacon	310	19	9	35	520	27	0	3	6
Cast Iron Orange-Herb Biscuits	380	19	10	35	580	41	0	2	7
Gruyère and Herb Buttermilk Biscuits	420	24	15	70	590	39	0	4	10
Butter and Lard Biscuits	570	34	17	60	760	55	0	4	9
Blueberry Biscuits	380	15	10	45	530	52	1	17	6
British-Style Currant Scones	260	9	5	60	340	39	1	13	6
Jalapeño-Cheddar Cornbread	370	18	11	95	830	39	2	5	12
Fresh Corn Muffins with Cardamom–Brown Sugar Butter	320	12	6	65	540	48	2	19	6
Rosemary-Parmesan Polenta Muffins	300	14	4.5	55	470	32	1	5	10
Manchego and Chorizo Muffins	290	14	8	50	550	28	0	2	10
Three-Ingredient Bread	210	0	0	0	610	42	2	4	5
Flourless Nut and Seed Loaf	380	26	7	0	115	31	10	9	11
Feta-Dill Zucchini Bread	340	16	10	125	640	36	2	2	11
Whole-Wheat Date-Nut Bread	440	18	2	30	390	64	7	32	10
Pumpkin Bread	400	16	1.5	45	400	58	0	40	5
Bacon-Onion Cheese Bread	390	19	9	75	900	35	0	3	18

	CALORIES	TOTAL FAT (G)	SAT FAT (G)	CHOL (MG)	SODIUM (MG)	TOTAL CARB (G)	DIETARY FIBER (G)	TOTAL SUGARS (G)	PROTEIN (G)
CHAPTER 1: QUICK BREADS (CONT.)									
Double-Chocolate Banana Bread	460	21	13	85	430	61	2	32	6
Maple-Sorghum Skillet Bread	390	22	9	90	390	42	2	14	7
Sweet Potato Cornbread	370	16	9	140	860	49	5	11	9
Bhature	240	13	1	0	310	27	0	1	4
Apple Cider Doughnuts	260	9	3	30	160	40	0	19	4
Soda Bread with Nuts and Cacao Nibs	400	15	3.5	5	670	56	11	5	13
Boston Brown Bread	310	6	3	15	650	61	4	29	7
Flavored Butters									
Ginger-Molasses Butter	110	11	7	30	35	1	0	1	0
Cardamom–Brown Sugar Butter	130	11	7	30	150	6	0	6	0
Honey Butter	130	11	7	30	150	9	0	8	0
Feta Butter	140	14	9	45	130	1	0	1	2
Nori Butter	100	11	7	30	80	0	0	0	0
Radish Butter	50	6	3.5	15	80	1	0	0	0
CHAPTER 2: ROLLS AND MORE									
White Dinner Rolls	260	7	3	25	340	42	0	7	6
Dutch Oven Pull-Apart Dinner Rolls	260	7	3	25	340	42	0	7	6
Knotted Rolls	260	7	3	25	340	42	0	7	6
Crescent Rolls	240	6	2.5	20	320	39	0	6	6
Chive Spiral Rolls	170	5	2.5	15	260	26	0	4	4
Scoop-and-Bake Dinner Rolls	170	6	3.5	15	200	24	0	4	3
Fluffy Dinner Rolls	160	5	3	15	210	23	1	2	4
Oatmeal Dinner Rolls	160	2.5	1.5	5	210	29	2	5	5
Brown-and-Serve Dinner Rolls	130	2	1	5	190	22	1	2	4
Hawaiian Sweet Rolls	230	5	3.5	25	330	39	0	7	5
Cast Iron Garlic-Herb Butter Rolls	120	6	4	15	170	14	0	2	2
Porcini-Truffle Crescent Rolls	230	10	5	50	210	27	0	5	5
Thai Curry Butter Fan Rolls	290	12	8	60	590	37	0	5	6
Rustic Dinner Rolls	120	0	0	0	220	23	1	1	4
Olive Rolls with Rosemary and Fennel	180	3	0	0	330	31	1	1	6
Hoagie Rolls	430	6	0.5	25	880	74	3	2	14
Pretzel Buns	320	3.5	0	0	860	57	2	3	10

	CALORIES	TOTAL FAT (G)	SAT FAT (G)	CHOL (MG)	SODIUM (MG)	TOTAL CARB (G)	DIETARY FIBER (G)	TOTAL SUGARS (G)	PROTEIN (G)
CHAPTER 2: ROLLS AND MORE (CONT.)									
Potato Burger Buns	230	3.5	2	25	270	39	2	2	7
English Muffins	290	4.5	2.5	10	390	51	2	6	10
Crumpets	320	1.5	0	0	500	65	1	0	9
Pão de Queijo	410	25	7	40	710	37	0	1	9
Za'atar Monkey Bread	360	16	2	0	440	45	2	1	8
Garlic and Herb Breadsticks	70	2	1	5	130	10	0	0	2
Pan de Coco	260	9	8	0	300	39	0	3	6
Lop Cheung Bao	230	10	3	20	360	28	1	6	7
CHAPTER 3: SANDWICH SLICES									
White Sandwich Bread	160	3	1.5	5	310	27	1	4	5
Parmesan–Black Pepper Sandwich Bread	290	7	4	20	700	39	1	3	14
Cinnamon Raisin Swirl Bread	180	4	2	10	310	31	1	6	5
Zhoug Swirl Bread	180	5	2	5	310	28	1	4	5
Sandwich Bread with Everything Bagel Crust	170	3.5	1.5	5	450	28	1	4	5
Easy Sandwich Bread	170	4	2	25	200	26	3	2	7
English Muffin Bread	290	4.5	2.5	10	390	51	2	6	10
Buttermilk Dill Bread	230	3	2	10	500	39	2	3	8
Oatmeal Sandwich Bread	150	3	1.5	5	250	26	1	4	4
Furikake Japanese Milk Bread	180	7	2.5	40	510	24	2	3	7
Whole-Wheat Sandwich Bread	170	3.5	1.5	5	310	30	2	5	5
Whole-Wheat Oatmeal Loaf	180	3	1.5	5	210	32	3	5	6
Quinoa Whole-Wheat Bread	200	4	0.5	15	380	33	3	4	7
CHAPTER 4: NO-KNEAD DUTCH OVEN BREADS									
No-Knead Rustic Loaf	200	0	0	0	440	40	2	0	7
No-Knead Rustic Bâtard	200	0	0	0	440	40	2	0	7
(Almost) No-Knead Rustic Flatbreads	210	0.5	0	0	670	40	2	0	7
No-Knead Rustic Rolls	120	0	0	0	220	23	1	1	4
No-Knead Rustic Sandwich Loaf	200	0	0	0	440	40	2	0	7
Whole-Wheat Rustic Loaf	220	0	0	0	440	43	3	0	8
Cranberry Walnut Bread	280	4.5	0	0	440	52	4	7	9
Seeded Oat Bread	270	5	0.5	0	440	45	5	0	10

	CALORIES	TOTAL FAT (G)	SAT FAT (G)	CHOL (MG)	SODIUM (MG)	TOTAL CARB (G)	DIETARY FIBER (G)	TOTAL SUGARS (G)	PROTEIN (G)
CHAPTER 4: NO-KNEAD DUTCH OVEN BREADS (CONT.)									
Sprouted Wheat Berry Bread	240	0	0	0	460	50	4	2	9
Spelt Bread	270	0.5	0	0	450	54	4	0	9
Spicy Olive Spelt Bread	260	4	0	0	740	44	3	0	8
Anadama Bread	260	0	0	0	470	54	3	9	8
Rye Bread	210	0	0	0	450	44	4	0	7
Cocoa Cherry Rye Bread	280	0.5	0	0	460	59	4	10	9
Sesame Durum Bread	280	7	0	0	480	43	4	1	10
Orange-Chocolate Durum Bread	280	6	3.5	0	450	50	3	2	8
CHAPTER 5: PIZZA AND FLATBREADS									
Thin-Crust Pizza	370	3	0	0	730	70	2	2	13
Shakshuka Breakfast Pizza	450	22	6	240	1100	43	2	4	17
Stuffed Pizza	650	35	16	100	1740	48	2	3	32
Broccoli Rabe and Salami Stromboli	520	24	12	105	1240	47	3	2	27
One-Hour Pizza	420	14	6	30	1640	52	3	6	20
Pepperoni Sheet-Pan Pizza	840	45	16	85	1820	76	4	6	32
Caprese Sheet-Pan Pizza	742	41	12	50	1042	65	4	5	26
Sheet-Pan Pizza with 'Nduja, Ricotta, and Cherry Peppers	863	48	25	138	1198	66	4	6	43
Detroit-Style Pizza	520	24	12	50	1030	55	3	4	22
Thin-Crust Whole-Wheat Pizza with Garlic Oil, Three Cheeses, and Basil	430	18	2.5	0	840	60	6	2	11
Pizza al Taglio with Potatoes and Soppressata	870	41	16	65	2100	81	3	2	39
Focaccia di Recco	420	20	6	25	1160	44	1	5	15
Mana'eesh Za'atar	390	15	2	0	730	56	3	0	8
Cheese Mana'eesh	490	22	7	25	1050	57	3	1	18
Tomato Mana'eesh	450	20	3	0	1610	60	4	3	9
Labneh Mana'eesh Za'atar	600	27	4	5	1470	79	5	5	12
Lahmajun	560	13	4.5	30	1280	88	1	2	20
Alu Parathas	480	21	9	35	750	66	3	1	9
Adjaruli Khachapuri	360	17	9	80	750	36	1	3	16
Mushroom Musakhan	590	29	4	0	1320	73	10	13	15
Coques with Spinach, Raisins, and Pine Nuts	580	28	3.5	0	1080	67	6	9	15
Socca with Sautéed Onions and Rosemary	210	14	2	0	710	17	3	4	6

	CALORIES	TOTAL FAT (G)	SAT FAT (G)	CHOL (MG)	SODIUM (MG)	TOTAL CARB (G)	DIETARY FIBER (G)	TOTAL SUGARS (G)	PROTEIN (G)
CHAPTER 5: PIZZA AND FLATBREADS (CONT.)									
Kesra Rakhsis	430	18	2.5	0	430	56	3	3	10
Pan-Grilled Flatbreads	530	15	5	16	490	85	4	7	15
Pita Bread	260	8	1	0	370	41	1	3	7
Whole-Wheat Pita Bread	260	8	1	0	370	41	4	3	7
Piadine	340	10	1	0	390	51	0	0	7
Chapatis	310	14	2	0	610	41	4	0	7
CHAPTER 6: ENRICHED BREADS									
No-Knead Brioche	180	9	5	80	220	19	1	3	5
Pumpkin Spice Brioche à Tête	190	9	5	80	220	29	1	4	5
Garlic-Thyme Pull-Apart Brioche	240	15	9	95	220	19	1	3	5
Brioche Cinnamon Buns	460	22	13	145	470	56	2	31	8
Brioche Burger Buns	270	13	8	100	250	29	1	5	7
Quicker Cinnamon Buns	530	19	12	50	480	81	1	43	8
Sticky Buns	450	19	8	65	370	63	2	30	7
Sausage and Chive Pull-Apart Rolls	430	23	11	110	720	33	2	4	20
Challah	150	3	0.5	45	180	23	1	3	5
Prosciutto and Fig Pinwheel Bread	180	8	4.5	60	370	21	0	7	6
Chocolate Babka	420	22	13	65	220	51	4	18	7
Pizza Babka	430	23	11	95	480	39	3	4	16
Cast Iron Cinnamon Swirl Bread	200	6	4	30	330	31	0	10	4
Spicy Cheese Bread	240	11	6	75	380	25	0	3	10
Bolos Lêvedos	330	8	4	65	330	55	0	13	8
Bolos Lêvedos with Lemon and Cinnamon	330	8	4	65	310	55	0	13	8
Glazed Doughnuts	480	14	6	40	350	81	2	40	7
Chocolate Frosting	80	0	0	0	15	21	1	19	0
Coffee Frosting	70	0	0	0	15	19	0	18	0
Matcha Frosting	70	0	0	0	15	19	0	18	0
Raspberry Frosting	120	3	1.5	0	15	25	0	23	1
Ham and Cheese Wool Roll	220	10	6	60	330	23	1	2	9
Conchas	480	22	10	65	440	57	2	13	9
Chocolate Conchas	470	23	10	65	440	55	2	14	9
Bolo Bao	190	6	4	45	170	27	0	7	4
Orange Blossom and Anise Brioche Buns	360	18	10	135	330	38	1	7	9

	CALORIES	TOTAL FAT (G)	SAT FAT (G)	CHOL (MG)	SODIUM (MG)	TOTAL CARB (G)	DIETARY FIBER (G)	TOTAL SUGARS (G)	PROTEIN (G)
APPENDIX: USE IT UP									
Enriched Bread French Toast	520	24	11	270	480	58	2	18	15
Almond-Crusted French Toast	630	31	12	270	480	66	4	23	18
Extra-Crisp French Toast	570	25	12	270	540	68	2	22	15
Everyday French Toast	420	11	5	160	850	60	2	12	16
Biscuits and Gravy	640	38	16	110	1060	48	0	6	23
Ham and Gruyère Breakfast Sandwiches	460	41	16	265	670	2	0	2	20
Skillet Strata with Cheddar and Thyme	580	34	19	355	1020	43	2	10	26
Sautéed Grape and Almond Butter Toast	500	21	2.5	0	510	67	8	18	15
Corn Ricotta Toast with Pickled Corn and Cherry Tomatoes	380	7	4	25	800	62	5	8	15
Brown Sugar Toast	310	14	9	35	400	40	1	17	5
Pita and Simple Hummus	370	16	2.5	0	630	48	3	3	10
Pita and Spicy Roasted Red Pepper Hummus	370	16	2.5	0	650	48	3	3	10
Ham and Swiss Football Sandwiches	850	41	20	110	1150	86	3	15	31
Grown-Up Grilled Cheese with Robiola and Chipotle	550	26	15	75	790	61	4	11	19
Grilled Cheese with Asiago and Dates	670	33	20	90	1140	66	6	13	27
Grilled Cheese with Cheddar and Shallot	630	34	21	100	1130	54	2	5	25
Grilled Cheese with Comté and Cornichon	660	35	20	105	1380	57	3	8	28
Grilled Cheese with Gruyère and Chives	650	35	20	105	1100	55	2	8	27
Savoy Cabbage Soup with Ham, Rye Bread, and Fontina	550	27	11	60	1890	50	8	5	25
Simple Tomato-Bread Soup	260	17	3	5	750	26	3	8	7
Acquacotta	510	21	2.5	40	790	63	7	6	17
Fattoush	380	29	4	0	200	29	4	6	5
Cornbread and Tomato Salad	700	43	17	140	1670	64	6	11	19
White Bean and Mushroom Gratin	560	23	2.5	0	1200	71	10	7	17
Pork Schnitzel	620	26	6	100	720	60	2	7	38
Berry Pudding	520	19	10	105	260	79	6	41	9
Apple-Blackberry Brown Betty	410	17	10	85	410	60	6	42	5

CONVERSIONS AND EQUIVALENTS

Baking is a science and an art, but geography has a hand in it, too. Flours and sugars manufactured in the United Kingdom and elsewhere will feel and taste different from those manufactured in the United States. So we cannot promise that a bread you bake in Canada or England will taste the same as a bread baked in the States, but we can offer guidelines for converting weights and measures. We also recommend that you rely on your instincts when making our recipes. Refer to the visual cues provided. If the dough hasn't "come together in a ball" as described, you may need to add more flour—even if the recipe doesn't tell you to. You be the judge.

The recipes in this book were developed using standard U.S. measures following U.S. government guidelines. The charts below offer equivalents for U.S. and metric measures. All conversions are approximate and have been rounded up or down to the nearest whole number.

EXAMPLE

1 teaspoon = 4.9292 milliliters, rounded up to 5 milliliters
1 ounce = 28.3495 grams, rounded down to 28 grams

VOLUME CONVERSIONS

U.S.	METRIC
1 teaspoon	5 milliliters
2 teaspoons	10 milliliters
1 tablespoon	15 milliliters
2 tablespoons	30 milliliters
¼ cup	59 milliliters
⅓ cup	79 milliliters
½ cup	118 milliliters
¾ cup	177 milliliters
1 cup	237 milliliters
1¼ cups	296 milliliters
1½ cups	355 milliliters
2 cups (1 pint)	473 milliliters
2½ cups	591 milliliters
3 cups	710 milliliters
4 cups (1 quart)	0.946 liter
1.06 quarts	1 liter
4 quarts (1 gallon)	3.8 liters

WEIGHT CONVERSIONS

OUNCES	GRAMS
½	14
¾	21
1	28
1½	43
2	57
2½	71
3	85
3½	99
4	113
4½	128
5	142
6	170
7	198
8	227
9	255
10	283
12	340
16 (1 pound)	454

CONVERSIONS FOR COMMON BAKING INGREDIENTS

Because measuring by weight is far more accurate than measuring by volume, and thus more likely to produce reliable results, in our recipes we provide ounce measures in addition to cup measures for many ingredients. Refer to the chart below to convert these measures into grams.

INGREDIENT	OUNCES	GRAMS
FLOUR		
1 cup all-purpose flour*	5	142
1 cup bread flour	5½	156
1 cup whole-wheat flour	5½	156
1 cup spelt flour	5½	156
1 cup rye flour	5½	156
1 cup durum flour	5	142
1 cup chickpea flour	3	85
1 cup cornmeal	5	142
SUGAR		
1 cup granulated (white) sugar	7	198
1 cup packed brown sugar (light or dark)	7	198
1 cup confectioners' sugar	4	113
FAT		
4 tablespoons lard	2	56
4 tablespoons (½ stick or ¼ cup) butter†	2	57
8 tablespoons (1 stick or ½ cup) butter†	4	113
16 tablespoons (2 sticks or 1 cup) butter†	8	227
LIQUIDS		
1 cup water	8	227
1 cup milk	8	227
1 cup heavy cream	8	227
1 cup buttermilk	8	227
1 cup sour cream	8	227
1 cup yogurt	8	227

* U.S. all-purpose flour does not contain leaveners, as some European flours do. These leavened flours are called self-rising or self-raising. If you are using self-rising flour, take this into consideration before adding leaveners to a recipe.

† In the United States, butter is sold both salted and unsalted. We recommend unsalted butter. If you are using salted butter, take this into consideration before adding salt to a recipe.

OVEN TEMPERATURES

FAHRENHEIT	CELSIUS	GAS MARK
225	105	¼
250	120	½
275	135	1
300	150	2
325	165	3
350	180	4
375	190	5
400	200	6
425	220	7
450	230	8
475	245	9

CONVERTING TEMPERATURES FROM AN INSTANT-READ THERMOMETER

We include doneness temperatures in many of the recipes in this book. We recommend an instant-read thermometer for the job. To convert Fahrenheit degrees to Celsius, use this simple formula:

Subtract 32 degrees from the Fahrenheit reading, then divide the result by 1.8 to find the Celsius reading.

EXAMPLE

"Bake until loaf registers 205 degrees, 30 to 35 minutes."

To convert:

205°F − 32 = 173°

173° ÷ 1.8 = 96.11°C, rounded down to 96°C

INDEX

Note: Page references in *italics* indicate photographs of completed recipes.

C